# Shinobi Life ™

## Vol. 1

### Created by
### Shoko Conami

HAMBURG // LONDON // LOS ANGELES // TOKYO

D0359225

## *Shinobi Life Vol. 1*
## Created by Shoko Conami

Translation - Lori Riser
English Adaptation - Ysabet Reinhardt MacFarlane
Copy Editor - Hope Donovan
Retouch and Lettering - Star Print Brokers
Production Artist - Vicente Rivera, Jr.
Cover Design - James Lee

Senior Editor - Bryce P. Coleman
Pre-Production Supervisor - Vicente Rivera, Jr.
Print-Production Specialist - Lucas Rivera
Managing Editor - Vy Nguyen
Senior Designer - Louis Csontos
Senior Designer - James Lee
Senior Editor - Jenna Winterberg
Associate Publisher - Marco F. Pavia
President and C.O.O. - John Parker
C.E.O. and Chief Creative Officer - Stu Levy

A **TOKYOPOP**® Manga

TOKYOPOP and ⊙ are trademarks or registered trademarks of TOKYOPOP Inc.

TOKYOPOP Inc.
5900 Wilshire Blvd. Suite 2000
Los Angeles, CA 90036

E-mail: info@TOKYOPOP.com
Come visit us online at www.TOKYOPOP.com

SHINOBI LIFE
© 2006 Shoko Conami
All rights reserved. First published in Japan in 2006 by
Akita Publishing Co., Ltd., Tokyo. English translation rights
in U.S.A. and Canada arranged with Akita Publishing Co., Ltd.
through Tuttle-Mori Agency, Inc., Tokyo
English text copyright © 2008 TOKYOPOP Inc.

All rights reserved. No portion of this book may be
reproduced or transmitted in any form or by any means
without written permission from the copyright holders.
This manga is a work of fiction. Any resemblance to
actual events or locales or persons, living or dead, is
entirely coincidental.

ISBN: 978-1-4278-1111-0

First TOKYOPOP printing: November 2008
10 9 8 7 6 5 4 3 2 1
Printed in the USA

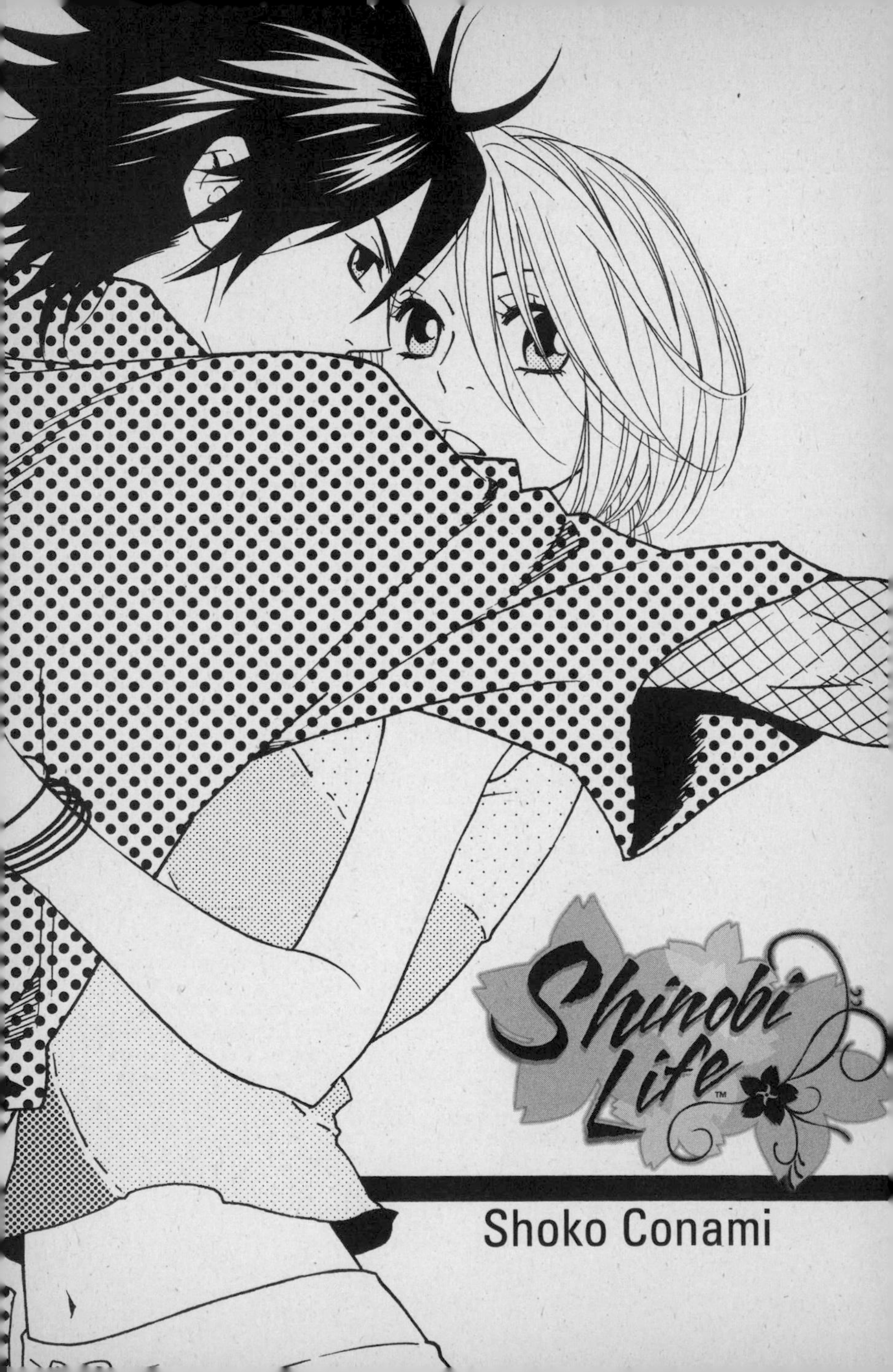

# Shinobi Life™

Shoko Conami

# CONTENTS

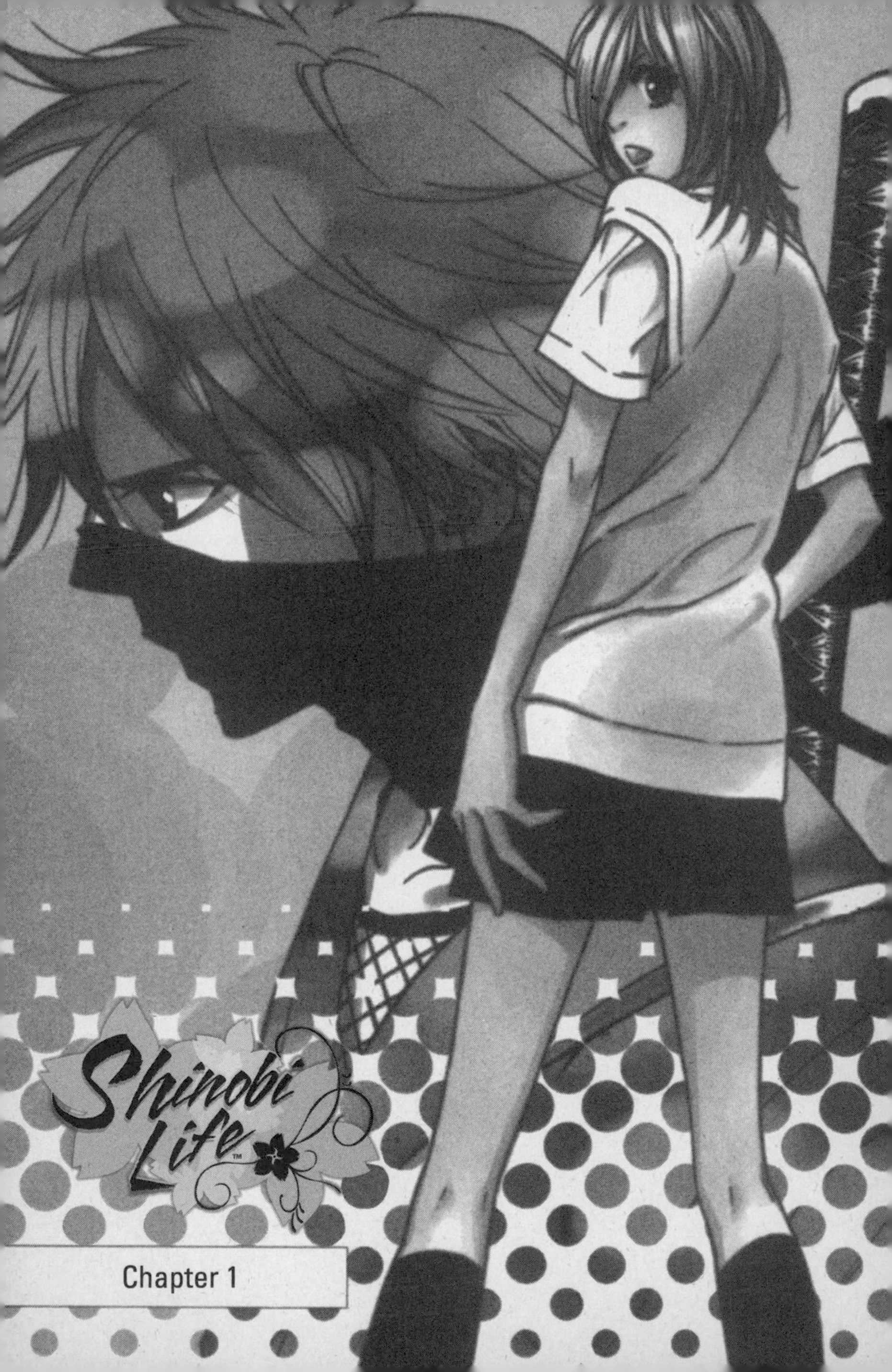
Shinobi Life™
Chapter 1

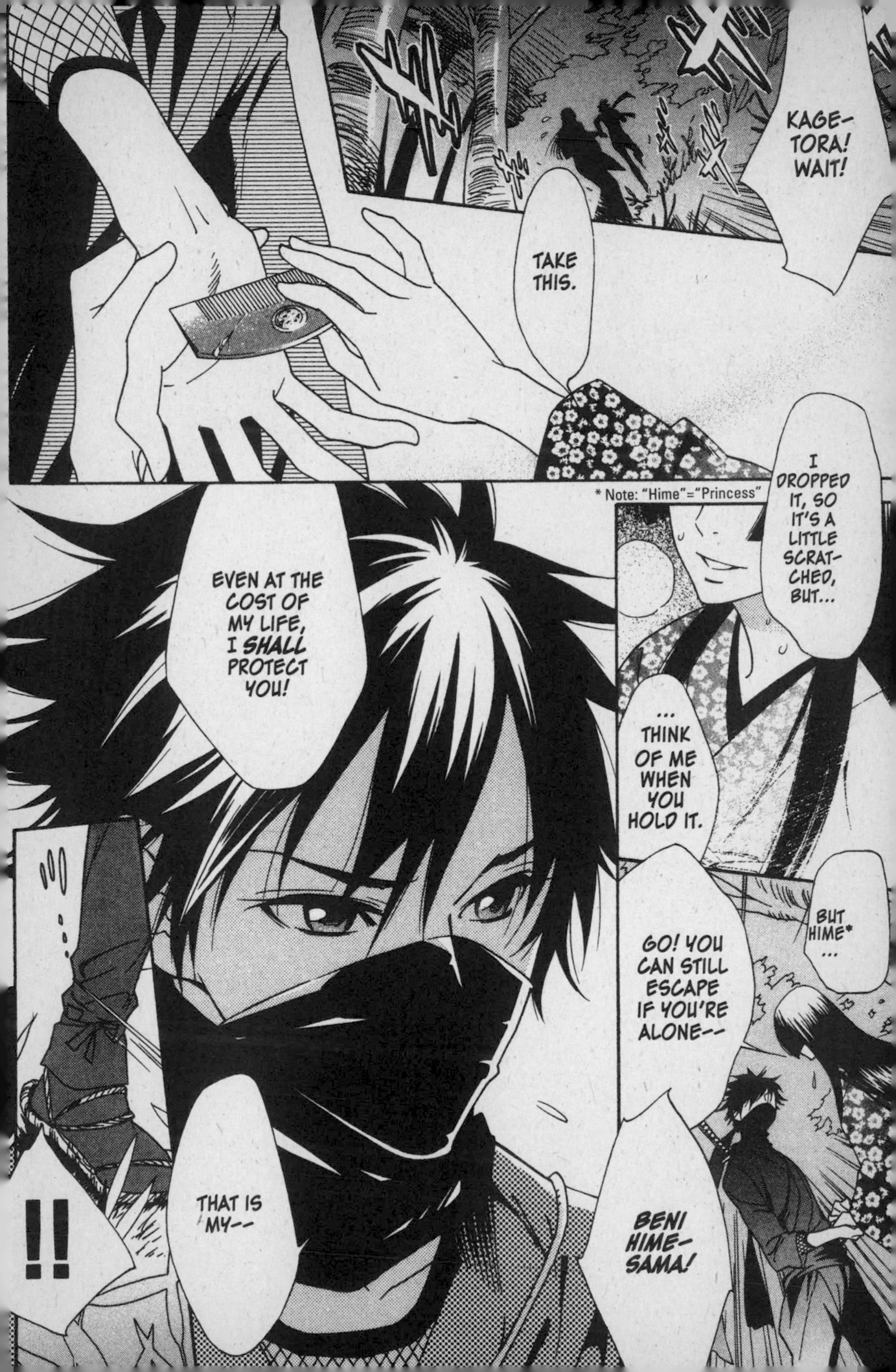
KAGE-TORA! WAIT!
TAKE THIS.
I DROPPED IT, SO IT'S A LITTLE SCRATCHED, BUT...
... THINK OF ME WHEN YOU HOLD IT.
BUT HIME* ...
GO! YOU CAN STILL ESCAPE IF YOU'RE ALONE--
BENI HIME-SAMA!
EVEN AT THE COST OF MY LIFE, I **SHALL** PROTECT YOU!
THAT IS MY--
!!

* Note: "Hime"="Princess"

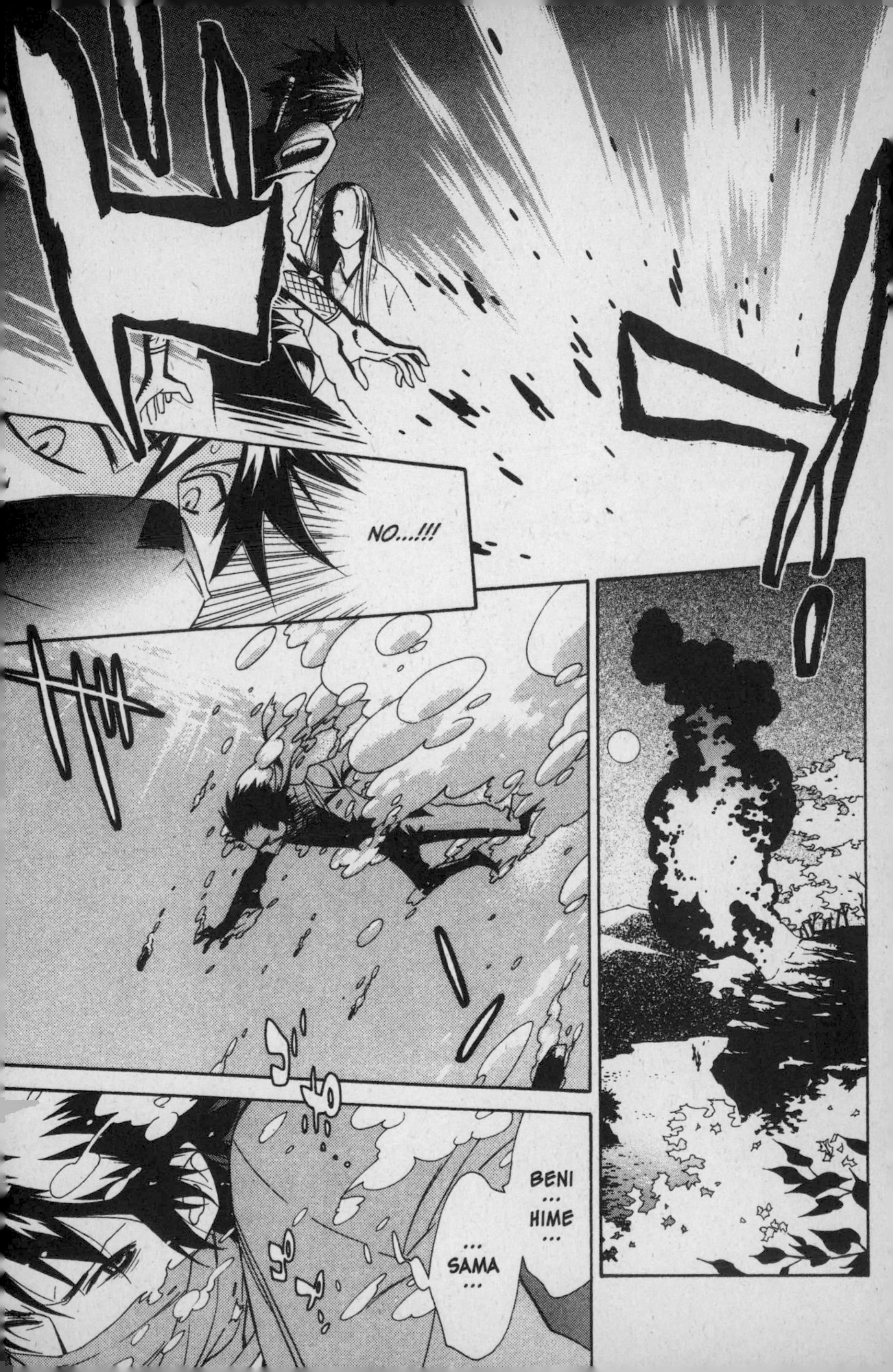
NO...!!!
BENI ... HIME ... SAMA ...

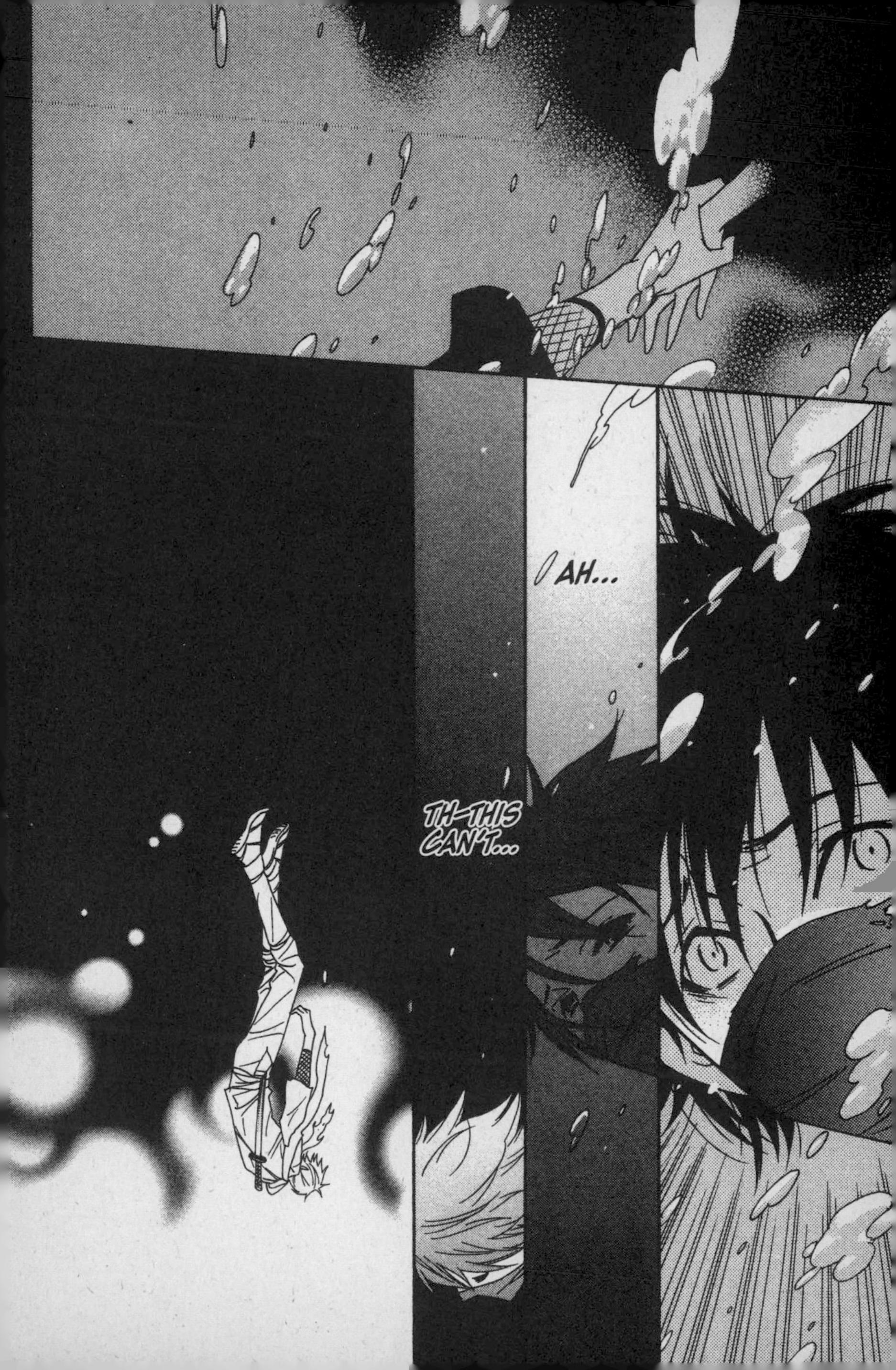
AH...
TH-THIS CAN'T...

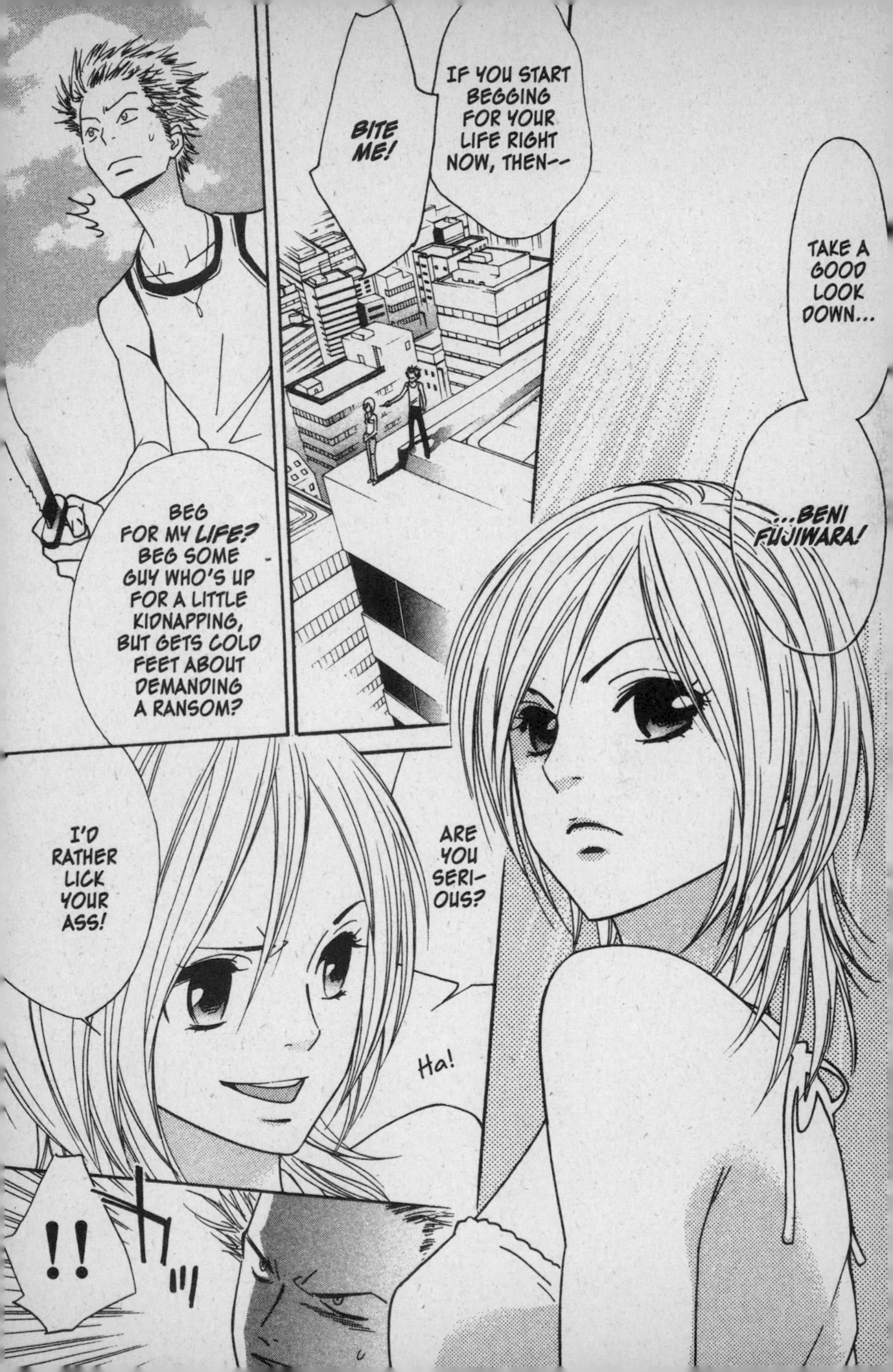
TAKE A GOOD LOOK DOWN...
...BENI FUJIWARA!
IF YOU START BEGGING FOR YOUR LIFE RIGHT NOW, THEN--
BITE ME!
BEG FOR MY LIFE? BEG SOME GUY WHO'S UP FOR A LITTLE KIDNAPPING, BUT GETS COLD FEET ABOUT DEMANDING A RANSOM?
ARE YOU SERIOUS?
I'D RATHER LICK YOUR ASS!
Ha!
!!

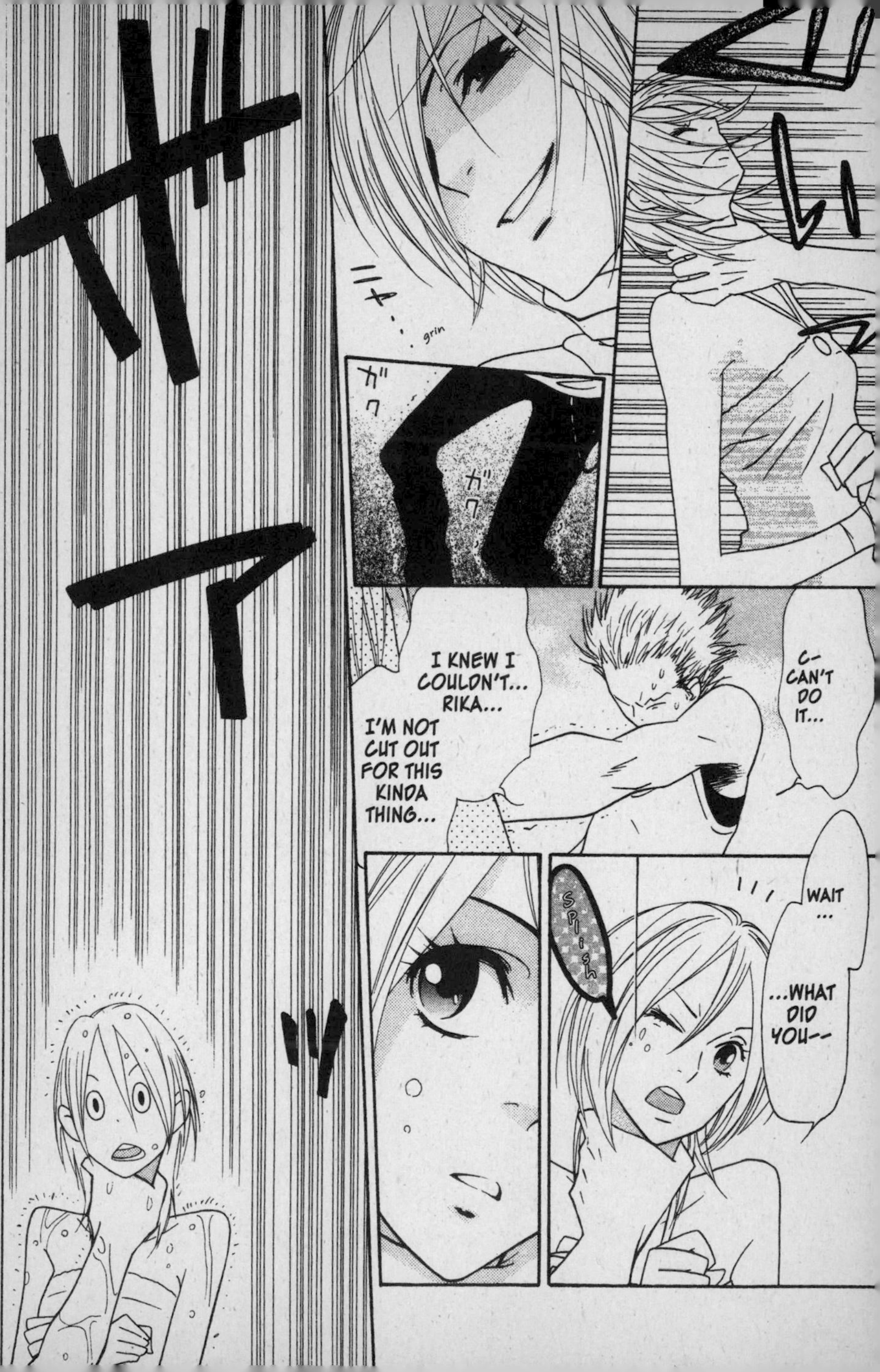
ニヤ…
grin
ガク
ガク
C-CAN'T DO IT...
I KNEW I COULDN'T... RIKA...
I'M NOT CUT OUT FOR THIS KINDA THING...
WAIT ...
...WHAT DID YOU--
Splish
ザア
ッ

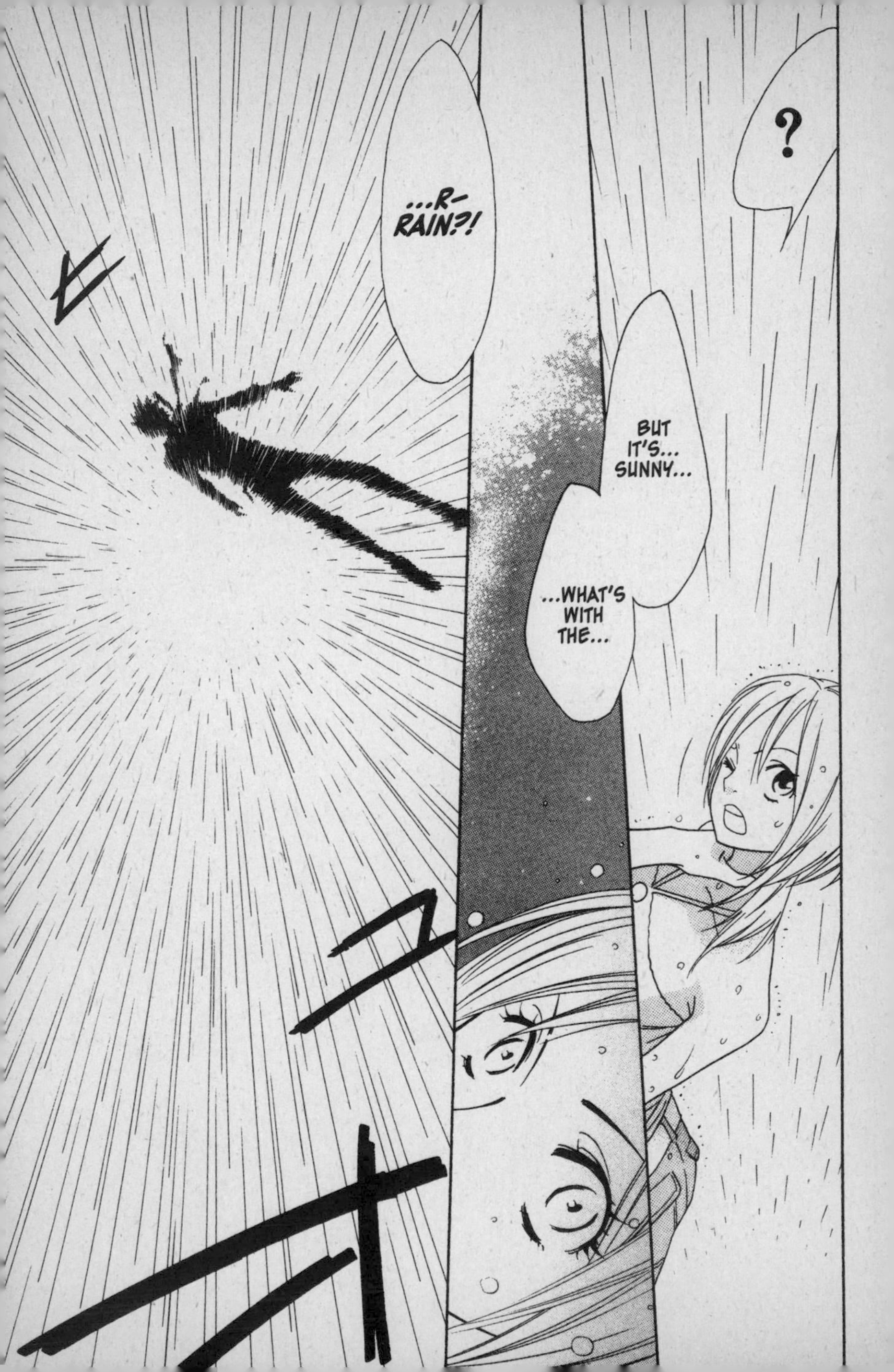
?
BUT IT'S... SUNNY...
...WHAT'S WITH THE...
...R-RAIN?!

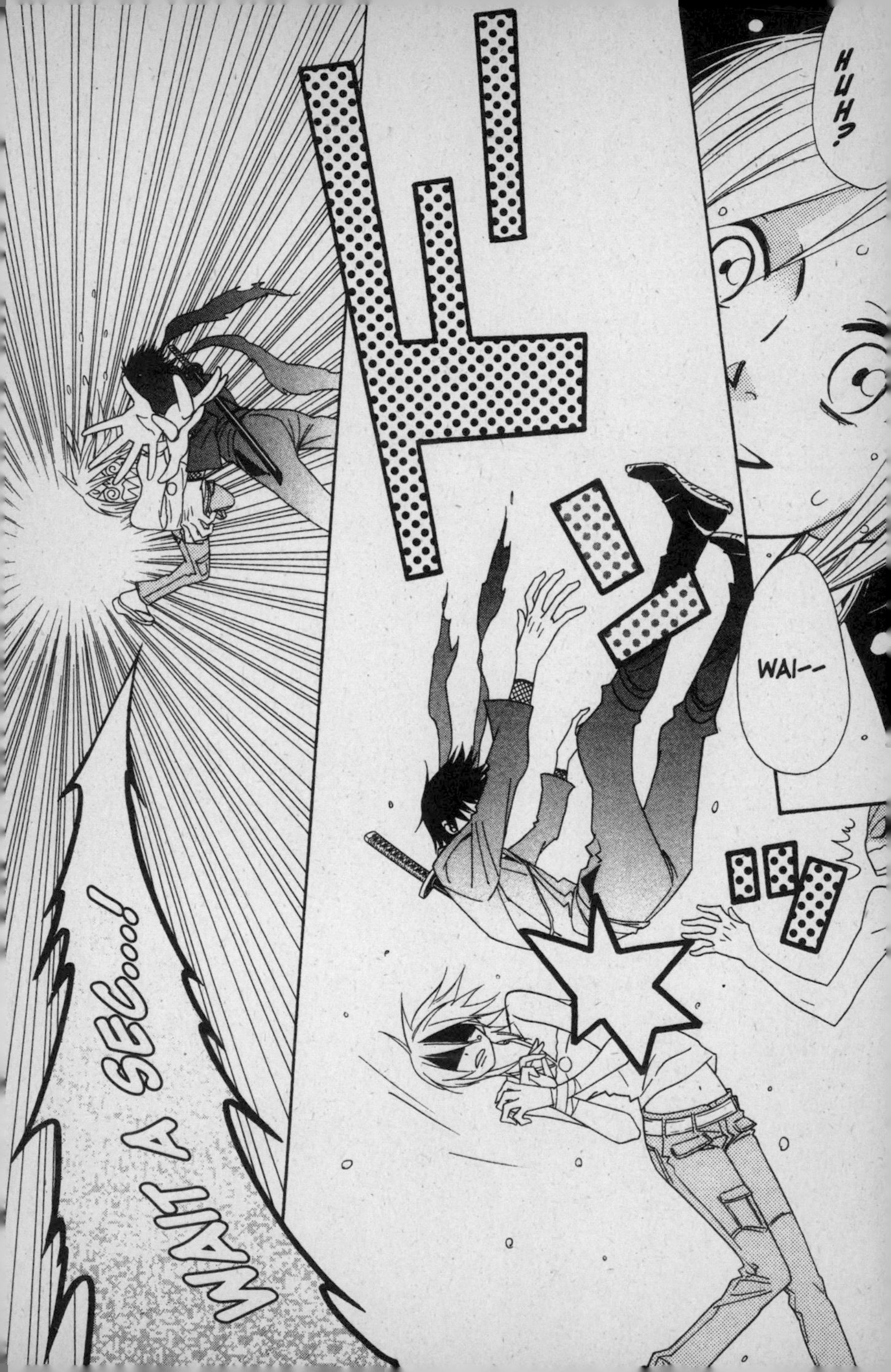
HUH?
WAI--
WAIT A SECoooo!

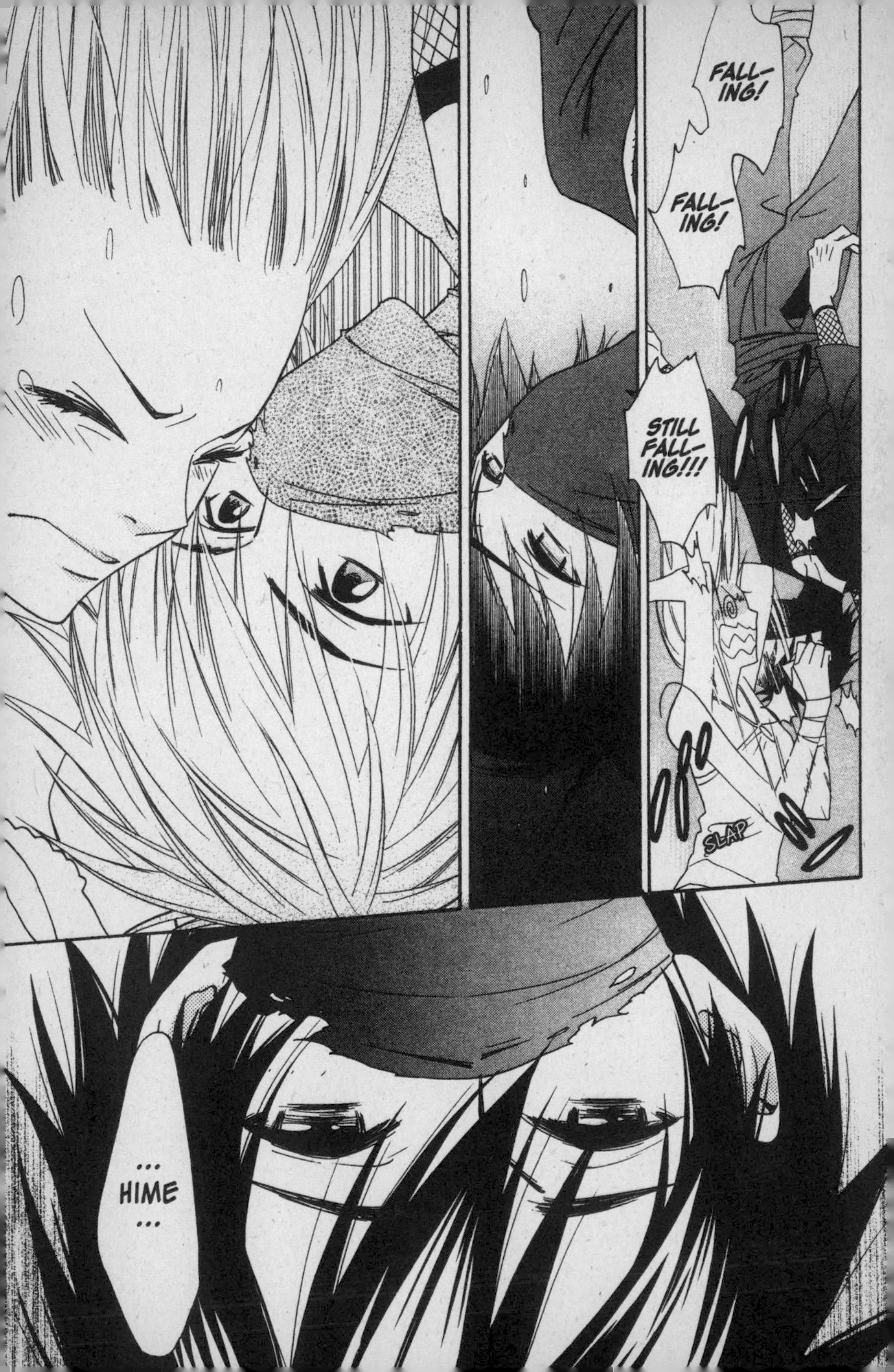
FALL-ING!
FALL-ING!
STILL FALL-ING!!!
SLAP
... HIME ...

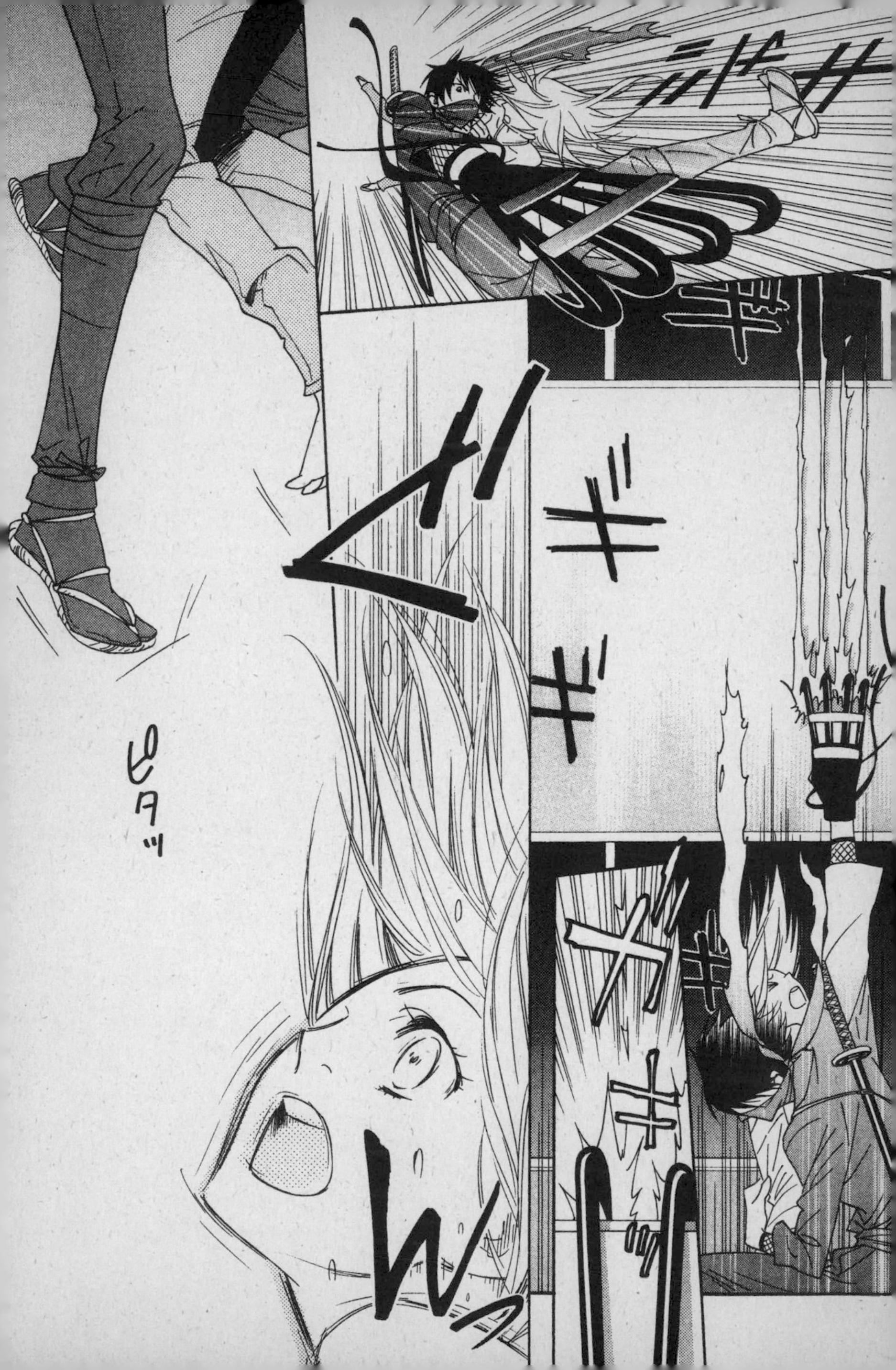
ピタッ

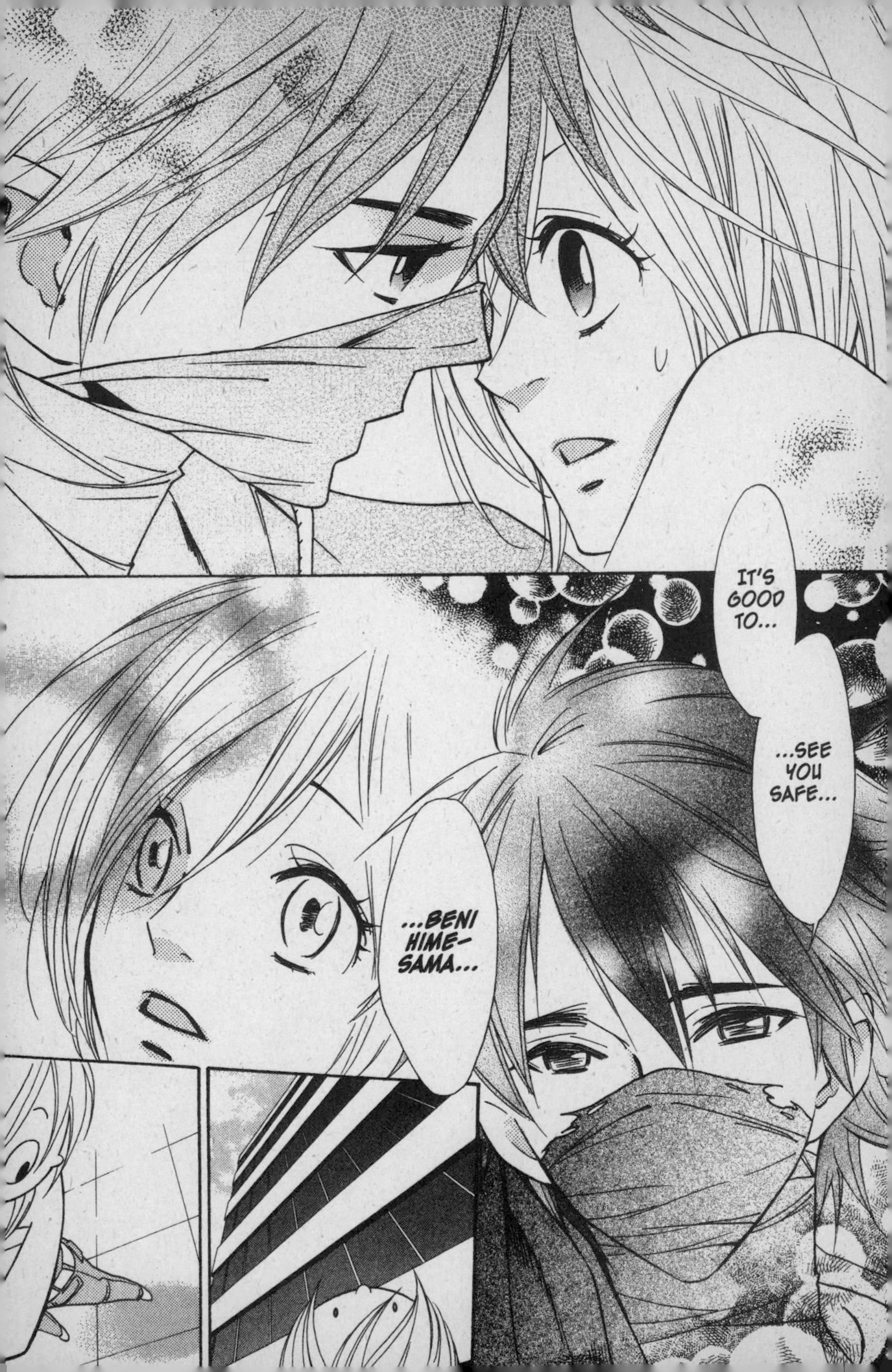
IT'S GOOD TO...
...SEE YOU SAFE...
...BENI HIME-SAMA...

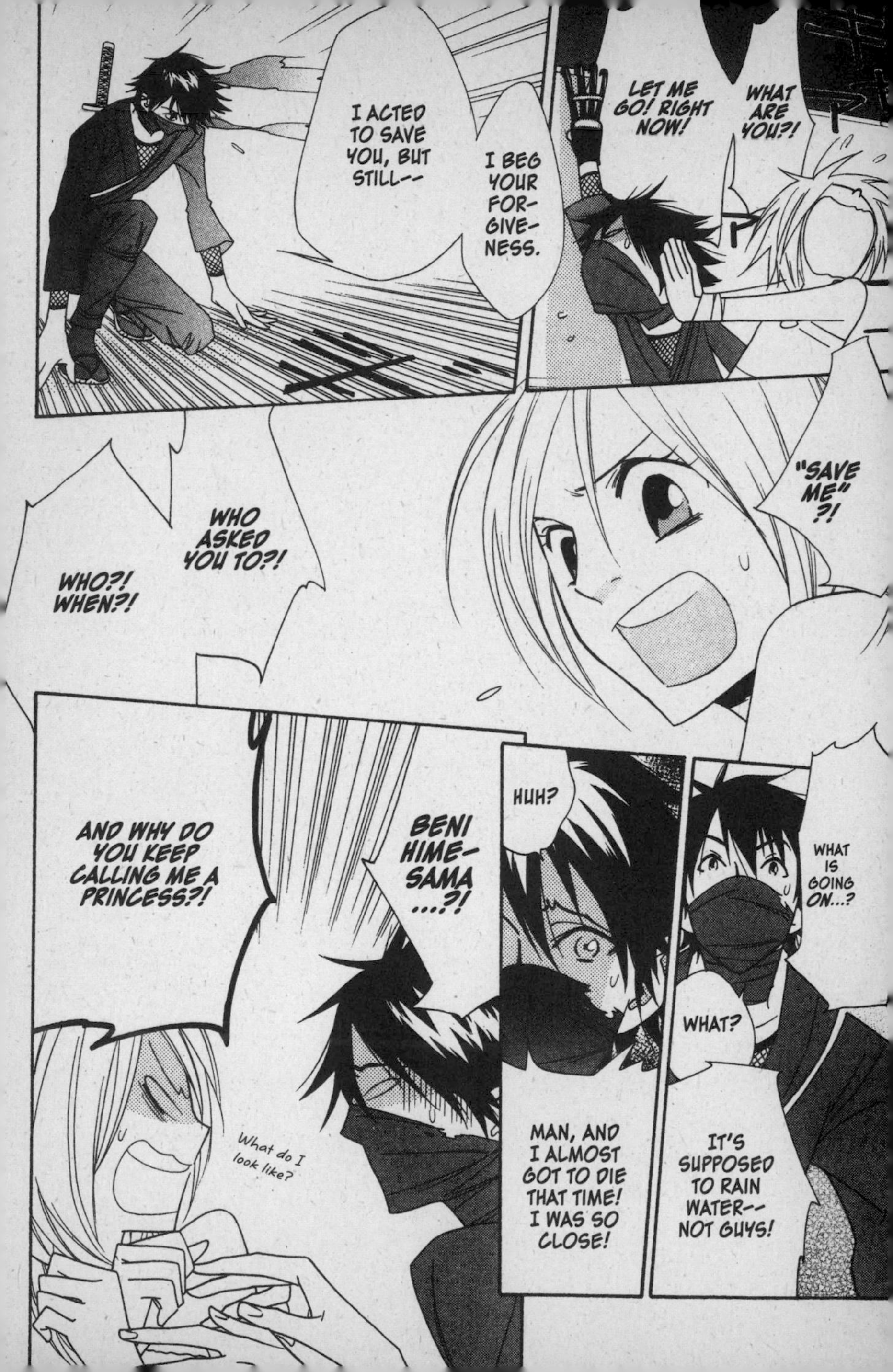
WHAT ARE YOU?!
LET ME GO! RIGHT NOW!
I ACTED TO SAVE YOU, BUT STILL--
I BEG YOUR FOR-GIVE-NESS.
"SAVE ME"?!
WHO ASKED YOU TO?!
WHO?! WHEN?!
WHAT IS GOING ON...?
WHAT?
IT'S SUPPOSED TO RAIN WATER--NOT GUYS!
HUH?
MAN, AND I ALMOST GOT TO DIE THAT TIME! I WAS SO CLOSE!
BENI HIME-SAMA...?!
AND WHY DO YOU KEEP CALLING ME A PRINCESS?!
What do I look like?

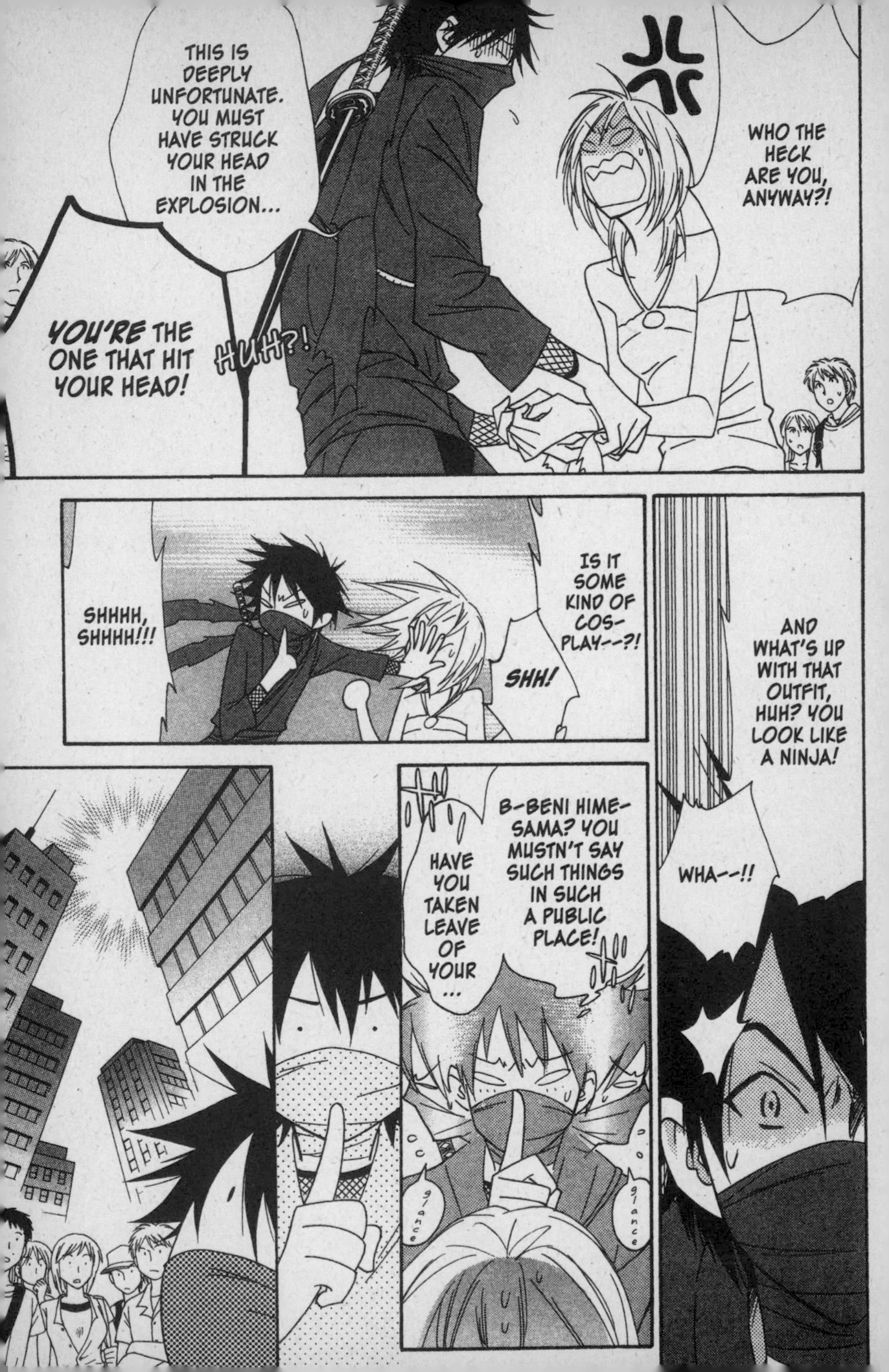

WHO THE HECK ARE YOU, ANYWAY?!
THIS IS DEEPLY UNFORTUNATE. YOU MUST HAVE STRUCK YOUR HEAD IN THE EXPLOSION...
HUH?!
YOU'RE THE ONE THAT HIT YOUR HEAD!
AND WHAT'S UP WITH THAT OUTFIT, HUH? YOU LOOK LIKE A NINJA!
IS IT SOME KIND OF COS-PLAY--?!
SHH!
SHHHH, SHHHH!!!
WHA--!!
B-BENI HIME-SAMA? YOU MUSTN'T SAY SUCH THINGS IN SUCH A PUBLIC PLACE!
glance
glance
HAVE YOU TAKEN LEAVE OF YOUR ...

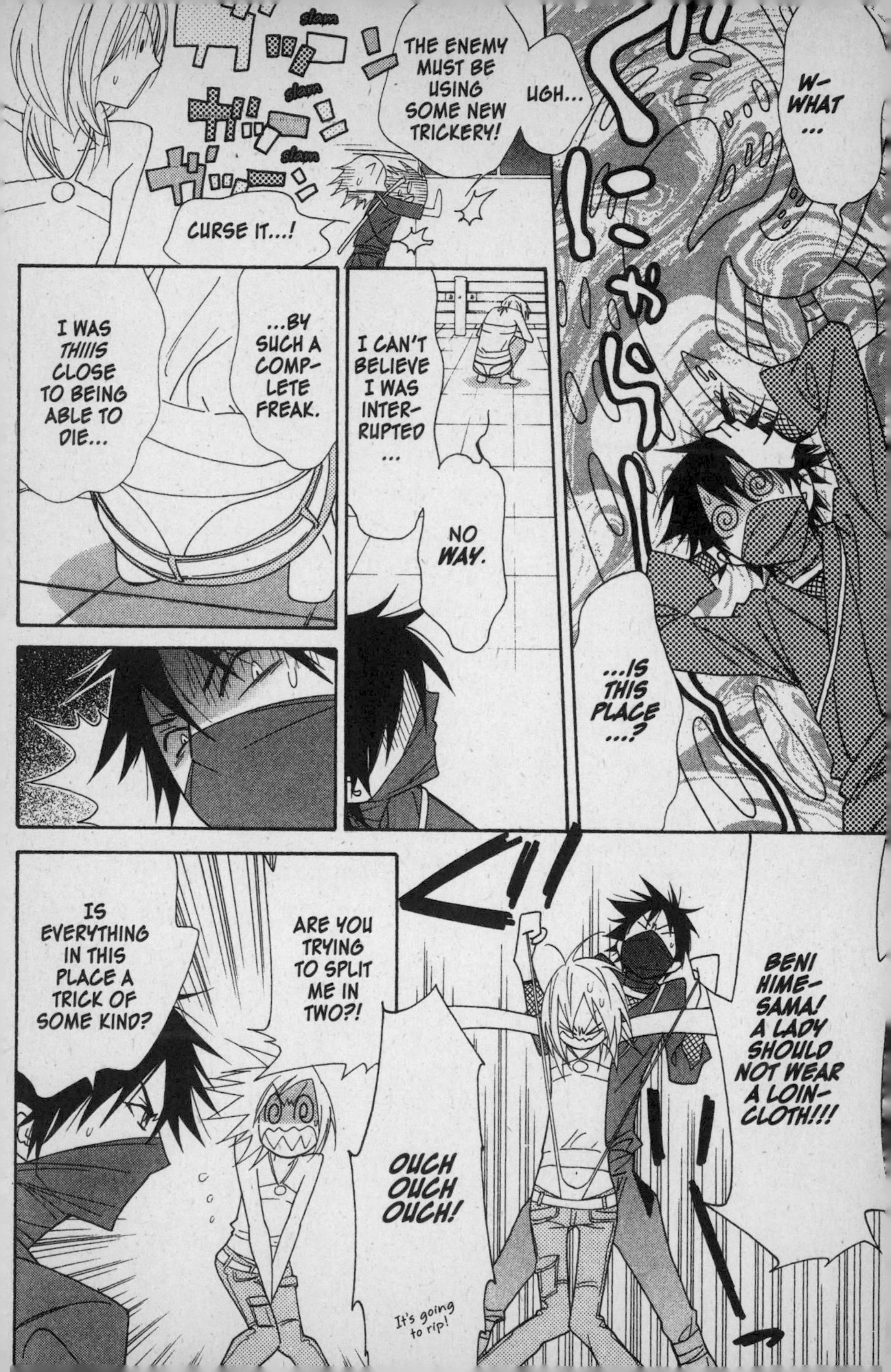
W-WHAT ...
...IS THIS PLACE ....?
UGH...
THE ENEMY MUST BE USING SOME NEW TRICKERY!
slam
slam
slam
CURSE IT...!
I CAN'T BELIEVE I WAS INTERRUPTED ...
NO WAY.
...BY SUCH A COMPLETE FREAK.
I WAS THIIIS CLOSE TO BEING ABLE TO DIE...
BENI HIME-SAMA! A LADY SHOULD NOT WEAR A LOINCLOTH!!!
OUCH OUCH OUCH!
It's going to rip!
ARE YOU TRYING TO SPLIT ME IN TWO?!
IS EVERYTHING IN THIS PLACE A TRICK OF SOME KIND?

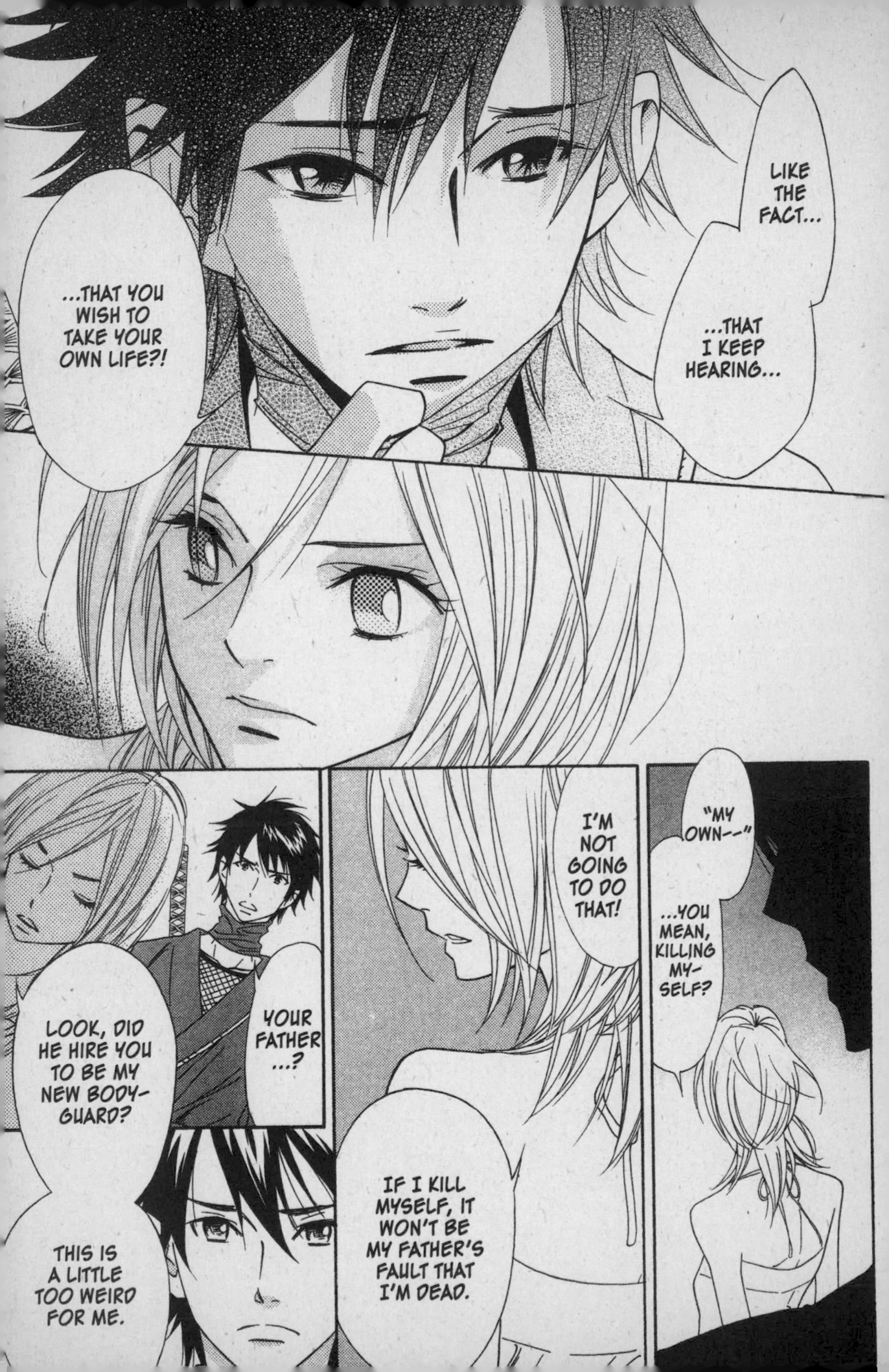
LIKE THE FACT...
...THAT I KEEP HEARING...
...THAT YOU WISH TO TAKE YOUR OWN LIFE?!
"MY OWN--"
...YOU MEAN, KILLING MY-SELF?
I'M NOT GOING TO DO THAT!
IF I KILL MYSELF, IT WON'T BE MY FATHER'S FAULT THAT I'M DEAD.
YOUR FATHER ...?
LOOK, DID HE HIRE YOU TO BE MY NEW BODY-GUARD?
THIS IS A LITTLE TOO WEIRD FOR ME.

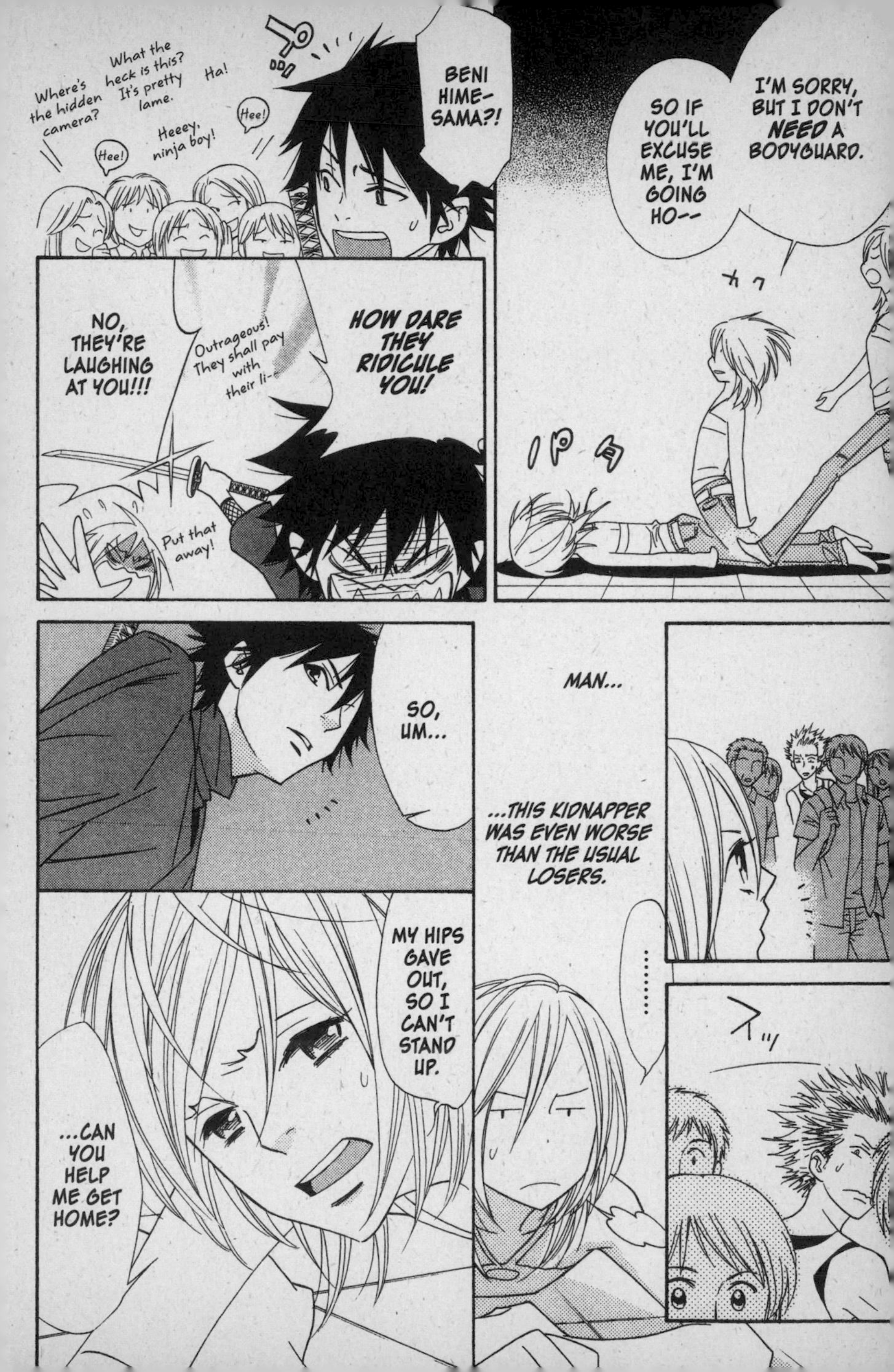
I'M SORRY, BUT I DON'T NEED A BODYGUARD.
SO IF YOU'LL EXCUSE ME, I'M GOING HO--
BENI HIME-SAMA?!
Ha!
Hee!
What the heck is this? It's pretty lame.
Heeey, ninja boy!
Where's the hidden camera?
Hee!
HOW DARE THEY RIDICULE YOU!
Outrageous! They shall pay with their li--
NO, THEY'RE LAUGHING AT YOU!!!
Put that away!
MAN...
...THIS KIDNAPPER WAS EVEN WORSE THAN THE USUAL LOSERS.
......
SO, UM...
...
スッ
MY HIPS GAVE OUT, SO I CAN'T STAND UP.
...CAN YOU HELP ME GET HOME?

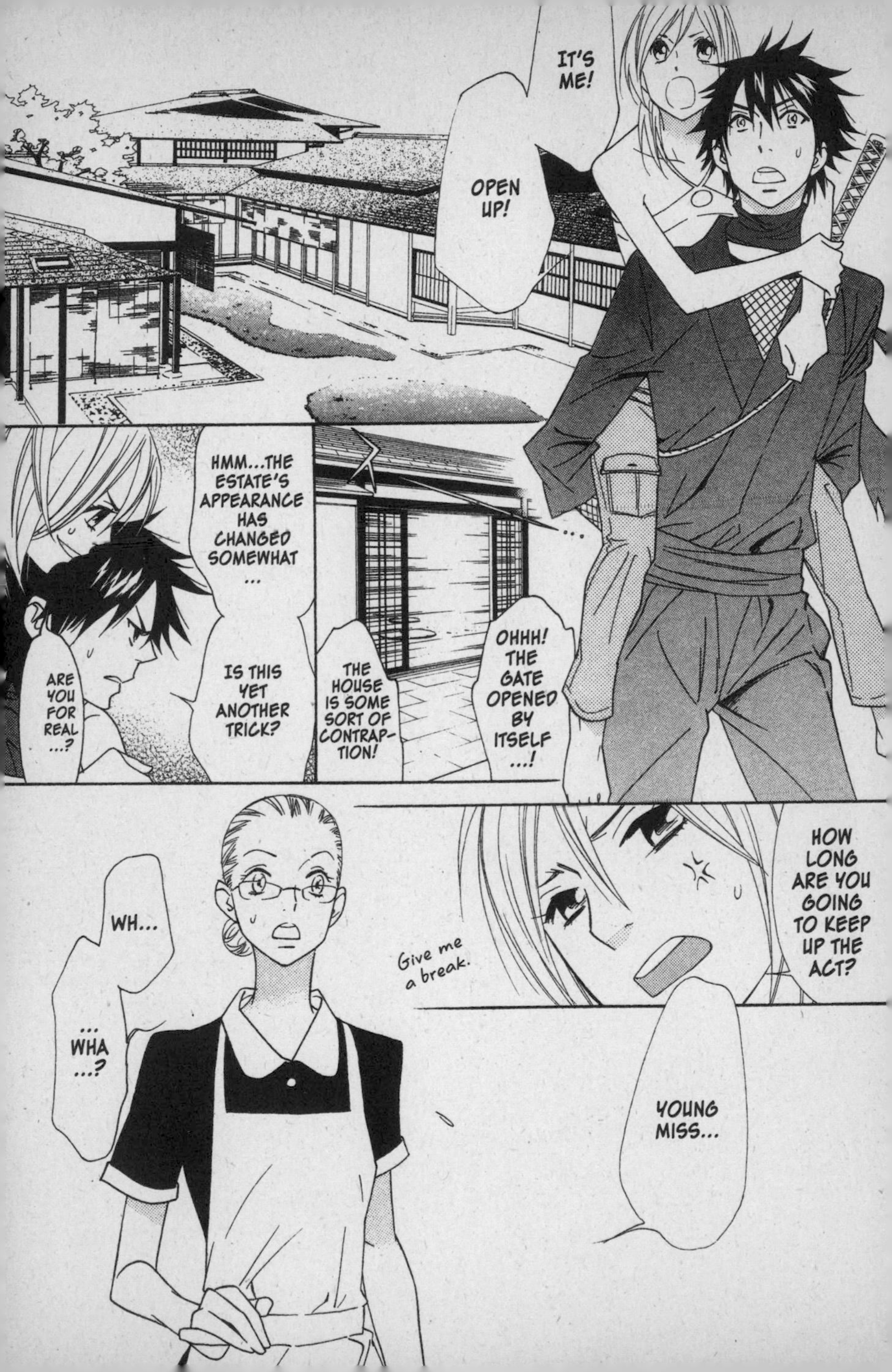
IT'S ME!
OPEN UP!
OHHH! THE GATE OPENED BY ITSELF ...!
...
THE HOUSE IS SOME SORT OF CONTRAPTION!
HMM...THE ESTATE'S APPEARANCE HAS CHANGED SOMEWHAT ...
IS THIS YET ANOTHER TRICK?
ARE YOU FOR REAL ...?
HOW LONG ARE YOU GOING TO KEEP UP THE ACT?
Give me a break.
YOUNG MISS...
WH...
... WHA ...?

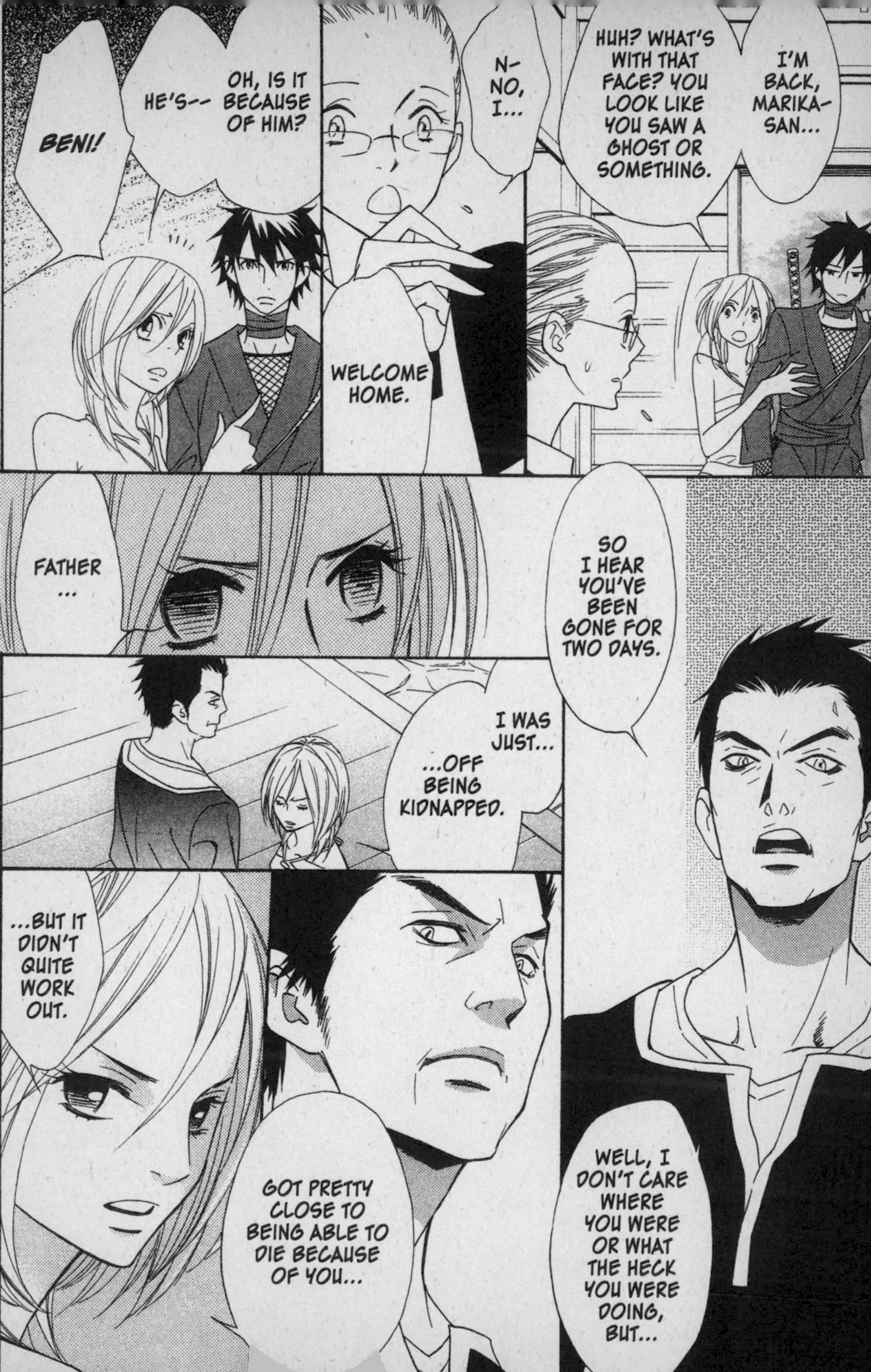
I'M BACK, MARIKA-SAN...
HUH? WHAT'S WITH THAT FACE? YOU LOOK LIKE YOU SAW A GHOST OR SOMETHING.
N-NO, I...
WELCOME HOME.
OH, IS IT BECAUSE OF HIM?
HE'S--
BENI!
SO I HEAR YOU'VE BEEN GONE FOR TWO DAYS.
WELL, I DON'T CARE WHERE YOU WERE OR WHAT THE HECK YOU WERE DOING, BUT...
FATHER...
I WAS JUST...
...OFF BEING KIDNAPPED.
...BUT IT DIDN'T QUITE WORK OUT.
GOT PRETTY CLOSE TO BEING ABLE TO DIE BECAUSE OF YOU...

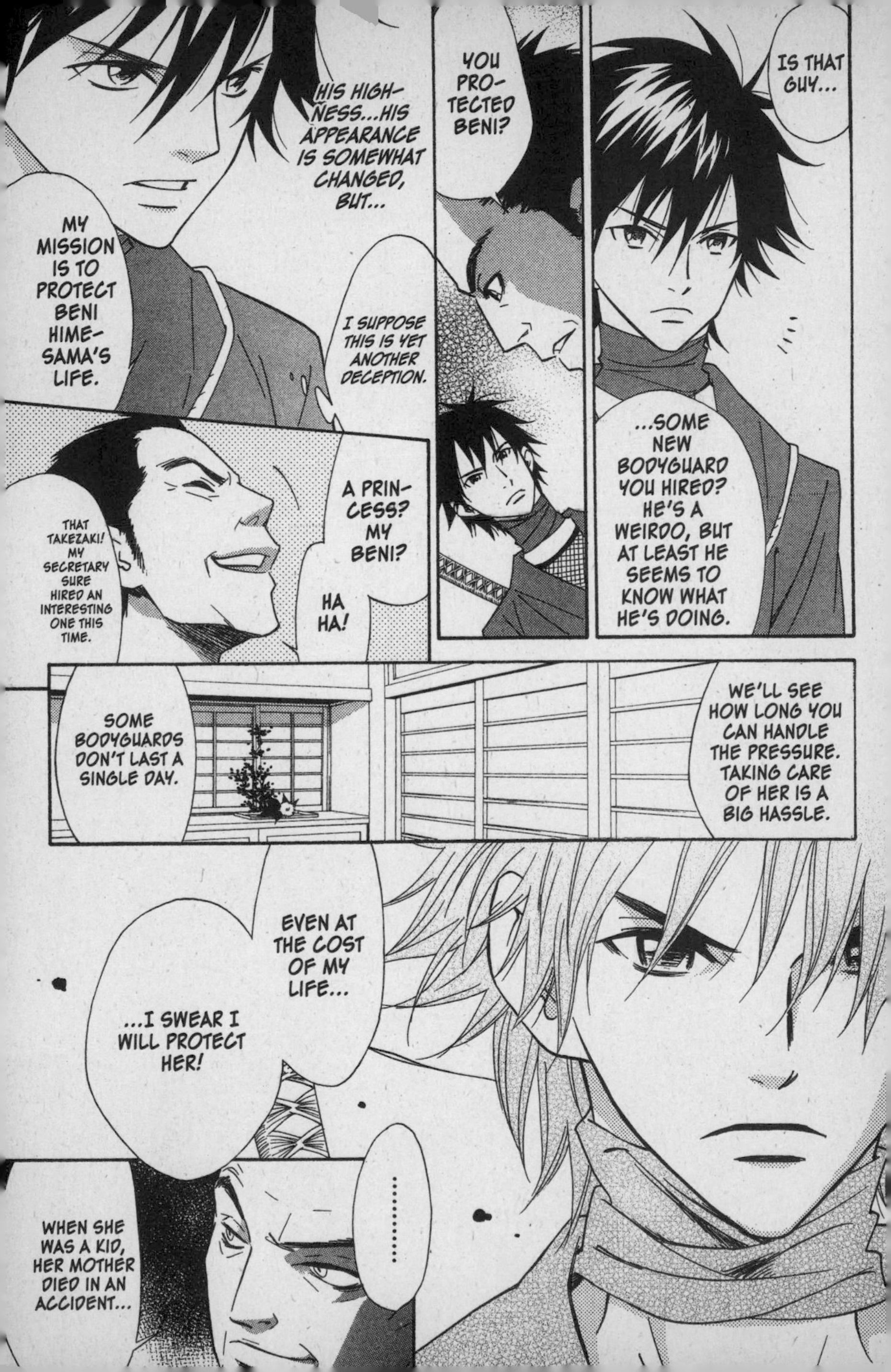
IS THAT GUY...
...SOME NEW BODYGUARD YOU HIRED? HE'S A WEIRDO, BUT AT LEAST HE SEEMS TO KNOW WHAT HE'S DOING.
YOU PROTECTED BENI?
HIS HIGHNESS...HIS APPEARANCE IS SOMEWHAT CHANGED, BUT...
MY MISSION IS TO PROTECT BENI HIME-SAMA'S LIFE.
I SUPPOSE THIS IS YET ANOTHER DECEPTION.
A PRINCESS? MY BENI?
HA HA!
THAT TAKEZAKI! MY SECRETARY SURE HIRED AN INTERESTING ONE THIS TIME.
WE'LL SEE HOW LONG YOU CAN HANDLE THE PRESSURE. TAKING CARE OF HER IS A BIG HASSLE.
SOME BODYGUARDS DON'T LAST A SINGLE DAY.
EVEN AT THE COST OF MY LIFE...
...I SWEAR I WILL PROTECT HER!
......
WHEN SHE WAS A KID, HER MOTHER DIED IN AN ACCIDENT...

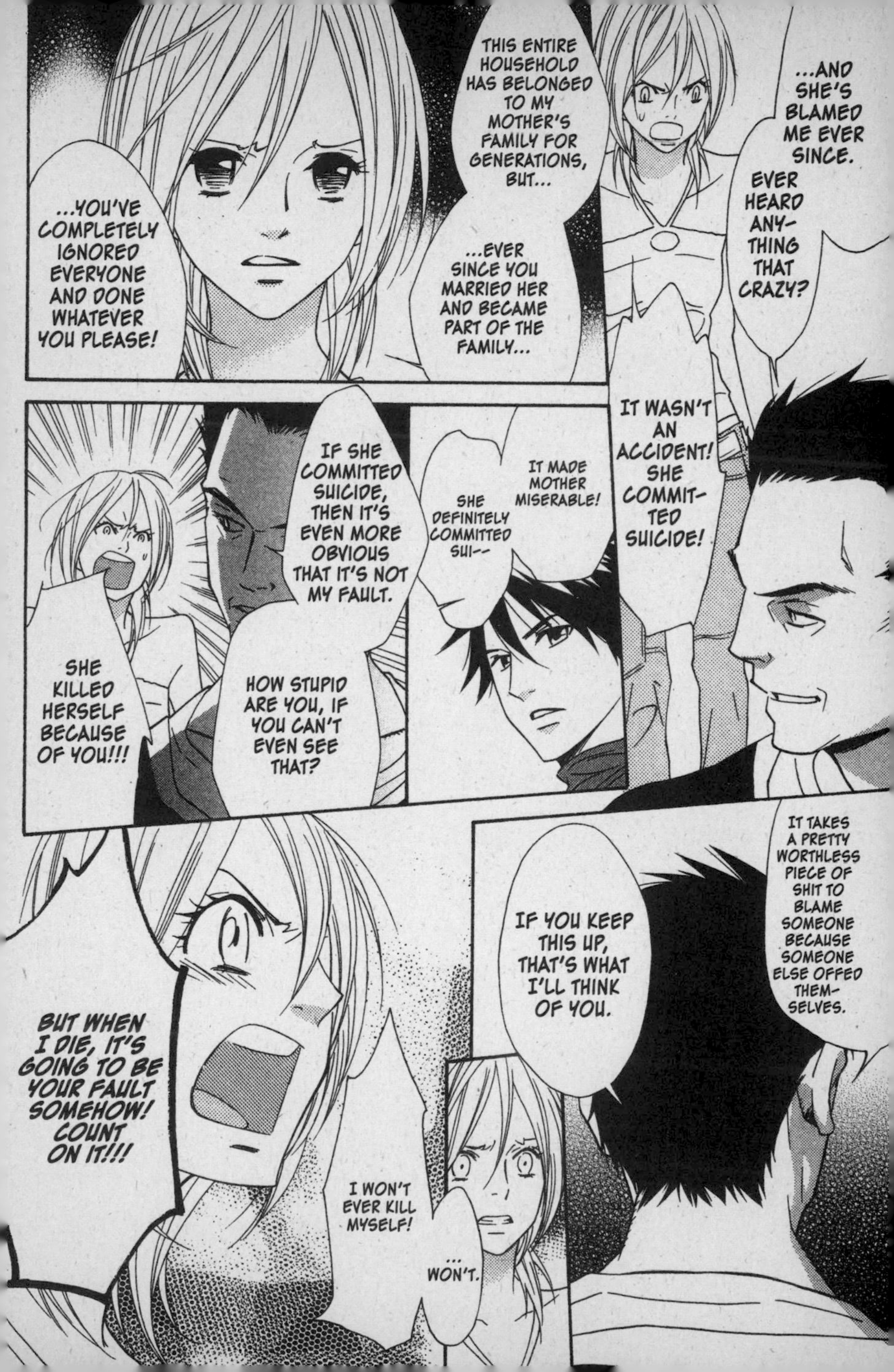
...AND SHE'S BLAMED ME EVER SINCE.
EVER HEARD ANYTHING THAT CRAZY?
IT WASN'T AN ACCIDENT! SHE COMMITTED SUICIDE!
THIS ENTIRE HOUSEHOLD HAS BELONGED TO MY MOTHER'S FAMILY FOR GENERATIONS, BUT...
...EVER SINCE YOU MARRIED HER AND BECAME PART OF THE FAMILY...
...YOU'VE COMPLETELY IGNORED EVERYONE AND DONE WHATEVER YOU PLEASE!
IT MADE MOTHER MISERABLE!
SHE DEFINITELY COMMITTED SUI--
IF SHE COMMITTED SUICIDE, THEN IT'S EVEN MORE OBVIOUS THAT IT'S NOT MY FAULT.
HOW STUPID ARE YOU, IF YOU CAN'T EVEN SEE THAT?
SHE KILLED HERSELF BECAUSE OF YOU!!!
IT TAKES A PRETTY WORTHLESS PIECE OF SHIT TO BLAME SOMEONE BECAUSE SOMEONE ELSE OFFED THEMSELVES.
IF YOU KEEP THIS UP, THAT'S WHAT I'LL THINK OF YOU.
I WON'T EVER KILL MYSELF!
... WON'T.
BUT WHEN I DIE, IT'S GOING TO BE YOUR FAULT SOMEHOW! COUNT ON IT!!!

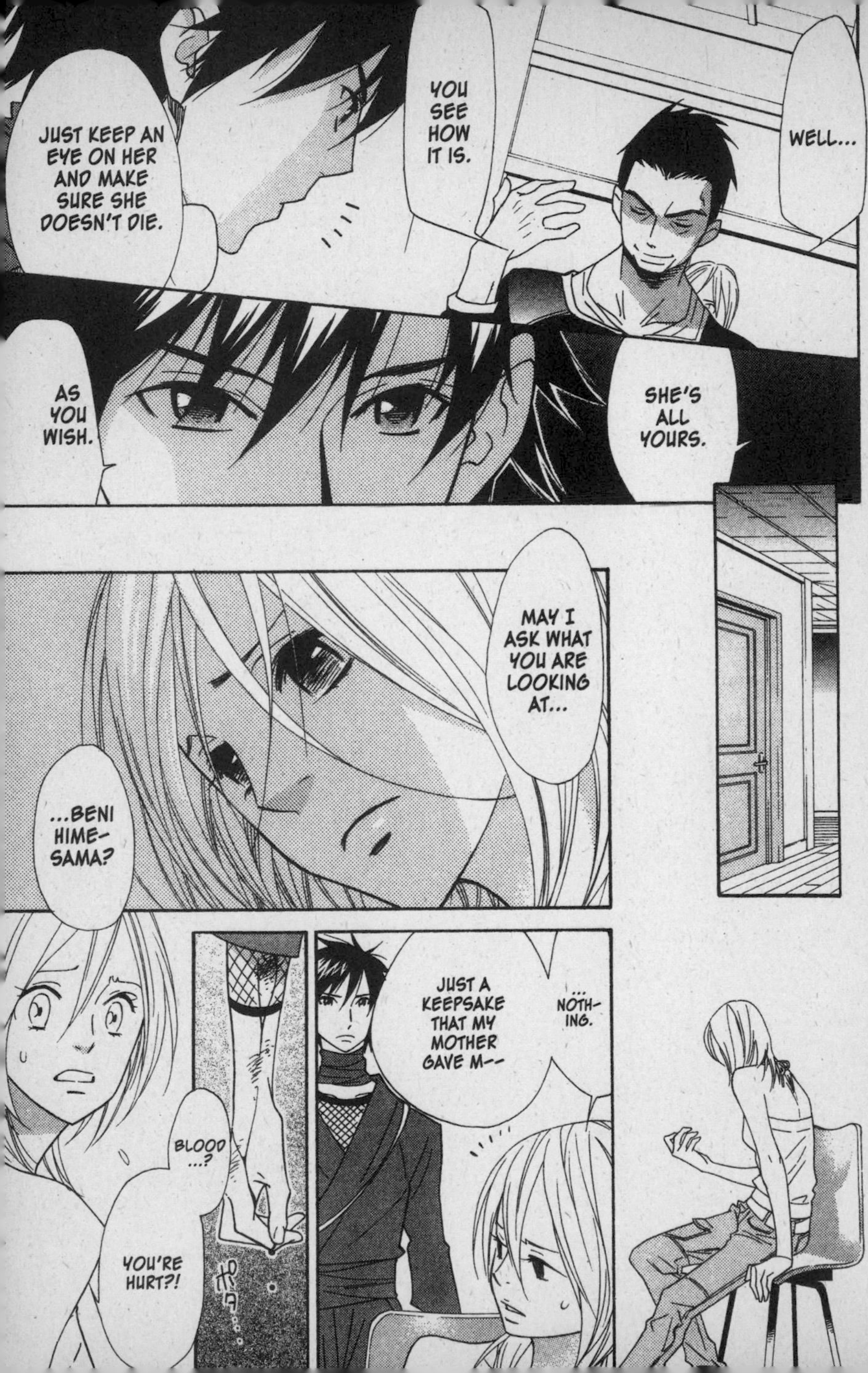

WELL...
YOU SEE HOW IT IS.
JUST KEEP AN EYE ON HER AND MAKE SURE SHE DOESN'T DIE.
SHE'S ALL YOURS.
AS YOU WISH.
MAY I ASK WHAT YOU ARE LOOKING AT...
...BENI HIME-SAMA?
...NOTH-ING.
JUST A KEEPSAKE THAT MY MOTHER GAVE M--
ポタ...
BLOOD...?
YOU'RE HURT?!

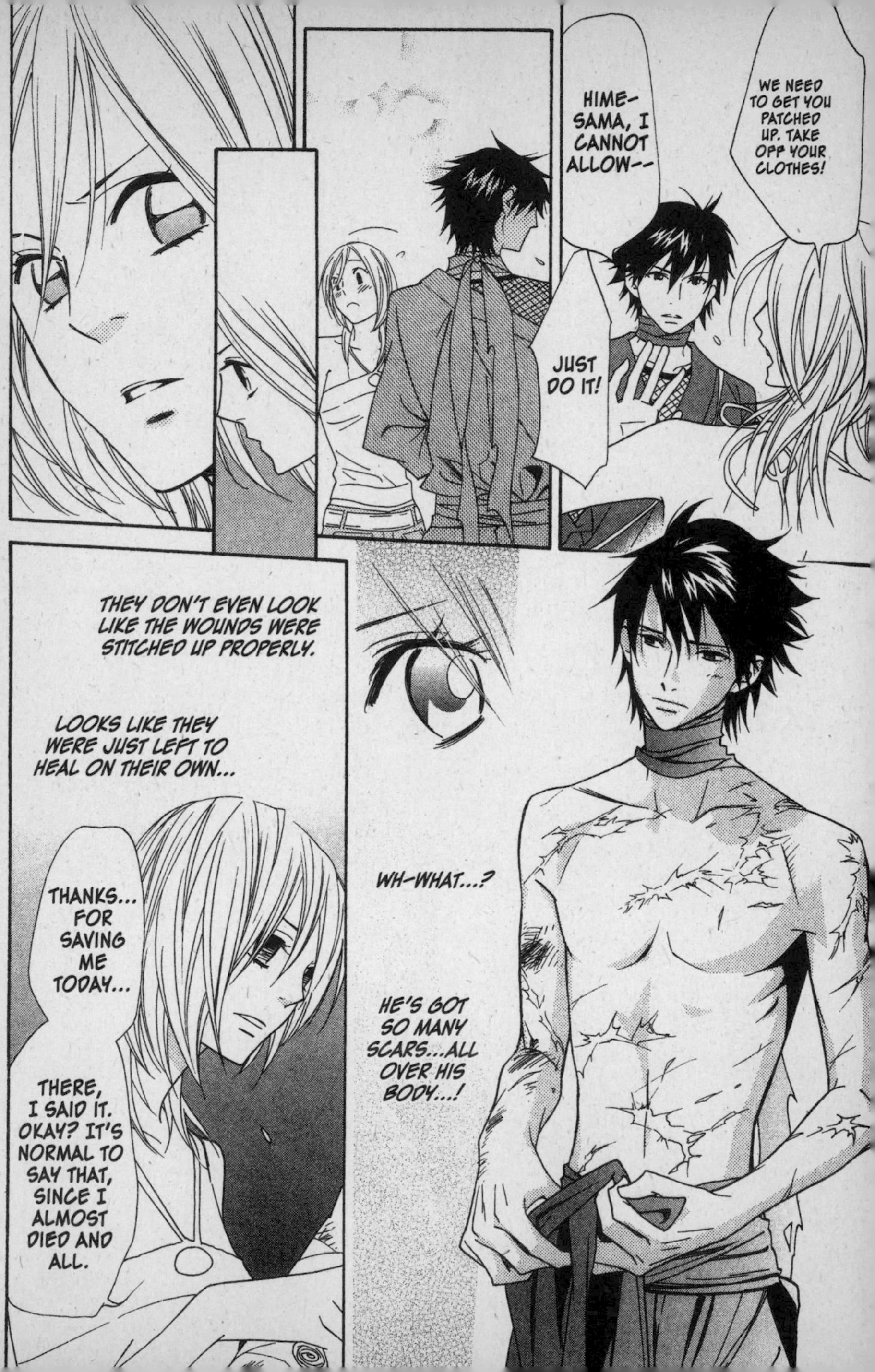

WE NEED TO GET YOU PATCHED UP. TAKE OFF YOUR CLOTHES!
HIME-SAMA, I CANNOT ALLOW--
JUST DO IT!
WH-WHAT...?
HE'S GOT SO MANY SCARS...ALL OVER HIS BODY...!
THEY DON'T EVEN LOOK LIKE THE WOUNDS WERE STITCHED UP PROPERLY.
LOOKS LIKE THEY WERE JUST LEFT TO HEAL ON THEIR OWN...
THANKS... FOR SAVING ME TODAY...
THERE, I SAID IT. OKAY? IT'S NORMAL TO SAY THAT, SINCE I ALMOST DIED AND ALL.

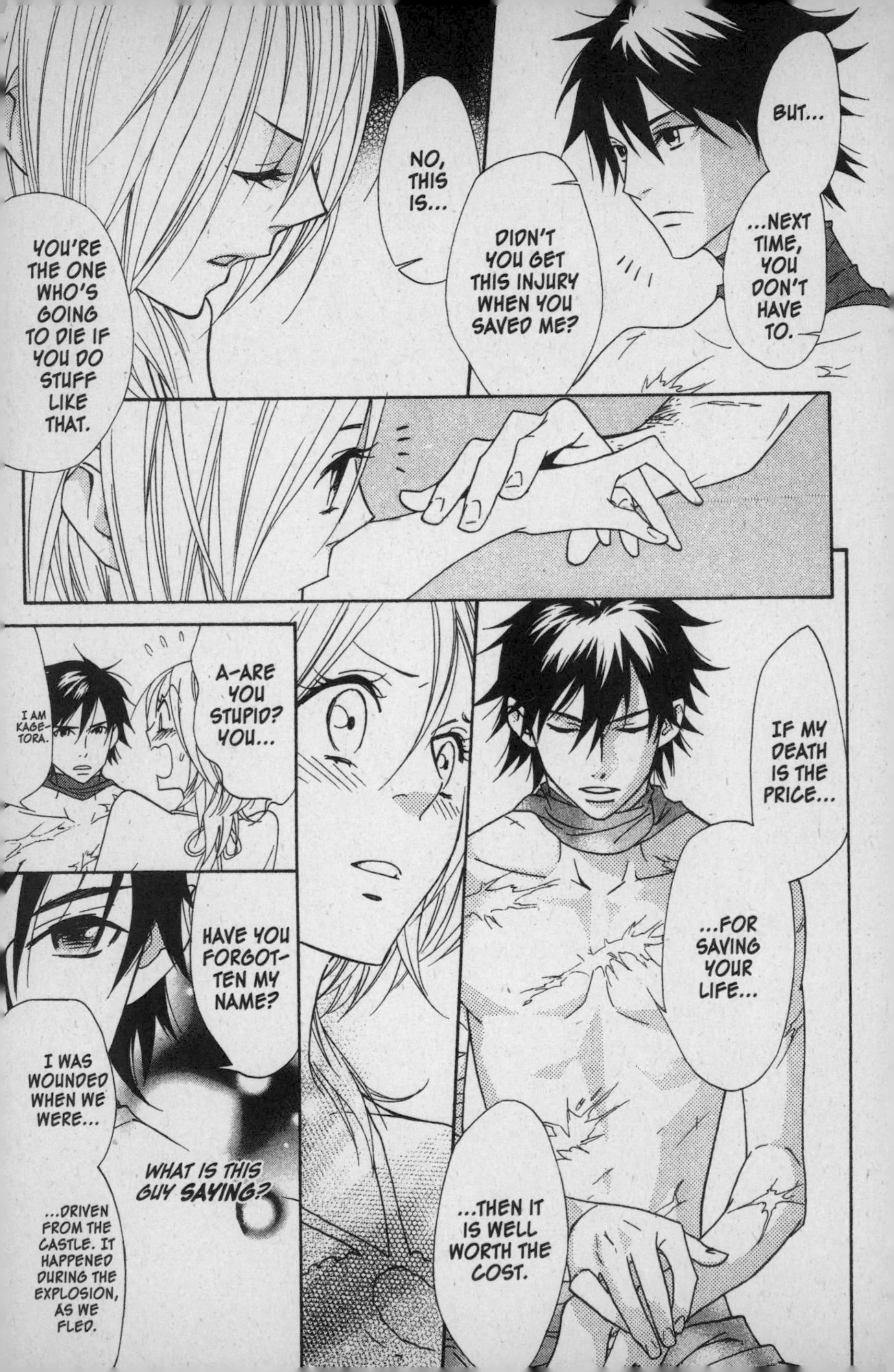

BUT...
...NEXT TIME, YOU DON'T HAVE TO.
DIDN'T YOU GET THIS INJURY WHEN YOU SAVED ME?
NO, THIS IS...
YOU'RE THE ONE WHO'S GOING TO DIE IF YOU DO STUFF LIKE THAT.
IF MY DEATH IS THE PRICE...
...FOR SAVING YOUR LIFE...
...THEN IT IS WELL WORTH THE COST.
A-ARE YOU STUPID? YOU...
I AM KAGETORA.
HAVE YOU FORGOTTEN MY NAME?
WHAT IS THIS GUY SAYING?
I WAS WOUNDED WHEN WE WERE...
...DRIVEN FROM THE CASTLE. IT HAPPENED DURING THE EXPLOSION, AS WE FLED.

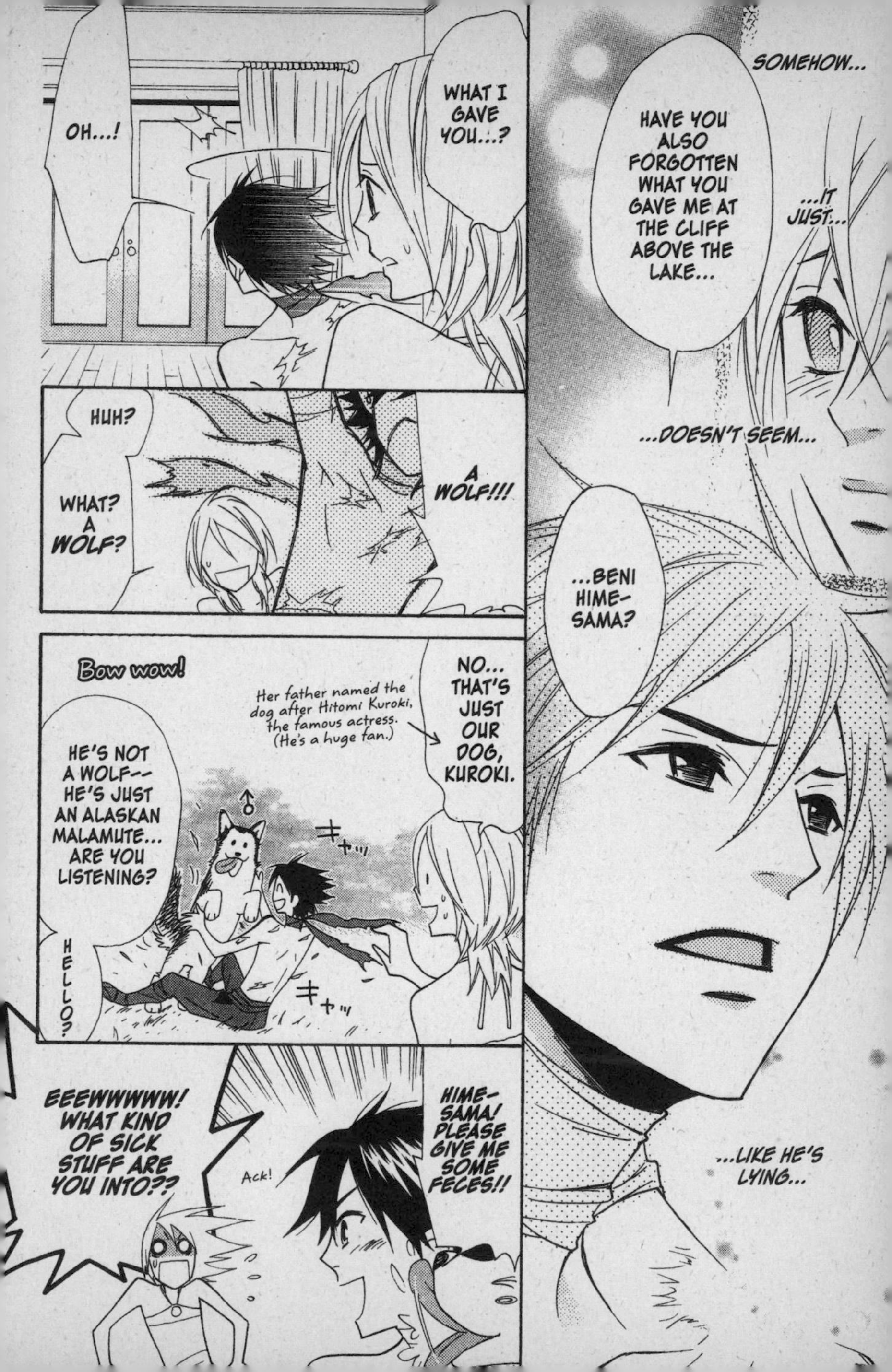
SOMEHOW...
HAVE YOU ALSO FORGOTTEN WHAT YOU GAVE ME AT THE CLIFF ABOVE THE LAKE...
...IT JUST...
...DOESN'T SEEM...
...BENI HIME-SAMA?
...LIKE HE'S LYING...
WHAT I GAVE YOU...?
OH...!
A WOLF!!!
HUH?
WHAT? A WOLF?
NO... THAT'S JUST OUR DOG, KUROKI.
Her father named the dog after Hitomi Kuroki, the famous actress. (He's a huge fan.)
Bow wow!
キャッ
キャッ
HE'S NOT A WOLF-- HE'S JUST AN ALASKAN MALAMUTE... ARE YOU LISTENING?
HELLO?
HIME-SAMA! PLEASE GIVE ME SOME FECES!!
Ack!
EEEWWWWW! WHAT KIND OF SICK STUFF ARE YOU INTO??

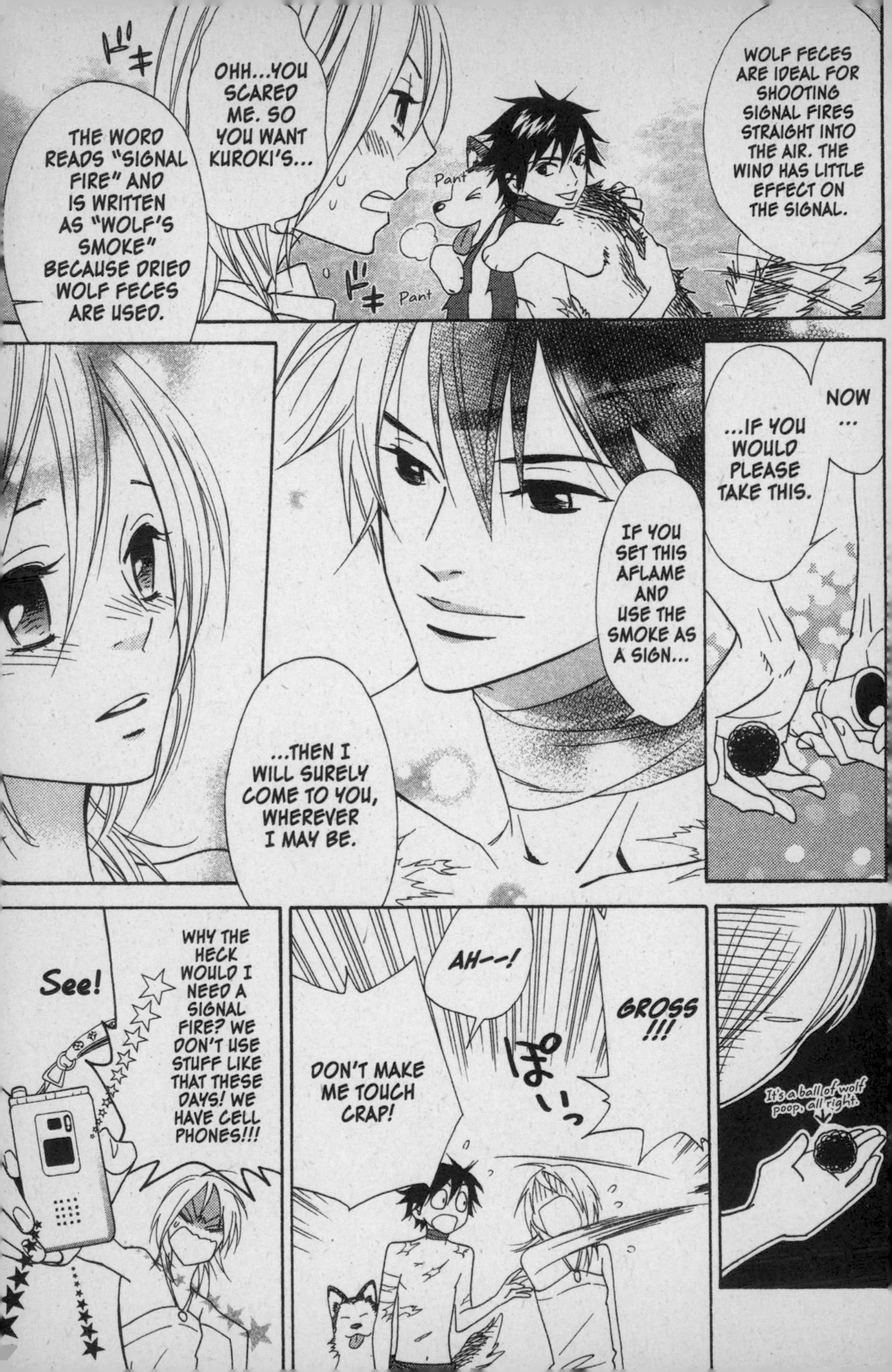
WOLF FECES ARE IDEAL FOR SHOOTING SIGNAL FIRES STRAIGHT INTO THE AIR. THE WIND HAS LITTLE EFFECT ON THE SIGNAL.
Pant
Pant
ドキ
OHH...YOU SCARED ME. SO YOU WANT KUROKI'S...
ドキ
THE WORD READS "SIGNAL FIRE" AND IS WRITTEN AS "WOLF'S SMOKE" BECAUSE DRIED WOLF FECES ARE USED.
NOW...
...IF YOU WOULD PLEASE TAKE THIS.
IF YOU SET THIS AFLAME AND USE THE SMOKE AS A SIGN...
...THEN I WILL SURELY COME TO YOU, WHEREVER I MAY BE.
It's a ball of wolf poop, all right.
GROSS!!!
ぽいっ
AH--!
DON'T MAKE ME TOUCH CRAP!
WHY THE HECK WOULD I NEED A SIGNAL FIRE? WE DON'T USE STUFF LIKE THAT THESE DAYS! WE HAVE CELL PHONES!!!
See!

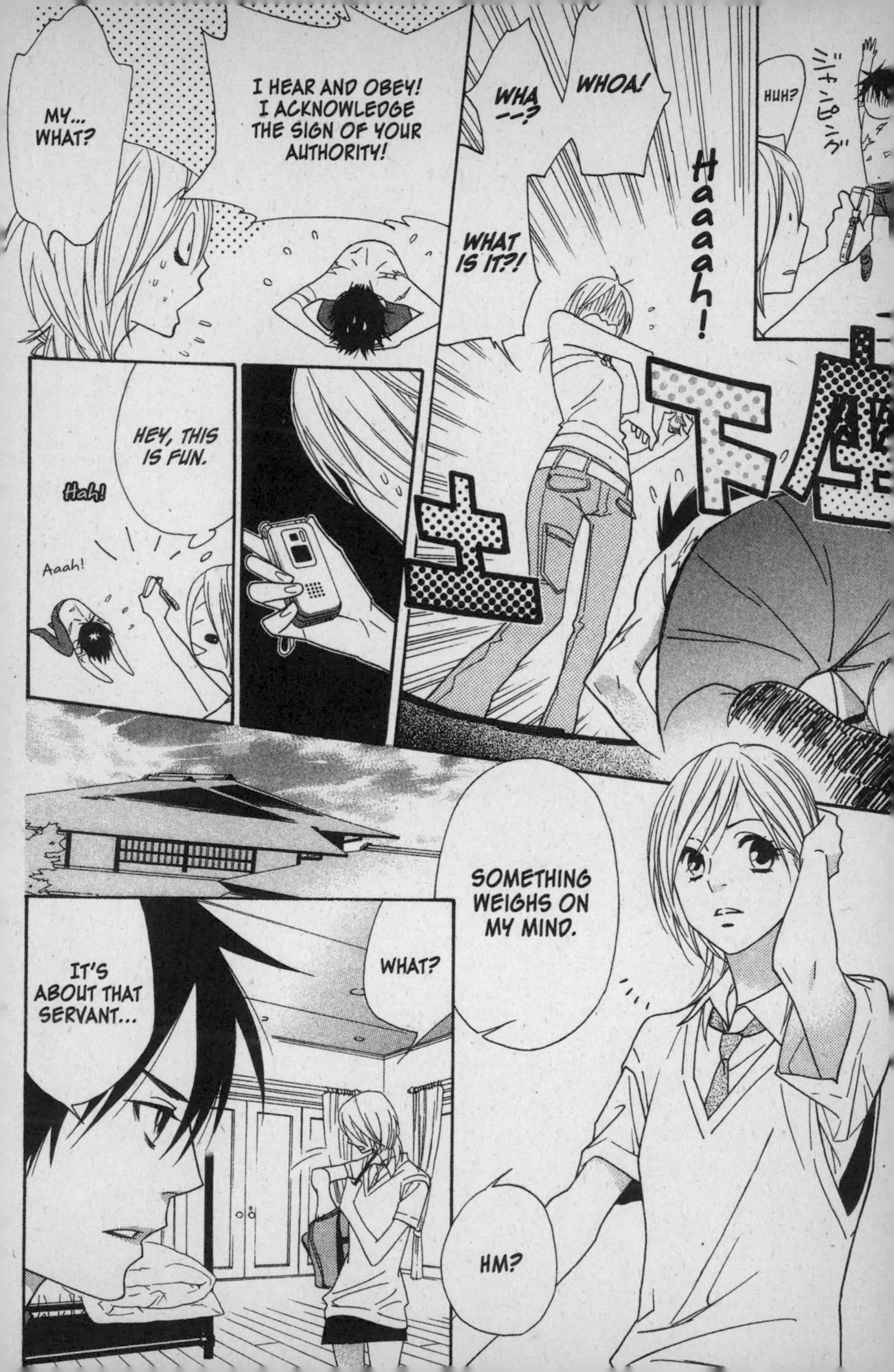
HUH?
WHA--?
WHOA!
WHAT IS IT?!
Haaaah!
I HEAR AND OBEY! I ACKNOWLEDGE THE SIGN OF YOUR AUTHORITY!
MY... WHAT?
HEY, THIS IS FUN.
Hah!
Aaah!
SOMETHING WEIGHS ON MY MIND.
HM?
WHAT?
IT'S ABOUT THAT SERVANT...

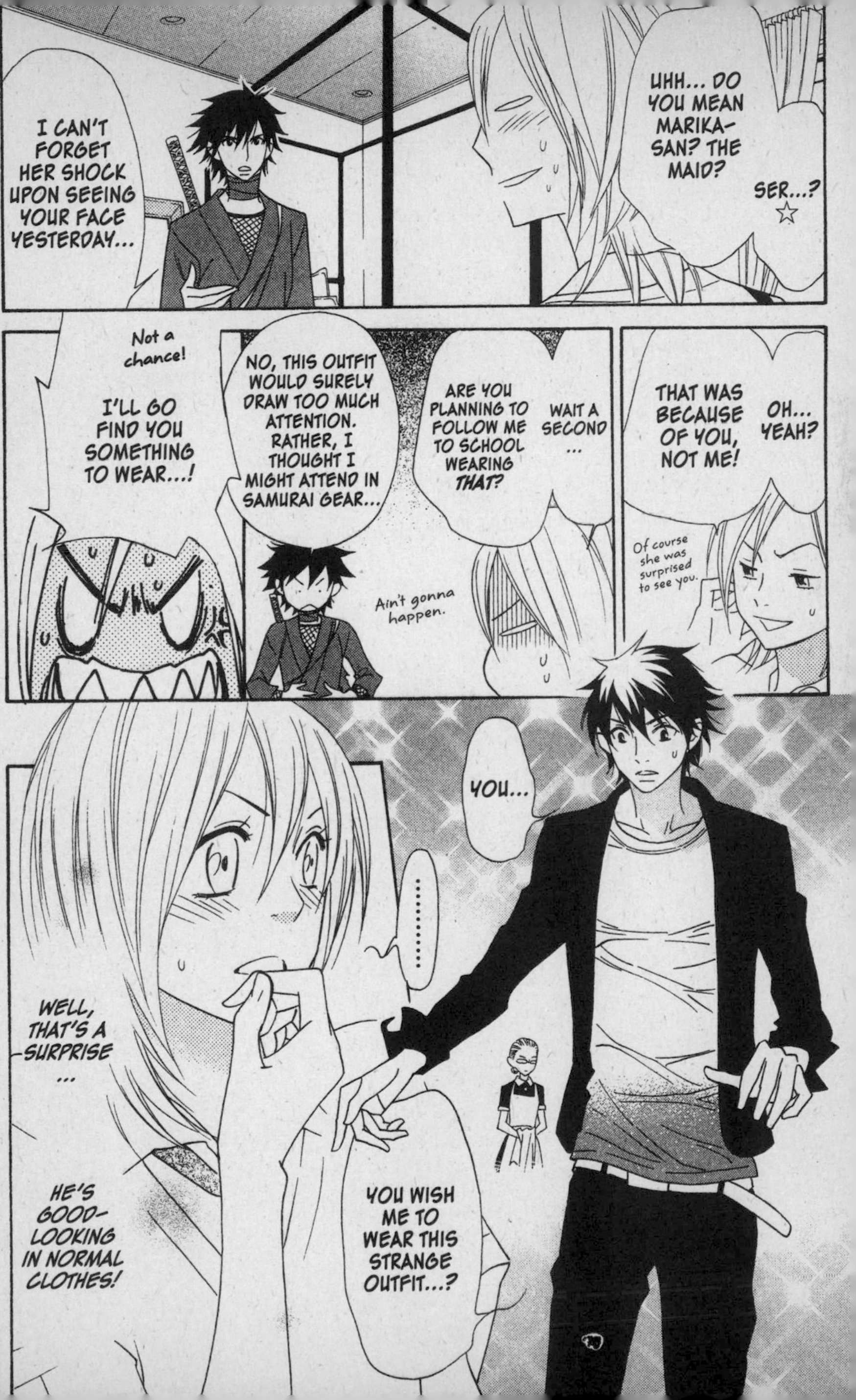
UHH... DO YOU MEAN MARIKA-SAN? THE MAID?
SER...? ☆
I CAN'T FORGET HER SHOCK UPON SEEING YOUR FACE YESTERDAY...
OH... YEAH?
THAT WAS BECAUSE OF YOU, NOT ME!
Of course she was surprised to see you.
WAIT A SECOND ...
ARE YOU PLANNING TO FOLLOW ME TO SCHOOL WEARING *THAT?*
NO, THIS OUTFIT WOULD SURELY DRAW TOO MUCH ATTENTION. RATHER, I THOUGHT I MIGHT ATTEND IN SAMURAI GEAR...
Ain't gonna happen.
Not a chance!
I'LL GO FIND YOU SOMETHING TO WEAR...!
YOU...
......
YOU WISH ME TO WEAR THIS STRANGE OUTFIT...?
WELL, THAT'S A SURPRISE...
HE'S GOOD-LOOKING IN NORMAL CLOTHES!

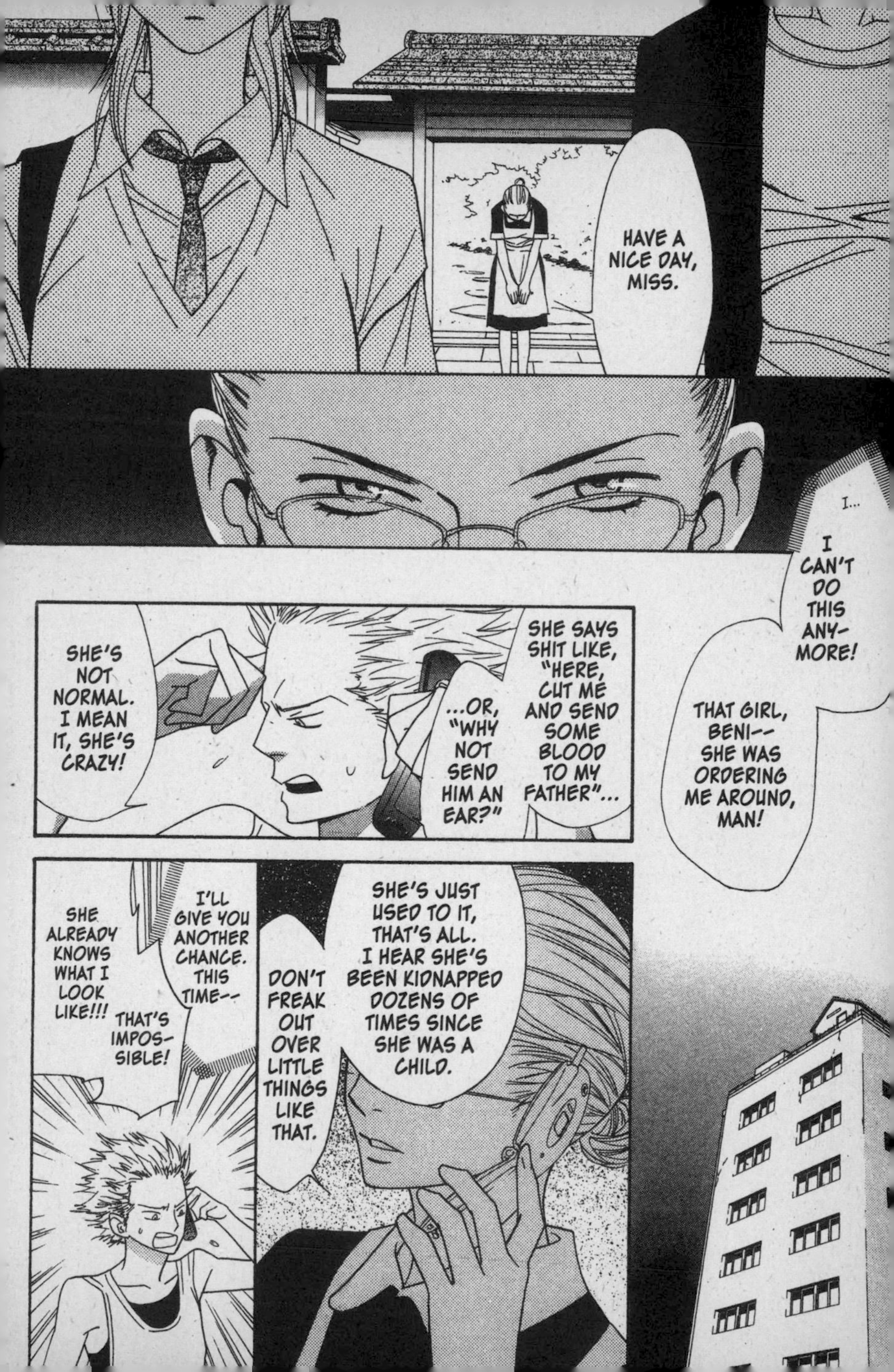
HAVE A NICE DAY, MISS.
I...
I CAN'T DO THIS ANY-MORE!
THAT GIRL, BENI-- SHE WAS ORDERING ME AROUND, MAN!
SHE SAYS SHIT LIKE, "HERE, CUT ME AND SEND SOME BLOOD TO MY FATHER"...
...OR, "WHY NOT SEND HIM AN EAR?"
SHE'S NOT NORMAL. I MEAN IT, SHE'S CRAZY!
SHE'S JUST USED TO IT, THAT'S ALL. I HEAR SHE'S BEEN KIDNAPPED DOZENS OF TIMES SINCE SHE WAS A CHILD.
DON'T FREAK OUT OVER LITTLE THINGS LIKE THAT.
I'LL GIVE YOU ANOTHER CHANCE. THIS TIME--
THAT'S IMPOS-SIBLE!
SHE ALREADY KNOWS WHAT I LOOK LIKE!!!

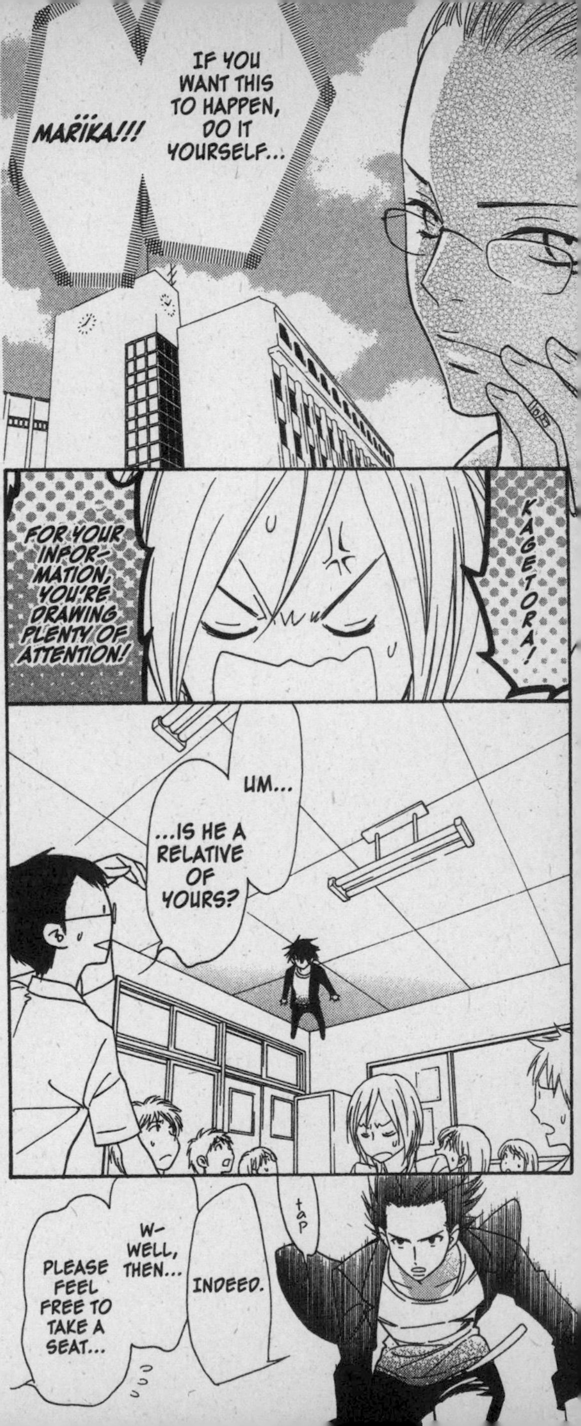
IF YOU WANT THIS TO HAPPEN, DO IT YOURSELF...
...MARIKA!!!
KAGETORA!
FOR YOUR INFORMATION, YOU'RE DRAWING PLENTY OF ATTENTION!
UM...
...IS HE A RELATIVE OF YOURS?
tap
INDEED.
W-WELL, THEN...
PLEASE FEEL FREE TO TAKE A SEAT...

Hello, this is Conami! Thank you for picking up my book.

This is my first book for Princess Comics.

As you can tell from the title, there's a ninja in this manga. I've wanted to draw this story for a long time now.

But when I first began to imagine the story, I never imagined my little tale of a ninja would take up a whole series like this.

I'll be so happy if you enjoy it, even a little bit.

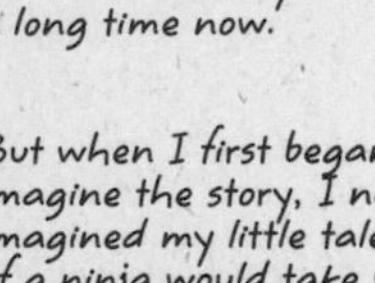
You can read it as you sit back and take a break.
If you like tea with your manga, I suggest Darjeeling.

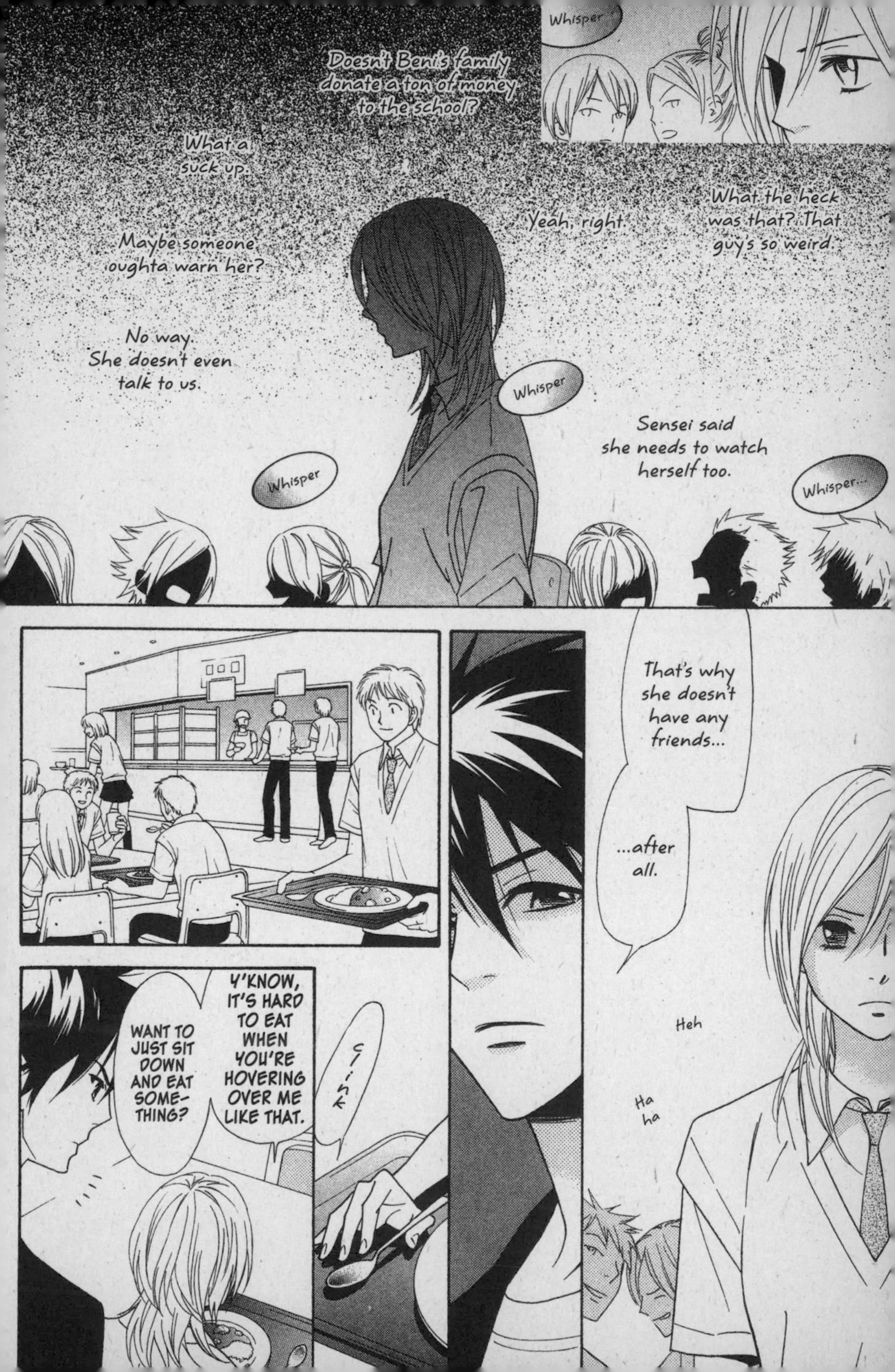
Whisper
Doesn't Beni's family donate a ton of money to the school?
What the heck was that? That guy's so weird.
Yeah, right.
What a suck up.
Maybe someone oughta warn her?
No way. She doesn't even talk to us.
Whisper
Sensei said she needs to watch herself too.
Whisper...
Whisper
That's why she doesn't have any friends...
...after all.
Heh
Ha ha
Y'KNOW, IT'S HARD TO EAT WHEN YOU'RE HOVERING OVER ME LIKE THAT.
WANT TO JUST SIT DOWN AND EAT SOMETHING?
Clink

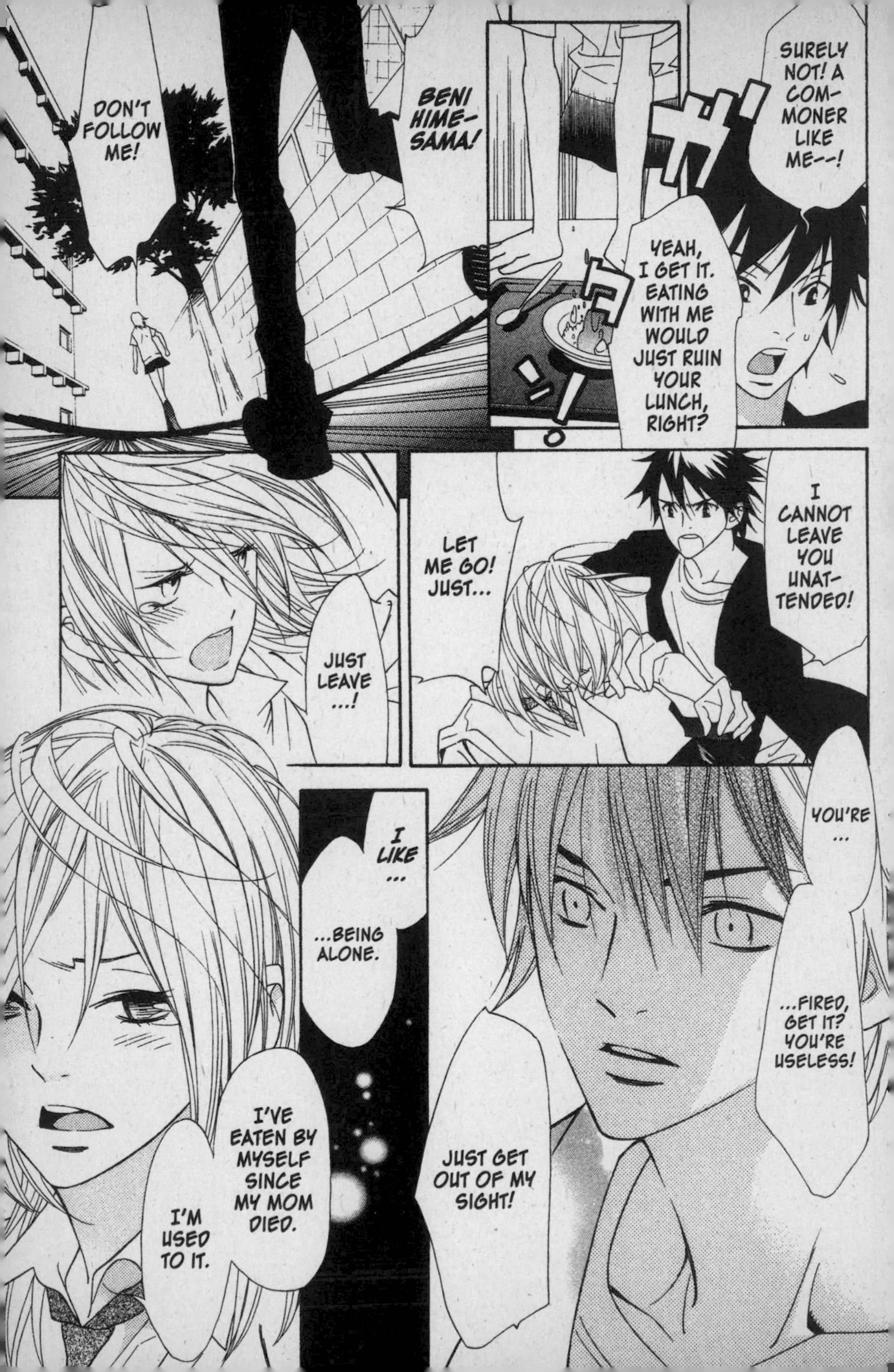
SURELY NOT! A COMMONER LIKE ME--!
YEAH, I GET IT. EATING WITH ME WOULD JUST RUIN YOUR LUNCH, RIGHT?
BENI HIME-SAMA!
DON'T FOLLOW ME!
I CANNOT LEAVE YOU UNATTENDED!
LET ME GO! JUST...
JUST LEAVE ...!
YOU'RE ...
...FIRED, GET IT? YOU'RE USELESS!
JUST GET OUT OF MY SIGHT!
I LIKE ...
...BEING ALONE.
I'VE EATEN BY MYSELF SINCE MY MOM DIED.
I'M USED TO IT.

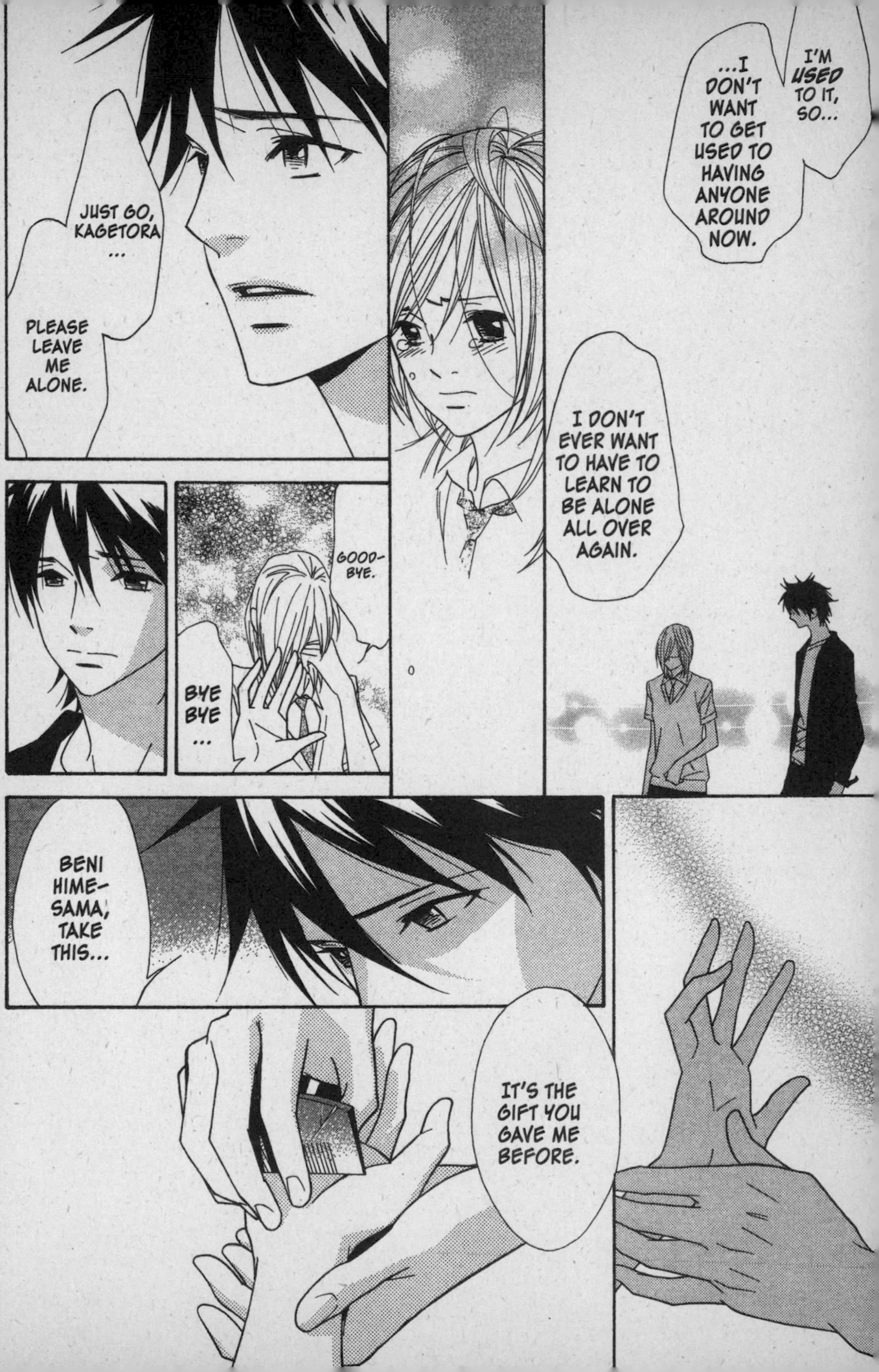
I'M USED TO IT, SO...
...I DON'T WANT TO GET USED TO HAVING ANYONE AROUND NOW.
I DON'T EVER WANT TO HAVE TO LEARN TO BE ALONE ALL OVER AGAIN.
JUST GO, KAGETORA ...
PLEASE LEAVE ME ALONE.
GOOD-BYE.
BYE BYE ...
BENI HIME-SAMA, TAKE THIS...
IT'S THE GIFT YOU GAVE ME BEFORE.

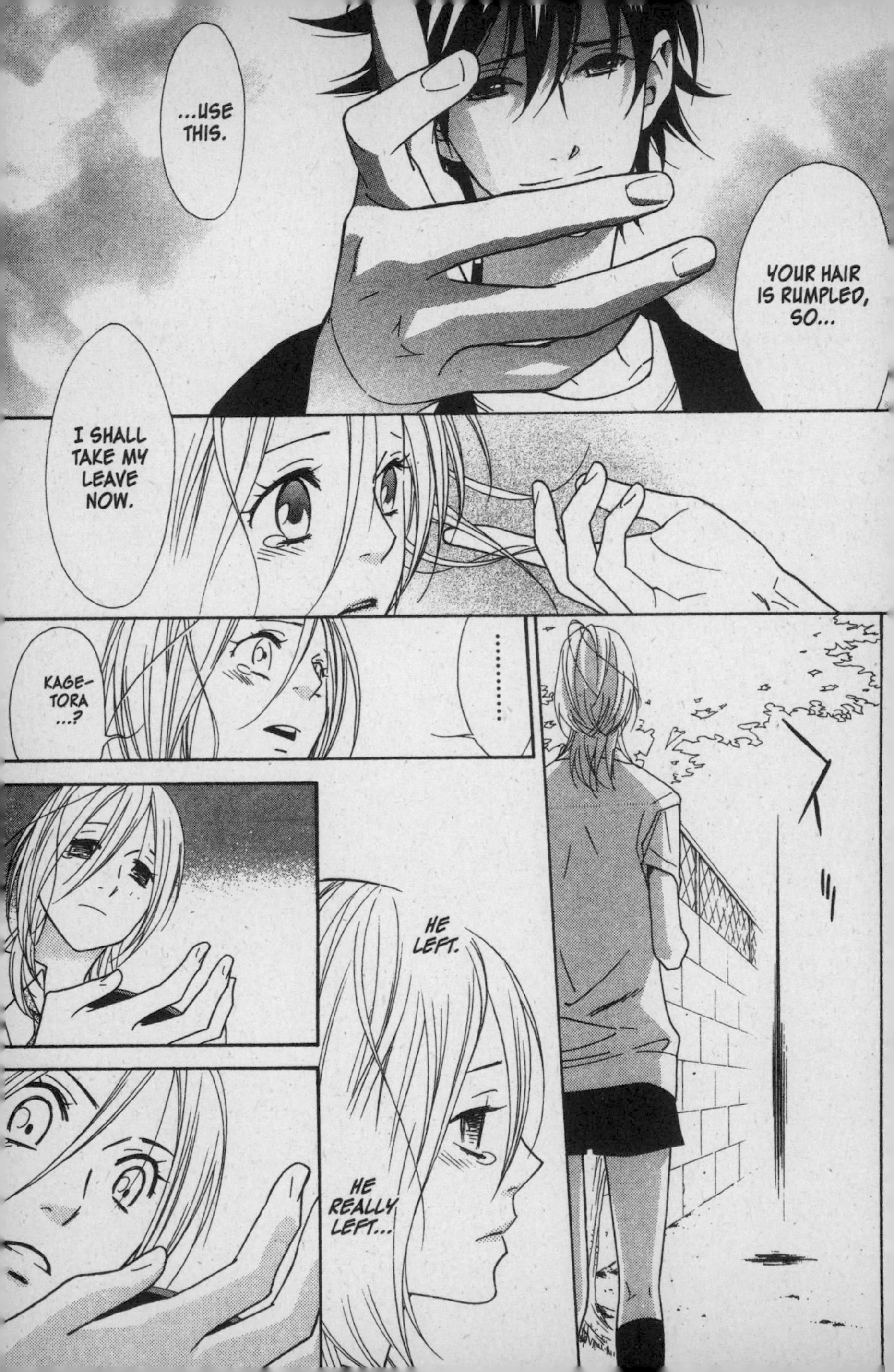
YOUR HAIR IS RUMPLED, SO...
...USE THIS.
I SHALL TAKE MY LEAVE NOW.
......
KAGE-TORA ...?
HE LEFT.
HE REALLY LEFT...

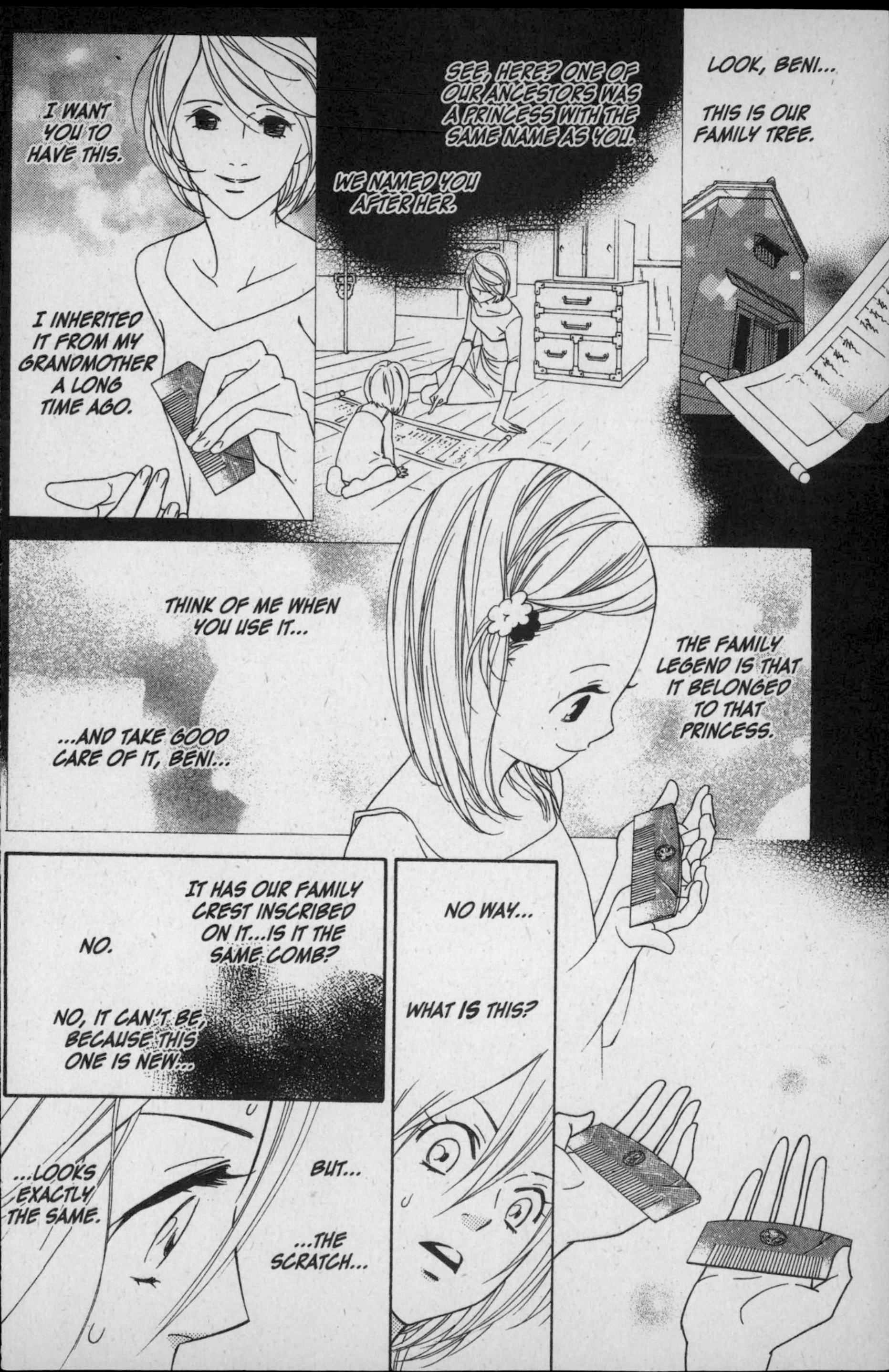

LOOK, BENI...
THIS IS OUR FAMILY TREE.
SEE, HERE? ONE OF OUR ANCESTORS WAS A PRINCESS WITH THE SAME NAME AS YOU.
WE NAMED YOU AFTER HER.
I WANT YOU TO HAVE THIS.
I INHERITED IT FROM MY GRANDMOTHER A LONG TIME AGO.
THE FAMILY LEGEND IS THAT IT BELONGED TO THAT PRINCESS.
THINK OF ME WHEN YOU USE IT...
...AND TAKE GOOD CARE OF IT, BENI...
NO WAY...
WHAT IS THIS?
IT HAS OUR FAMILY CREST INSCRIBED ON IT...IS IT THE SAME COMB?
NO.
NO, IT CAN'T BE, BECAUSE THIS ONE IS NEW...
BUT...
...THE SCRATCH...
...LOOKS EXACTLY THE SAME.

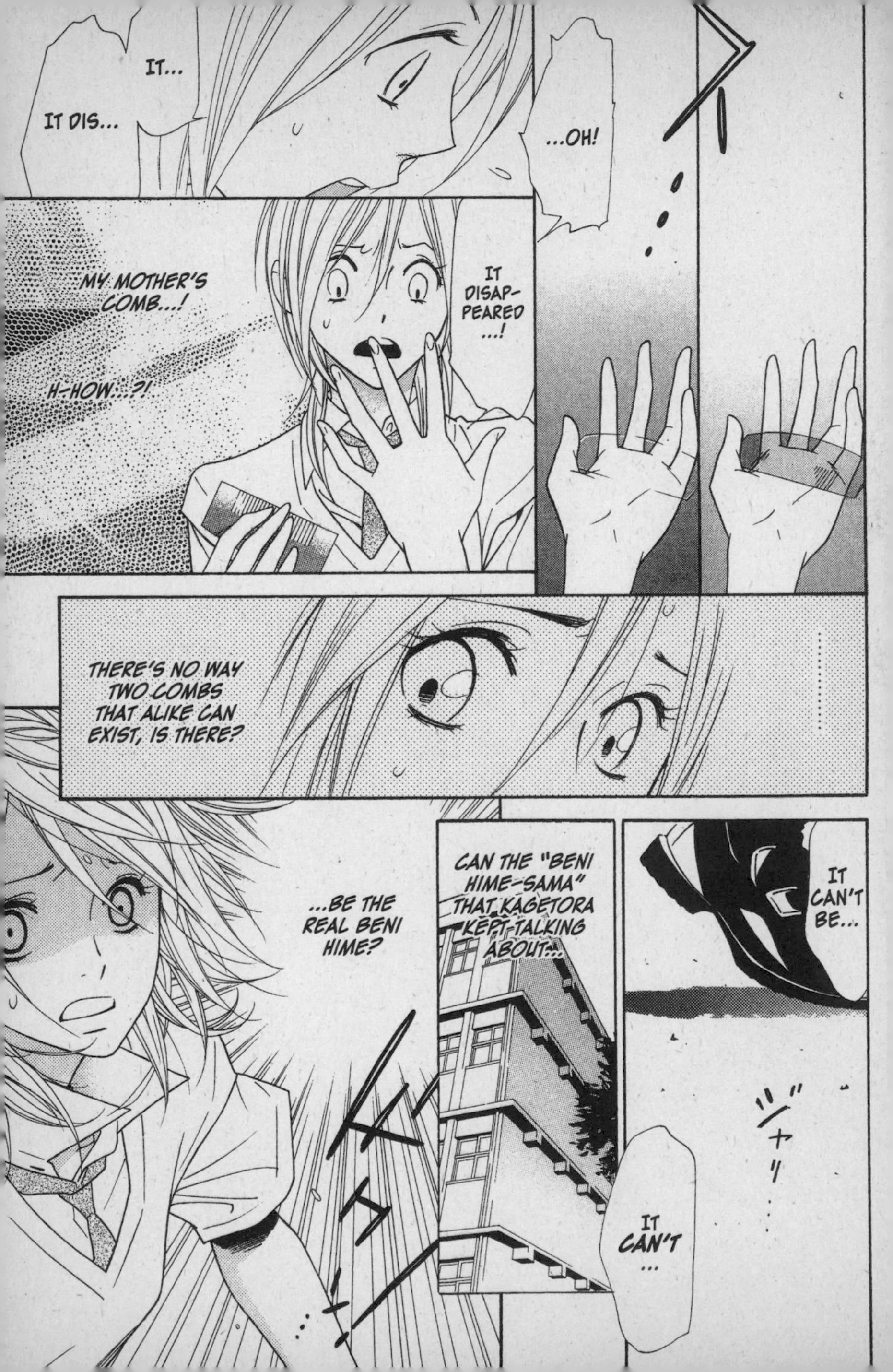
!
......
...OH!
IT...
IT DIS...
IT DISAPPEARED...!
MY MOTHER'S COMB...!
H-HOW...?!
......
THERE'S NO WAY TWO COMBS THAT ALIKE CAN EXIST, IS THERE?
IT CAN'T BE...
ジャリ...
IT CAN'T ...
CAN THE "BENI HIME-SAMA" THAT KAGETORA KEPT TALKING ABOUT...
...BE THE REAL BENI HIME?

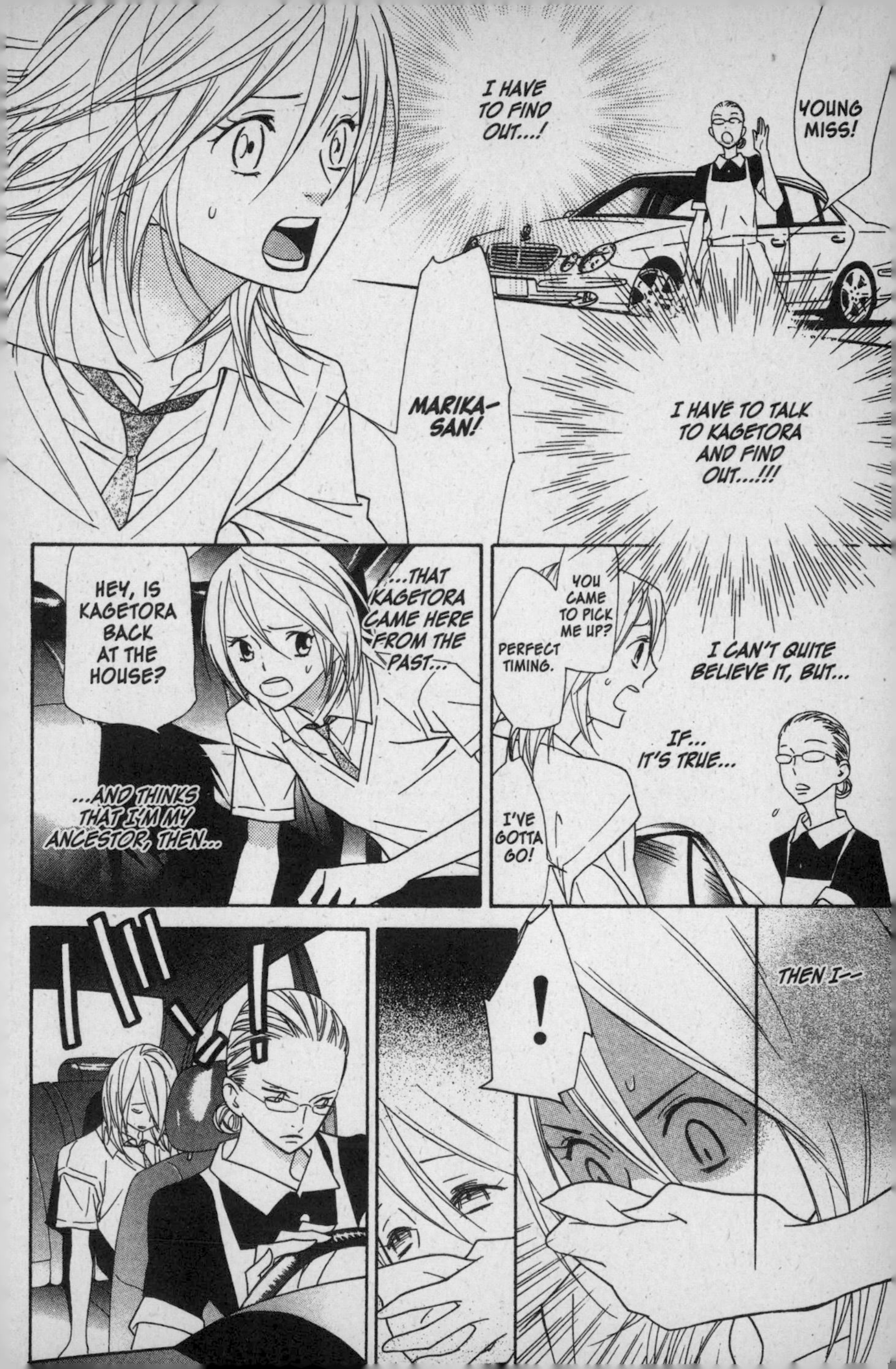
YOUNG MISS!
I HAVE TO FIND OUT...!
I HAVE TO TALK TO KAGETORA AND FIND OUT...!!!
MARIKA-SAN!
I CAN'T QUITE BELIEVE IT, BUT...
YOU CAME TO PICK ME UP?
PERFECT TIMING.
IF... IT'S TRUE...
I'VE GOTTA GO!
...THAT KAGETORA CAME HERE FROM THE PAST...
HEY, IS KAGETORA BACK AT THE HOUSE?
...AND THINKS THAT I'M MY ANCESTOR, THEN...
THEN I--
!

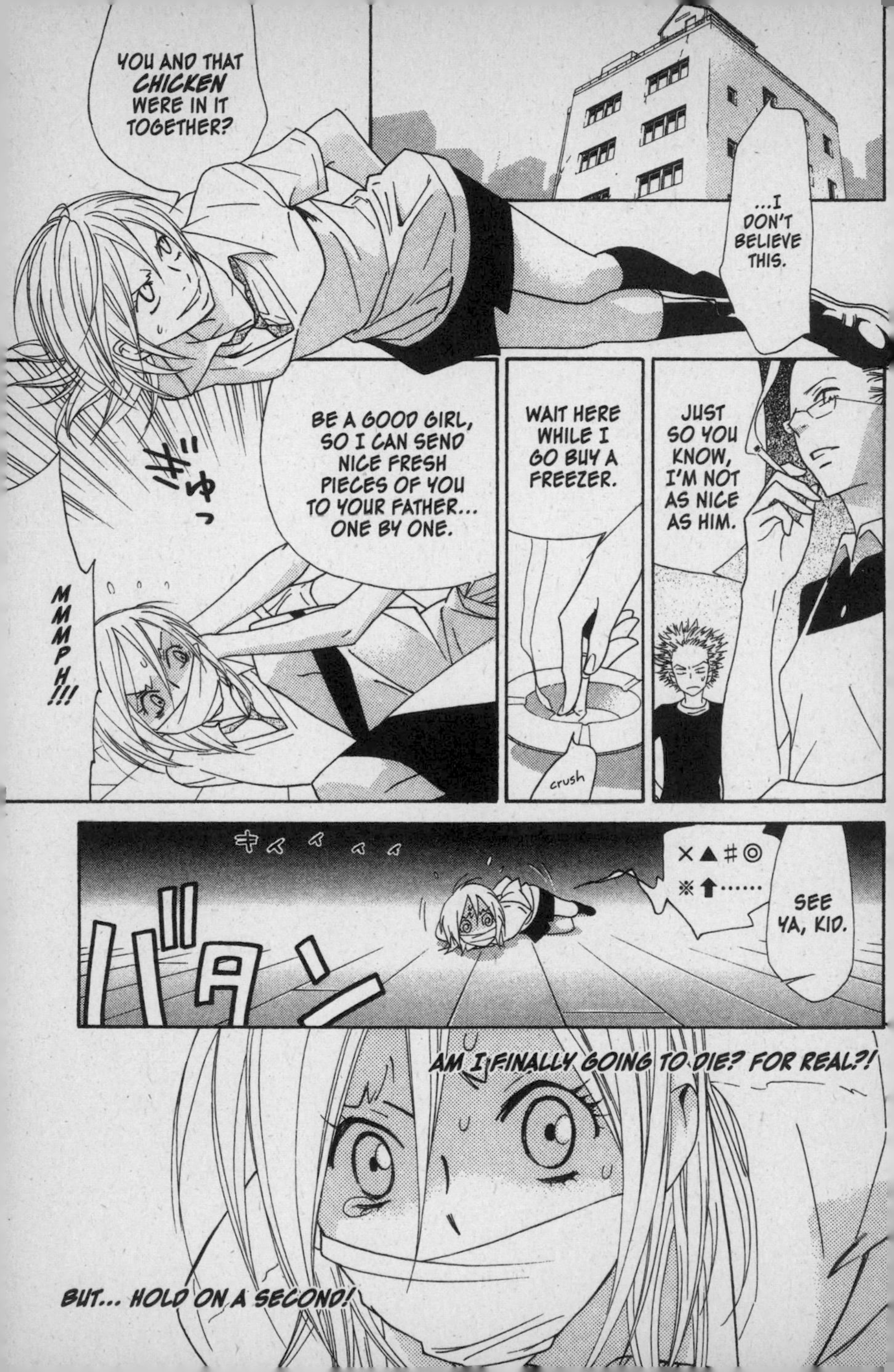
...I DON'T BELIEVE THIS.
YOU AND THAT CHICKEN WERE IN IT TOGETHER?
JUST SO YOU KNOW, I'M NOT AS NICE AS HIM.
WAIT HERE WHILE I GO BUY A FREEZER.
crush
BE A GOOD GIRL, SO I CAN SEND NICE FRESH PIECES OF YOU TO YOUR FATHER... ONE BY ONE.
ギュっ
MMMPH!!!
SEE YA, KID.
×▲#◎ ※⬆……
キイイイイ
バタン
AM I FINALLY GOING TO DIE? FOR REAL?!
BUT... HOLD ON A SECOND!

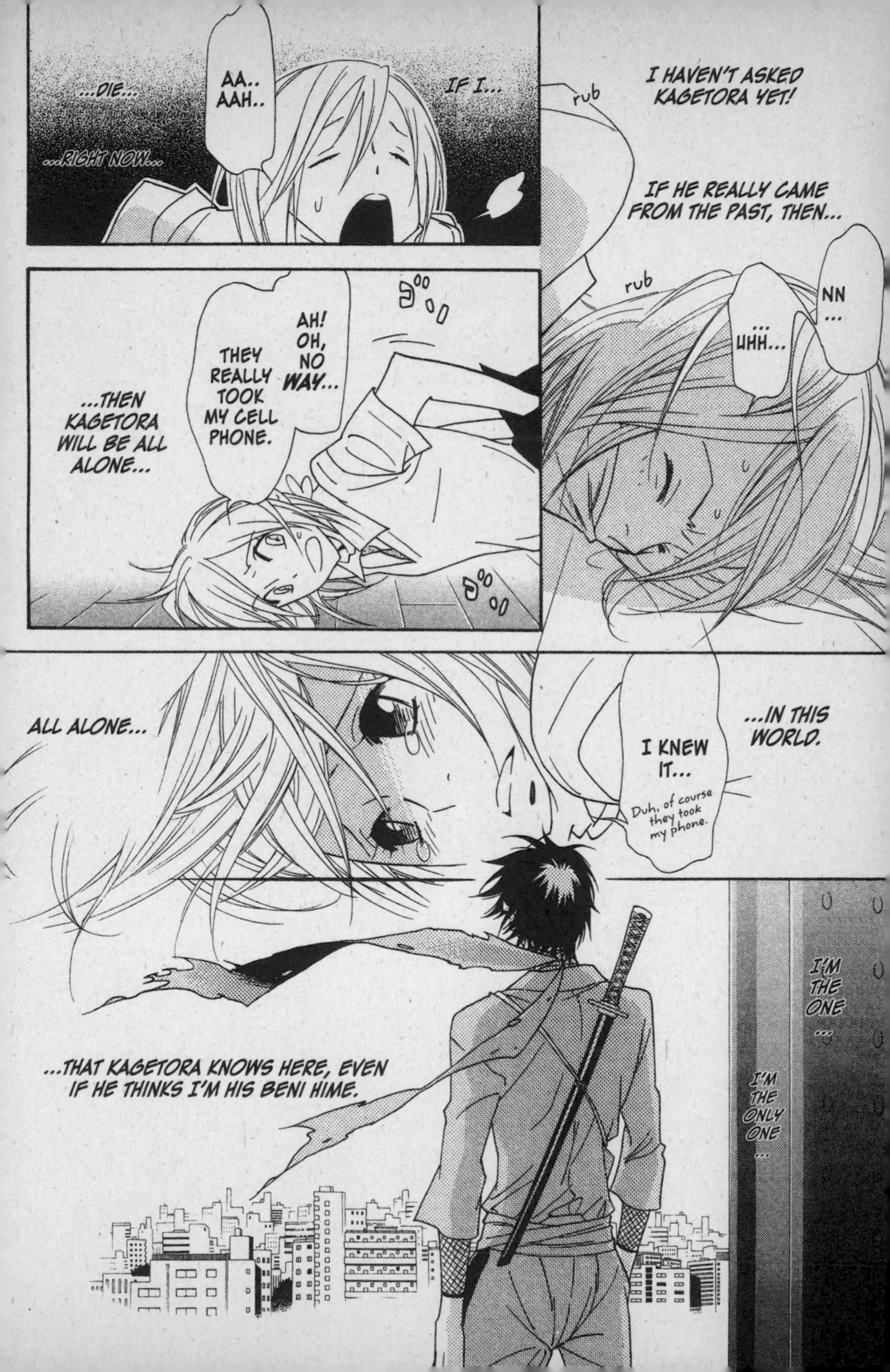
I HAVEN'T ASKED KAGETORA YET!
rub
IF HE REALLY CAME FROM THE PAST, THEN...
rub
NN ...
... UHH...
IF I...
AA.. AAH..
...DIE...
...RIGHT NOW...
AH! OH, NO WAY...
THEY REALLY TOOK MY CELL PHONE.
...THEN KAGETORA WILL BE ALL ALONE...
...IN THIS WORLD.
I KNEW IT...
Duh, of course they took my phone.
ALL ALONE...
I'M THE ONE...
I'M THE ONLY ONE...
...THAT KAGETORA KNOWS HERE, EVEN IF HE THINKS I'M HIS BENI HIME.

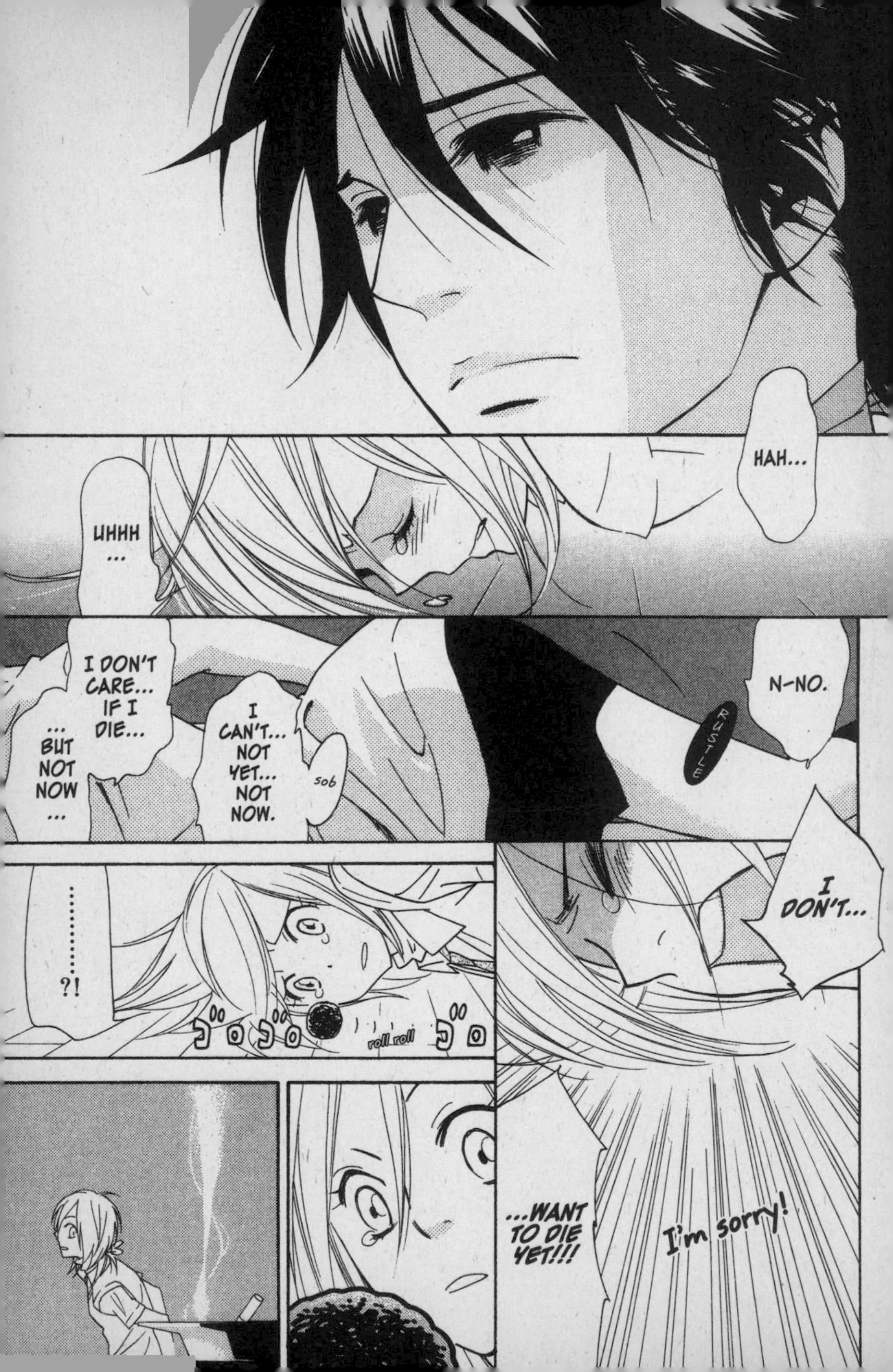
HAH...
UHHH ...
N-NO.
RUSTLE
sob
I CAN'T... NOT YET... NOT NOW.
I DON'T CARE... IF I DIE...
... BUT NOT NOW ...
I DON'T...
...WANT TO DIE YET!!!
I'm sorry!
........?!
roll roll

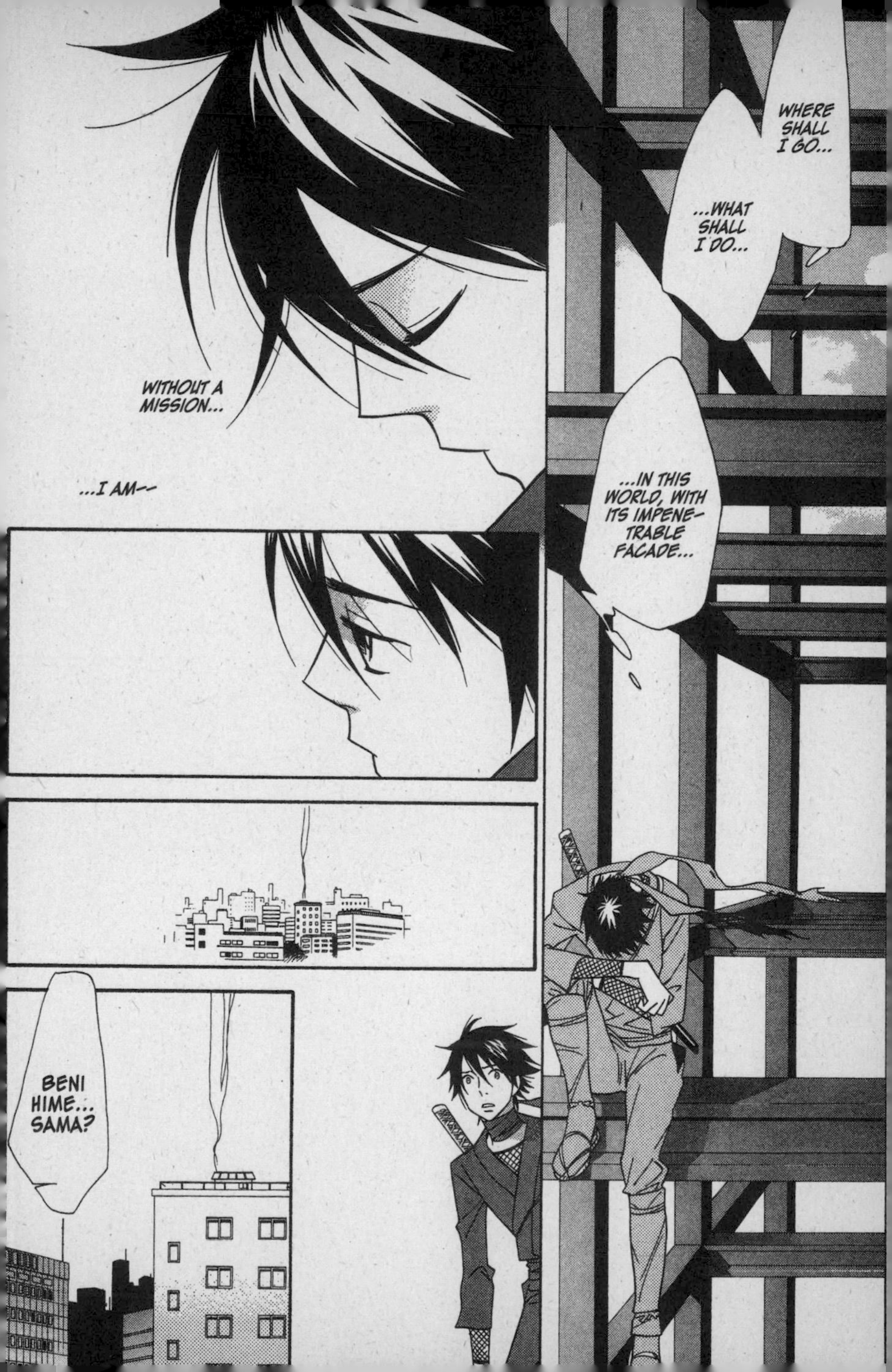
WHERE SHALL I GO...
...WHAT SHALL I DO...
...IN THIS WORLD, WITH ITS IMPENE-TRABLE FACADE...
WITHOUT A MISSION...
...I AM--
BENI HIME... SAMA?

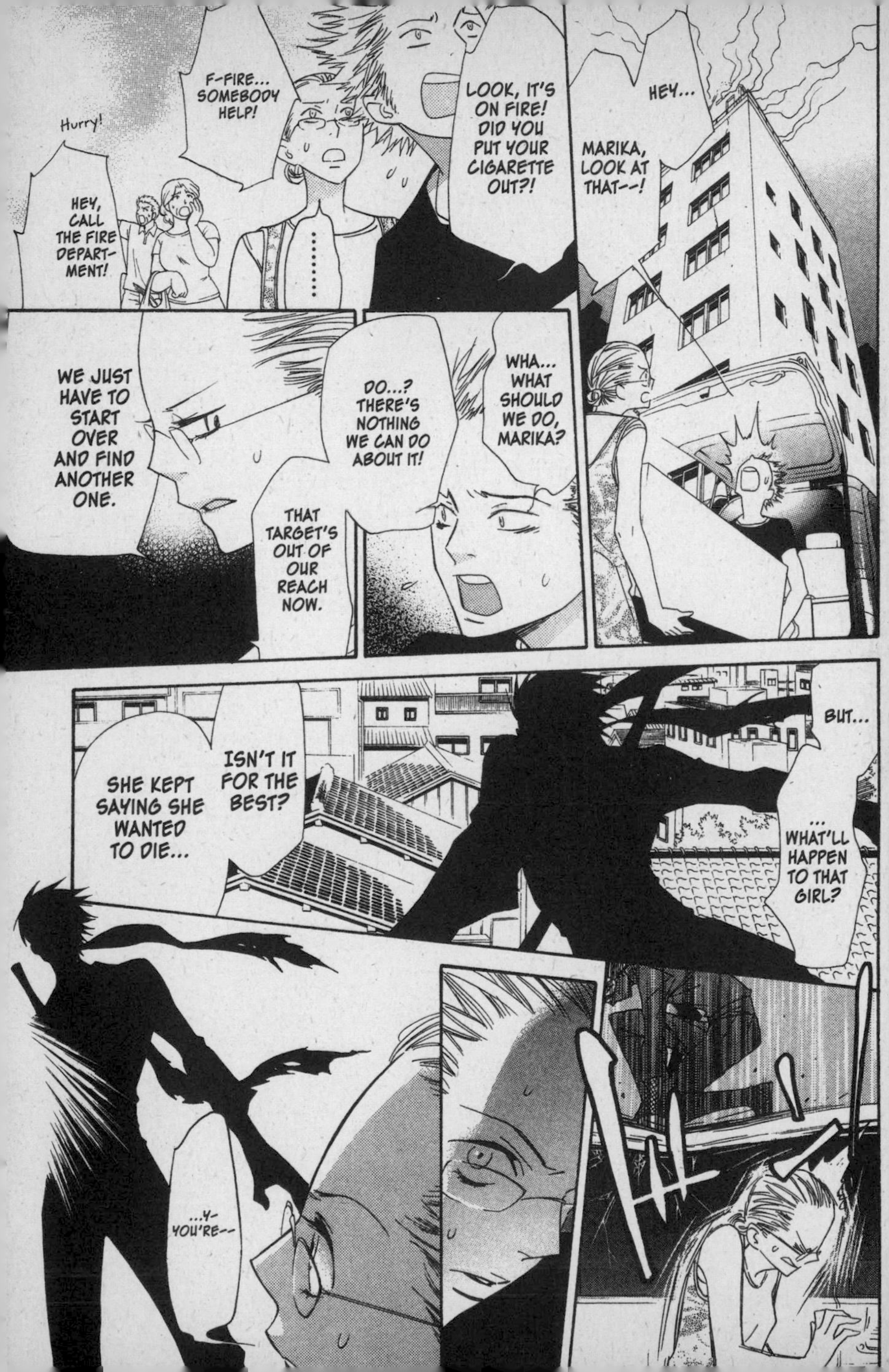
HEY...
MARIKA, LOOK AT THAT--!
LOOK, IT'S ON FIRE! DID YOU PUT YOUR CIGARETTE OUT?!
F-FIRE... SOMEBODY HELP!
Hurry!
......
HEY, CALL THE FIRE DEPARTMENT!
WHA... WHAT SHOULD WE DO, MARIKA?
DO...? THERE'S NOTHING WE CAN DO ABOUT IT!
THAT TARGET'S OUT OF OUR REACH NOW.
WE JUST HAVE TO START OVER AND FIND ANOTHER ONE.
BUT...
...WHAT'LL HAPPEN TO THAT GIRL?
ISN'T IT FOR THE BEST?
SHE KEPT SAYING SHE WANTED TO DIE...
...Y-YOU'RE--

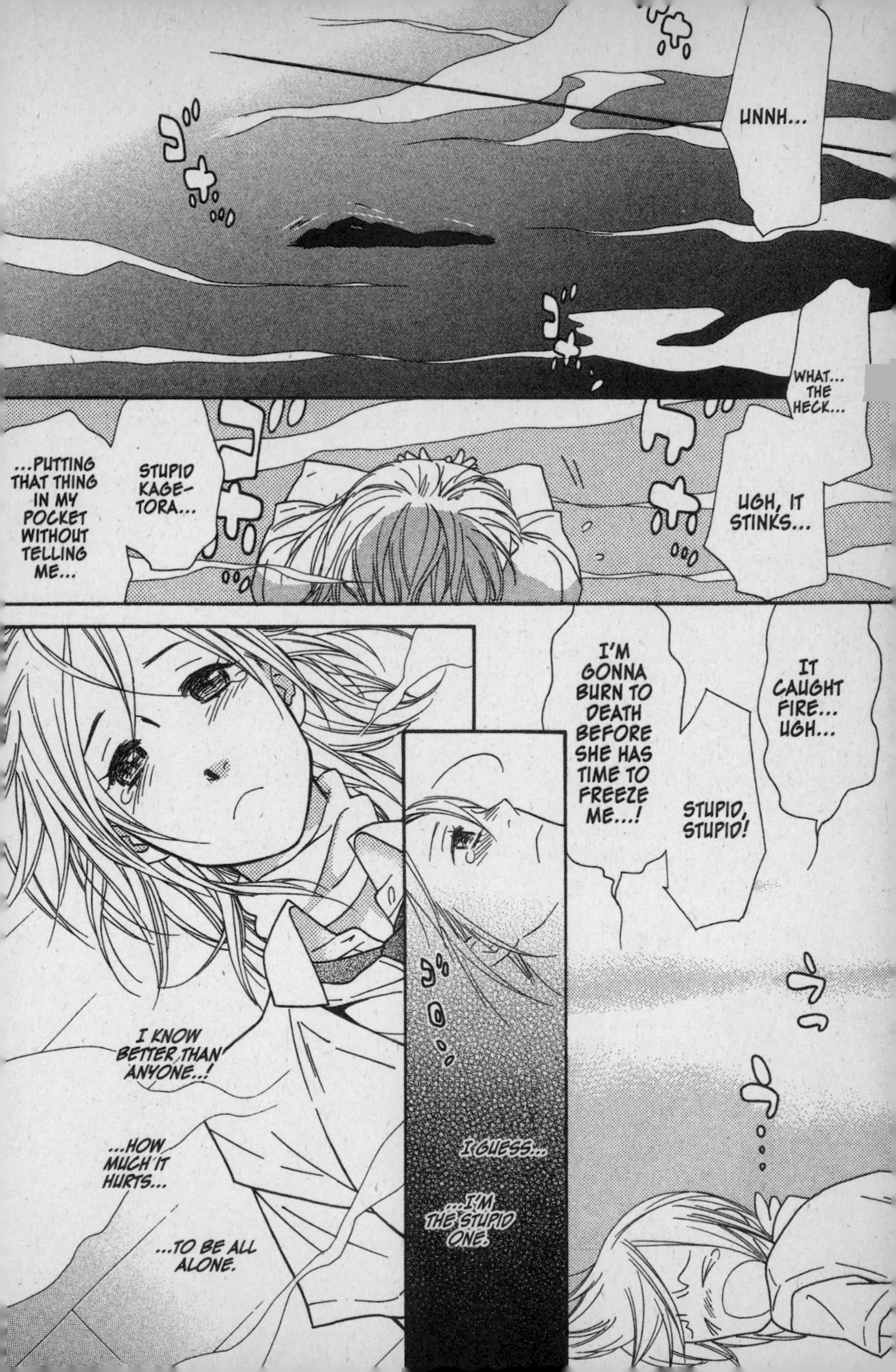
UNNH...
WHAT... THE HECK...
UGH, IT STINKS...
STUPID KAGE-TORA...
...PUTTING THAT THING IN MY POCKET WITHOUT TELLING ME...
IT CAUGHT FIRE... UGH...
STUPID, STUPID!
I'M GONNA BURN TO DEATH BEFORE SHE HAS TIME TO FREEZE ME...!
I GUESS...
...I'M THE STUPID ONE.
I KNOW BETTER THAN ANYONE..!
...HOW MUCH IT HURTS...
...TO BE ALL ALONE.

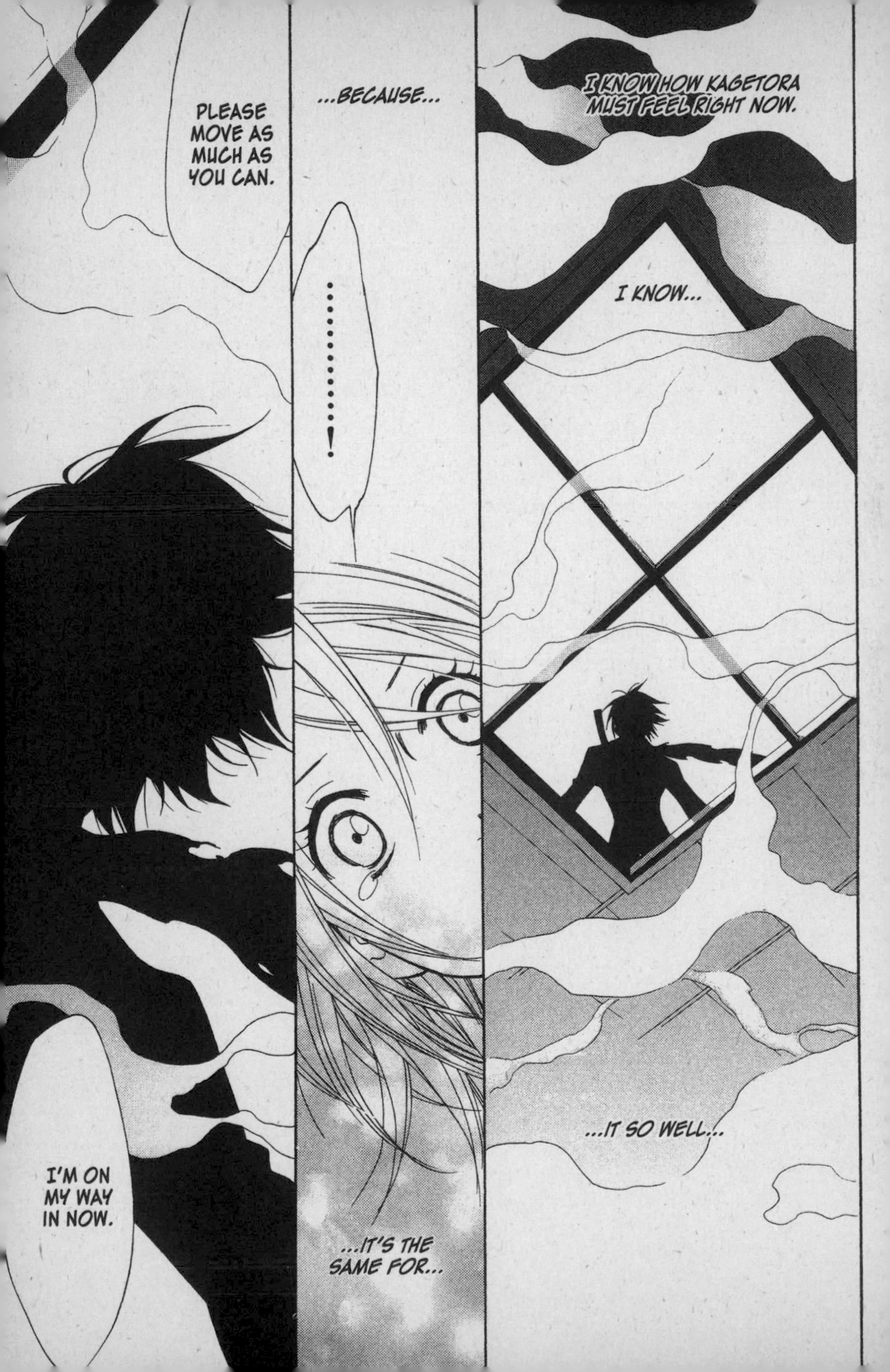
I KNOW HOW KAGETORA MUST FEEL RIGHT NOW.
I KNOW...
...IT SO WELL...
...BECAUSE...
......!
...IT'S THE SAME FOR...
PLEASE MOVE AS MUCH AS YOU CAN.
I'M ON MY WAY IN NOW.

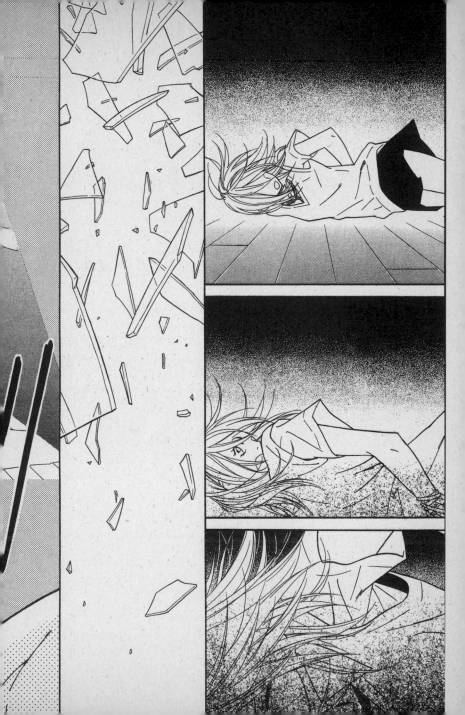

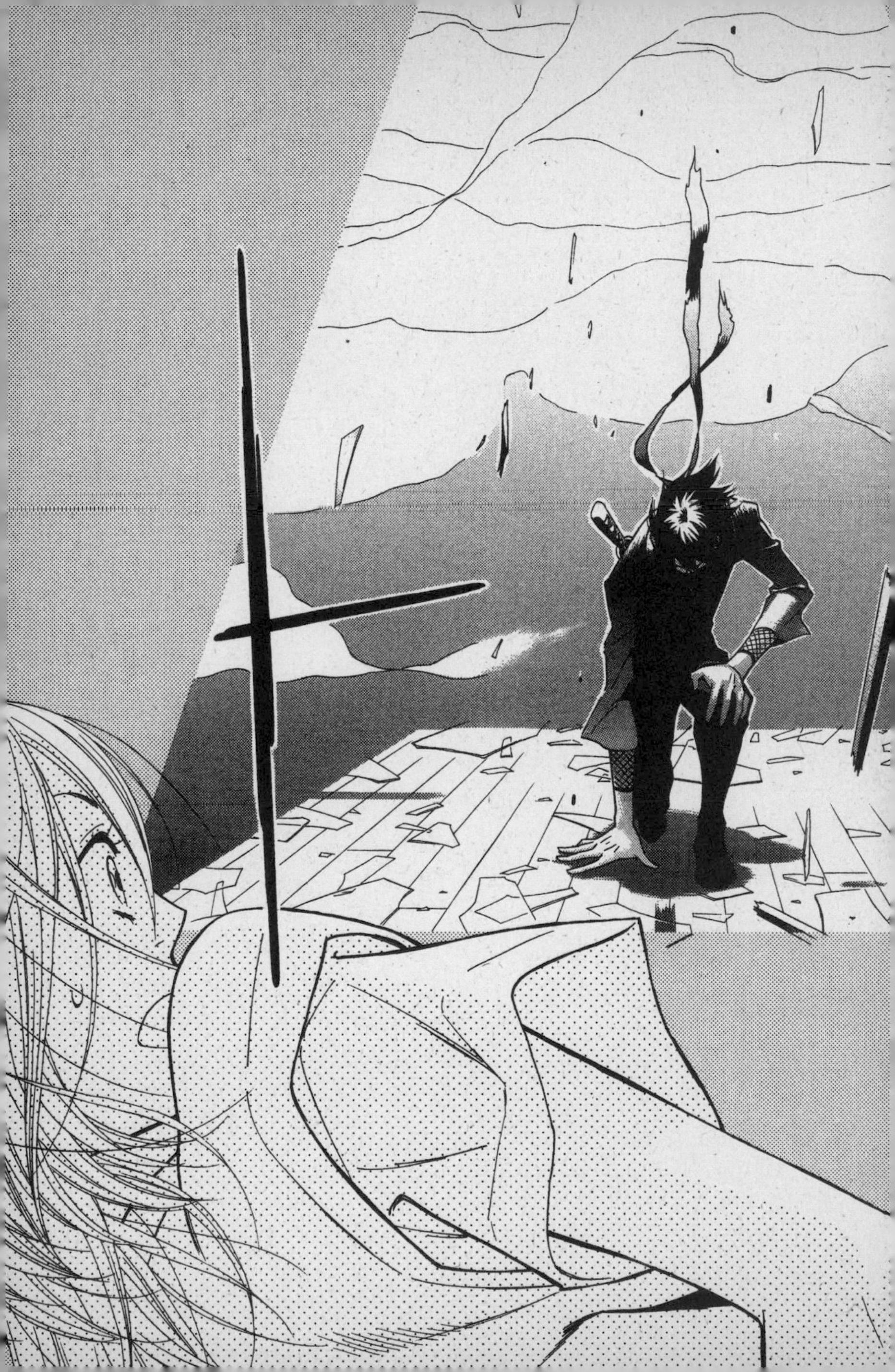

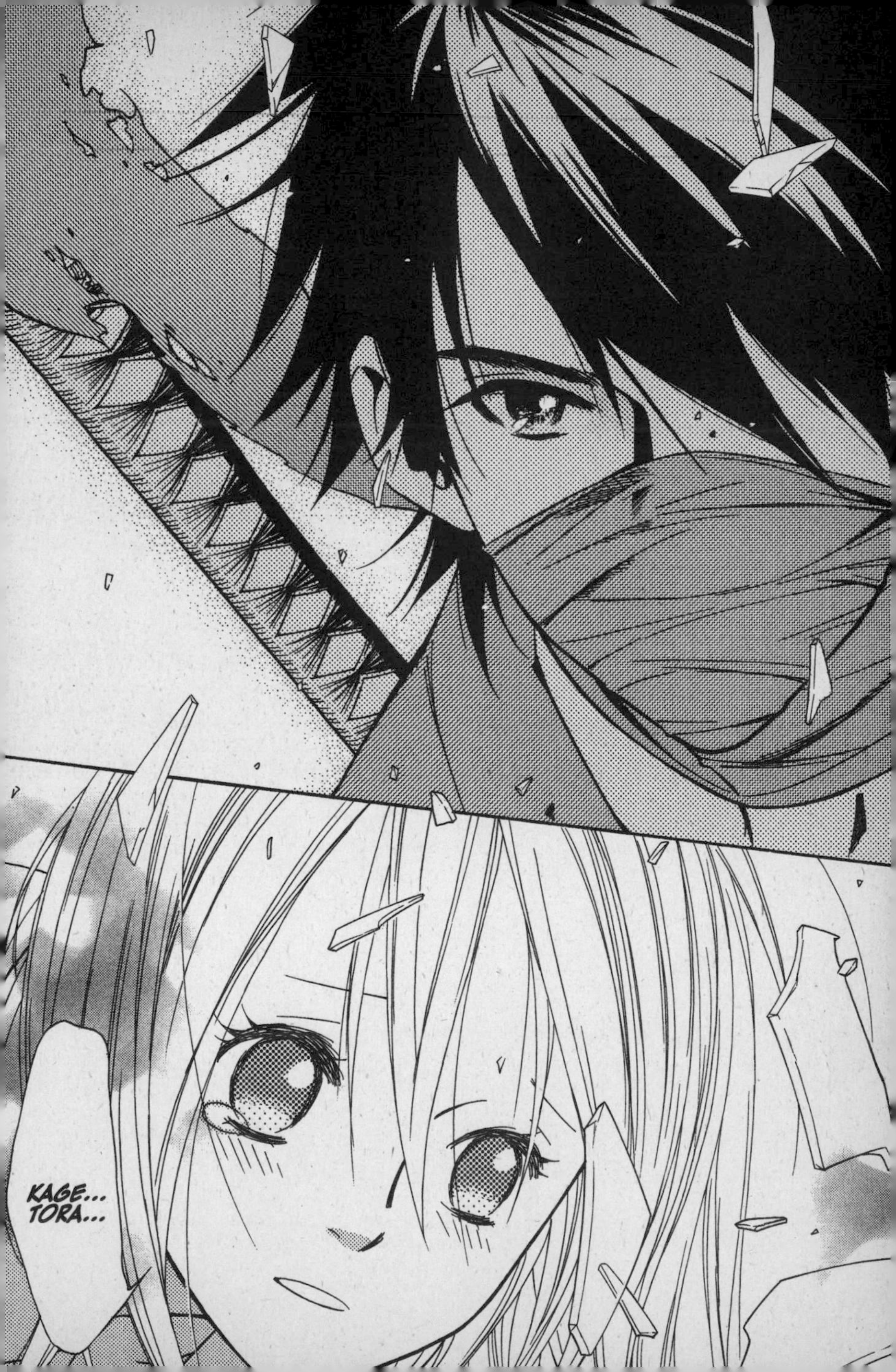
KAGE... TORA...

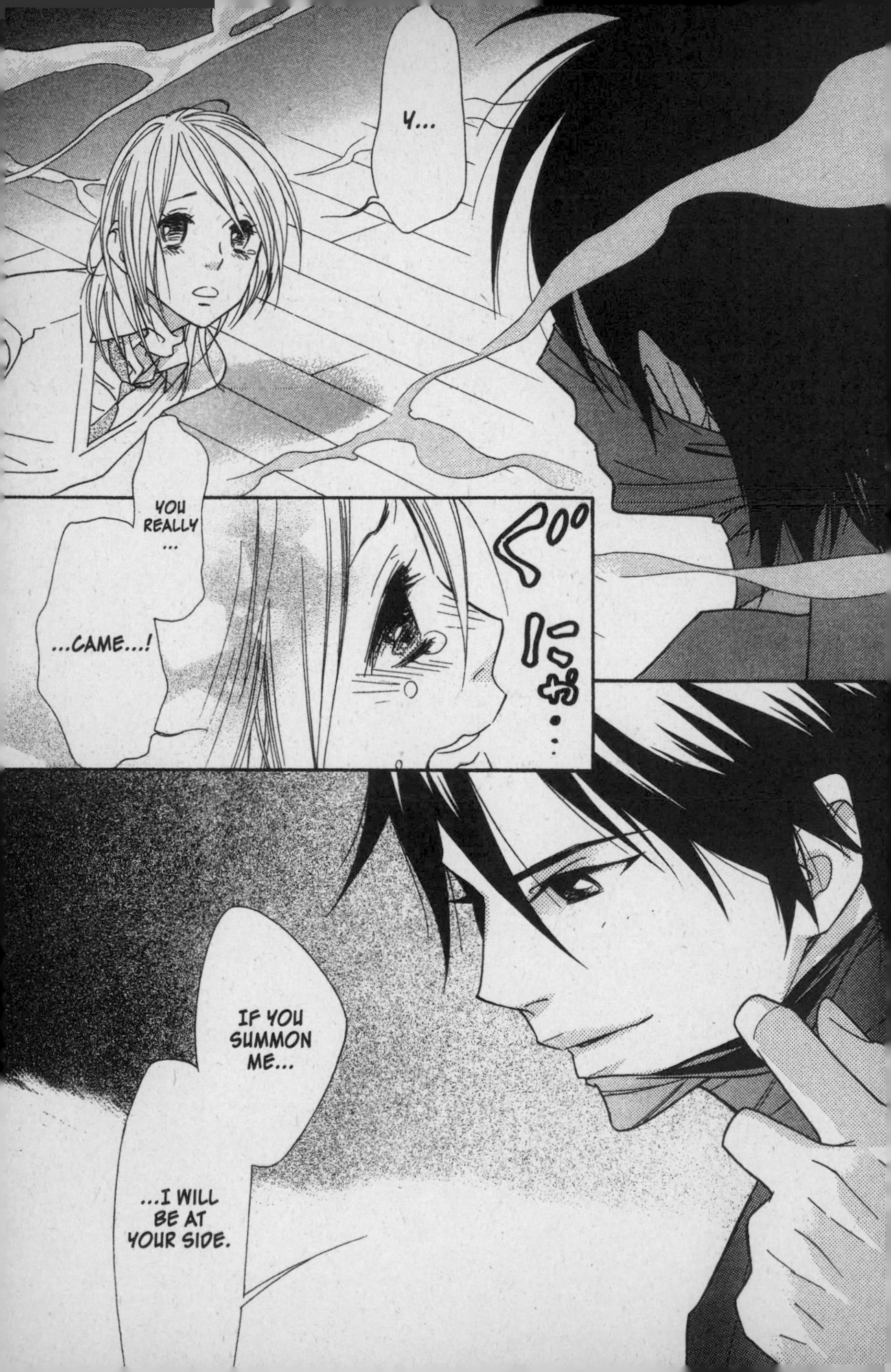
Y...
YOU REALLY ...
...CAME...!
IF YOU SUMMON ME...
...I WILL BE AT YOUR SIDE.

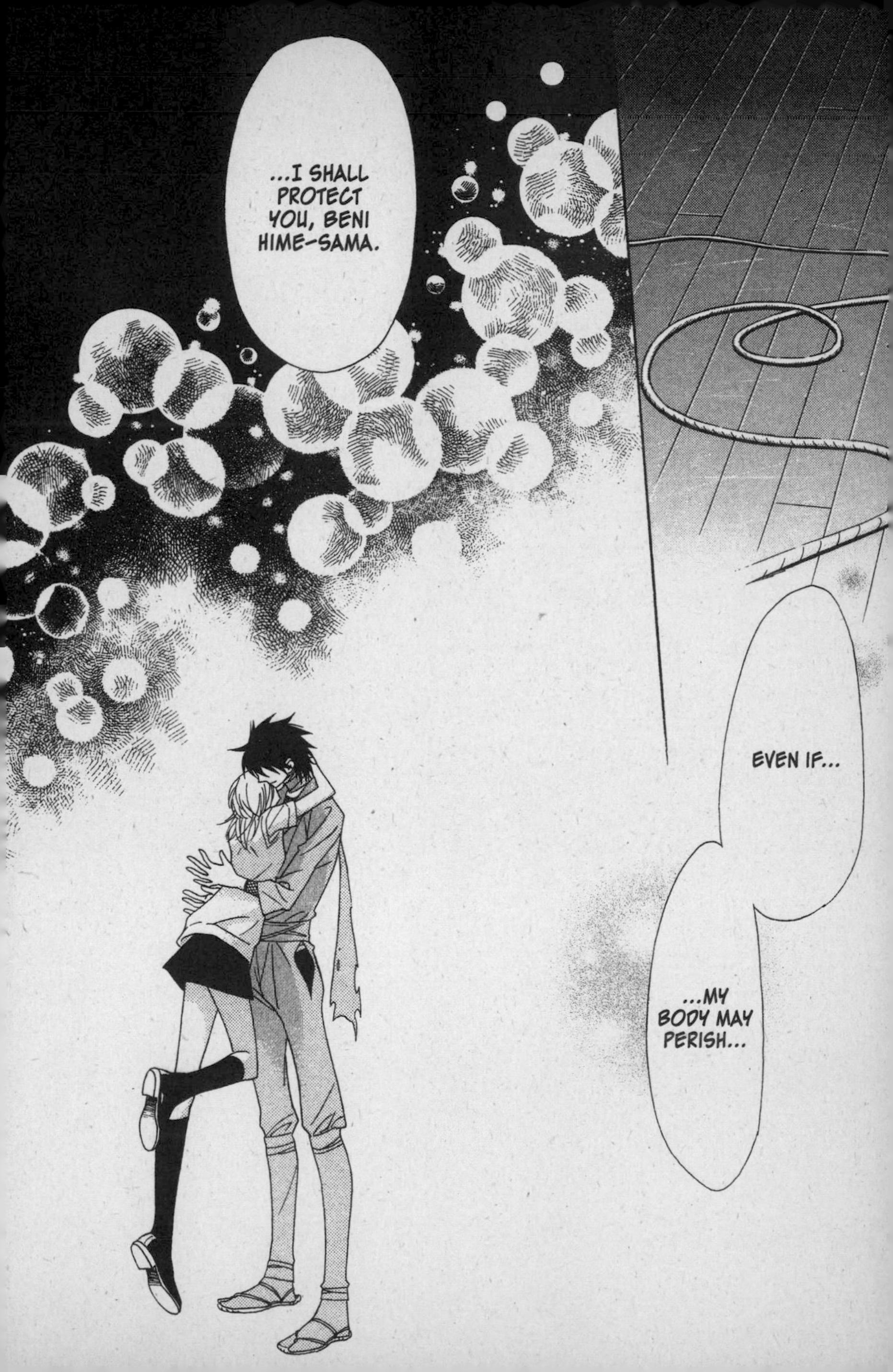
EVEN IF...
...MY BODY MAY PERISH...
...I SHALL PROTECT YOU, BENI HIME-SAMA.

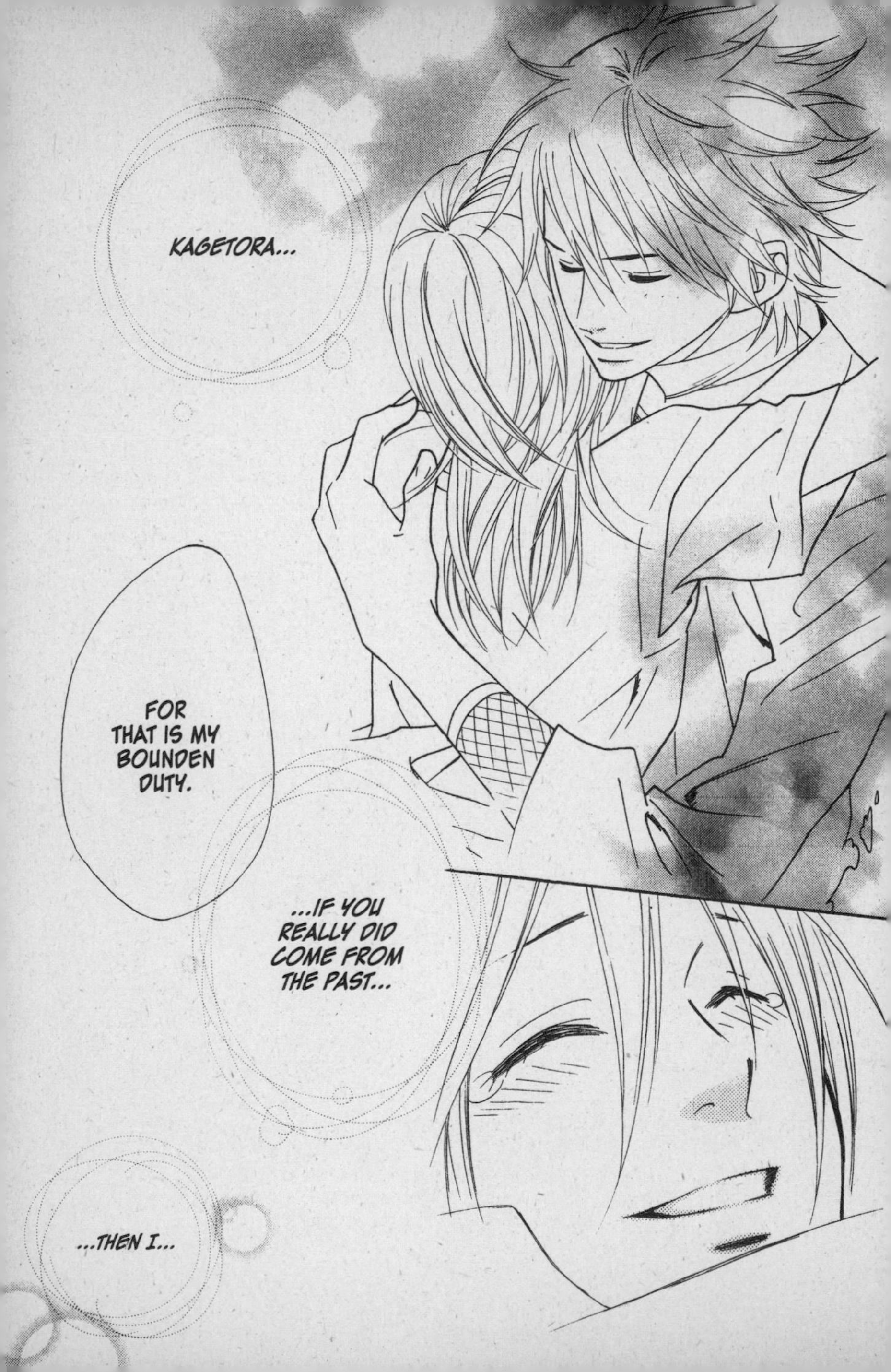
KAGETORA...
FOR THAT IS MY BOUNDEN DUTY.
...IF YOU REALLY DID COME FROM THE PAST...
...THEN I...

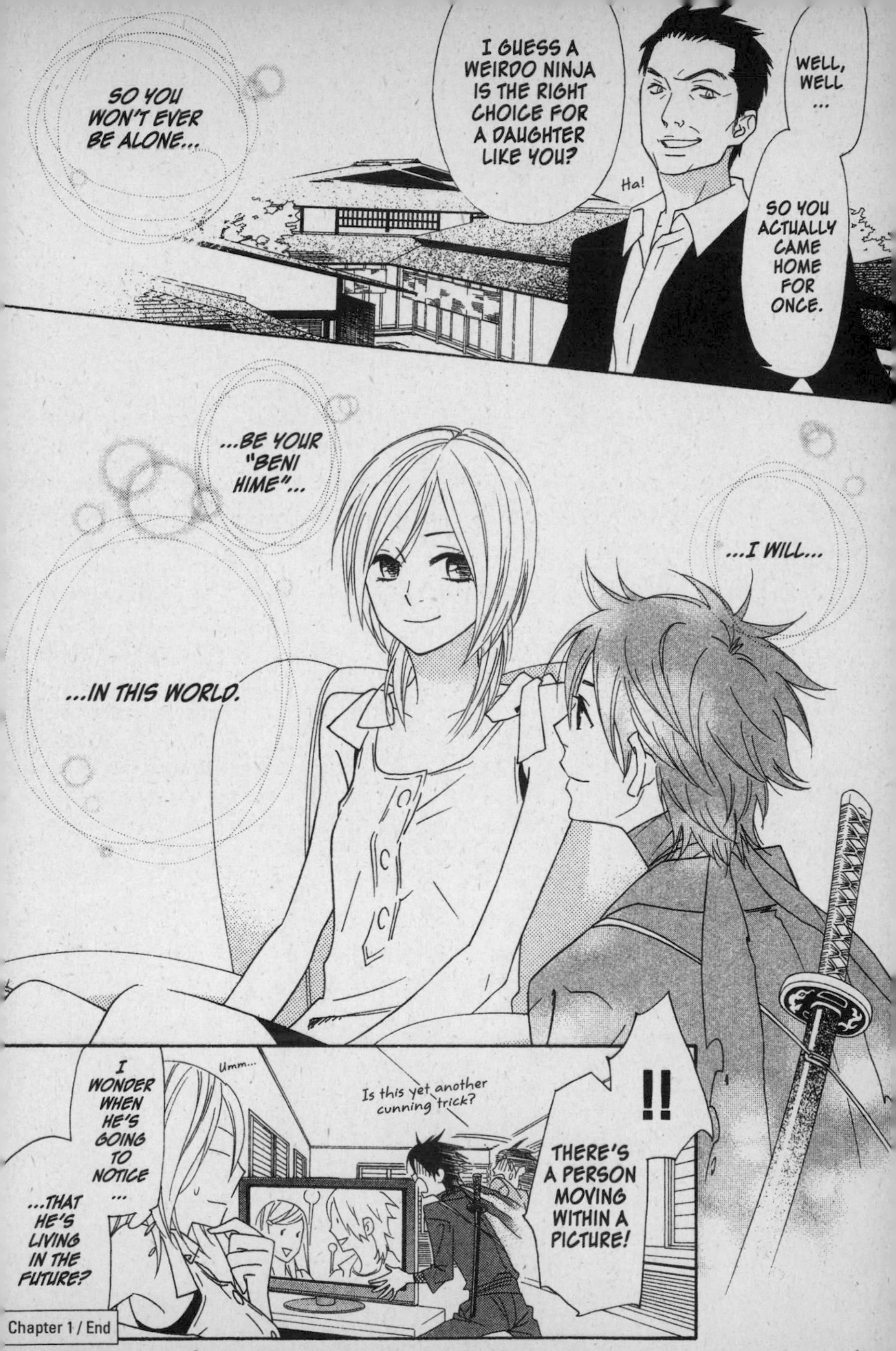
WELL, WELL ...
SO YOU ACTUALLY CAME HOME FOR ONCE.
Ha!
I GUESS A WEIRDO NINJA IS THE RIGHT CHOICE FOR A DAUGHTER LIKE YOU?
SO YOU WON'T EVER BE ALONE...
...I WILL...
...BE YOUR "BENI HIME"...
...IN THIS WORLD.
!!
THERE'S A PERSON MOVING WITHIN A PICTURE!
Is this yet another cunning trick?
Umm...
I WONDER WHEN HE'S GOING TO NOTICE ...
...THAT HE'S LIVING IN THE FUTURE?
Chapter 1 / End

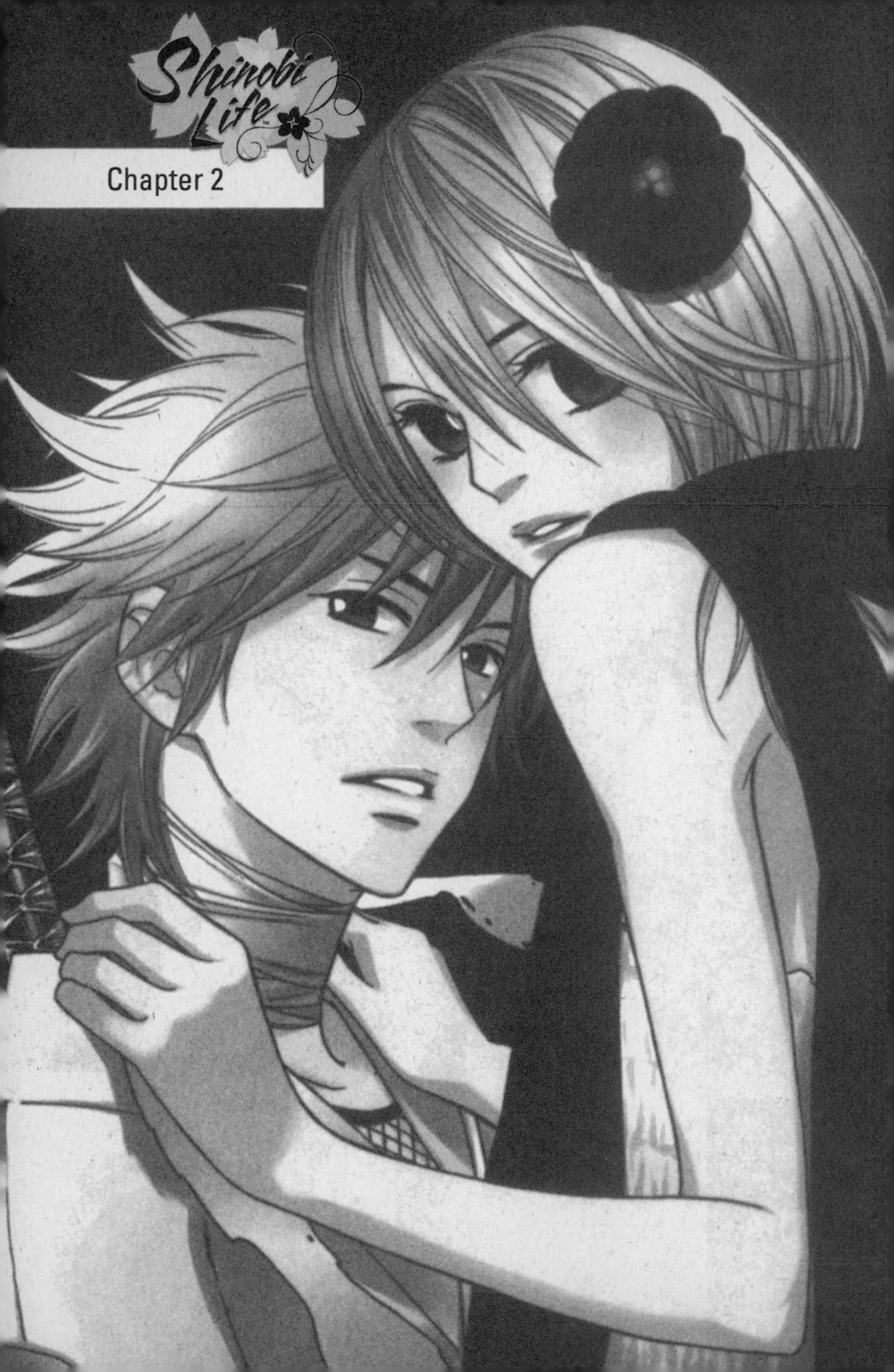
Shinobi Life
Chapter 2

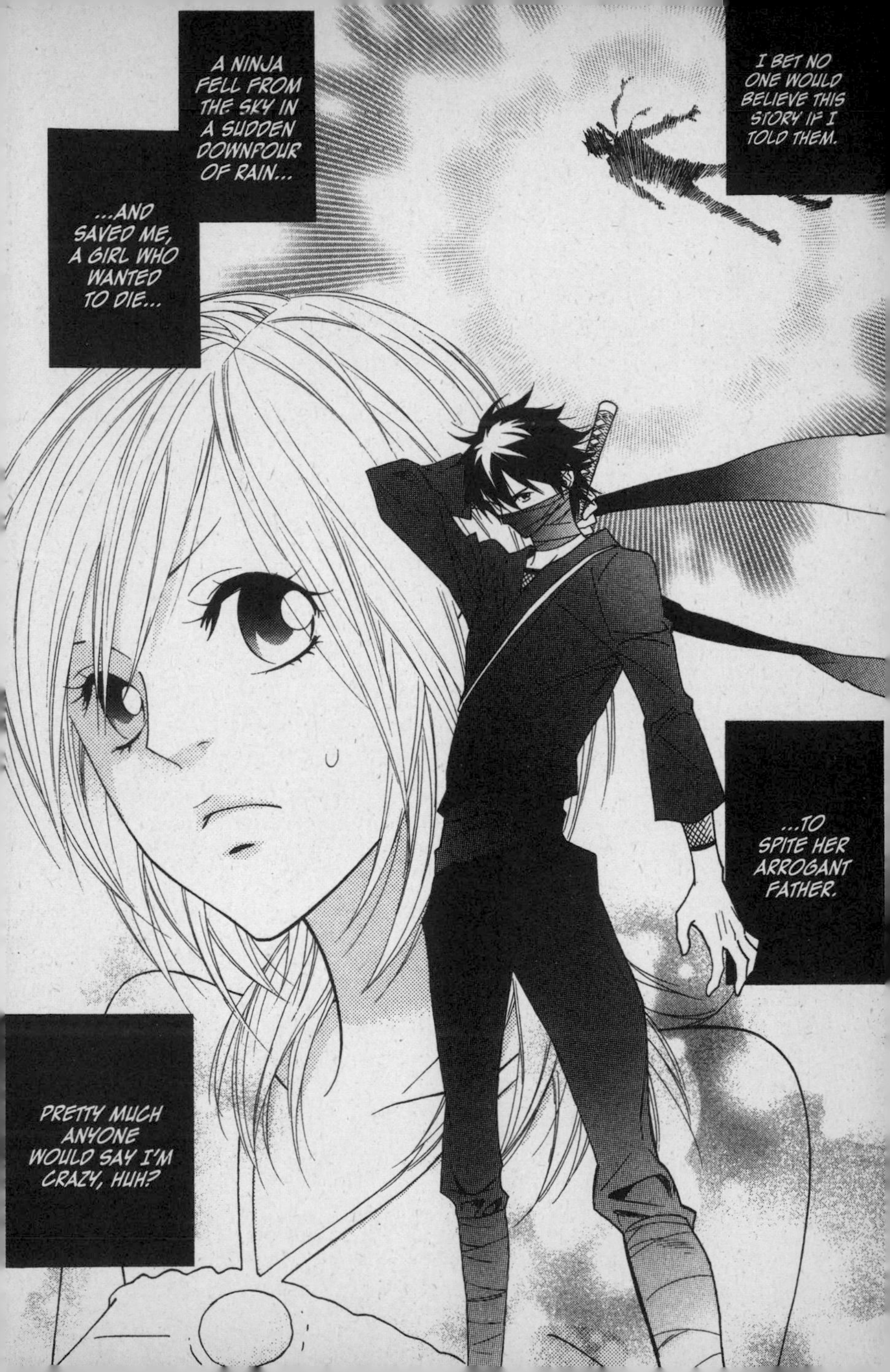
I BET NO ONE WOULD BELIEVE THIS STORY IF I TOLD THEM.
A NINJA FELL FROM THE SKY IN A SUDDEN DOWNPOUR OF RAIN...
...AND SAVED ME, A GIRL WHO WANTED TO DIE...
...TO SPITE HER ARROGANT FATHER.
PRETTY MUCH ANYONE WOULD SAY I'M CRAZY, HUH?

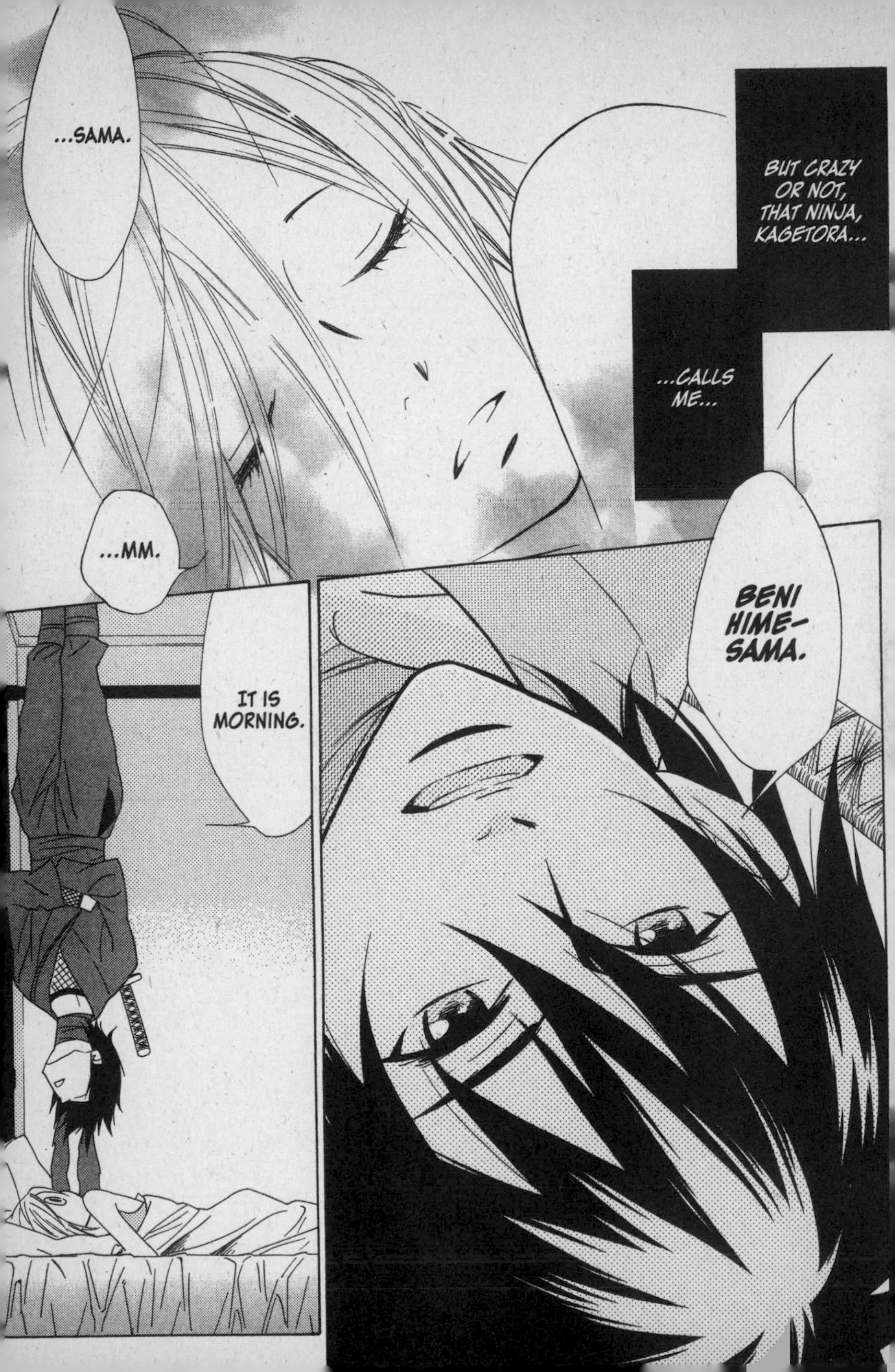
BUT CRAZY OR NOT, THAT NINJA, KAGETORA...
...CALLS ME...
BENI HIME-SAMA.
...SAMA.
...MM.
IT IS MORNING.

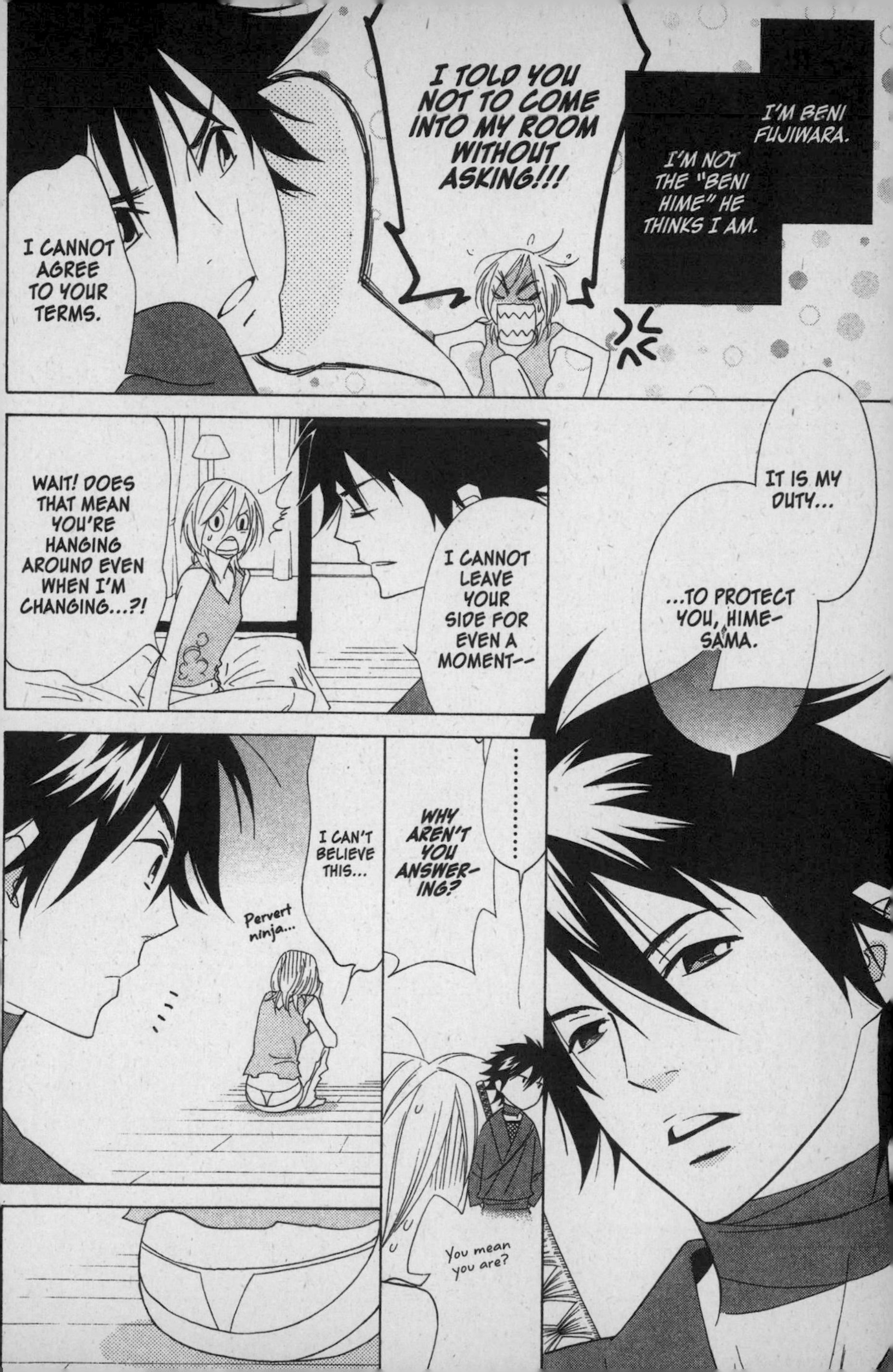
I'M BENI FUJIWARA.
I'M NOT THE "BENI HIME" HE THINKS I AM.
I TOLD YOU NOT TO COME INTO MY ROOM WITHOUT ASKING!!!
I CANNOT AGREE TO YOUR TERMS.
IT IS MY DUTY...
...TO PROTECT YOU, HIME-SAMA.
I CANNOT LEAVE YOUR SIDE FOR EVEN A MOMENT--
WAIT! DOES THAT MEAN YOU'RE HANGING AROUND EVEN WHEN I'M CHANGING...?!
......
WHY AREN'T YOU ANSWERING?
You mean you are?
I CAN'T BELIEVE THIS...
Pervert ninja...

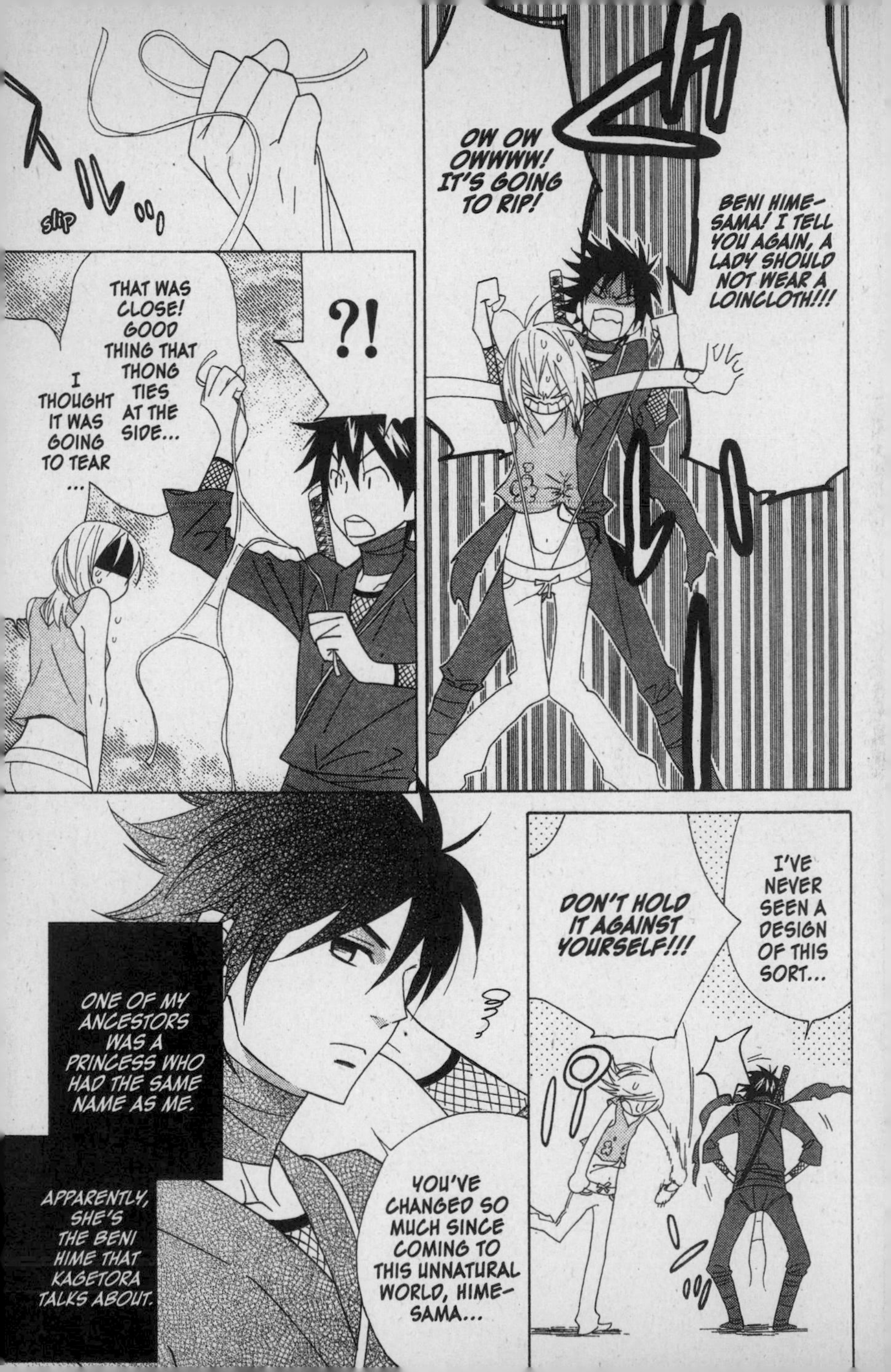

OW OW OWWWW! IT'S GOING TO RIP!
BENI HIME-SAMA! I TELL YOU AGAIN, A LADY SHOULD NOT WEAR A LOINCLOTH!!!
slip
?!
THAT WAS CLOSE! GOOD THING THAT THONG TIES AT THE SIDE...
I THOUGHT IT WAS GOING TO TEAR...
I'VE NEVER SEEN A DESIGN OF THIS SORT...
DON'T HOLD IT AGAINST YOURSELF!!!
YOU'VE CHANGED SO MUCH SINCE COMING TO THIS UNNATURAL WORLD, HIME-SAMA...
ONE OF MY ANCESTORS WAS A PRINCESS WHO HAD THE SAME NAME AS ME.
APPARENTLY, SHE'S THE BENI HIME THAT KAGETORA TALKS ABOUT.

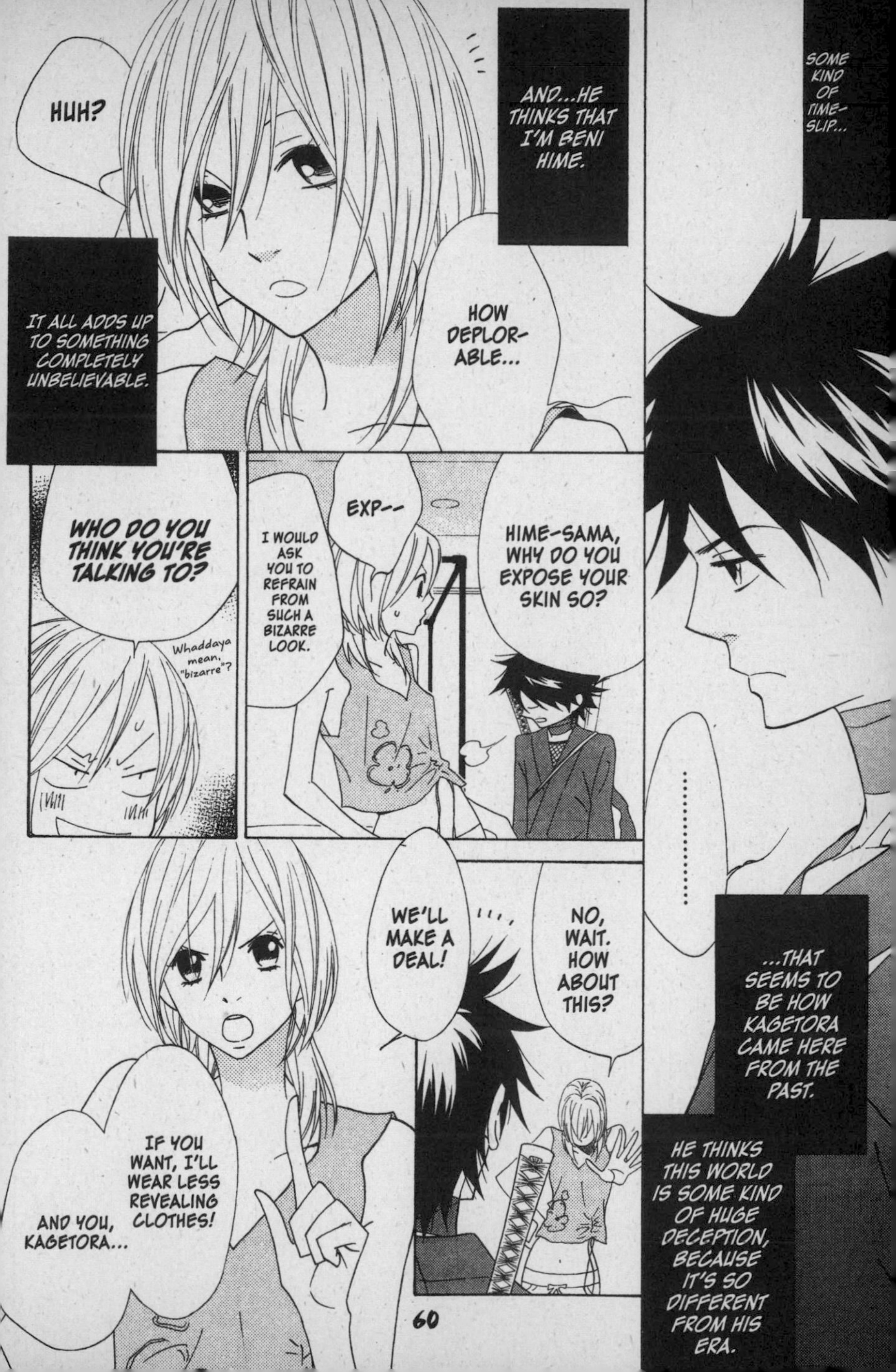

SOME KIND OF TIME-SLIP...
......
...THAT SEEMS TO BE HOW KAGETORA CAME HERE FROM THE PAST.
HE THINKS THIS WORLD IS SOME KIND OF HUGE DECEPTION, BECAUSE IT'S SO DIFFERENT FROM HIS ERA.
AND...HE THINKS THAT I'M BENI HIME.
HOW DEPLOR-ABLE...
HUH?
IT ALL ADDS UP TO SOMETHING COMPLETELY UNBELIEVABLE.
HIME-SAMA, WHY DO YOU EXPOSE YOUR SKIN SO?
EXP--
I WOULD ASK YOU TO REFRAIN FROM SUCH A BIZARRE LOOK.
Whaddaya mean, "bizarre"?
WHO DO YOU THINK YOU'RE TALKING TO?
NO, WAIT. HOW ABOUT THIS?
WE'LL MAKE A DEAL!
IF YOU WANT, I'LL WEAR LESS REVEALING CLOTHES!
AND YOU, KAGETORA...

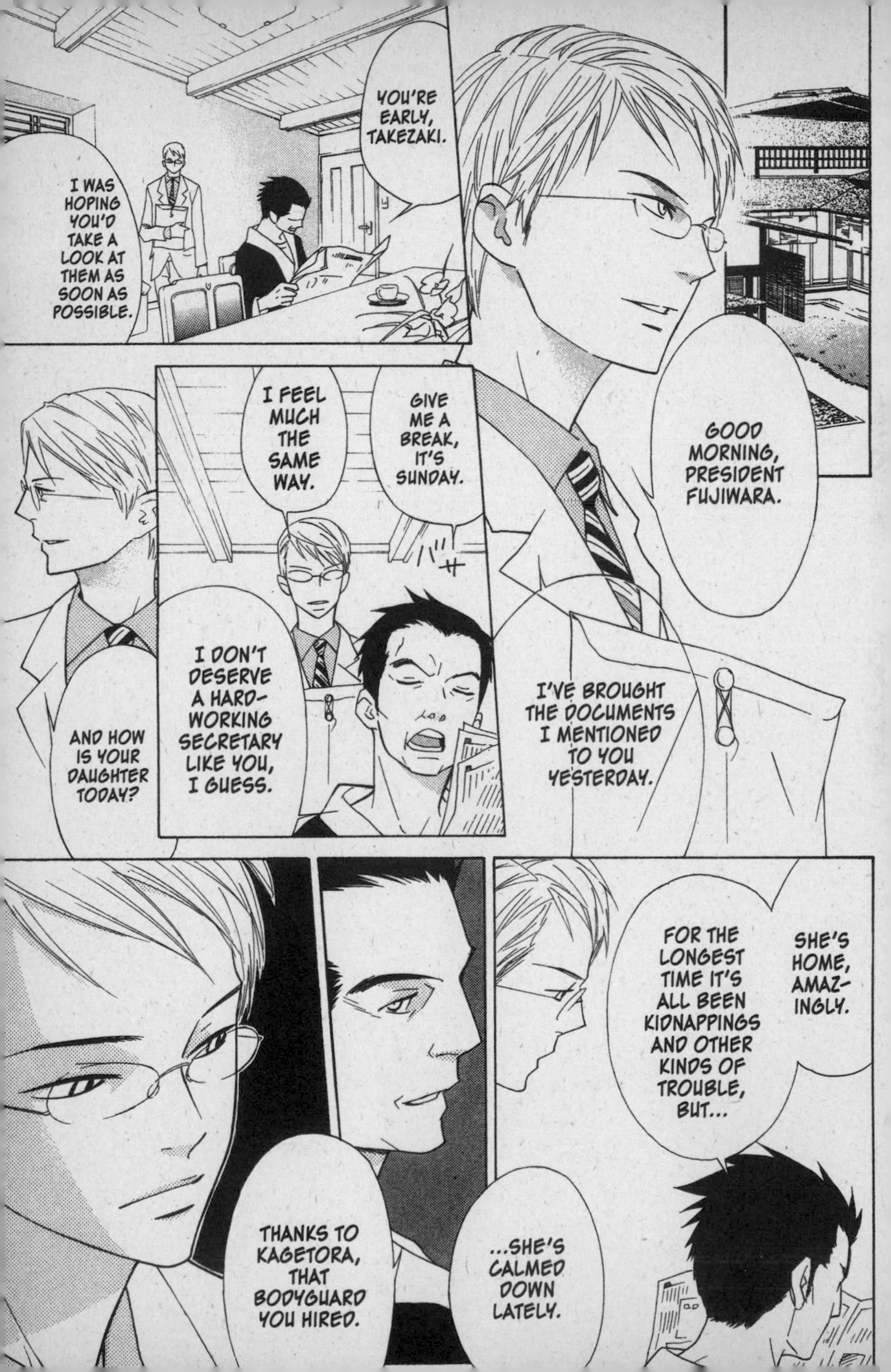
GOOD MORNING, PRESIDENT FUJIWARA.
YOU'RE EARLY, TAKEZAKI.
I'VE BROUGHT THE DOCUMENTS I MENTIONED TO YOU YESTERDAY.
I WAS HOPING YOU'D TAKE A LOOK AT THEM AS SOON AS POSSIBLE.
GIVE ME A BREAK, IT'S SUNDAY.
I FEEL MUCH THE SAME WAY.
I DON'T DESERVE A HARD-WORKING SECRETARY LIKE YOU, I GUESS.
AND HOW IS YOUR DAUGHTER TODAY?
SHE'S HOME, AMAZINGLY.
FOR THE LONGEST TIME IT'S ALL BEEN KIDNAPPINGS AND OTHER KINDS OF TROUBLE, BUT...
...SHE'S CALMED DOWN LATELY.
THANKS TO KAGETORA, THAT BODYGUARD YOU HIRED.

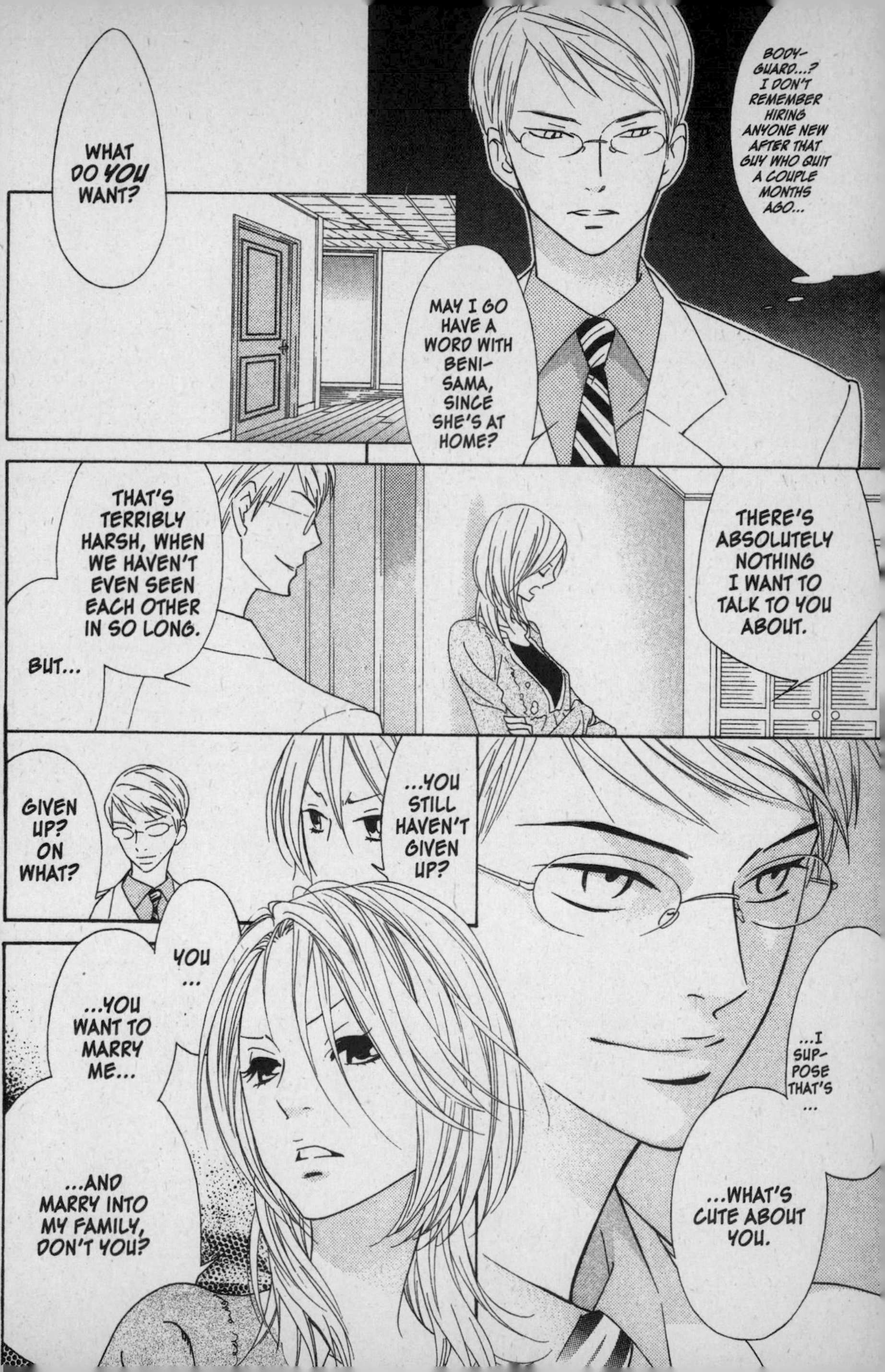
BODY-GUARD...? I DON'T REMEMBER HIRING ANYONE NEW AFTER THAT GUY WHO QUIT A COUPLE MONTHS AGO...
MAY I GO HAVE A WORD WITH BENI-SAMA, SINCE SHE'S AT HOME?
WHAT DO YOU WANT?
THERE'S ABSOLUTELY NOTHING I WANT TO TALK TO YOU ABOUT.
THAT'S TERRIBLY HARSH, WHEN WE HAVEN'T EVEN SEEN EACH OTHER IN SO LONG.
BUT...
...YOU STILL HAVEN'T GIVEN UP?
GIVEN UP? ON WHAT?
YOU ...
...YOU WANT TO MARRY ME...
...AND MARRY INTO MY FAMILY, DON'T YOU?
...I SUPPOSE THAT'S ...
...WHAT'S CUTE ABOUT YOU.

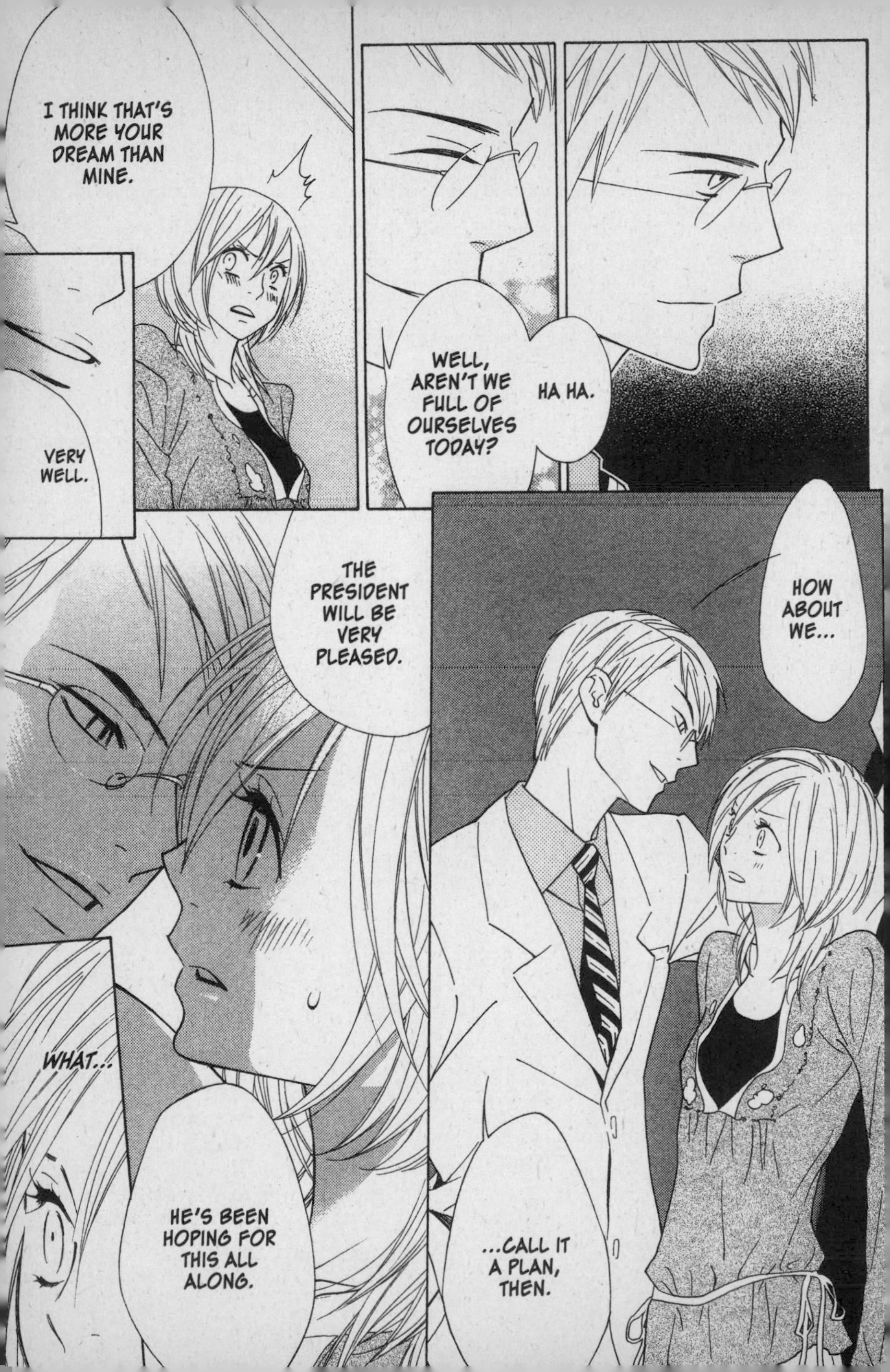
HA HA.
WELL, AREN'T WE FULL OF OURSELVES TODAY?
I THINK THAT'S MORE YOUR DREAM THAN MINE.
VERY WELL.
HOW ABOUT WE...
...CALL IT A PLAN, THEN.
THE PRESIDENT WILL BE VERY PLEASED.
HE'S BEEN HOPING FOR THIS ALL ALONG.
WHAT...

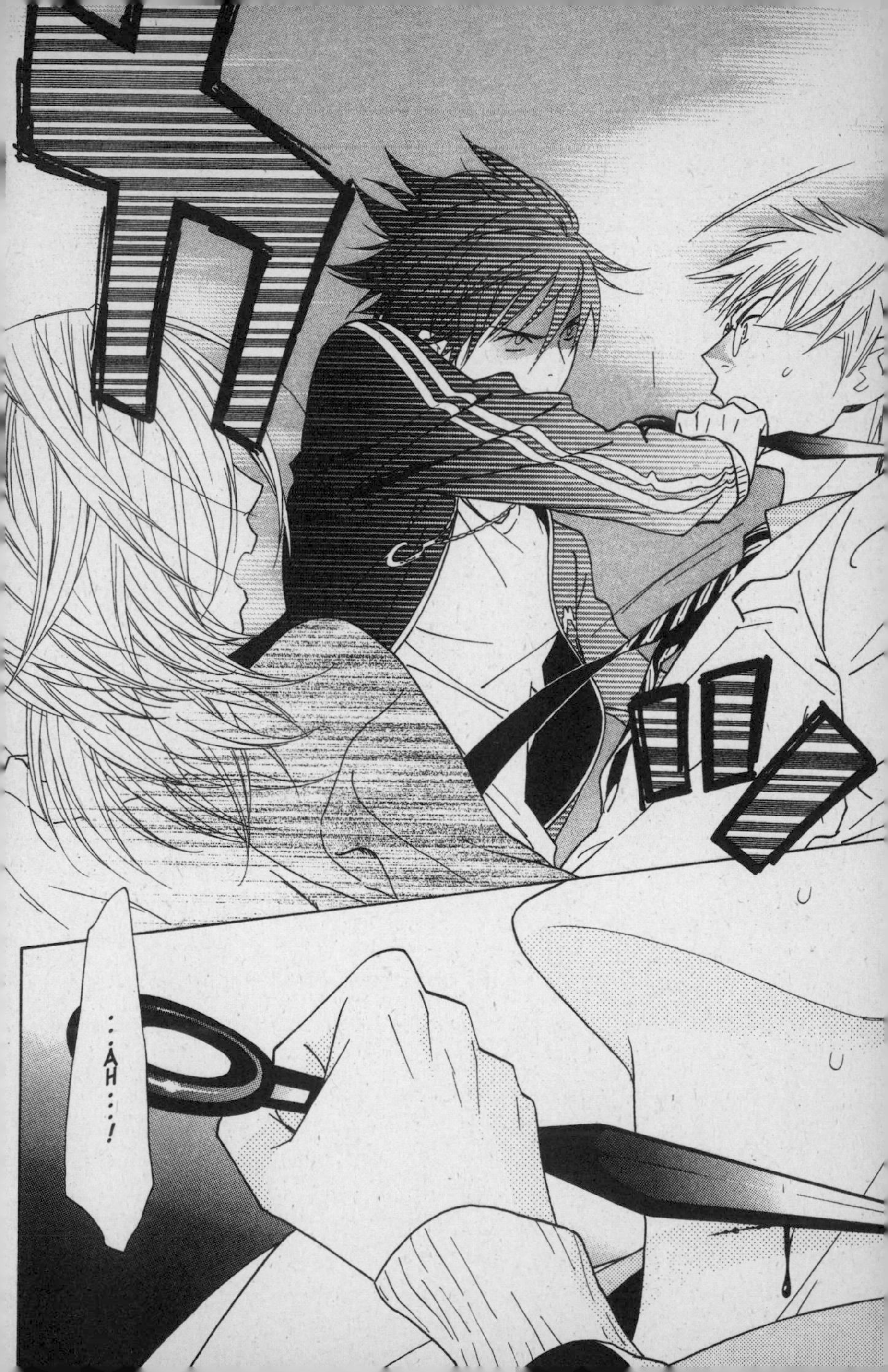
...AH...!

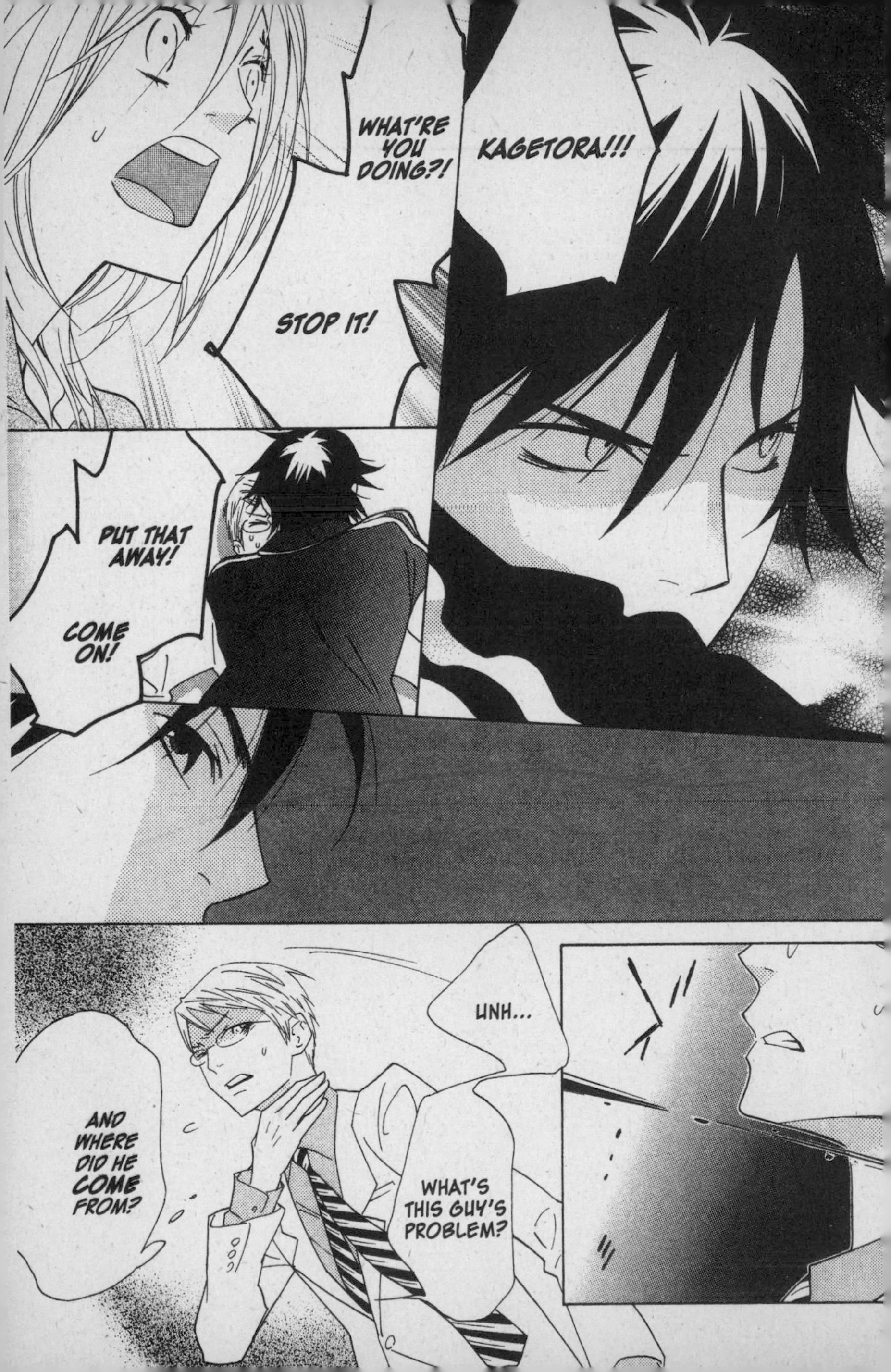
KAGETORA!!!
WHAT'RE YOU DOING?!
STOP IT!
PUT THAT AWAY!
COME ON!
UNH...
WHAT'S THIS GUY'S PROBLEM?
AND WHERE DID HE COME FROM?

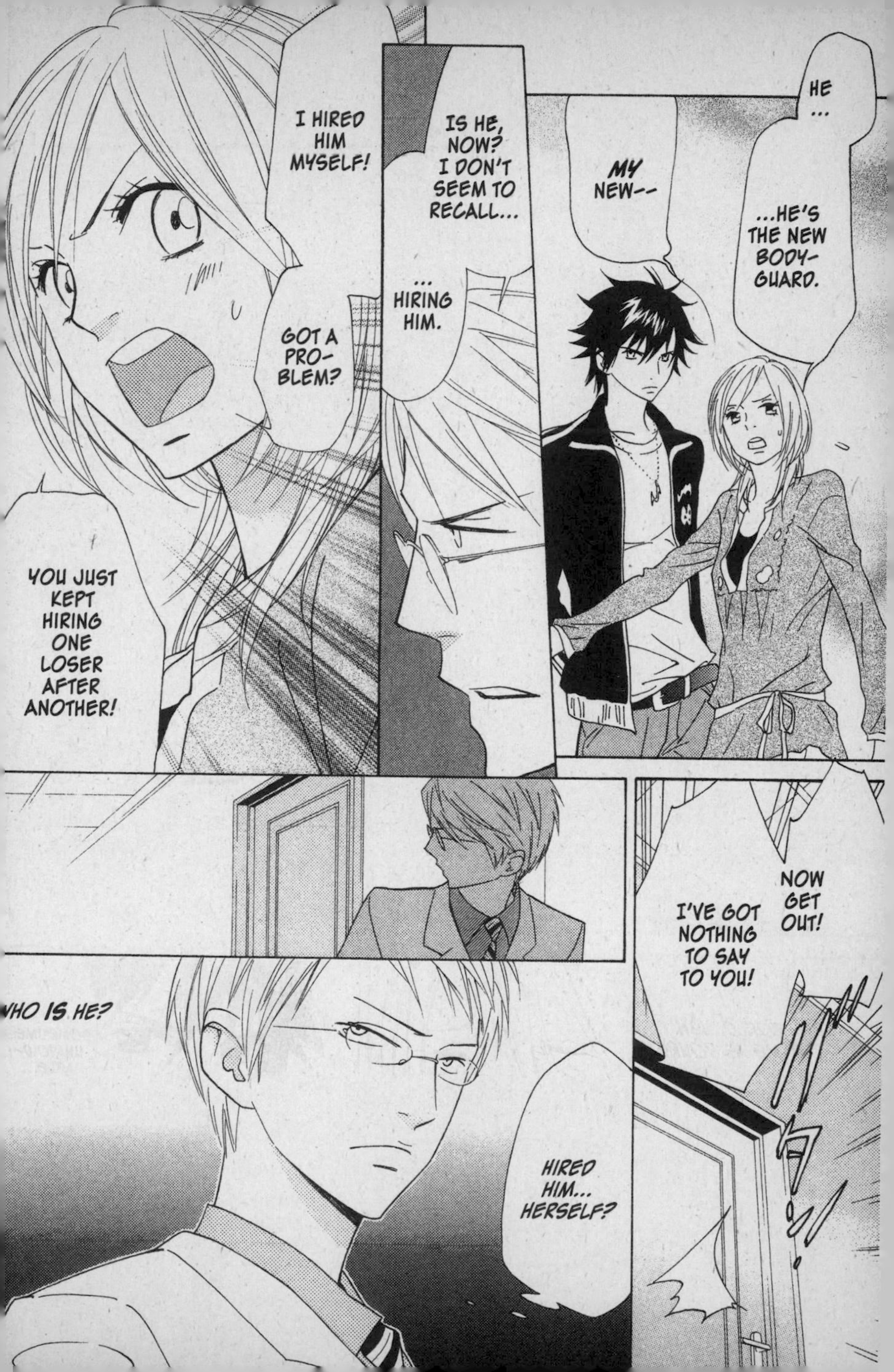
HE ...
...HE'S THE NEW BODY-GUARD.
MY NEW--
IS HE, NOW? I DON'T SEEM TO RECALL...
...HIRING HIM.
I HIRED HIM MYSELF!
GOT A PRO-BLEM?
YOU JUST KEPT HIRING ONE LOSER AFTER ANOTHER!
NOW GET OUT!
I'VE GOT NOTHING TO SAY TO YOU!
HIRED HIM... HERSELF?
WHO IS HE?

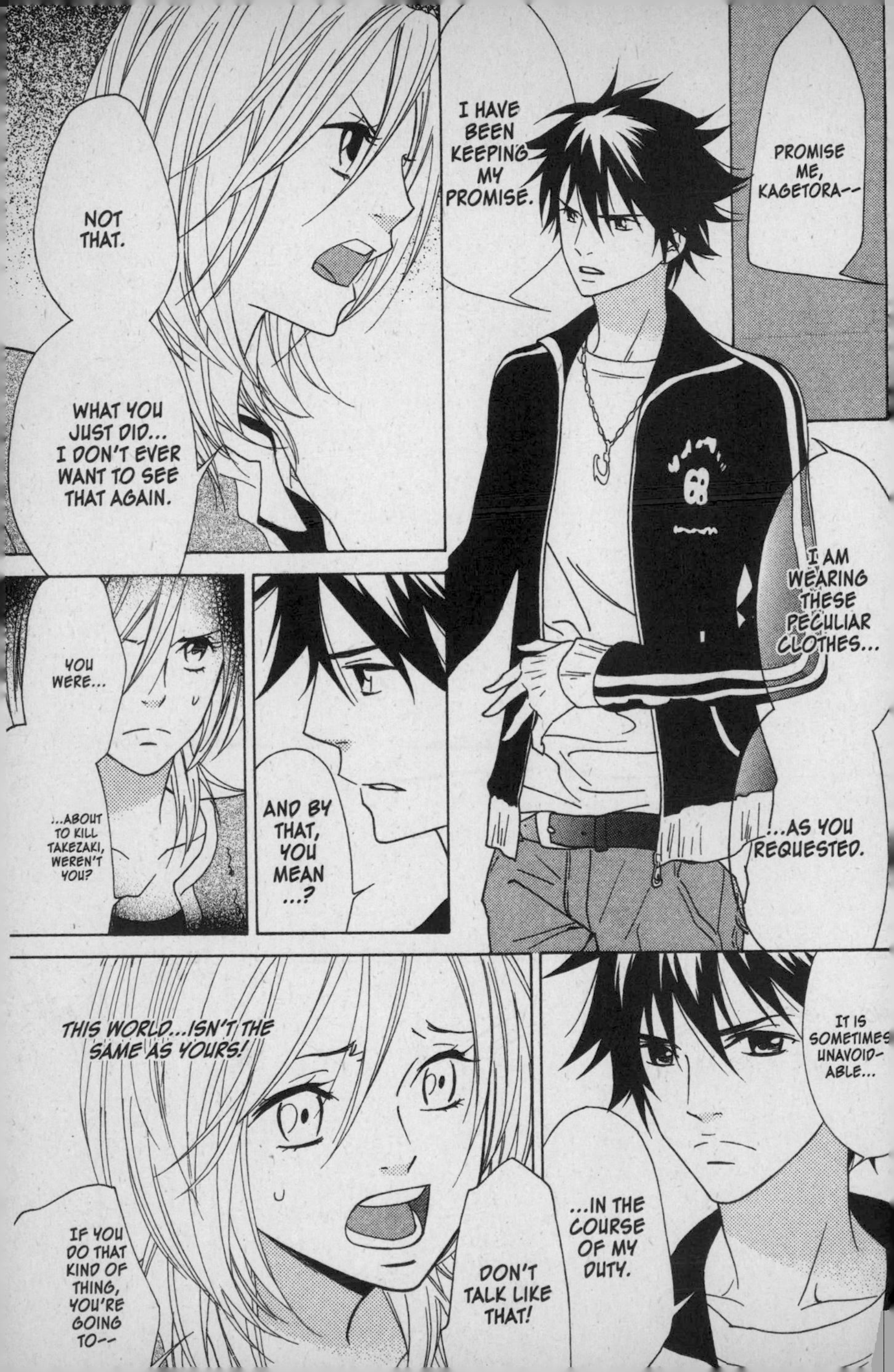

PROMISE ME, KAGETORA--
I HAVE BEEN KEEPING MY PROMISE.
I AM WEARING THESE PECULIAR CLOTHES...
...AS YOU REQUESTED.
NOT THAT.
WHAT YOU JUST DID... I DON'T EVER WANT TO SEE THAT AGAIN.
AND BY THAT, YOU MEAN ...?
YOU WERE...
...ABOUT TO KILL TAKEZAKI, WEREN'T YOU?
IT IS SOMETIMES UNAVOID-ABLE...
...IN THE COURSE OF MY DUTY.
DON'T TALK LIKE THAT!
THIS WORLD...ISN'T THE SAME AS YOURS!
IF YOU DO THAT KIND OF THING, YOU'RE GOING TO--

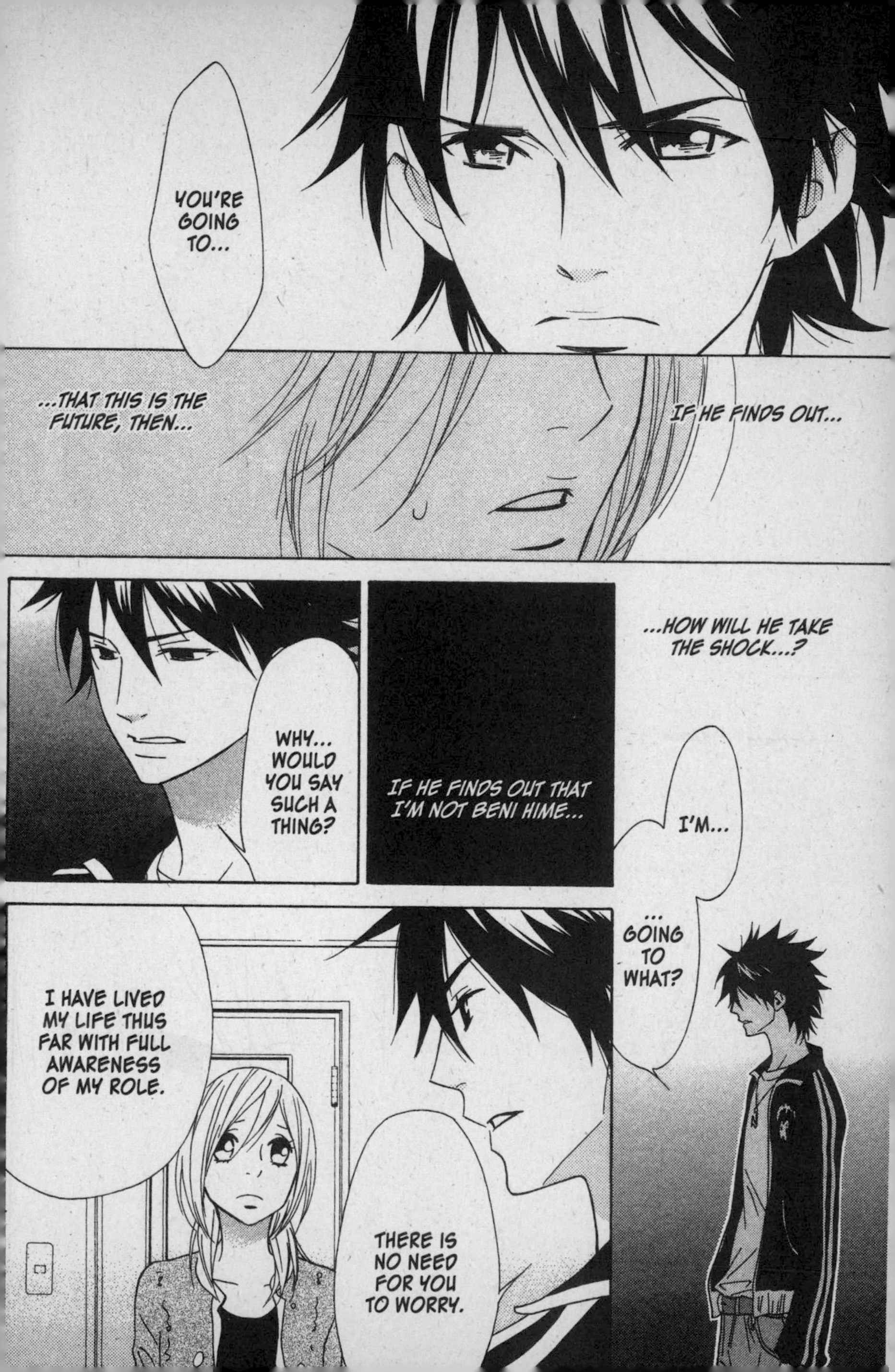
YOU'RE GOING TO...
IF HE FINDS OUT...
...THAT THIS IS THE FUTURE, THEN...
...HOW WILL HE TAKE THE SHOCK...?
I'M...
IF HE FINDS OUT THAT I'M NOT BENI HIME...
WHY... WOULD YOU SAY SUCH A THING?
... GOING TO WHAT?
I HAVE LIVED MY LIFE THUS FAR WITH FULL AWARENESS OF MY ROLE.
THERE IS NO NEED FOR YOU TO WORRY.

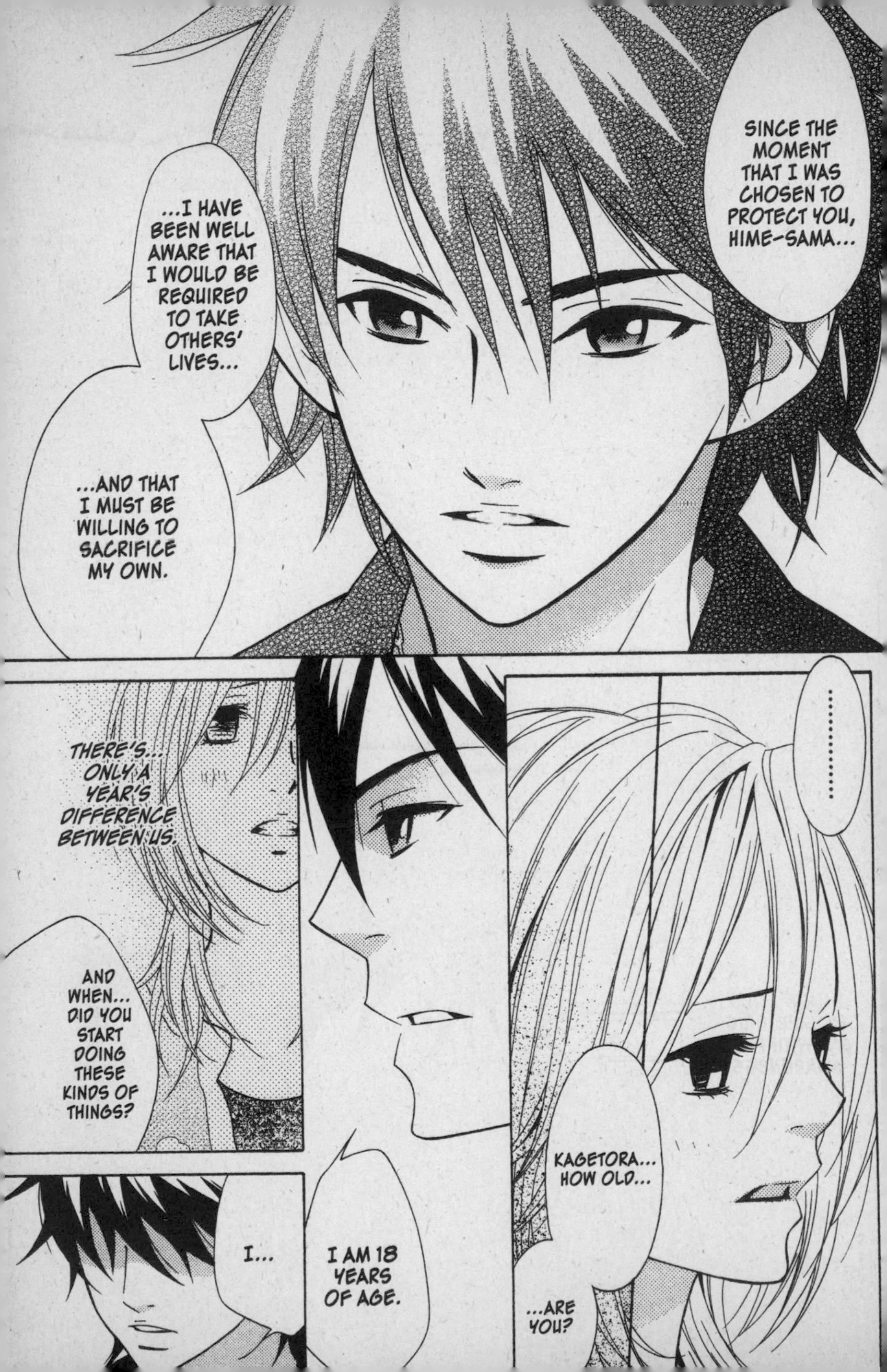
SINCE THE MOMENT THAT I WAS CHOSEN TO PROTECT YOU, HIME-SAMA...
...I HAVE BEEN WELL AWARE THAT I WOULD BE REQUIRED TO TAKE OTHERS' LIVES...
...AND THAT I MUST BE WILLING TO SACRIFICE MY OWN.
......
KAGETORA... HOW OLD...
...ARE YOU?
I...
I AM 18 YEARS OF AGE.
THERE'S... ONLY A YEAR'S DIFFERENCE BETWEEN US.
AND WHEN... DID YOU START DOING THESE KINDS OF THINGS?

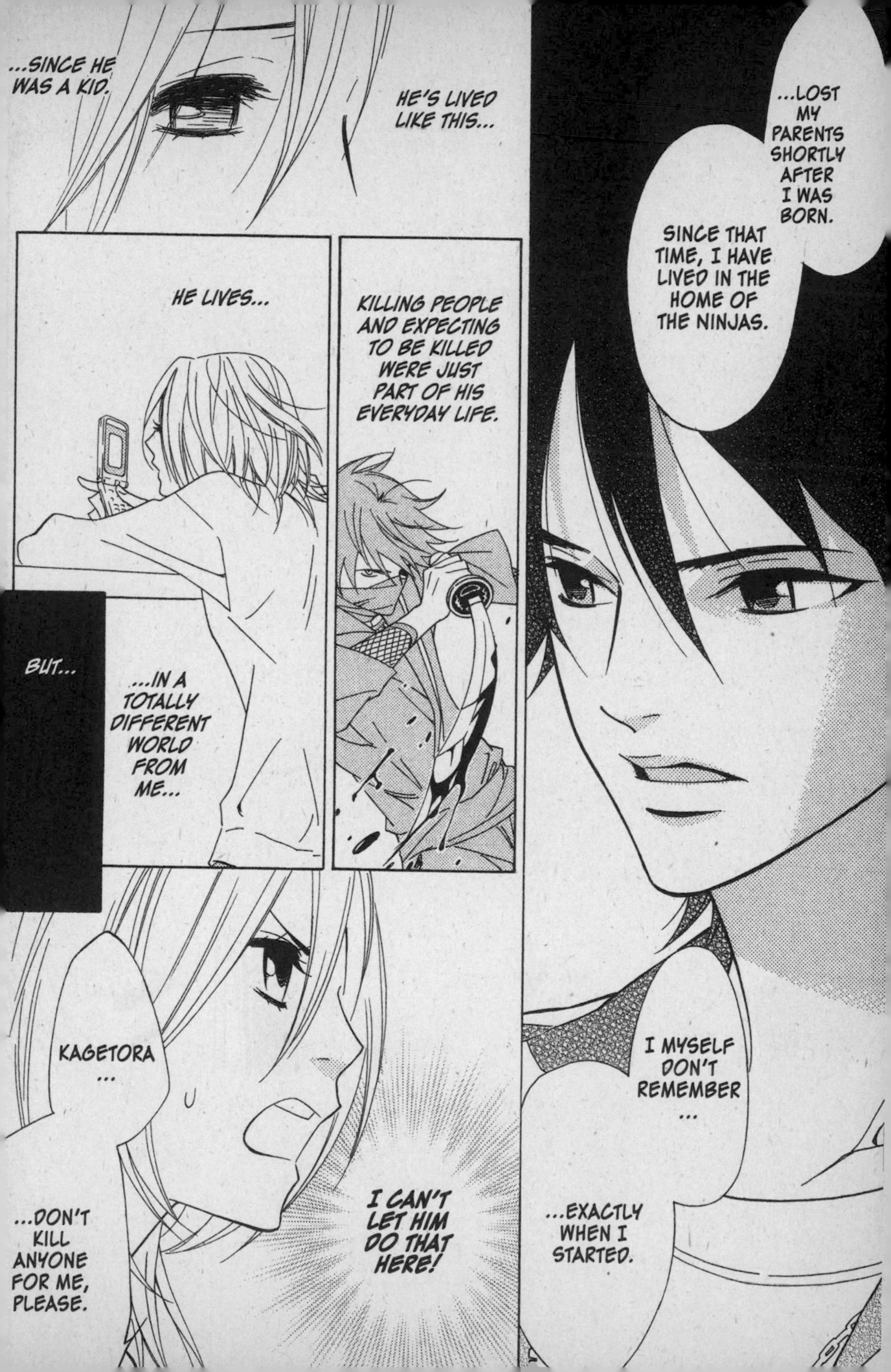
...LOST MY PARENTS SHORTLY AFTER I WAS BORN.
SINCE THAT TIME, I HAVE LIVED IN THE HOME OF THE NINJAS.
I MYSELF DON'T REMEMBER...
...EXACTLY WHEN I STARTED.
HE'S LIVED LIKE THIS...
...SINCE HE WAS A KID.
KILLING PEOPLE AND EXPECTING TO BE KILLED WERE JUST PART OF HIS EVERYDAY LIFE.
HE LIVES...
...IN A TOTALLY DIFFERENT WORLD FROM ME...
BUT...
KAGETORA...
I CAN'T LET HIM DO THAT HERE!
...DON'T KILL ANYONE FOR ME, PLEASE.

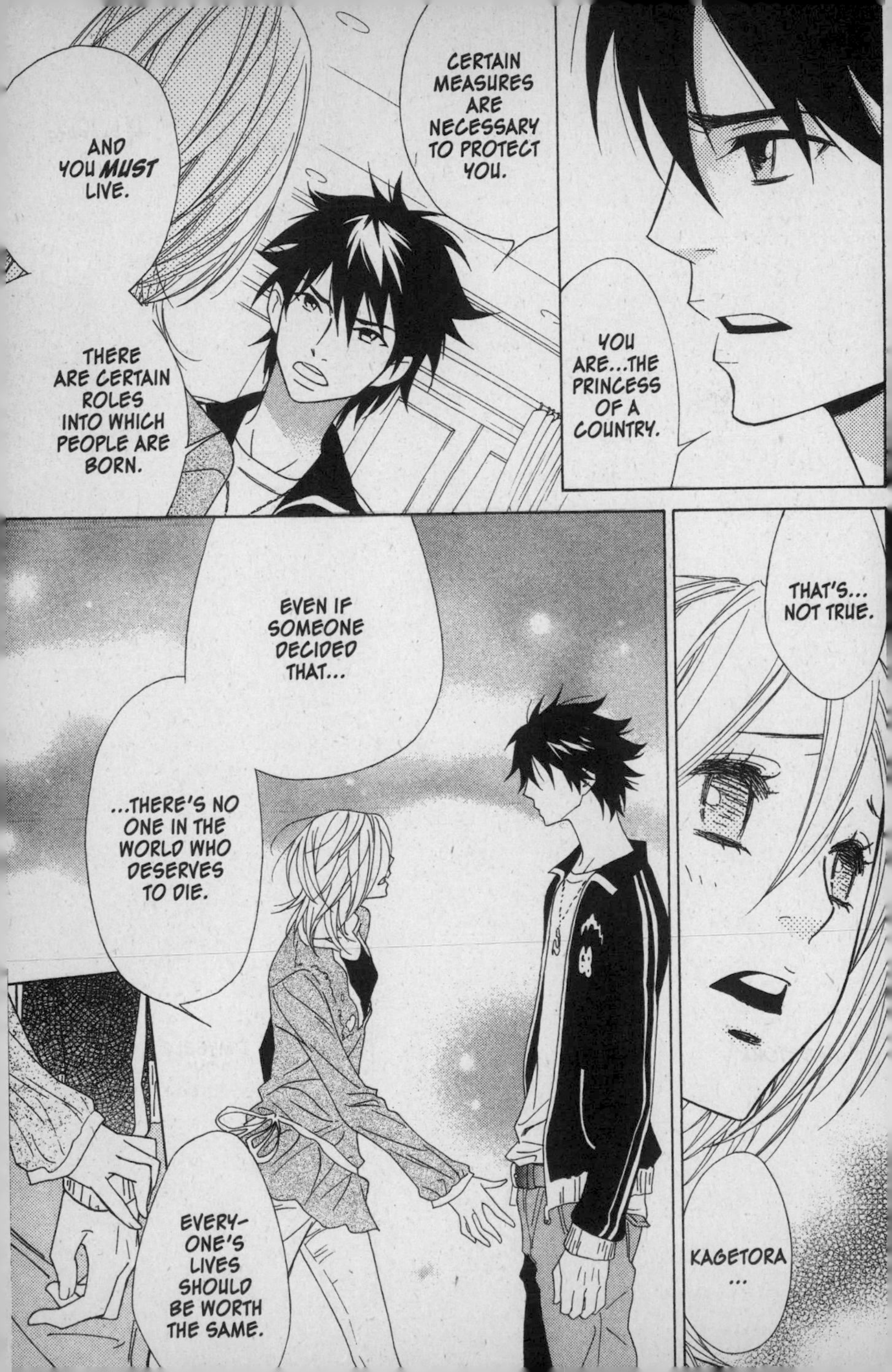
YOU ARE...THE PRINCESS OF A COUNTRY.
CERTAIN MEASURES ARE NECESSARY TO PROTECT YOU.
THERE ARE CERTAIN ROLES INTO WHICH PEOPLE ARE BORN.
AND YOU ***MUST*** LIVE.
THAT'S... NOT TRUE.
KAGETORA ...
EVEN IF SOMEONE DECIDED THAT...
...THERE'S NO ONE IN THE WORLD WHO DESERVES TO DIE.
EVERY-ONE'S LIVES SHOULD BE WORTH THE SAME.

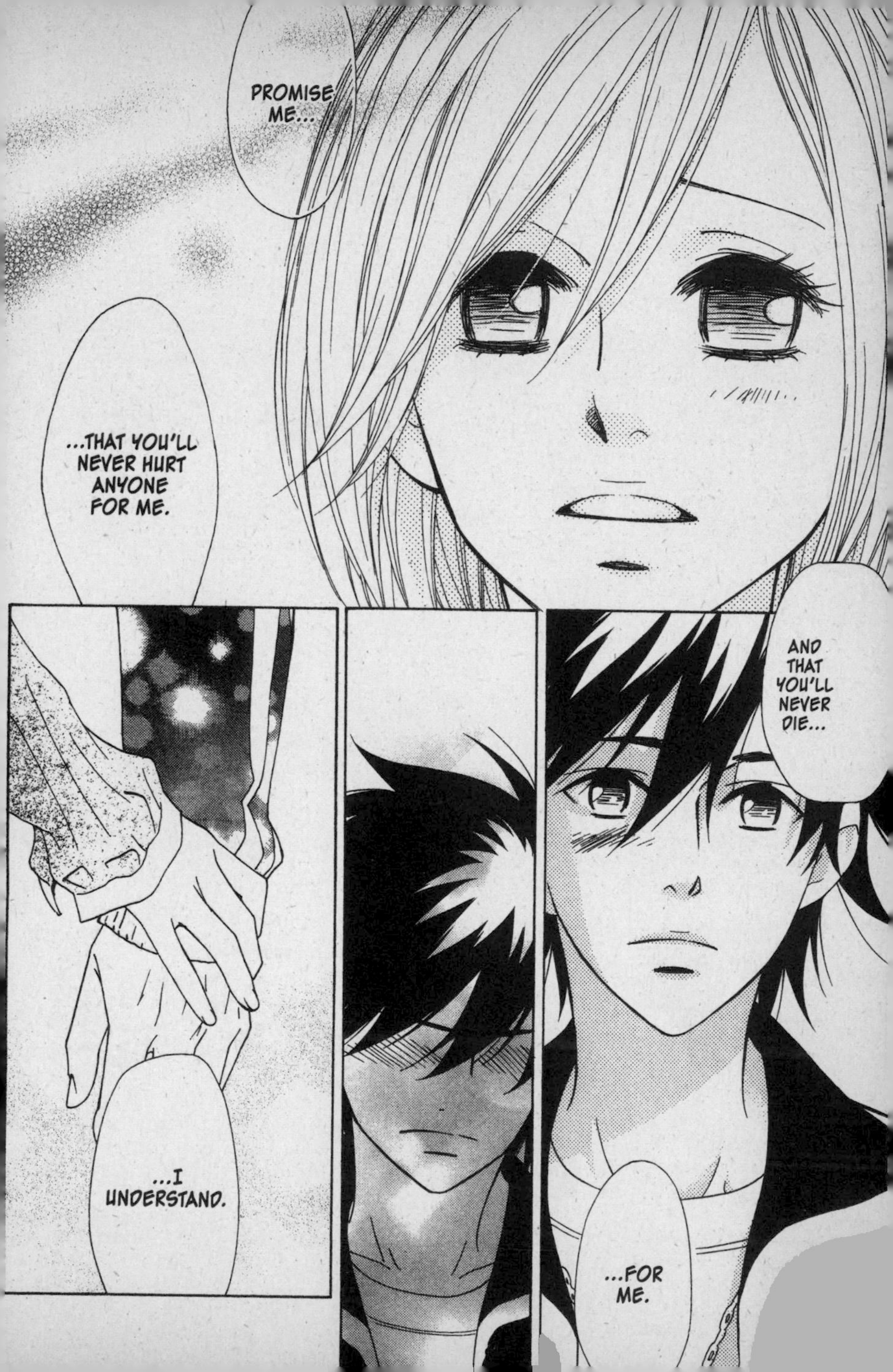
PROMISE ME...
...THAT YOU'LL NEVER HURT ANYONE FOR ME.
AND THAT YOU'LL NEVER DIE...
...FOR ME.
...I UNDERSTAND.

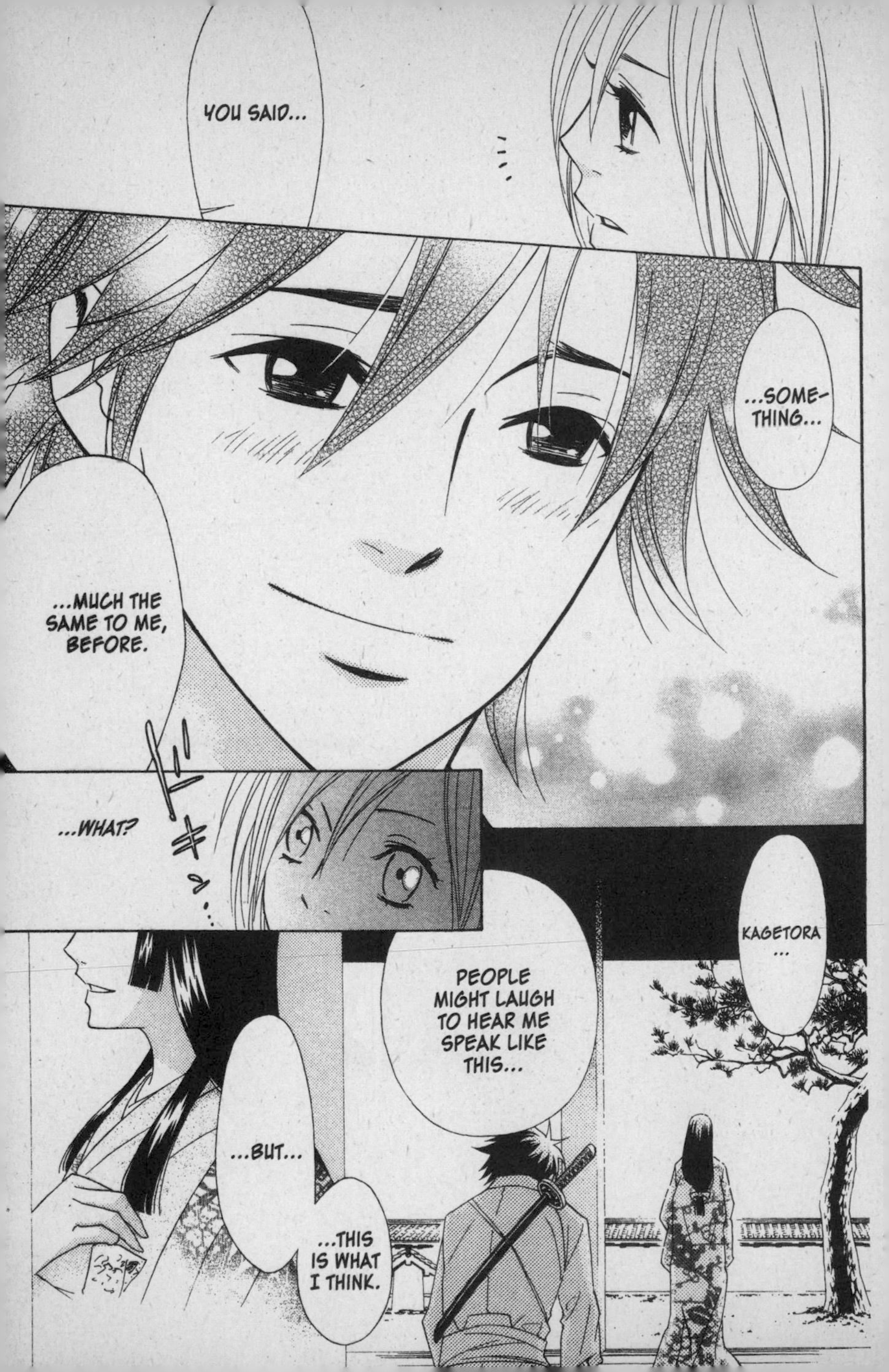
YOU SAID...
...SOME-THING...
...MUCH THE SAME TO ME, BEFORE.
...WHAT?
KAGETORA ...
PEOPLE MIGHT LAUGH TO HEAR ME SPEAK LIKE THIS...
...BUT...
...THIS IS WHAT I THINK.

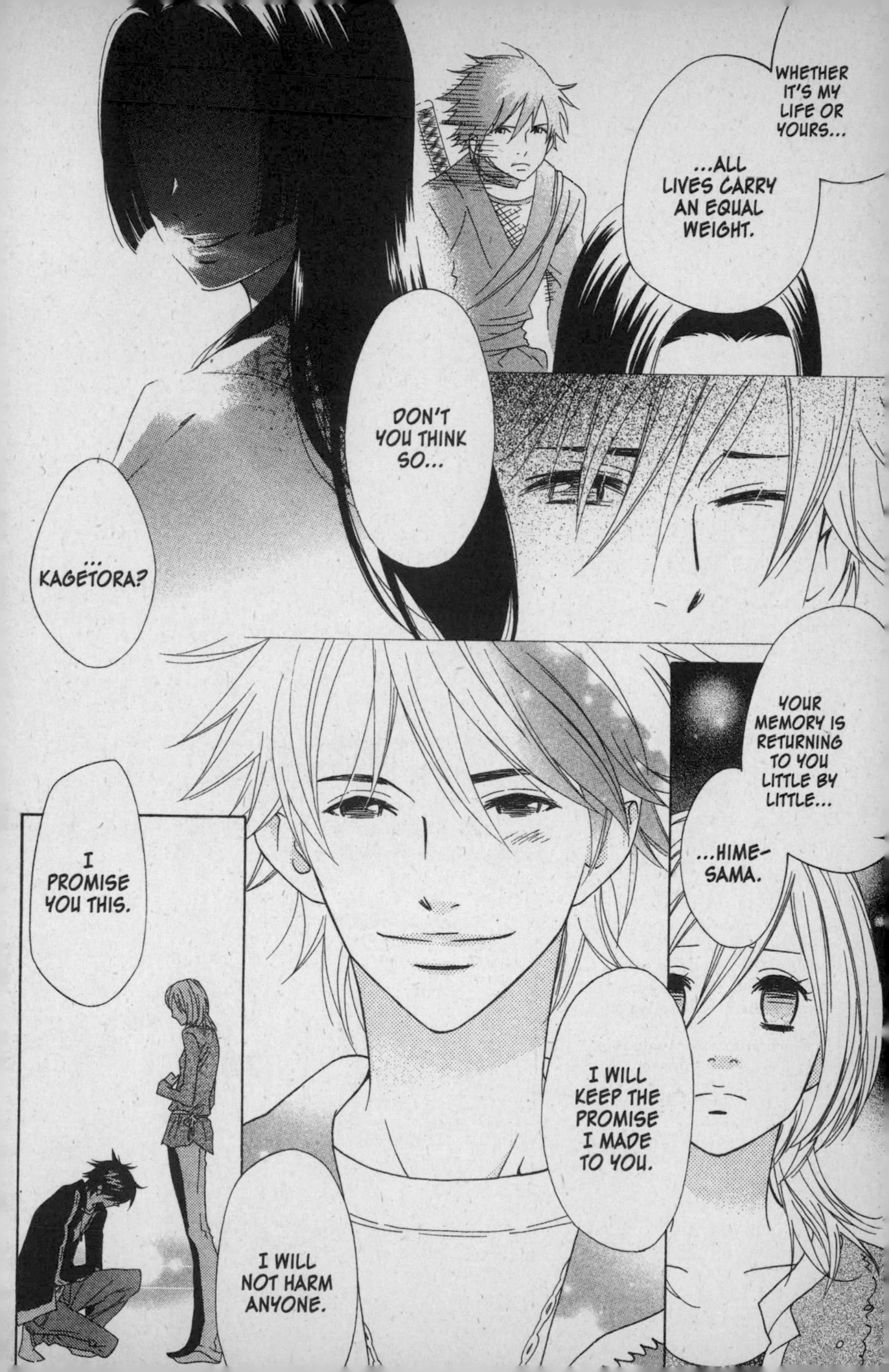
WHETHER IT'S MY LIFE OR YOURS...
...ALL LIVES CARRY AN EQUAL WEIGHT.
DON'T YOU THINK SO...
...KAGETORA?
YOUR MEMORY IS RETURNING TO YOU LITTLE BY LITTLE...
...HIME-SAMA.
I WILL KEEP THE PROMISE I MADE TO YOU.
I WILL NOT HARM ANYONE.
I PROMISE YOU THIS.

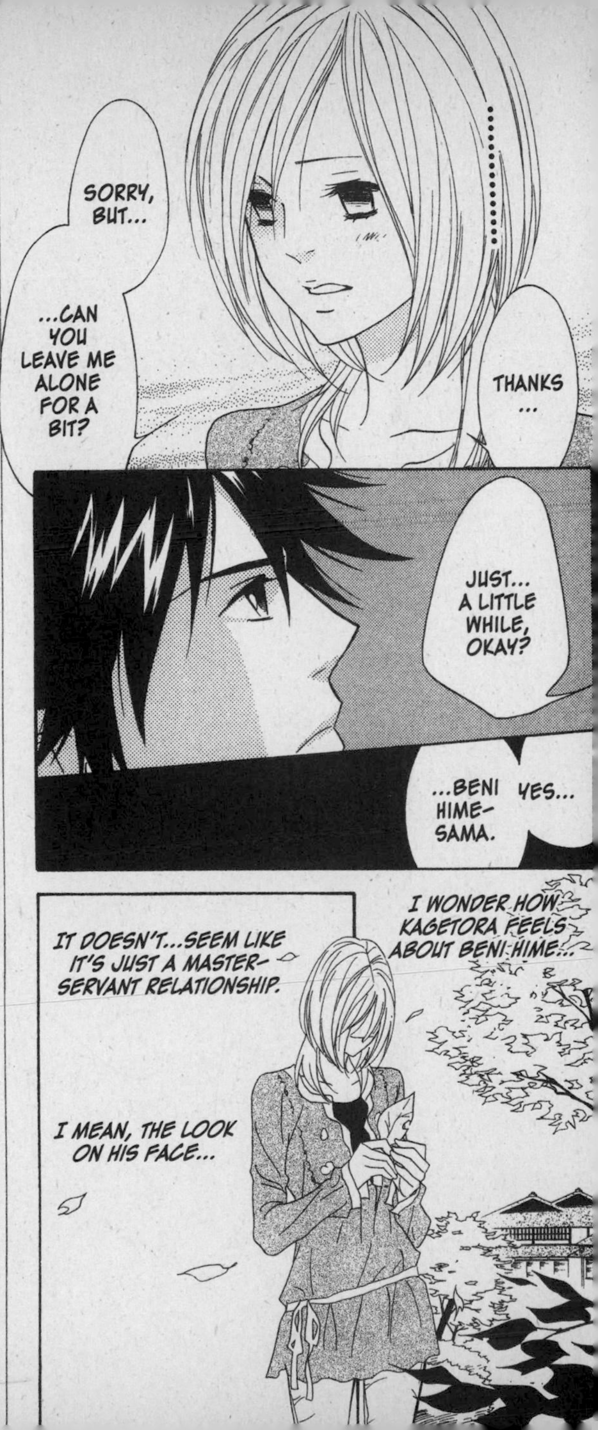
SORRY, BUT...
...CAN YOU LEAVE ME ALONE FOR A BIT?
THANKS ...
JUST... A LITTLE WHILE, OKAY?
YES...
...BENI HIME-SAMA.
I WONDER HOW KAGETORA FEELS ABOUT BENI-HIME...
IT DOESN'T...SEEM LIKE IT'S JUST A MASTER-SERVANT RELATIONSHIP.
I MEAN, THE LOOK ON HIS FACE...

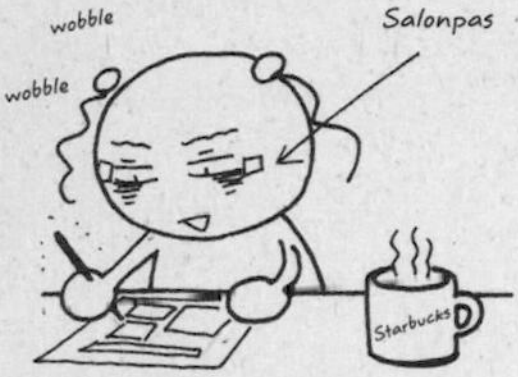
wobble
wobble
Salonpas
Starbucks

Your author is someone who usually gets enough sleep, but there often isn't enough production time when working on "Shinobi Life." Sleeping time is the first thing to go, in order to get the manuscripts finished by the deadline. All-nighters are not unheard-of.

Sometimes people ask, "What do you do when you get sleepy?" I tell them that those caffeine pills you can buy make my hand tremble so much that I can't draw, so I have to get by with really, really strong green tea--green tea so thick you can barely see the bottom of my favorite Starbucks mug. To calm my nerves, I try sticking salonpas to the corners of my eyes, but it doesn't work so well...

If there are better ways to stay awake, please let me know.

* Note: Salonpas are a pain-relieving medicinal patch.

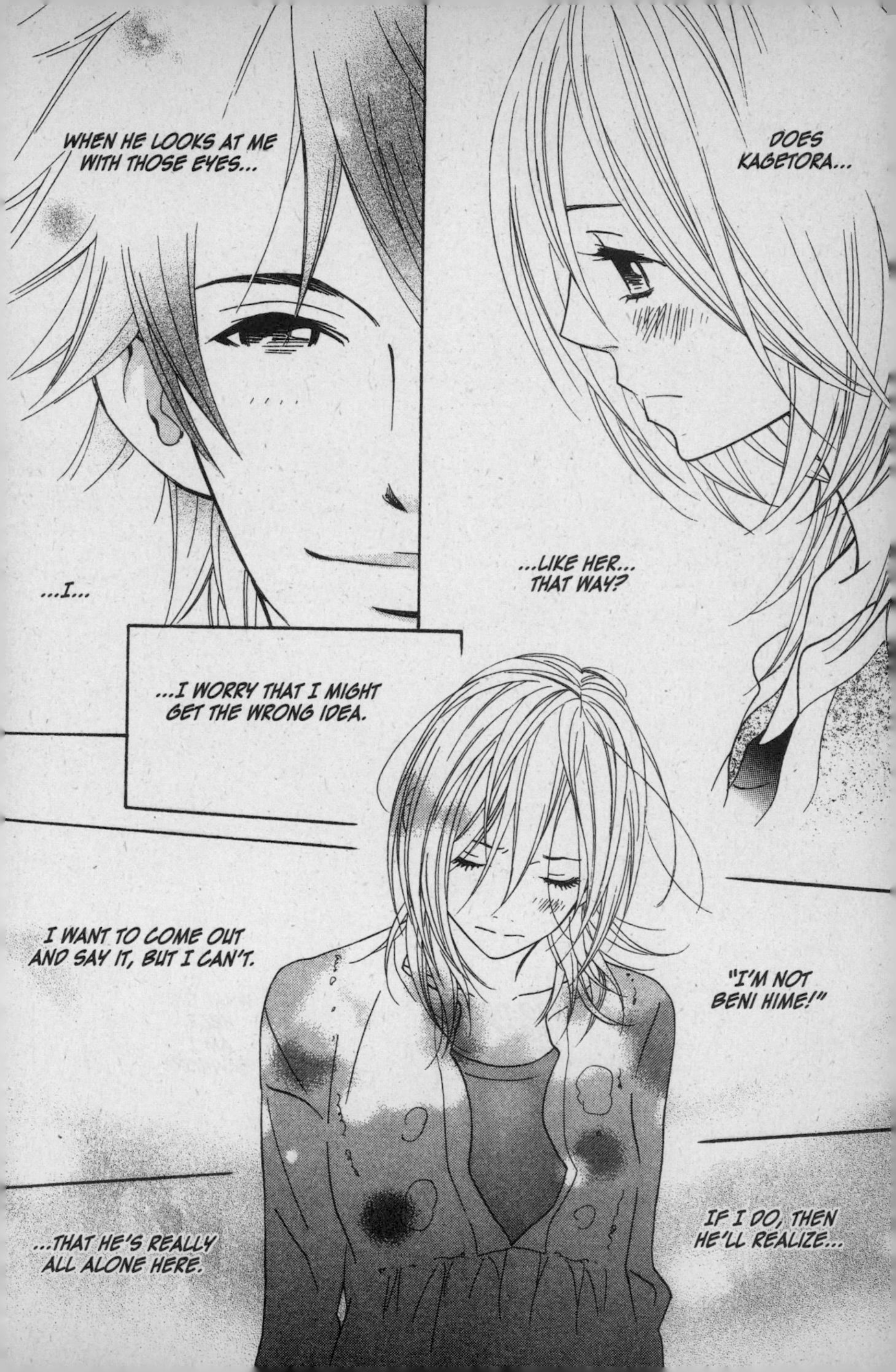
DOES KAGETORA...
...LIKE HER... THAT WAY?
WHEN HE LOOKS AT ME WITH THOSE EYES...
...I...
...I WORRY THAT I MIGHT GET THE WRONG IDEA.
"I'M NOT BENI HIME!"
I WANT TO COME OUT AND SAY IT, BUT I CAN'T.
IF I DO, THEN HE'LL REALIZE...
...THAT HE'S REALLY ALL ALONE HERE.

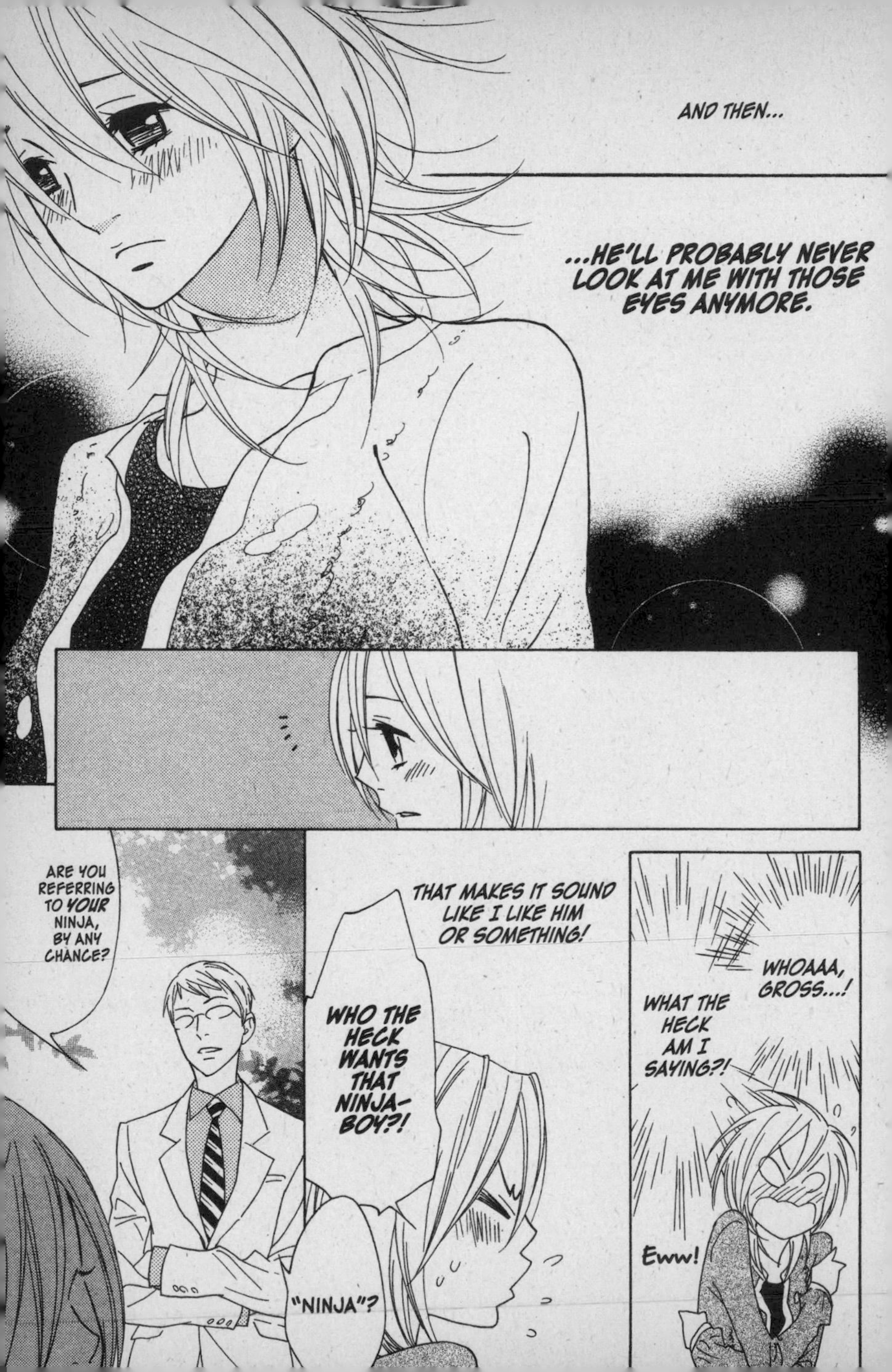
AND THEN...
...HE'LL PROBABLY NEVER LOOK AT ME WITH THOSE EYES ANYMORE.
WHOAAA, GROSS...!
WHAT THE HECK AM I SAYING?!
Eww!
THAT MAKES IT SOUND LIKE I LIKE HIM OR SOMETHING!
WHO THE HECK WANTS THAT NINJA-BOY?!
"NINJA"?
ARE YOU REFERRING TO YOUR NINJA, BY ANY CHANCE?

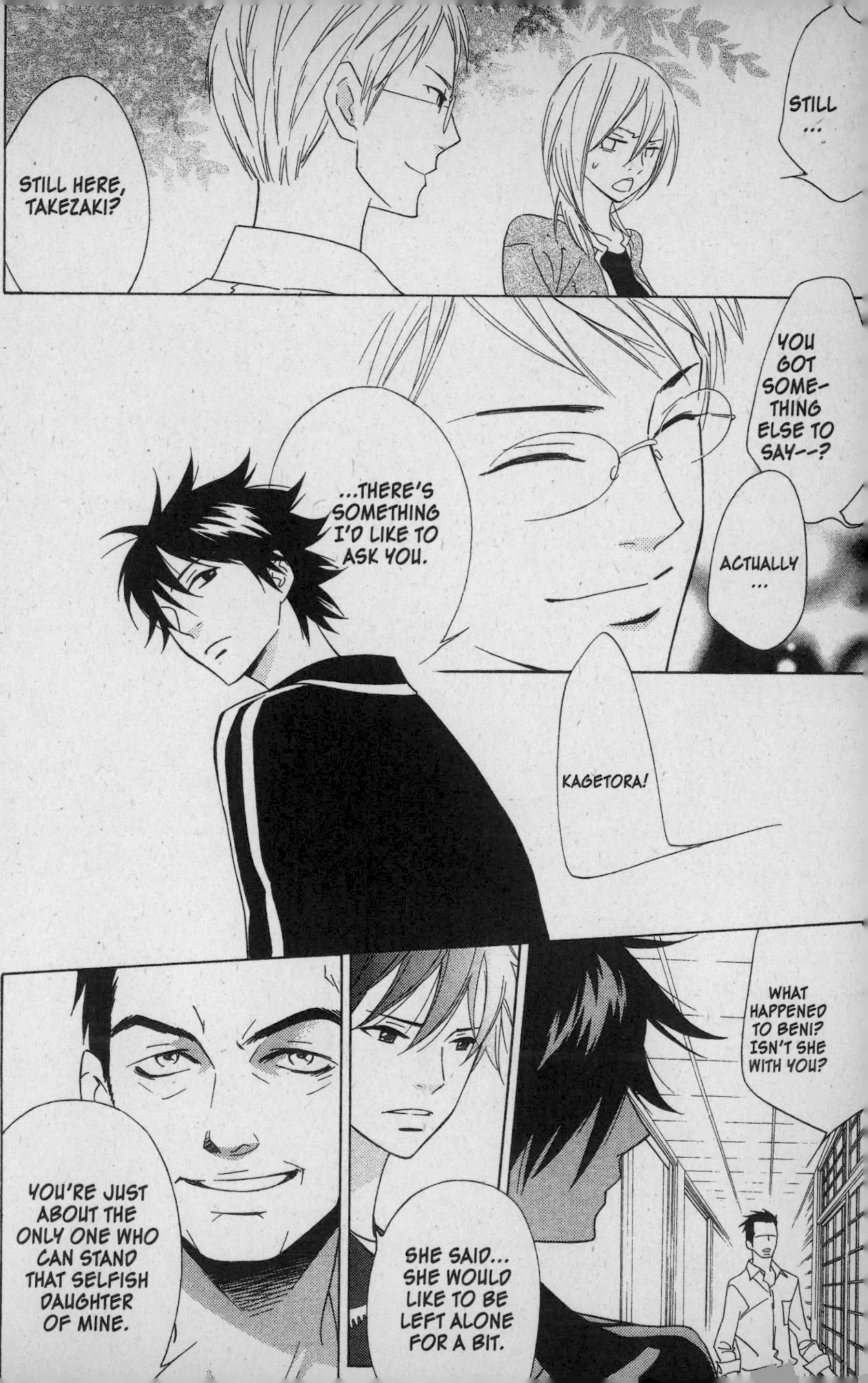

STILL...
STILL HERE, TAKEZAKI?
YOU GOT SOMETHING ELSE TO SAY--?
ACTUALLY...
...THERE'S SOMETHING I'D LIKE TO ASK YOU.
KAGETORA!
WHAT HAPPENED TO BENI? ISN'T SHE WITH YOU?
SHE SAID... SHE WOULD LIKE TO BE LEFT ALONE FOR A BIT.
YOU'RE JUST ABOUT THE ONLY ONE WHO CAN STAND THAT SELFISH DAUGHTER OF MINE.

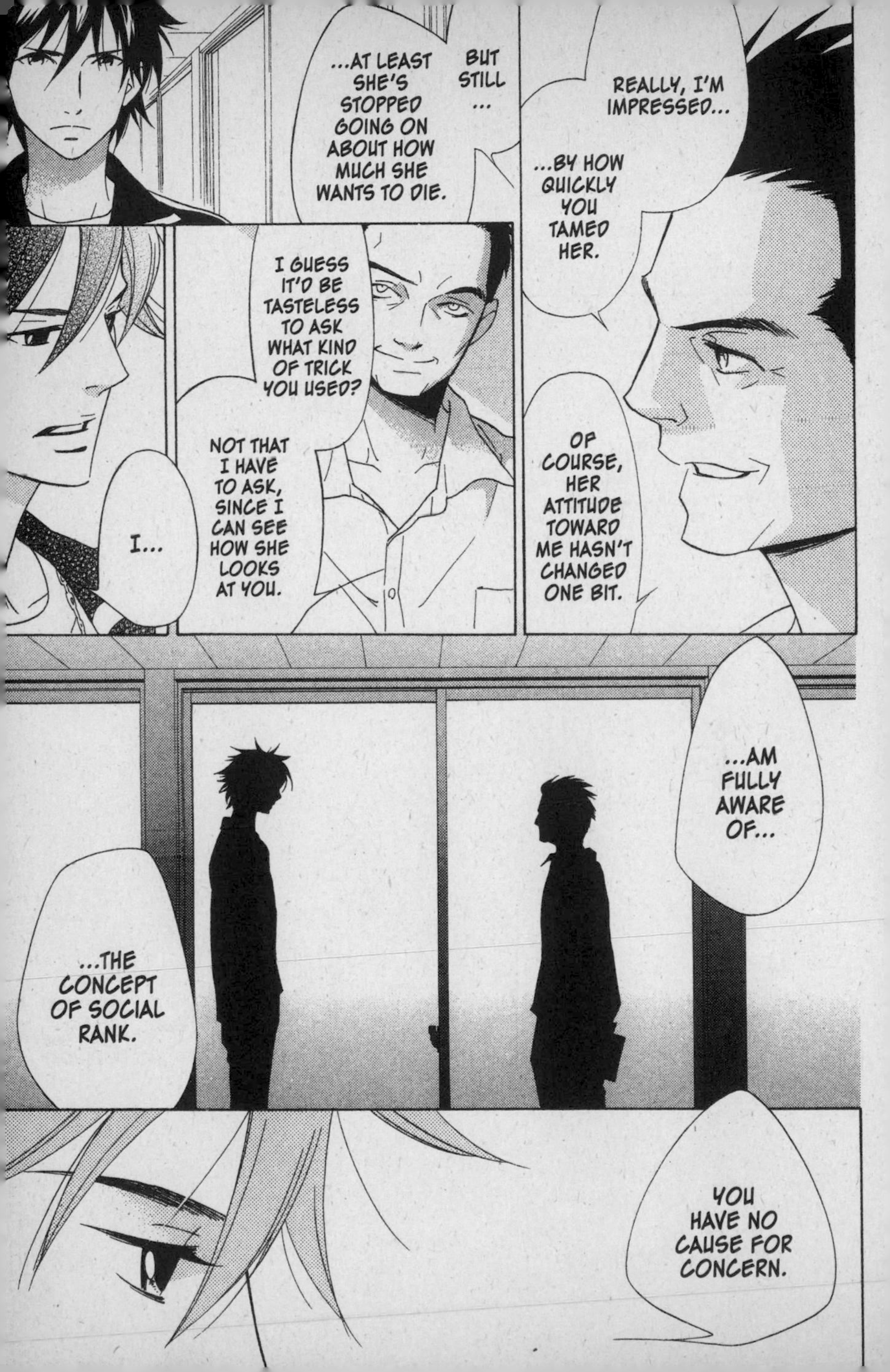
REALLY, I'M IMPRESSED...
...BY HOW QUICKLY YOU TAMED HER.
OF COURSE, HER ATTITUDE TOWARD ME HASN'T CHANGED ONE BIT.
BUT STILL...
...AT LEAST SHE'S STOPPED GOING ON ABOUT HOW MUCH SHE WANTS TO DIE.
I GUESS IT'D BE TASTELESS TO ASK WHAT KIND OF TRICK YOU USED?
NOT THAT I HAVE TO ASK, SINCE I CAN SEE HOW SHE LOOKS AT YOU.
I...
...AM FULLY AWARE OF...
...THE CONCEPT OF SOCIAL RANK.
YOU HAVE NO CAUSE FOR CONCERN.

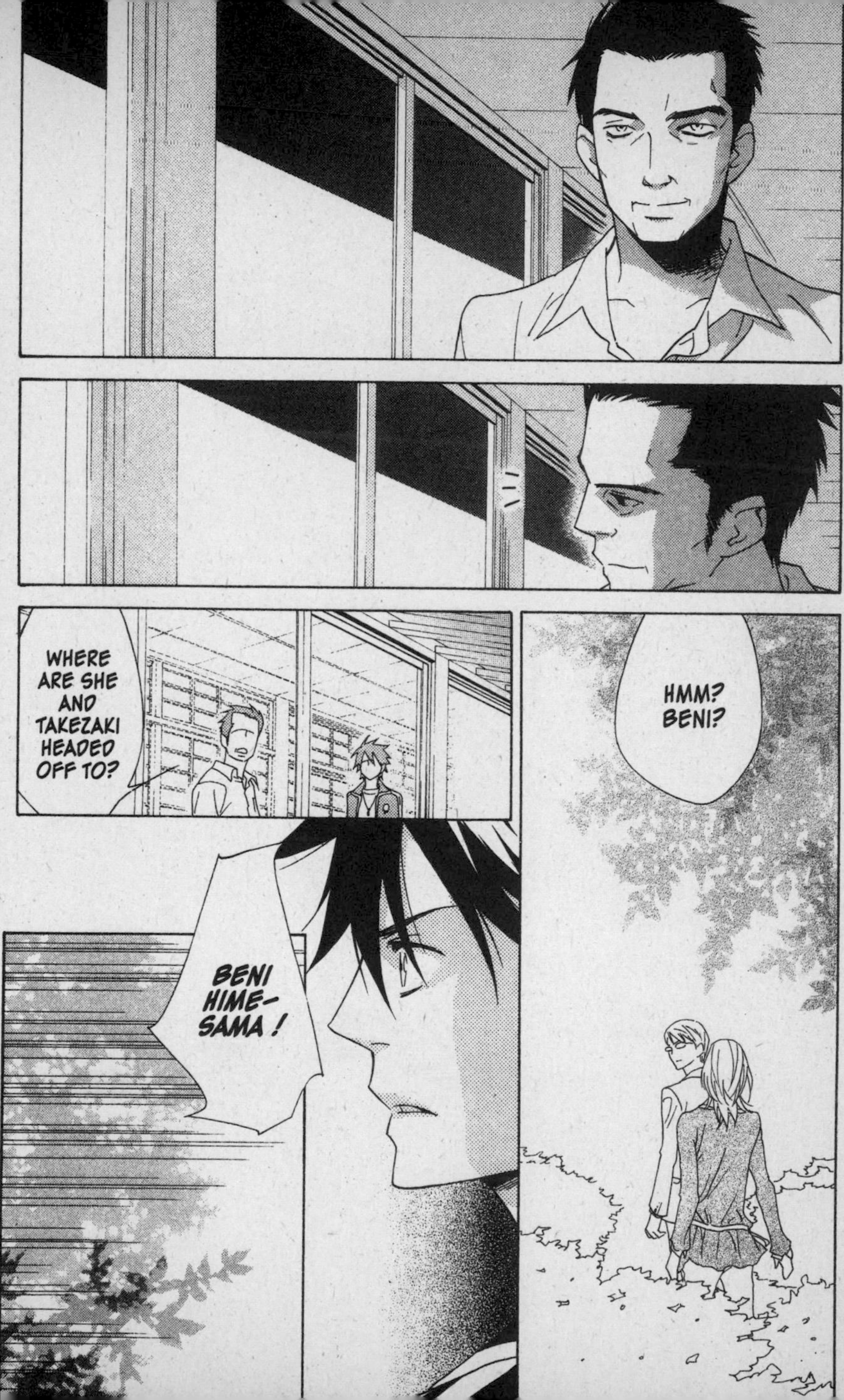
HMM? BENI?
WHERE ARE SHE AND TAKEZAKI HEADED OFF TO?
BENI HIME-SAMA!

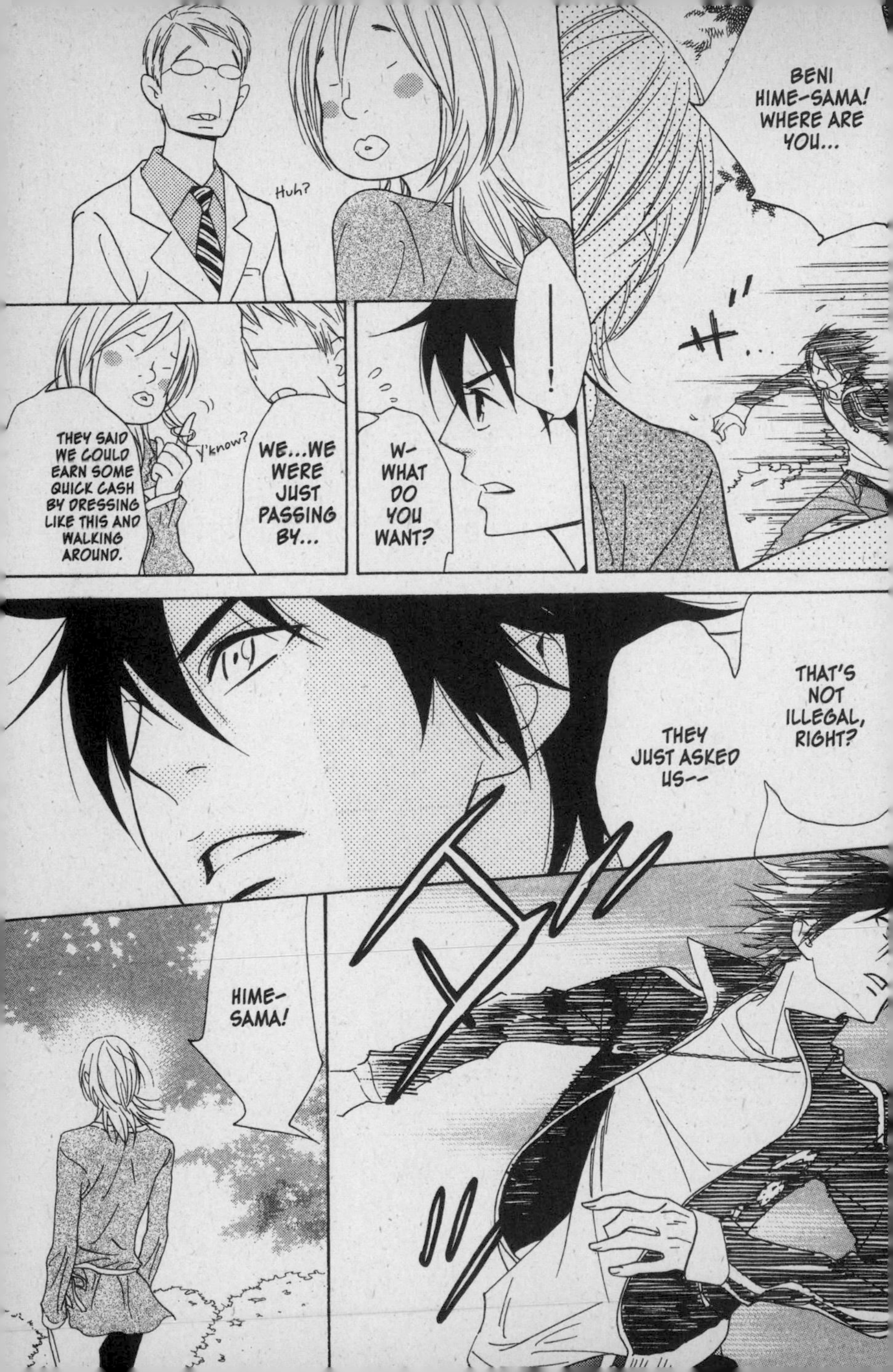
BENI HIME-SAMA! WHERE ARE YOU...
Huh?
!
W-WHAT DO YOU WANT?
WE...WE WERE JUST PASSING BY...
THEY SAID WE COULD EARN SOME QUICK CASH BY DRESSING LIKE THIS AND WALKING AROUND.
Y'know?
THAT'S NOT ILLEGAL, RIGHT?
THEY JUST ASKED US--
HIME-SAMA!

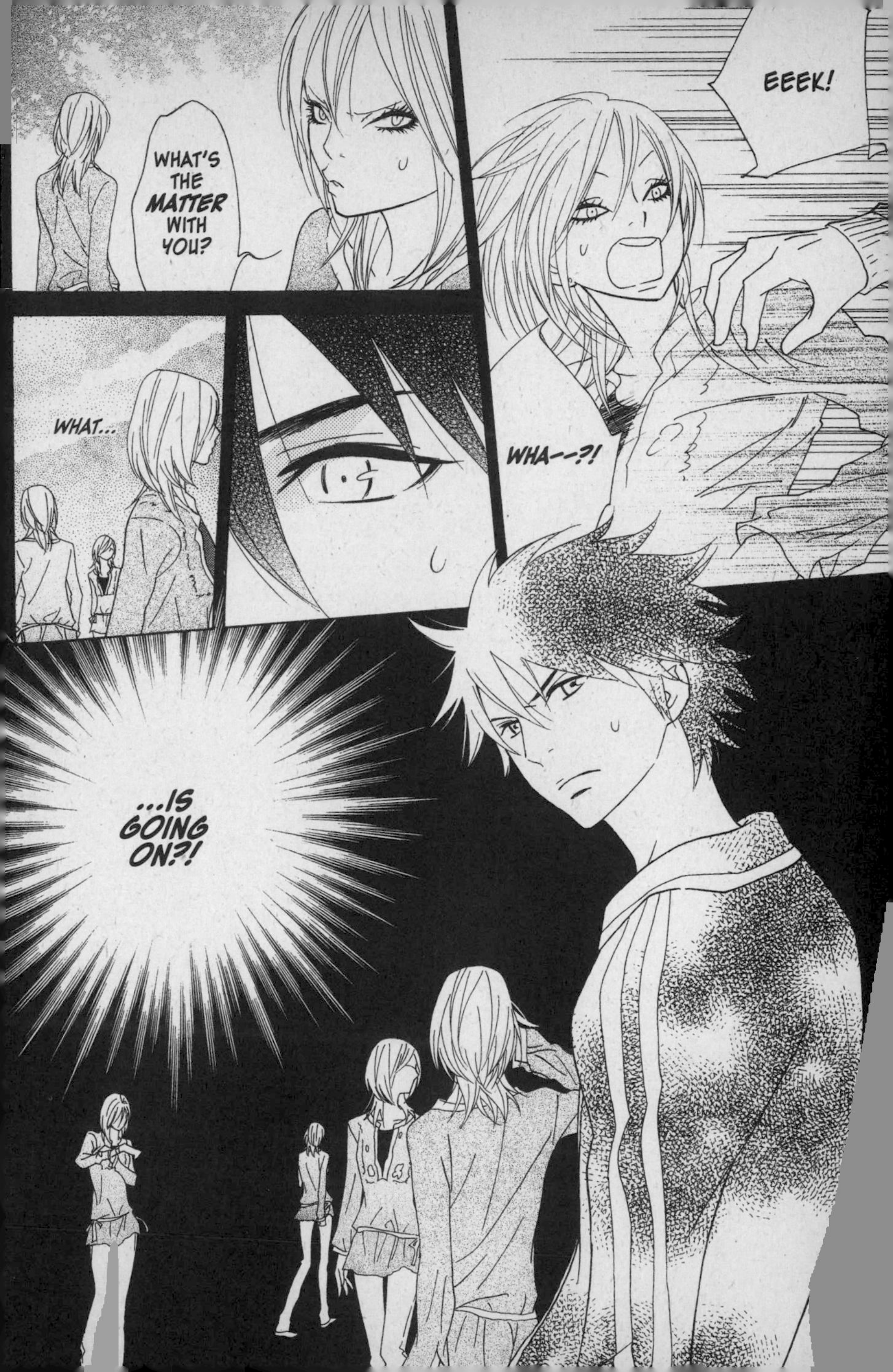
EEEK!
WHA--?!
WHAT'S THE MATTER WITH YOU?
WHAT...
...IS GOING ON?!

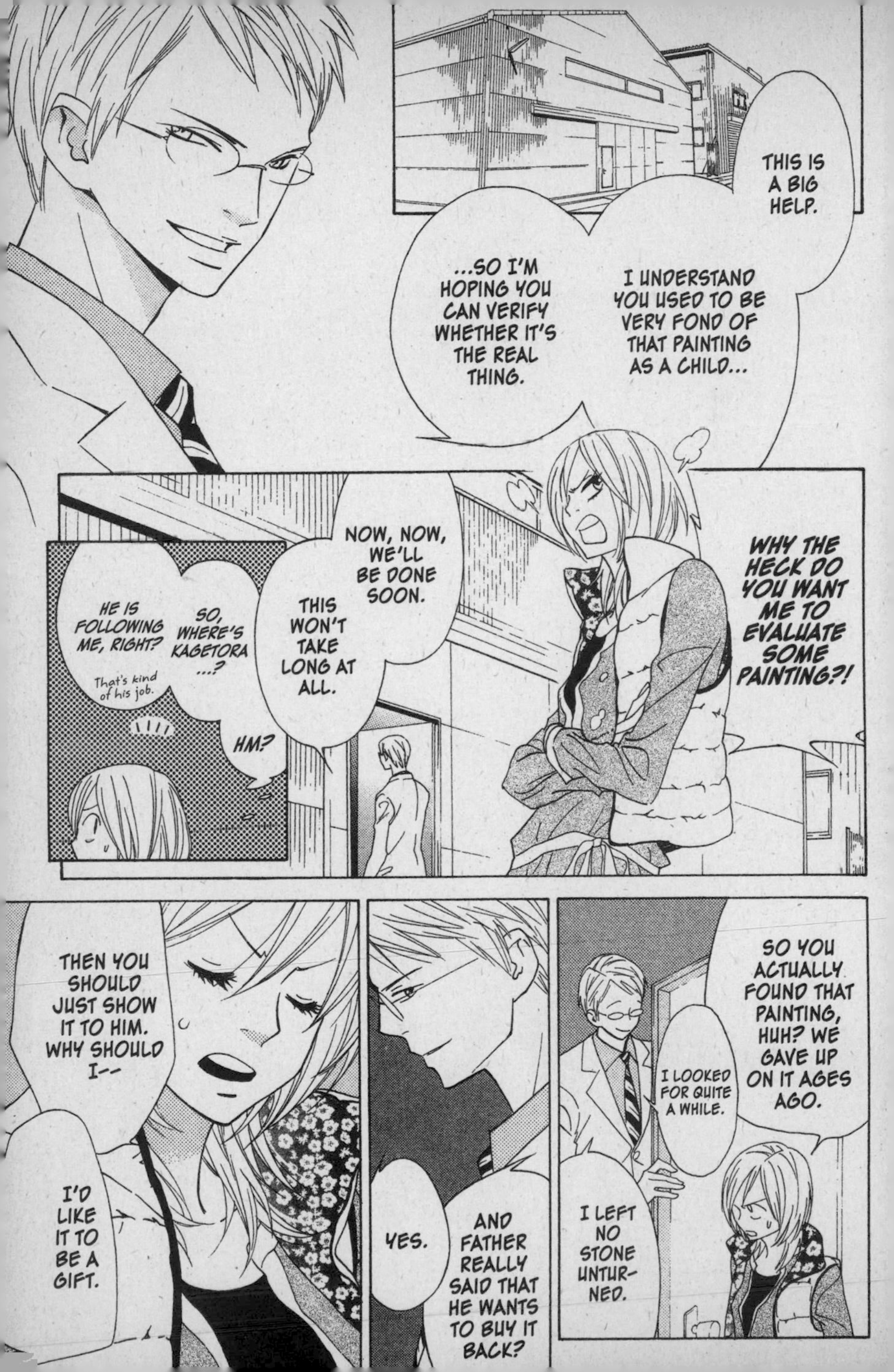
THIS IS A BIG HELP.
I UNDERSTAND YOU USED TO BE VERY FOND OF THAT PAINTING AS A CHILD...
...SO I'M HOPING YOU CAN VERIFY WHETHER IT'S THE REAL THING.
WHY THE HECK DO YOU WANT ME TO EVALUATE SOME PAINTING?!
NOW, NOW, WE'LL BE DONE SOON.
THIS WON'T TAKE LONG AT ALL.
SO, WHERE'S KAGETORA ...?
HE IS FOLLOWING ME, RIGHT?
That's kind of his job.
HM?
SO YOU ACTUALLY FOUND THAT PAINTING, HUH? WE GAVE UP ON IT AGES AGO.
I LOOKED FOR QUITE A WHILE.
I LEFT NO STONE UNTUR-NED.
AND FATHER REALLY SAID THAT HE WANTS TO BUY IT BACK?
YES.
THEN YOU SHOULD JUST SHOW IT TO HIM. WHY SHOULD I--
I'D LIKE IT TO BE A GIFT.

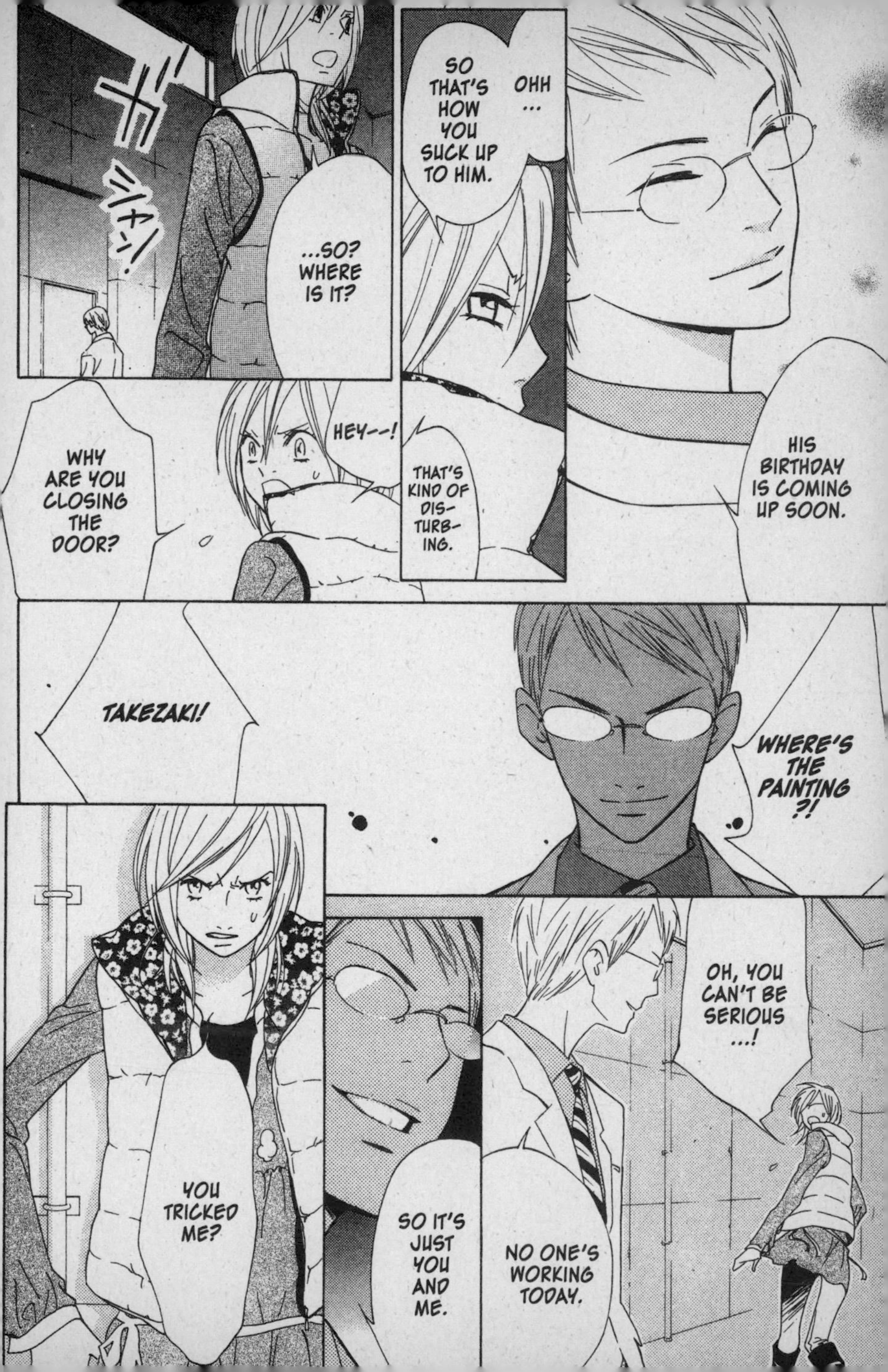
OHH ...
SO THAT'S HOW YOU SUCK UP TO HIM.
HIS BIRTHDAY IS COMING UP SOON.
THAT'S KIND OF DIS-TURB-ING.
ガシャン!
...SO? WHERE IS IT?
HEY--!
WHY ARE YOU CLOSING THE DOOR?
WHERE'S THE PAINTING?!
TAKEZAKI!
OH, YOU CAN'T BE SERIOUS ...!
NO ONE'S WORKING TODAY.
SO IT'S JUST YOU AND ME.
YOU TRICKED ME?

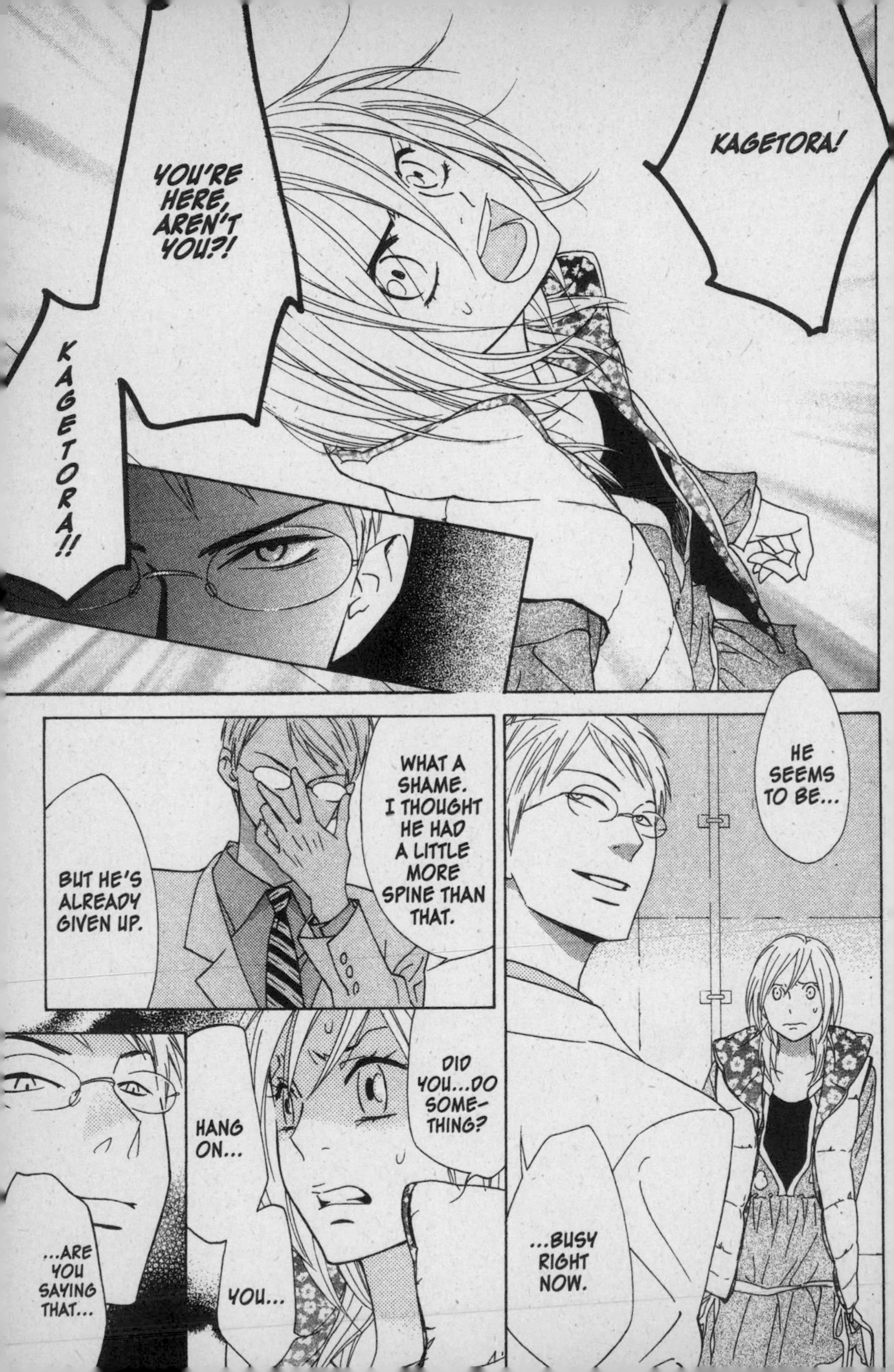
KAGETORA!
YOU'RE HERE, AREN'T YOU?!
KAGETORA!!
HE SEEMS TO BE...
...BUSY RIGHT NOW.
WHAT A SHAME. I THOUGHT HE HAD A LITTLE MORE SPINE THAN THAT.
BUT HE'S ALREADY GIVEN UP.
DID YOU...DO SOMETHING?
HANG ON...
YOU...
...ARE YOU SAYING THAT...

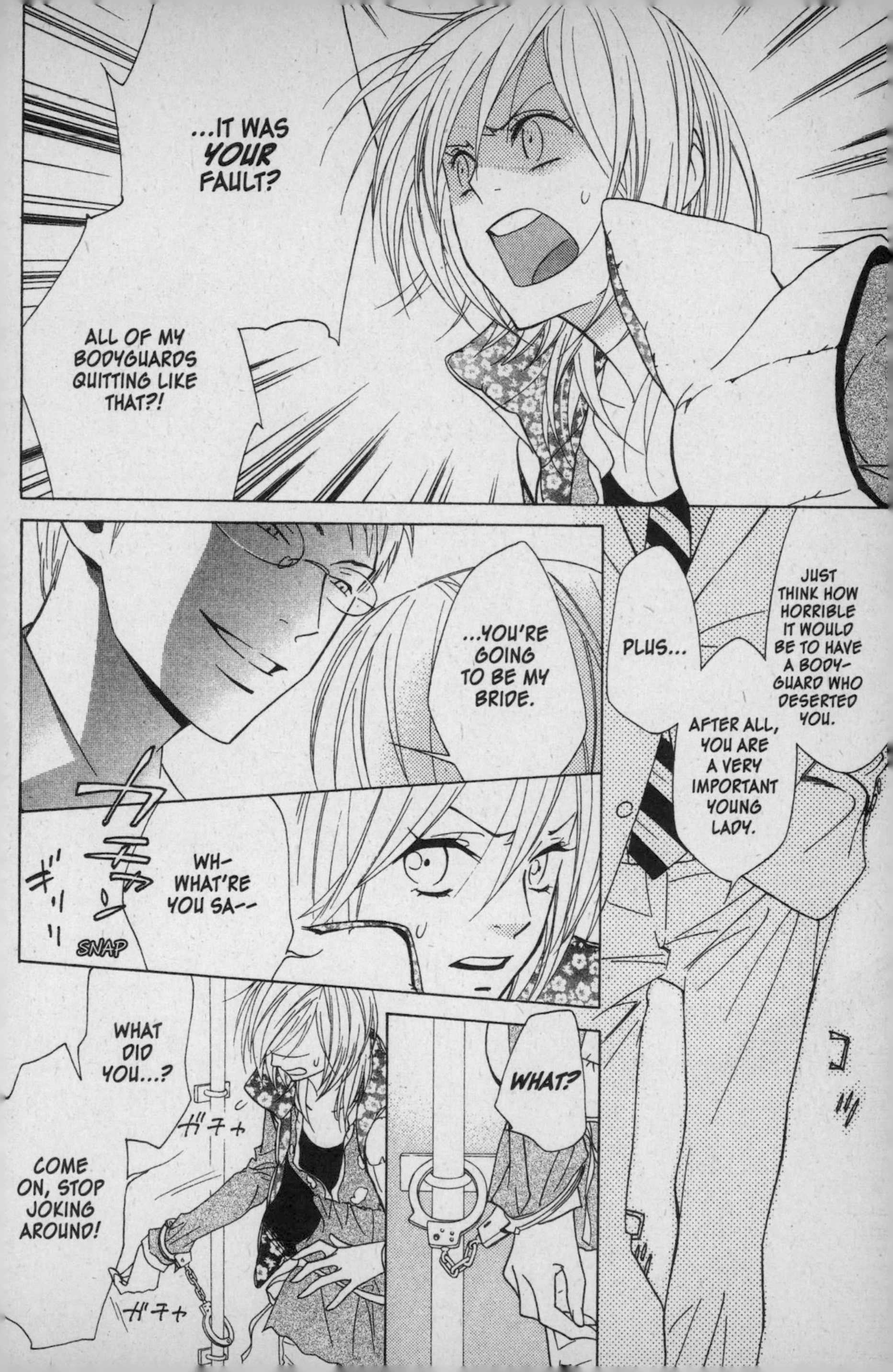
...IT WAS YOUR FAULT?
ALL OF MY BODYGUARDS QUITTING LIKE THAT?!
JUST THINK HOW HORRIBLE IT WOULD BE TO HAVE A BODY-GUARD WHO DESERTED YOU.
PLUS...
AFTER ALL, YOU ARE A VERY IMPORTANT YOUNG LADY.
...YOU'RE GOING TO BE MY BRIDE.
WH- WHAT'RE YOU SA--
SNAP
WHAT?
WHAT DID YOU...?
COME ON, STOP JOKING AROUND!

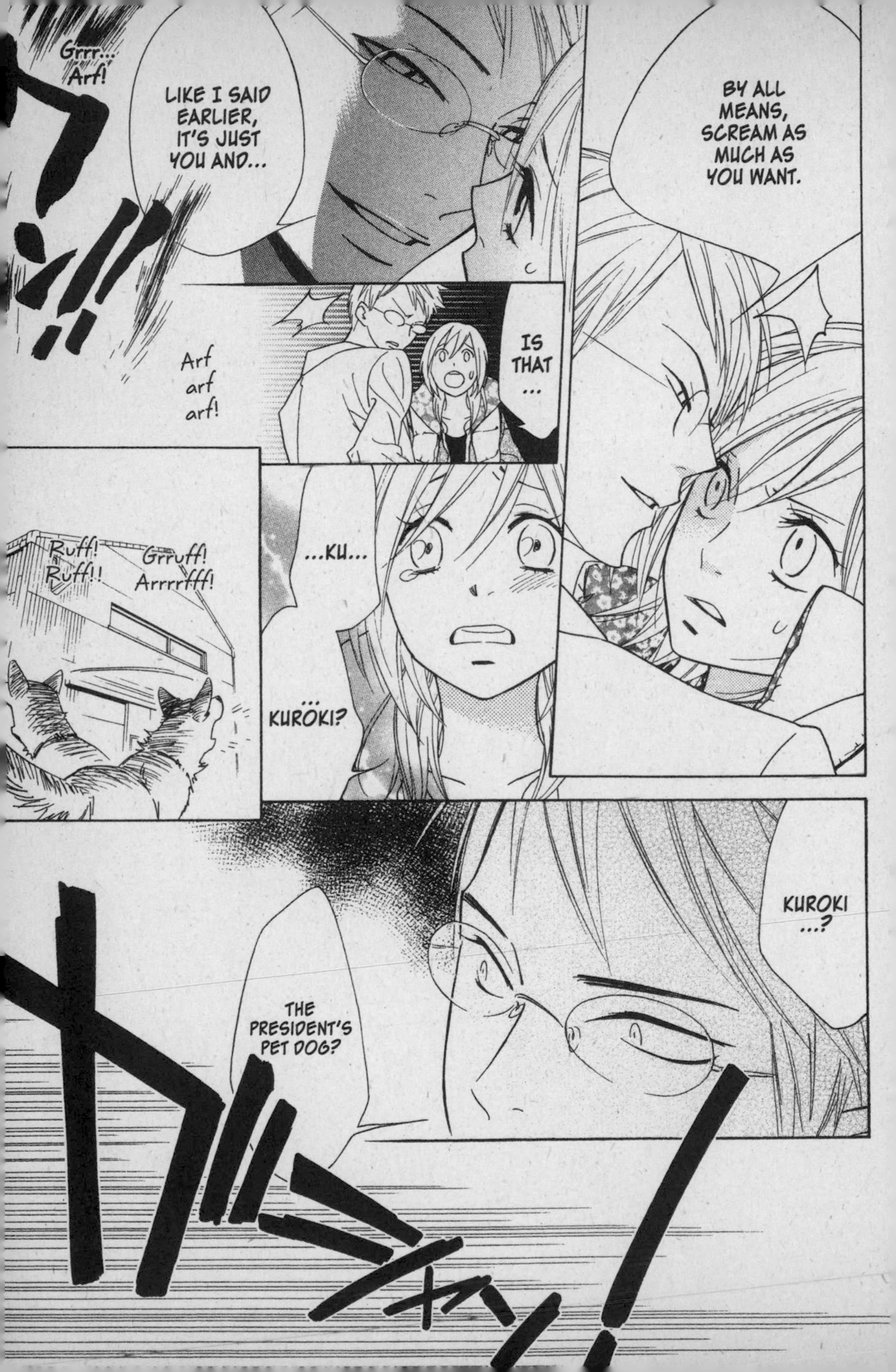
BY ALL MEANS, SCREAM AS MUCH AS YOU WANT.
LIKE I SAID EARLIER, IT'S JUST YOU AND...
Grrr... Arf!
IS THAT ...
Arf arf arf!
...KU...
... KUROKI?
Ruff! Ruff!!
Grruff! Arrrrfff!
KUROKI ...?
THE PRESIDENT'S PET DOG?

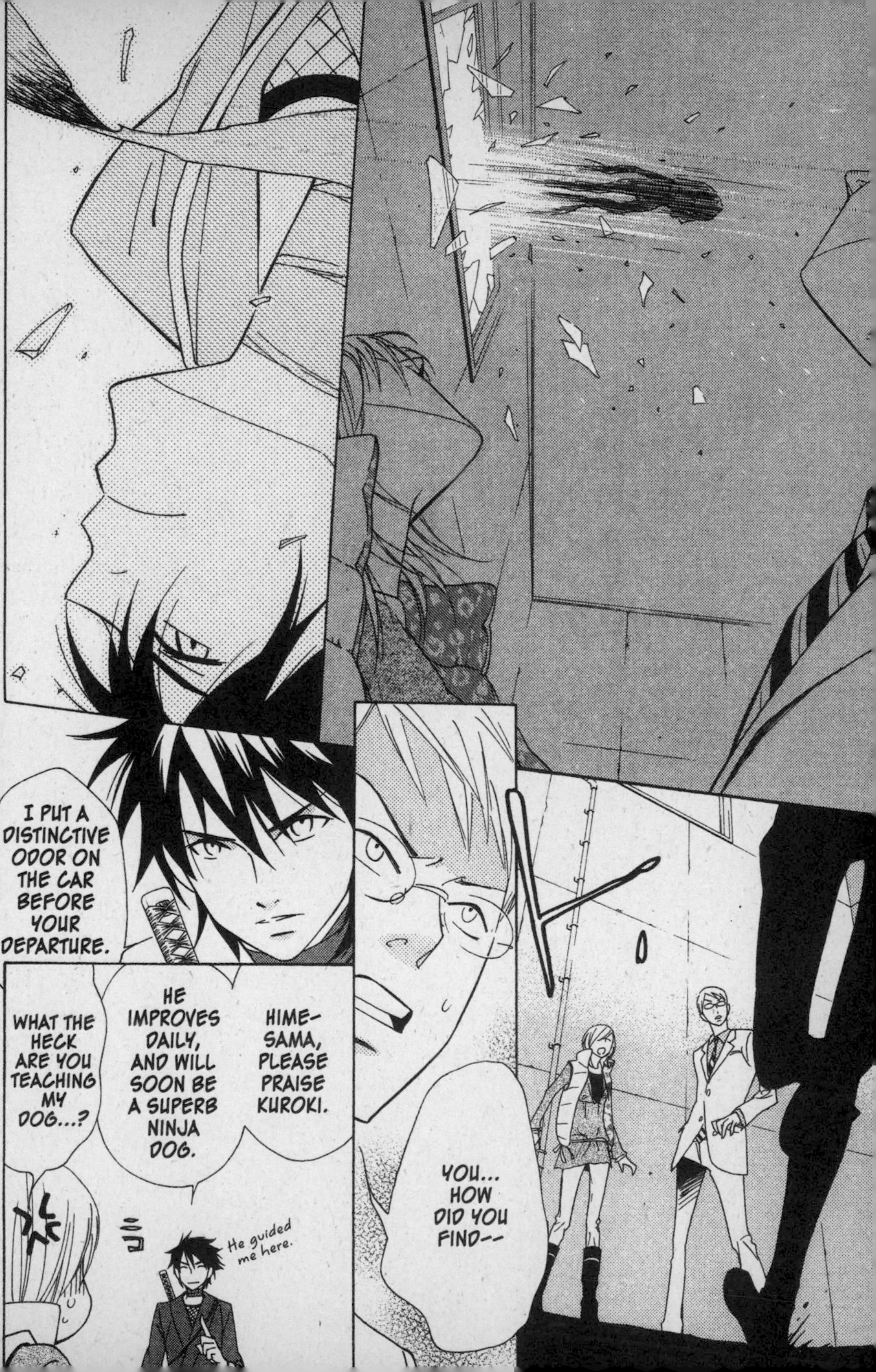
YOU... HOW DID YOU FIND--
I PUT A DISTINCTIVE ODOR ON THE CAR BEFORE YOUR DEPARTURE.
HIME-SAMA, PLEASE PRAISE KUROKI.
HE IMPROVES DAILY, AND WILL SOON BE A SUPERB NINJA DOG.
WHAT THE HECK ARE YOU TEACHING MY DOG...?
He guided me here.

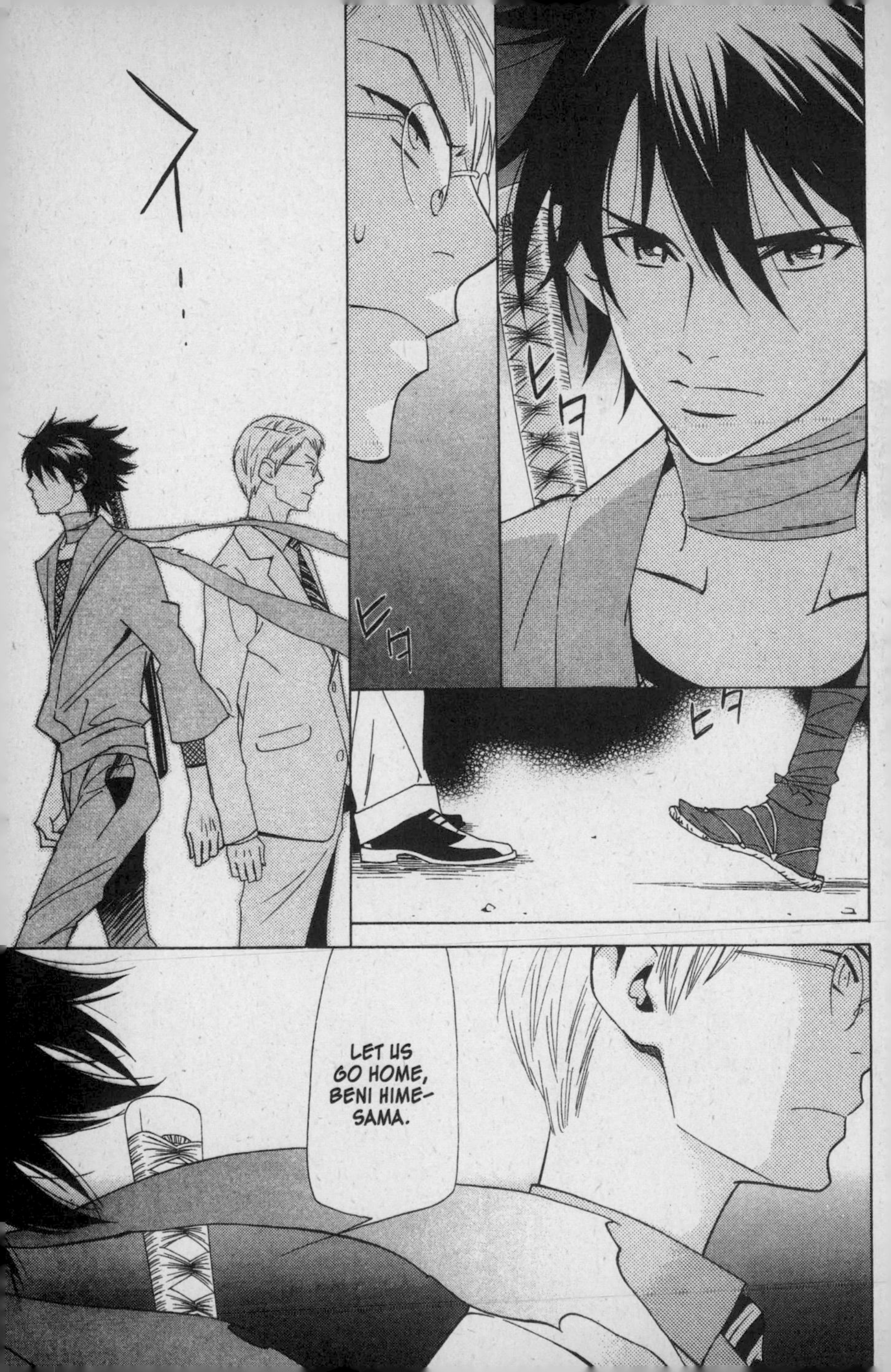
LET US GO HOME, BENI HIME-SAMA.

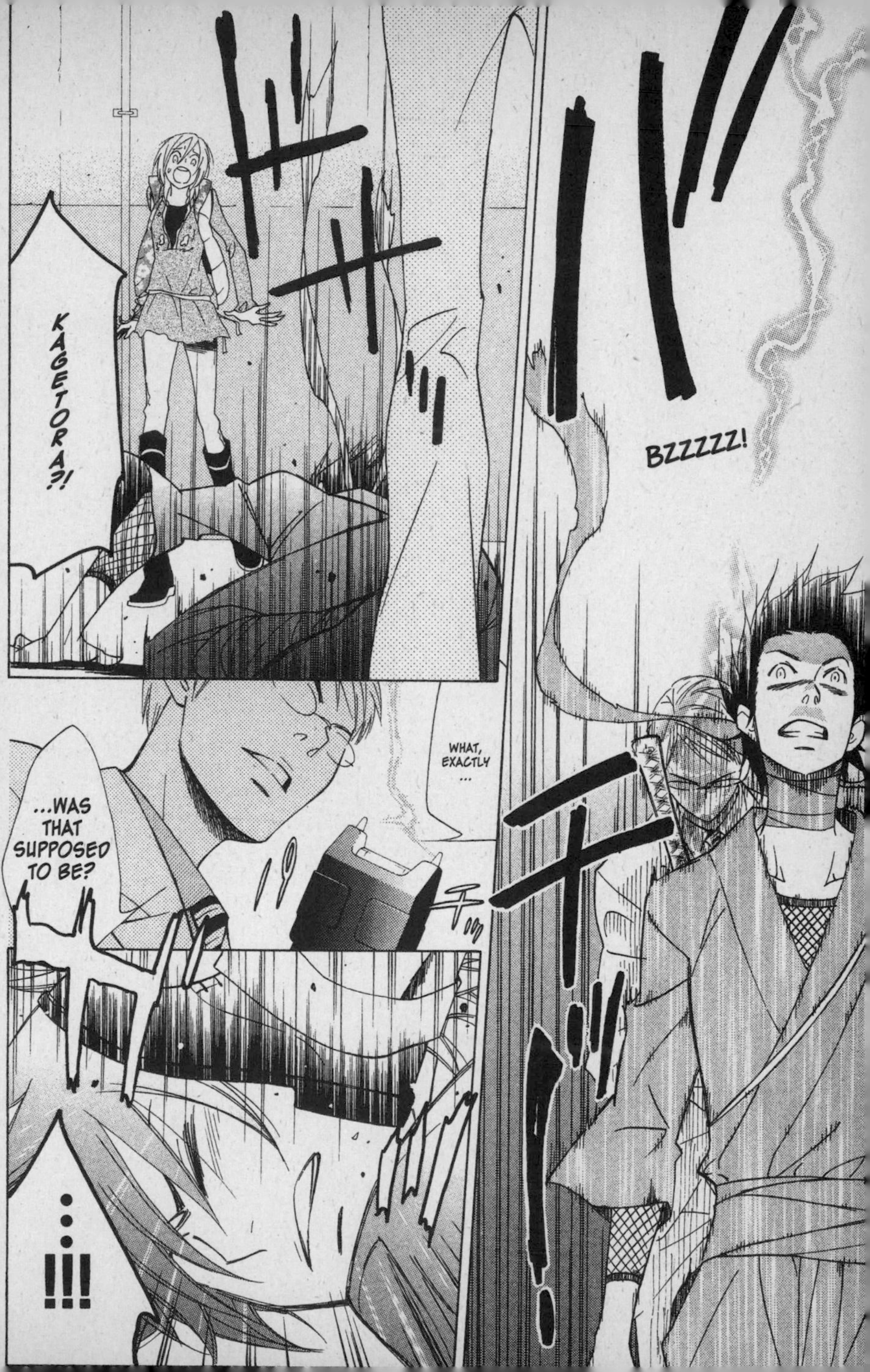
BZZZZZ!
KAGETORA?!
WHAT, EXACTLY...
...WAS THAT SUPPOSED TO BE?
...!!!

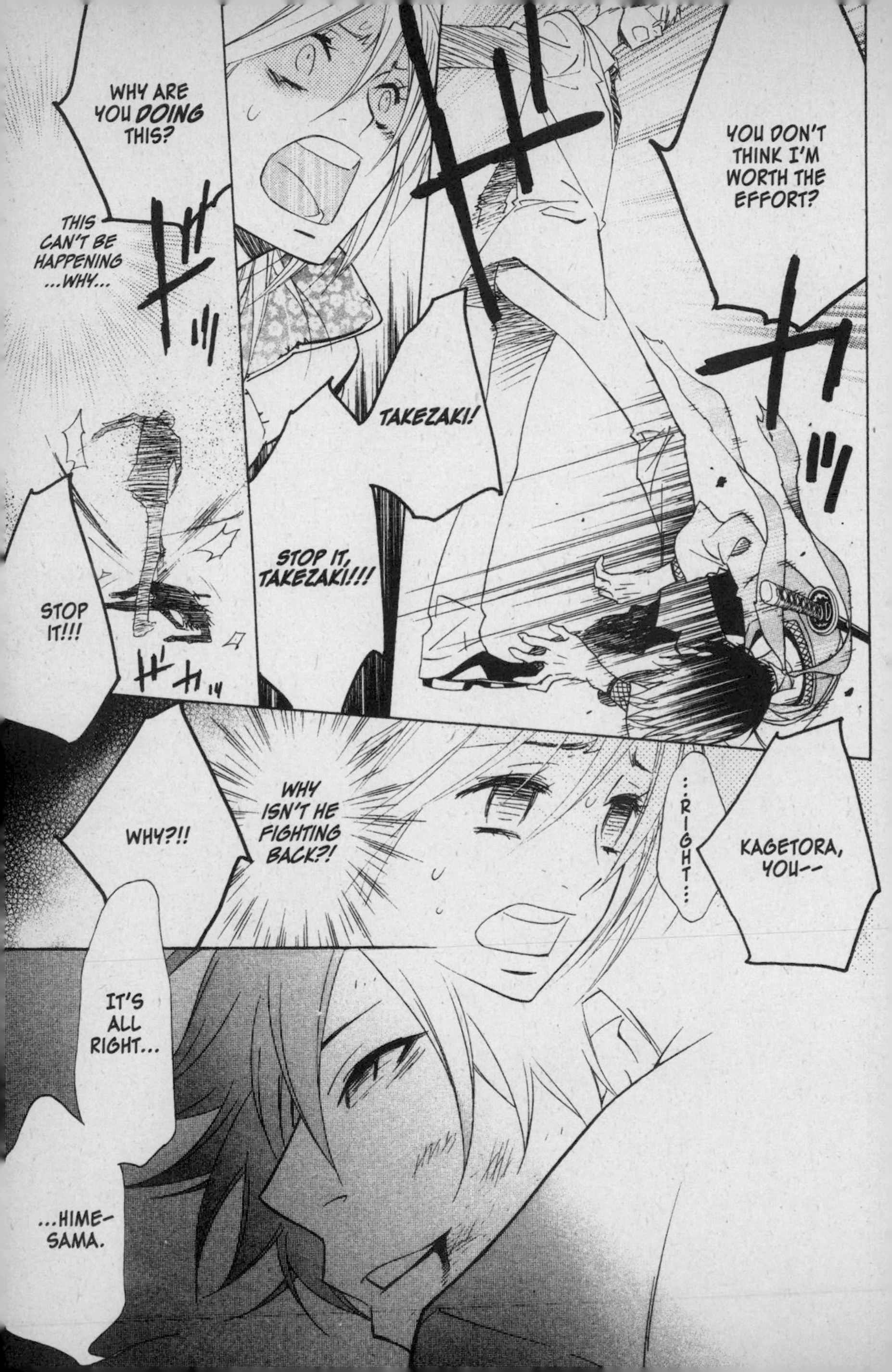
YOU DON'T THINK I'M WORTH THE EFFORT?
TAKEZAKI!
STOP IT, TAKEZAKI!!!
WHY ARE YOU DOING THIS?
THIS CAN'T BE HAPPENING ...WHY...
STOP IT!!!
KAGETORA, YOU--
...RIGHT...
WHY ISN'T HE FIGHTING BACK?!
WHY?!!
IT'S ALL RIGHT...
...HIME-SAMA.

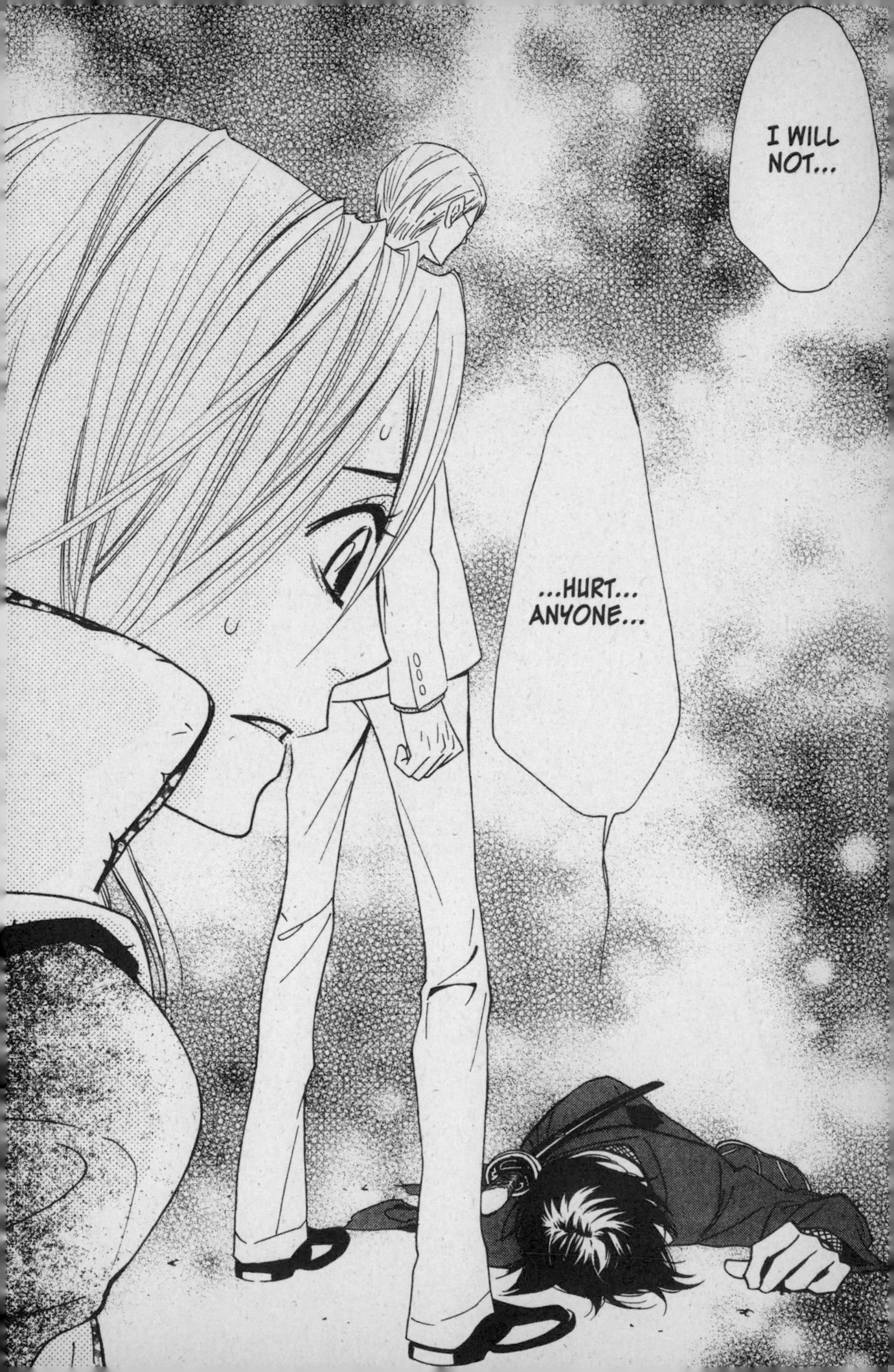
I WILL NOT...
...HURT... ANYONE...

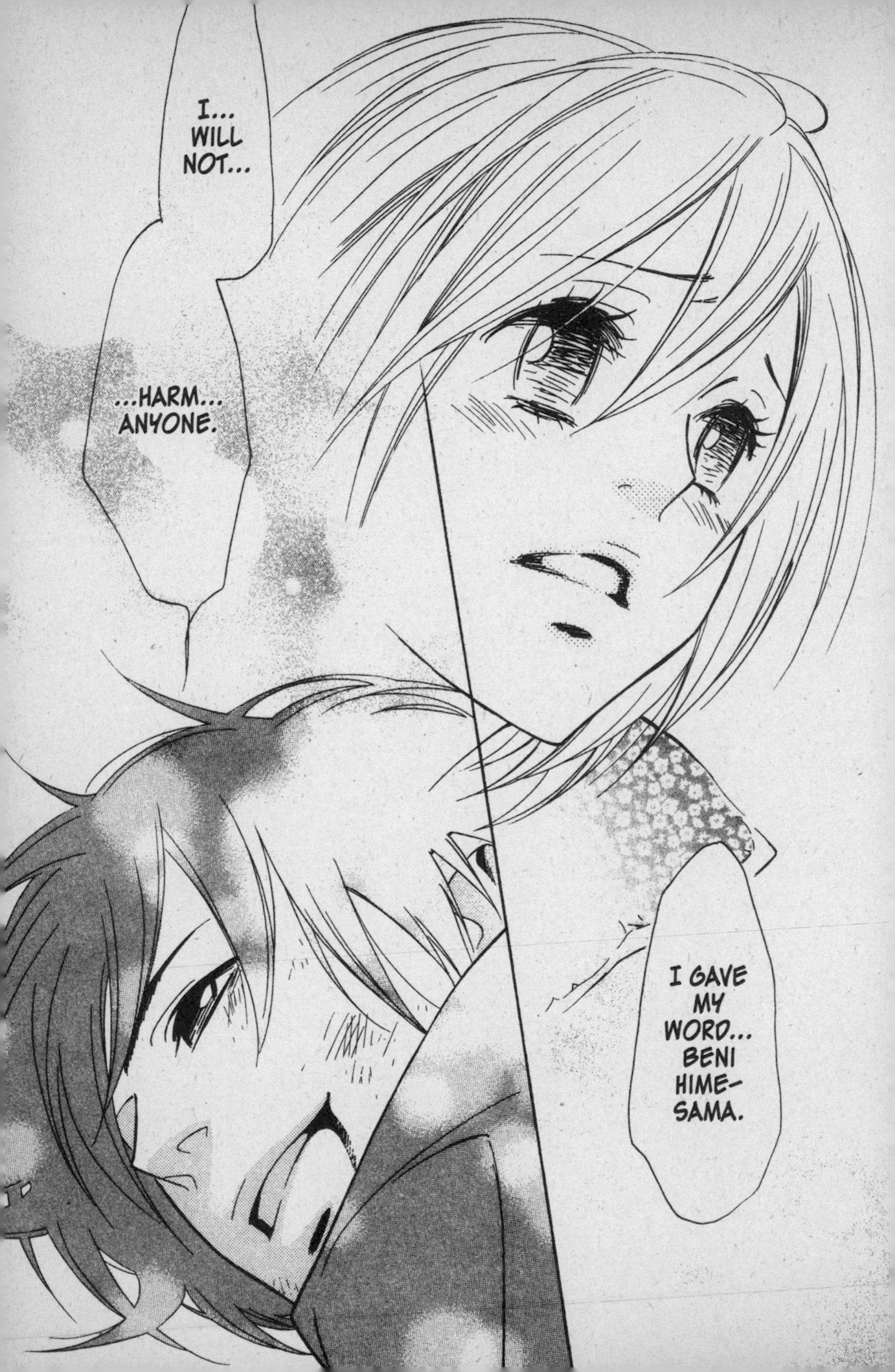
I GAVE MY WORD... BENI HIME-SAMA.
I... WILL NOT...
...HARM... ANYONE.

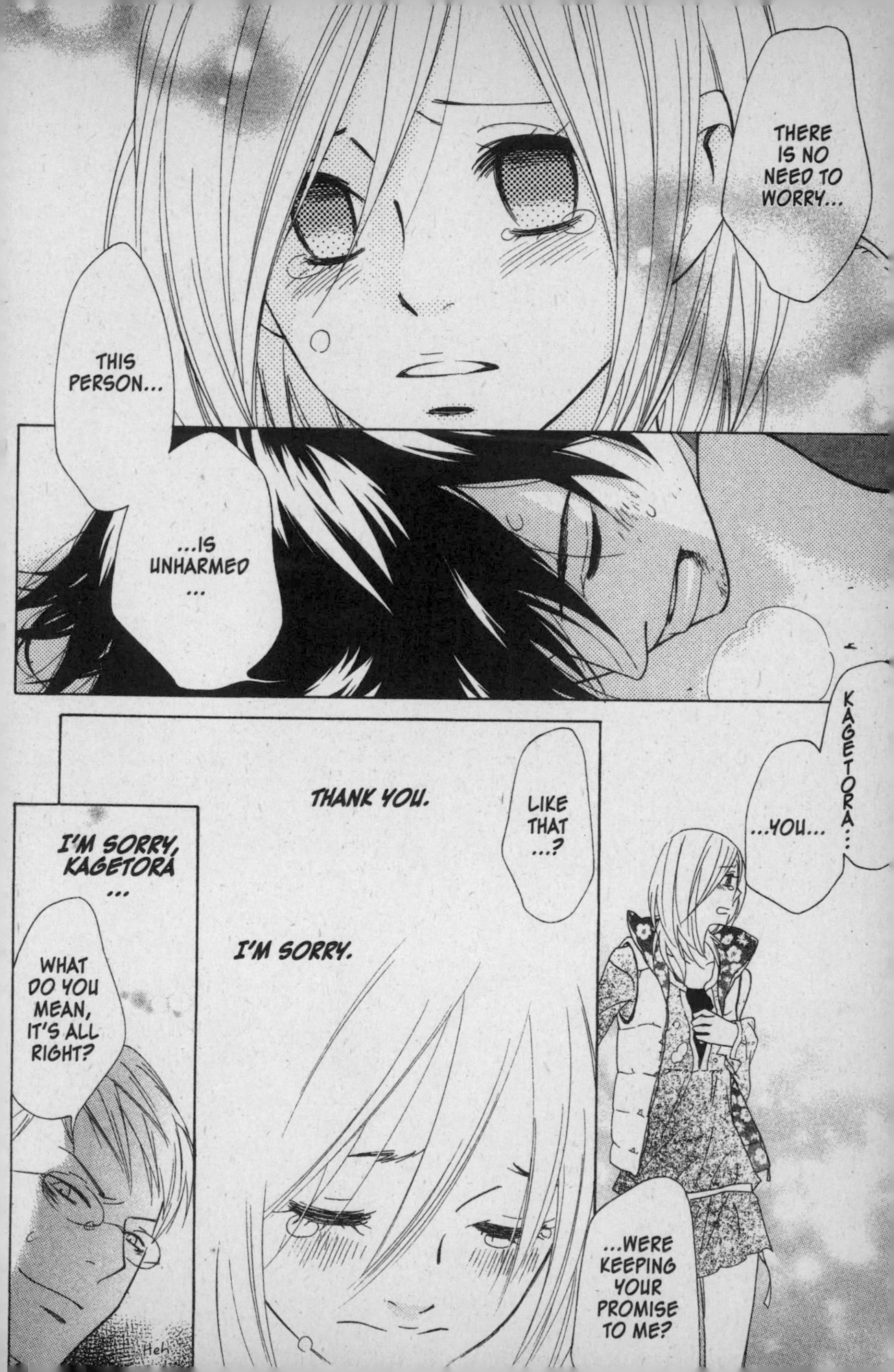
THERE IS NO NEED TO WORRY...
THIS PERSON...
...IS UNHARMED ...
KAGETORA...
...YOU...
...WERE KEEPING YOUR PROMISE TO ME?
LIKE THAT ...?
THANK YOU.
I'M SORRY.
I'M SORRY, KAGETORA ...
WHAT DO YOU MEAN, IT'S ALL RIGHT?
Heh

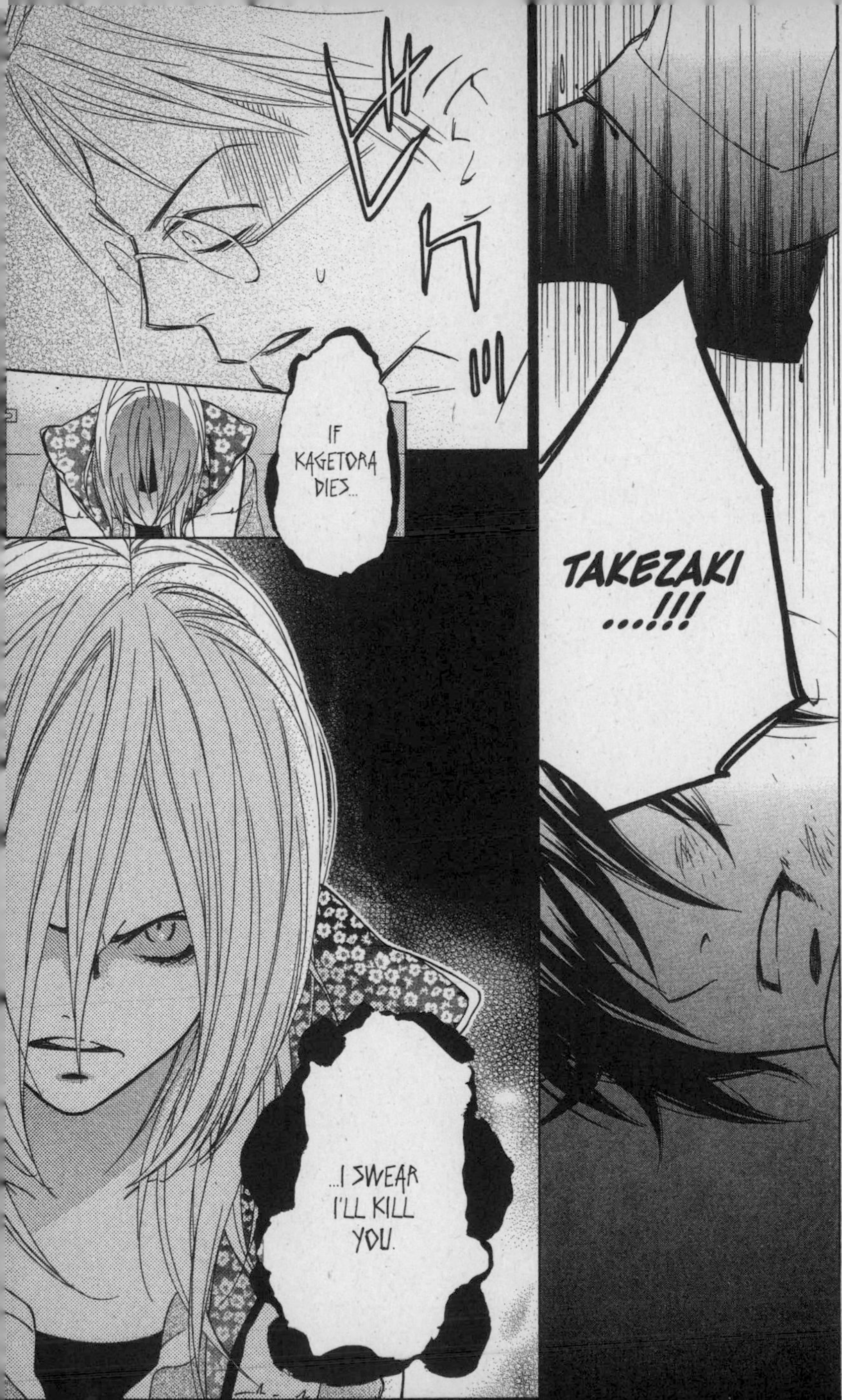
TAKEZAKI ...!!!
IF KAGETORA DIES...
...I SWEAR I'LL KILL YOU.

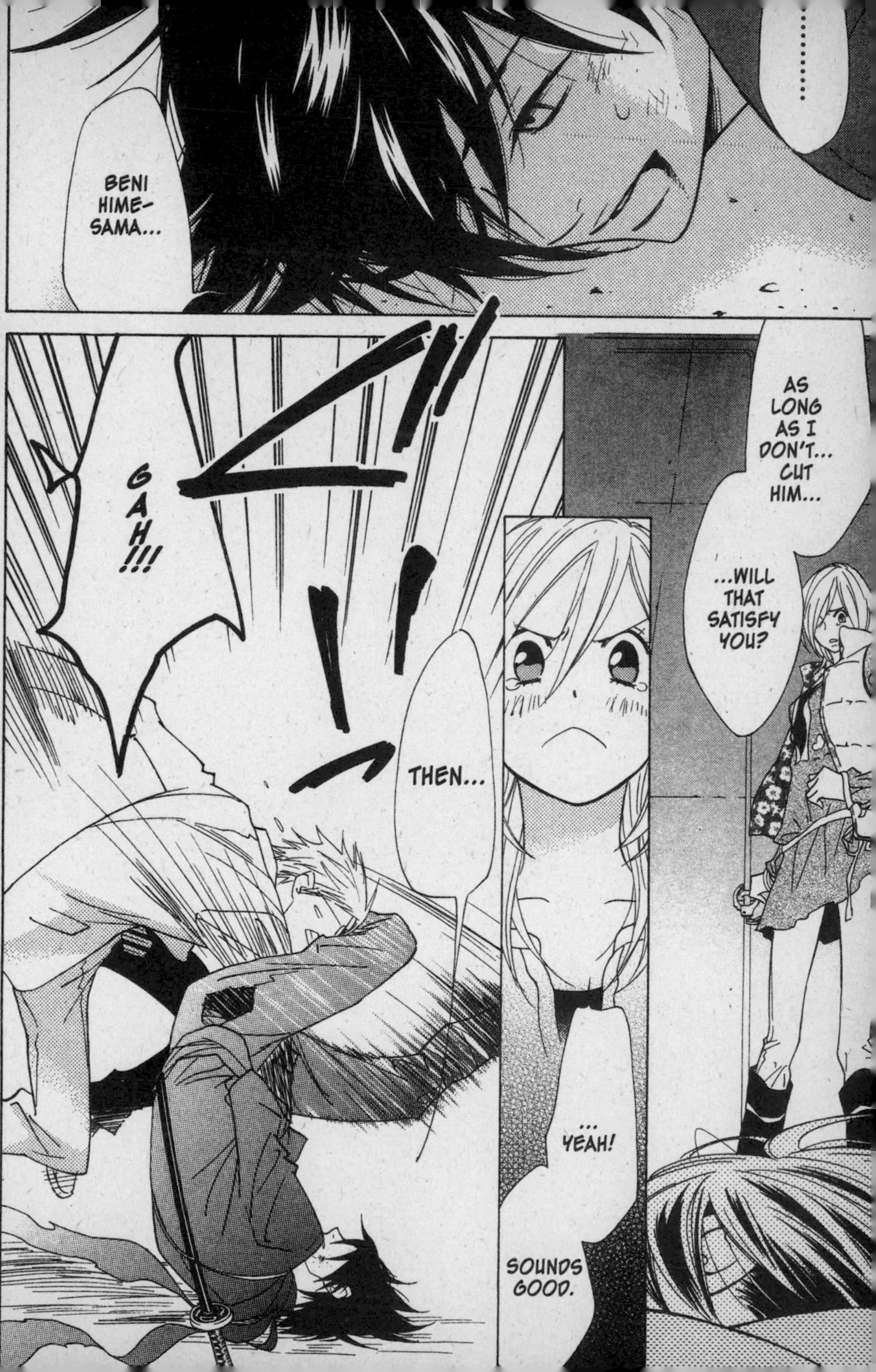
......
BENI HIME-SAMA...
AS LONG AS I DON'T... CUT HIM...
...WILL THAT SATISFY YOU?
THEN...
...YEAH!
SOUNDS GOOD.
GAH!!!

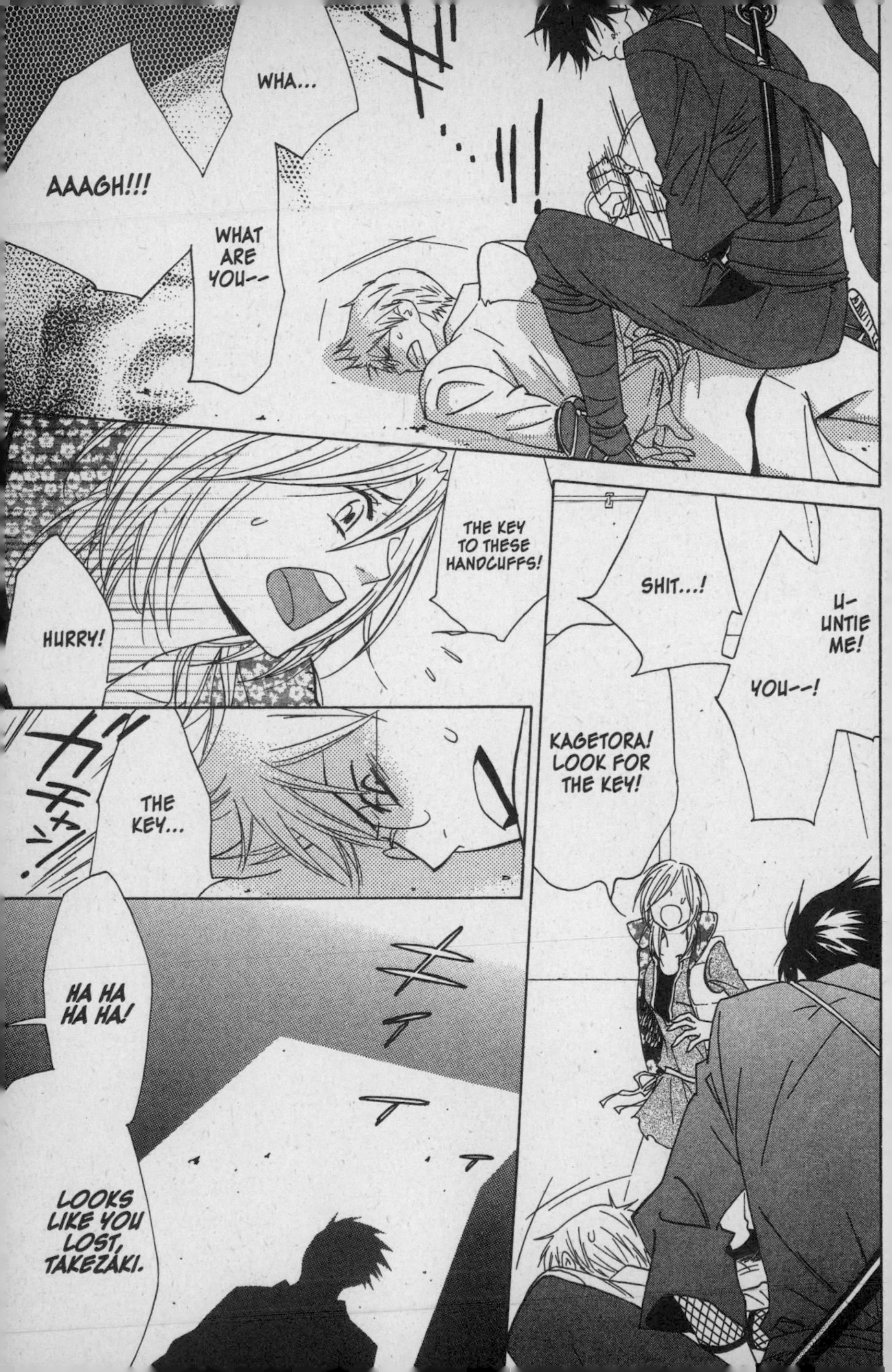
WHA...
AAAGH!!!
WHAT ARE YOU--
U-UNTIE ME!
SHIT...!
YOU--!
KAGETORA! LOOK FOR THE KEY!
THE KEY TO THESE HANDCUFFS!
HURRY!
THE KEY...
HA HA HA HA!
LOOKS LIKE YOU LOST, TAKEZAKI.

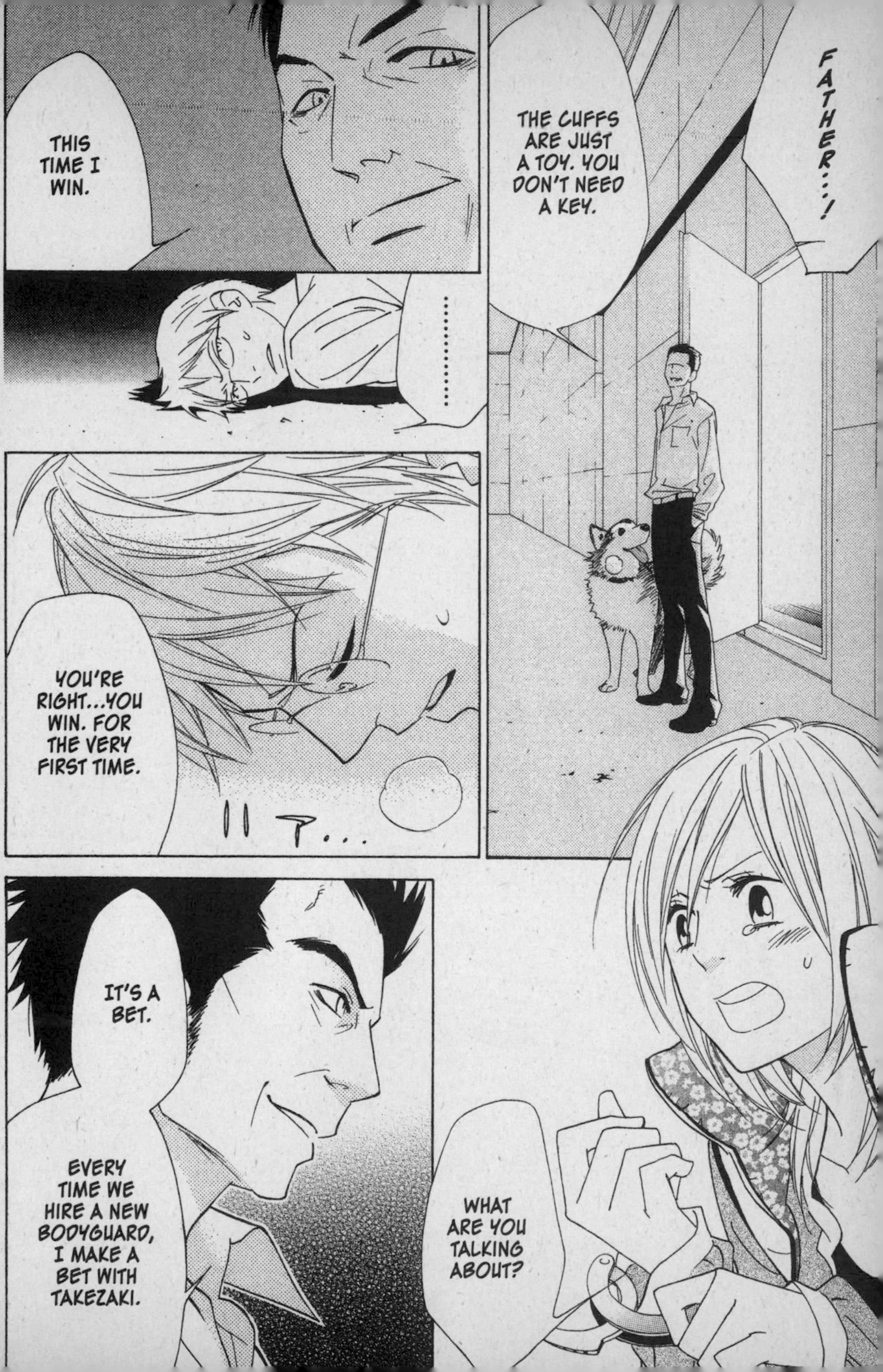
FATHER...!
THE CUFFS ARE JUST A TOY. YOU DON'T NEED A KEY.
THIS TIME I WIN.
......
YOU'RE RIGHT...YOU WIN. FOR THE VERY FIRST TIME.
WHAT ARE YOU TALKING ABOUT?
IT'S A BET.
EVERY TIME WE HIRE A NEW BODYGUARD, I MAKE A BET WITH TAKEZAKI.

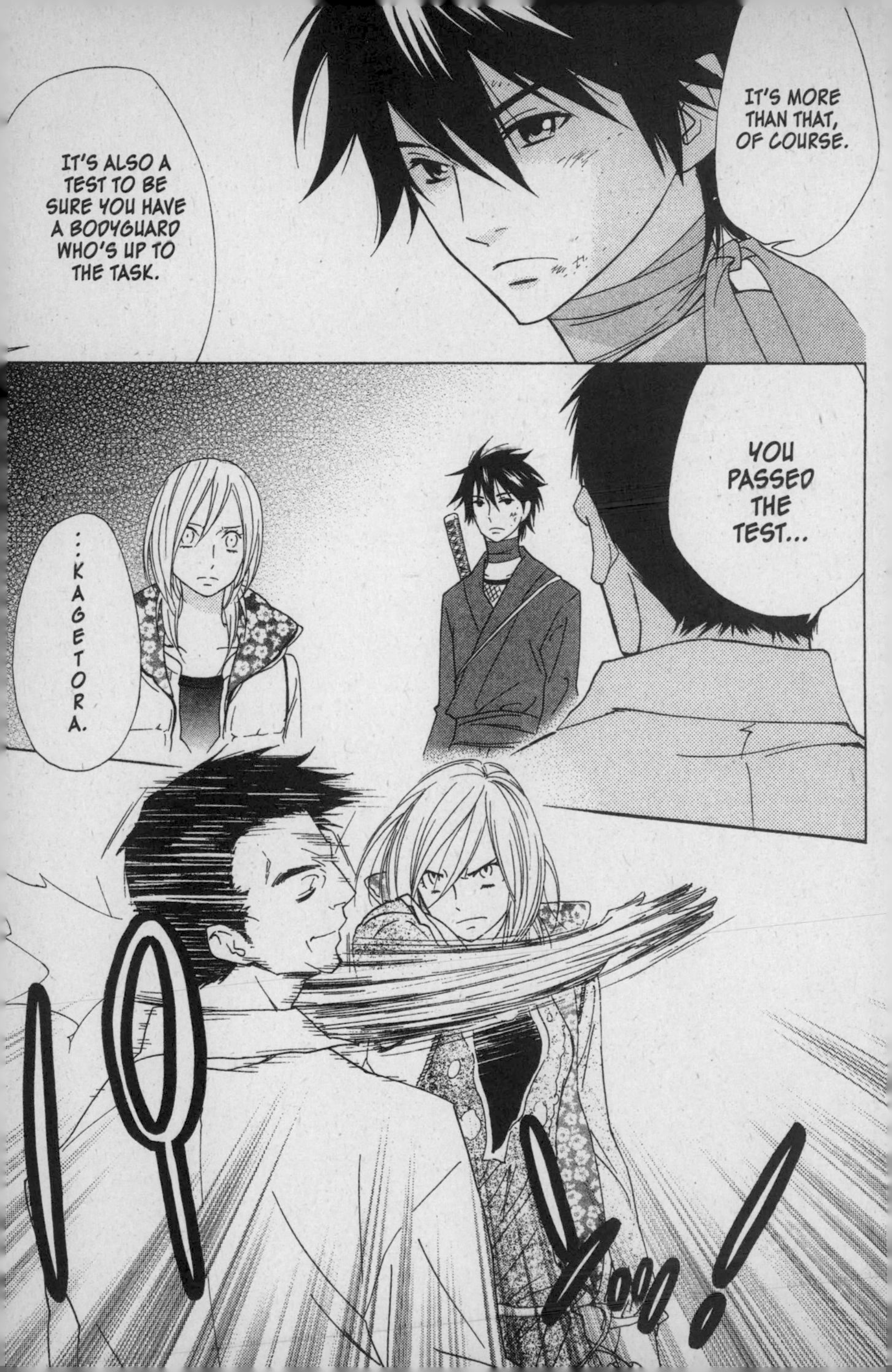
IT'S MORE THAN THAT, OF COURSE.
IT'S ALSO A TEST TO BE SURE YOU HAVE A BODYGUARD WHO'S UP TO THE TASK.
YOU PASSED THE TEST...
...KAGETORA.

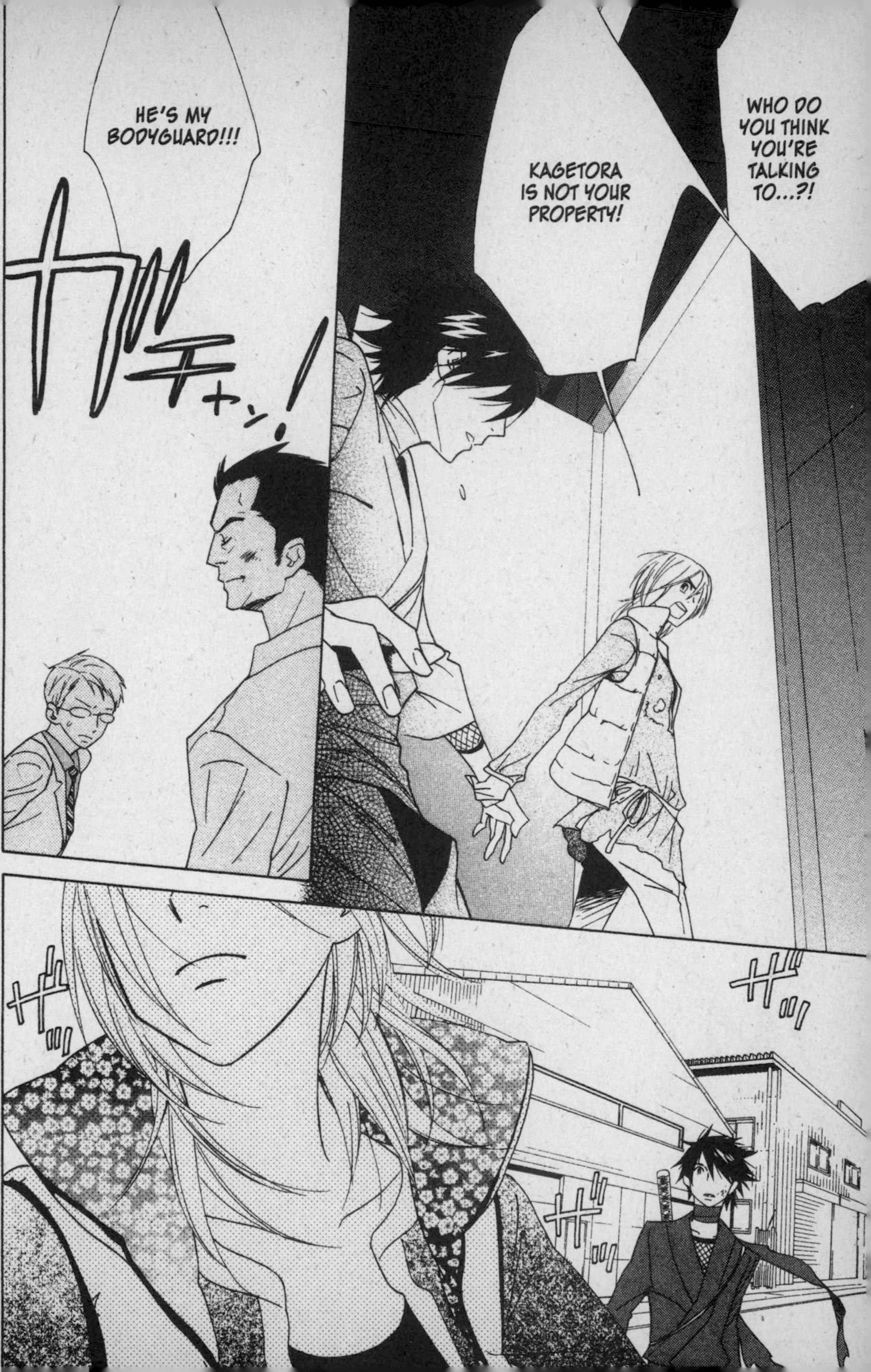
WHO DO YOU THINK YOU'RE TALKING TO...?!
KAGETORA IS NOT YOUR PROPERTY!
HE'S MY BODYGUARD!!!

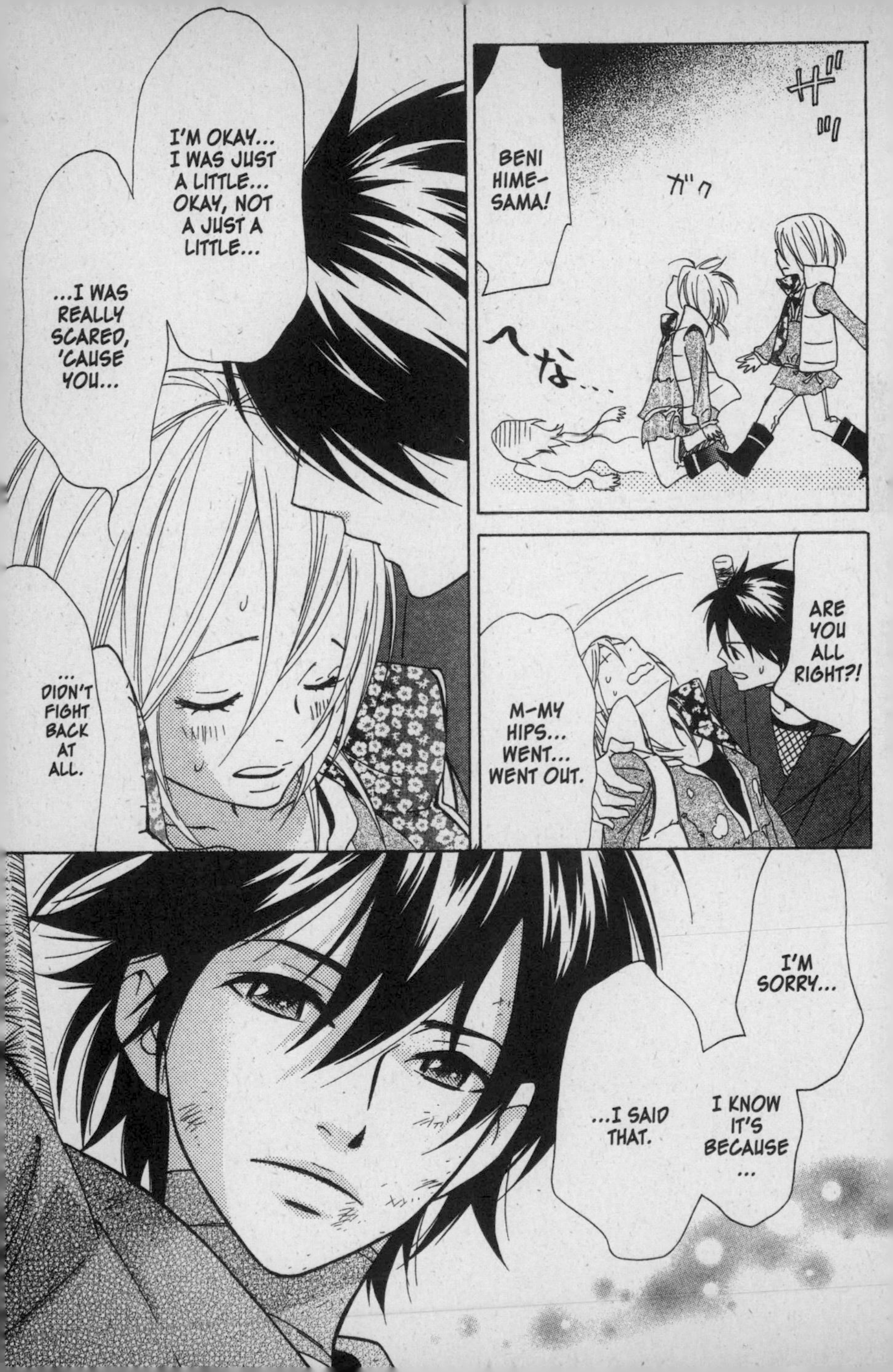

BENI HIME-SAMA!
ガク
へな…
ARE YOU ALL RIGHT?!
M-MY HIPS... WENT... WENT OUT.
I'M OKAY... I WAS JUST A LITTLE... OKAY, NOT A JUST A LITTLE...
...I WAS REALLY SCARED, 'CAUSE YOU...
...DIDN'T FIGHT BACK AT ALL.
I'M SORRY...
I KNOW IT'S BECAUSE ...
...I SAID THAT.

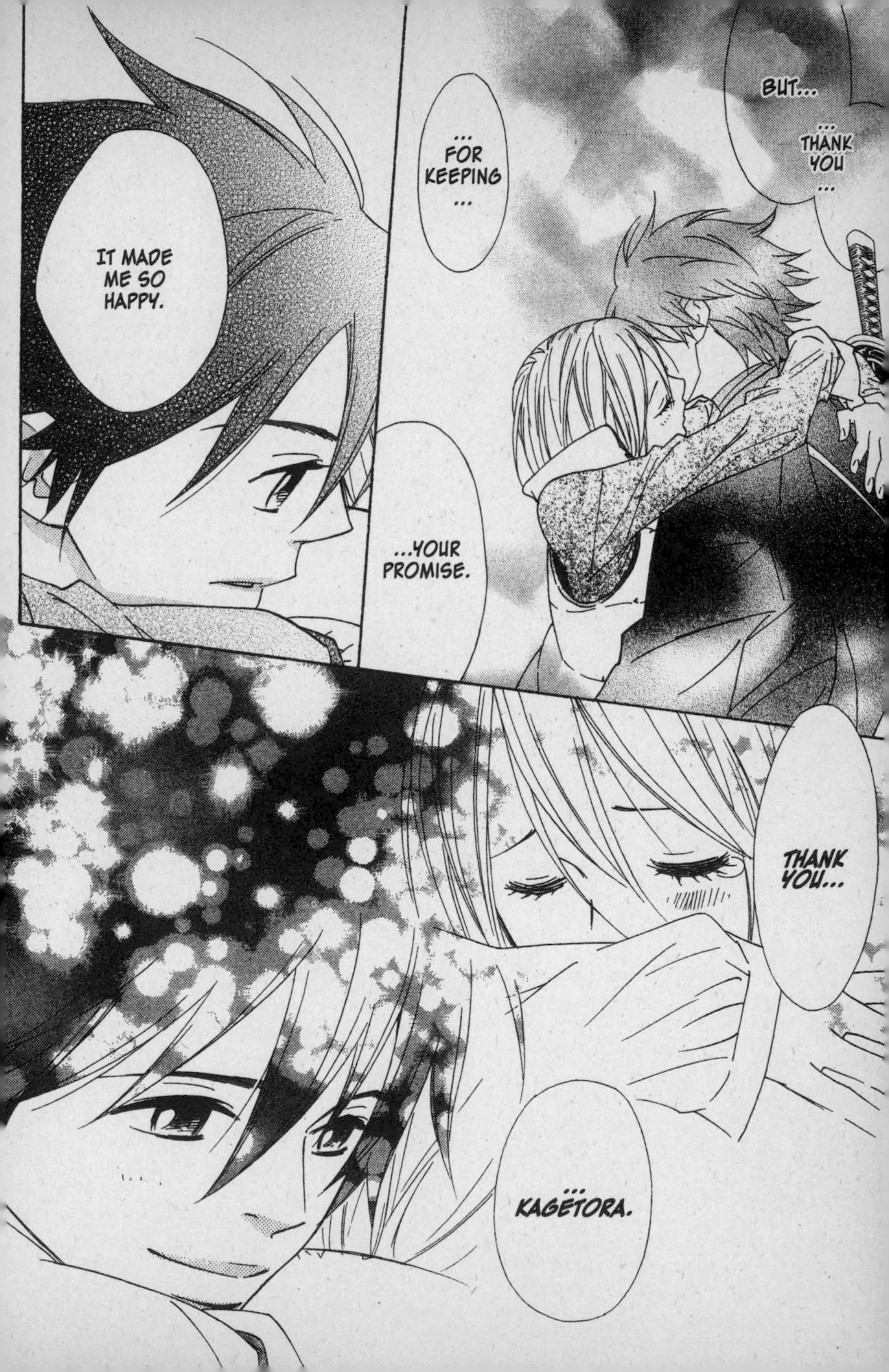
BUT...
...THANK YOU...
...FOR KEEPING...
...YOUR PROMISE.
IT MADE ME SO HAPPY.
THANK YOU...
...KAGETORA.

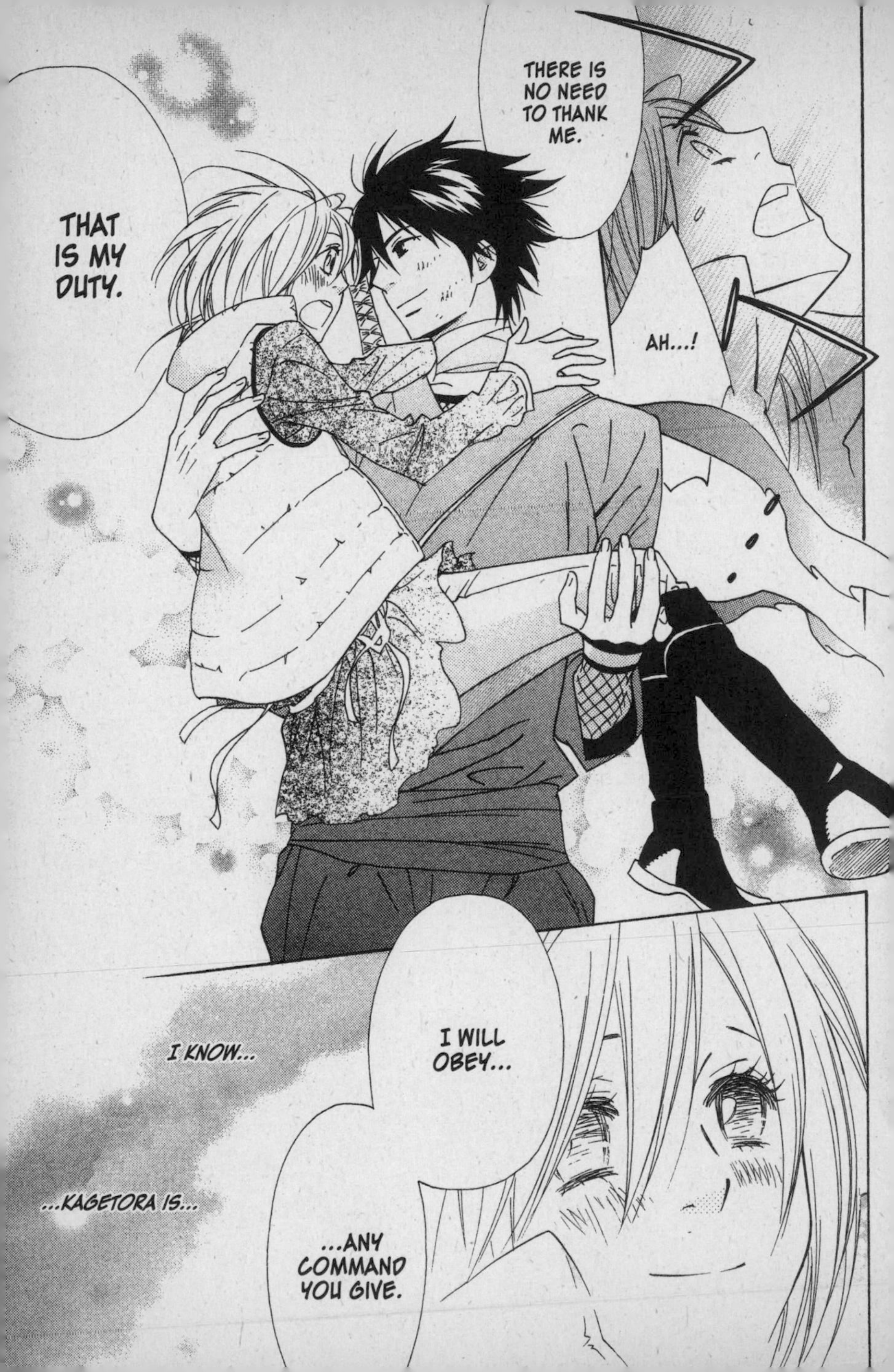

THERE IS NO NEED TO THANK ME.
THAT IS MY DUTY.
AH...!
I WILL OBEY...
...ANY COMMAND YOU GIVE.
I KNOW...
...KAGETORA IS...

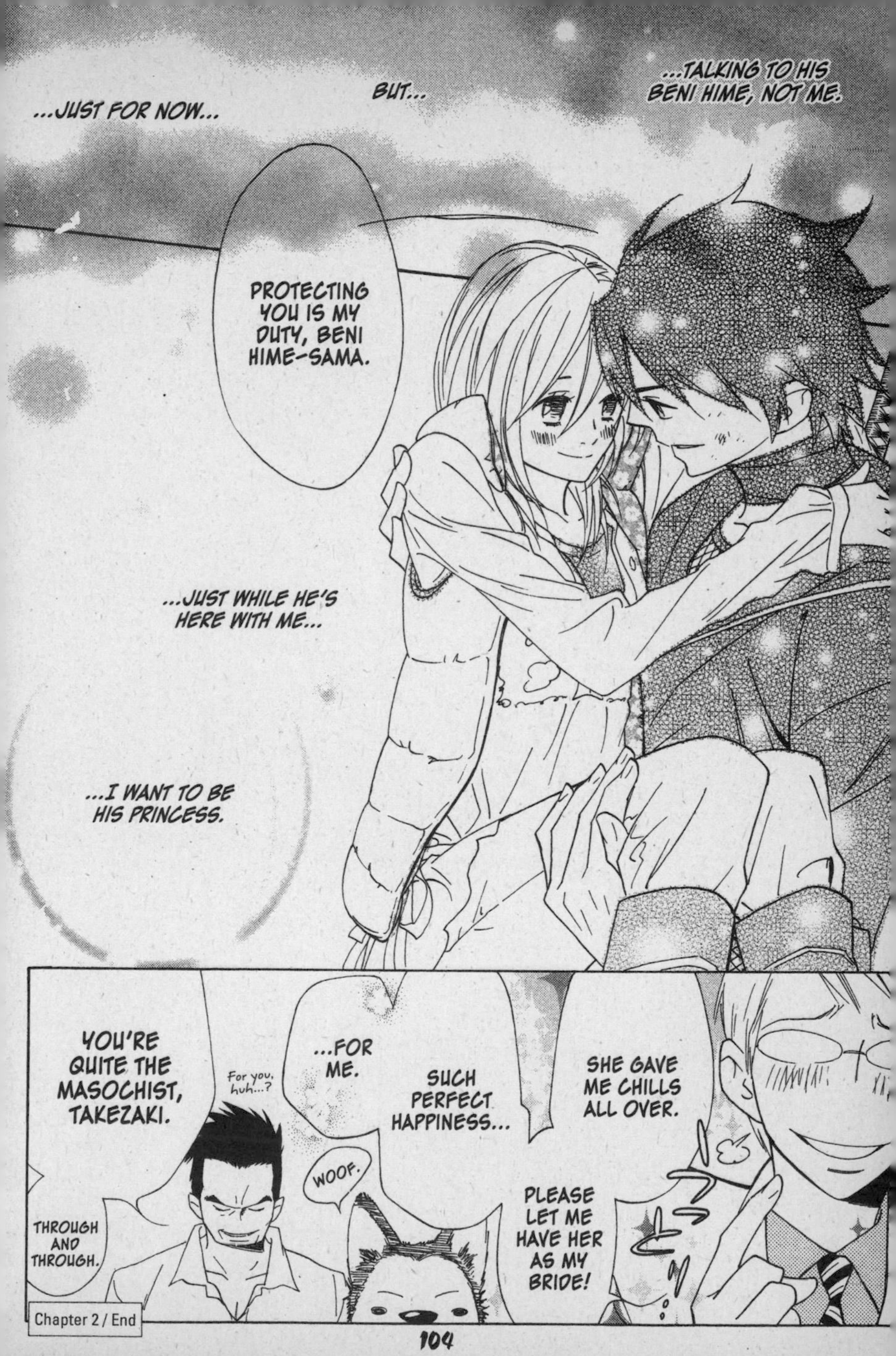
...TALKING TO HIS BENI HIME, NOT ME.
BUT...
...JUST FOR NOW...
PROTECTING YOU IS MY DUTY, BENI HIME-SAMA.
...JUST WHILE HE'S HERE WITH ME...
...I WANT TO BE HIS PRINCESS.
SHE GAVE ME CHILLS ALL OVER.
PLEASE LET ME HAVE HER AS MY BRIDE!
SUCH PERFECT HAPPINESS...
...FOR ME.
WOOF.
For you, huh...?
YOU'RE QUITE THE MASOCHIST, TAKEZAKI.
THROUGH AND THROUGH.
Chapter 2 / End

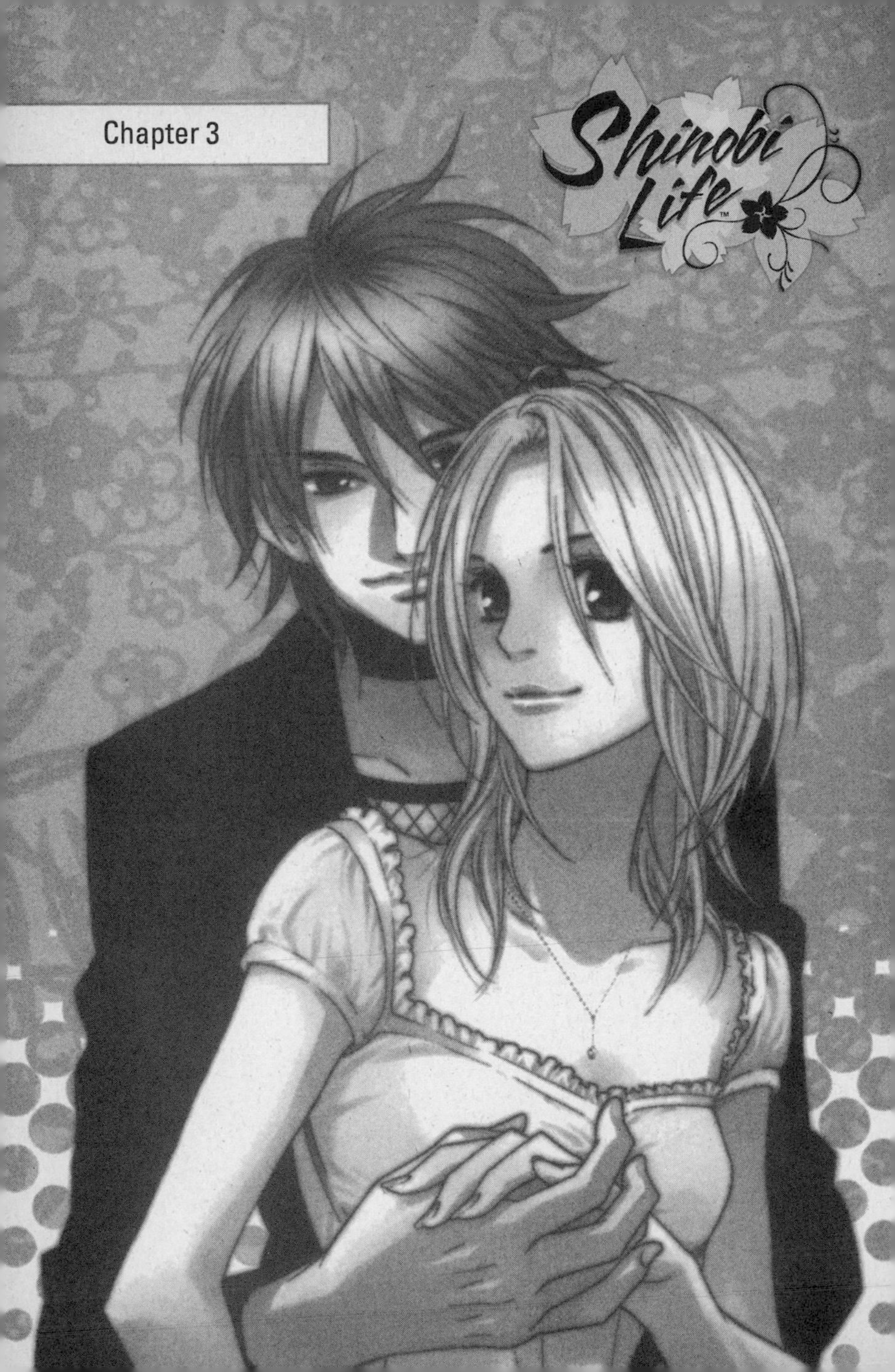
Chapter 3
Shinobi Life™

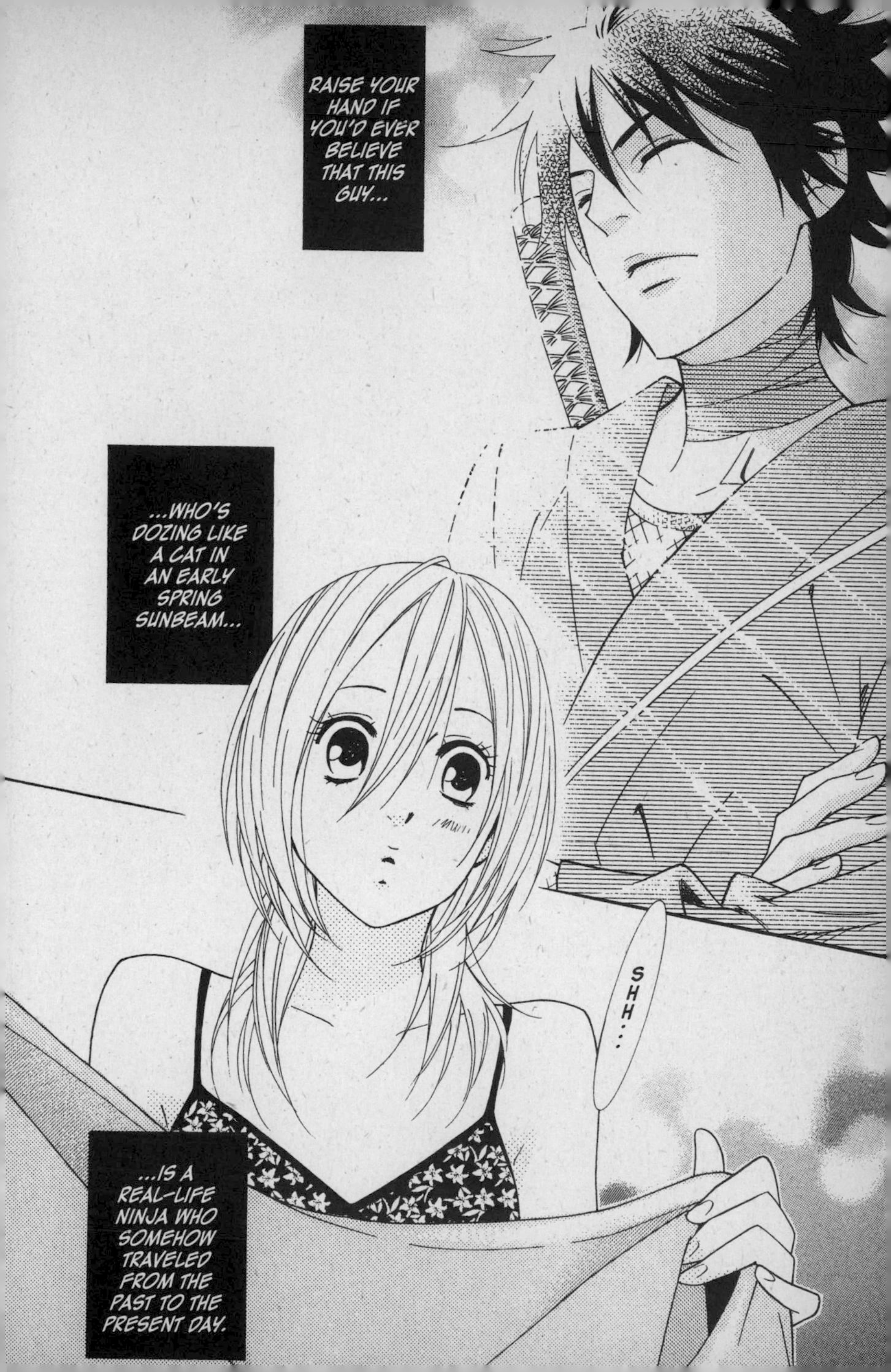
RAISE YOUR HAND IF YOU'D EVER BELIEVE THAT THIS GUY...
...WHO'S DOZING LIKE A CAT IN AN EARLY SPRING SUNBEAM...
SHH...
...IS A REAL-LIFE NINJA WHO SOMEHOW TRAVELED FROM THE PAST TO THE PRESENT DAY.

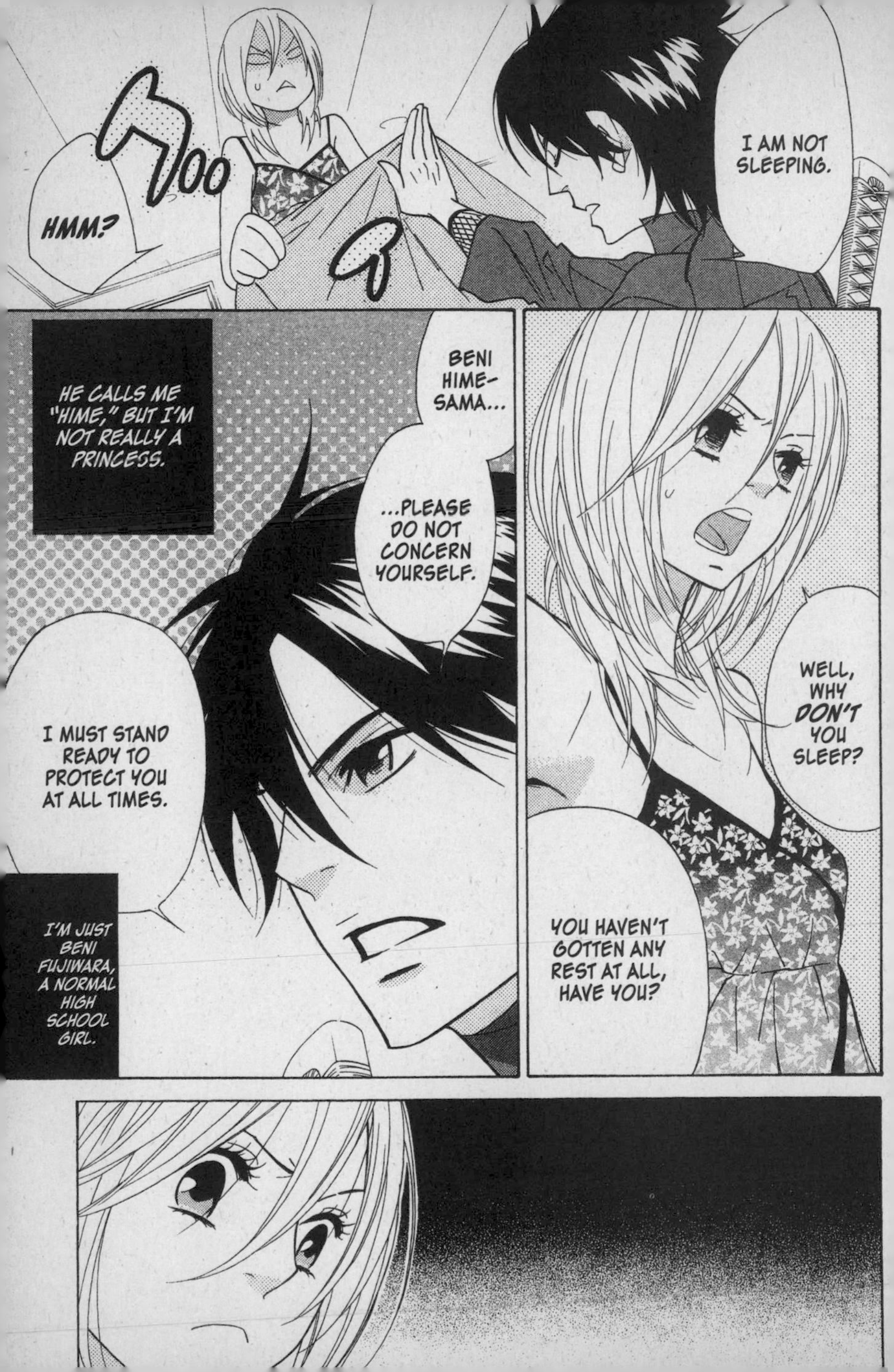
I AM NOT SLEEPING.
MOO
HMM?
WELL, WHY DON'T YOU SLEEP?
YOU HAVEN'T GOTTEN ANY REST AT ALL, HAVE YOU?
BENI HIME-SAMA...
...PLEASE DO NOT CONCERN YOURSELF.
HE CALLS ME "HIME," BUT I'M NOT REALLY A PRINCESS.
I MUST STAND READY TO PROTECT YOU AT ALL TIMES.
I'M JUST BENI FUJIWARA, A NORMAL HIGH SCHOOL GIRL.

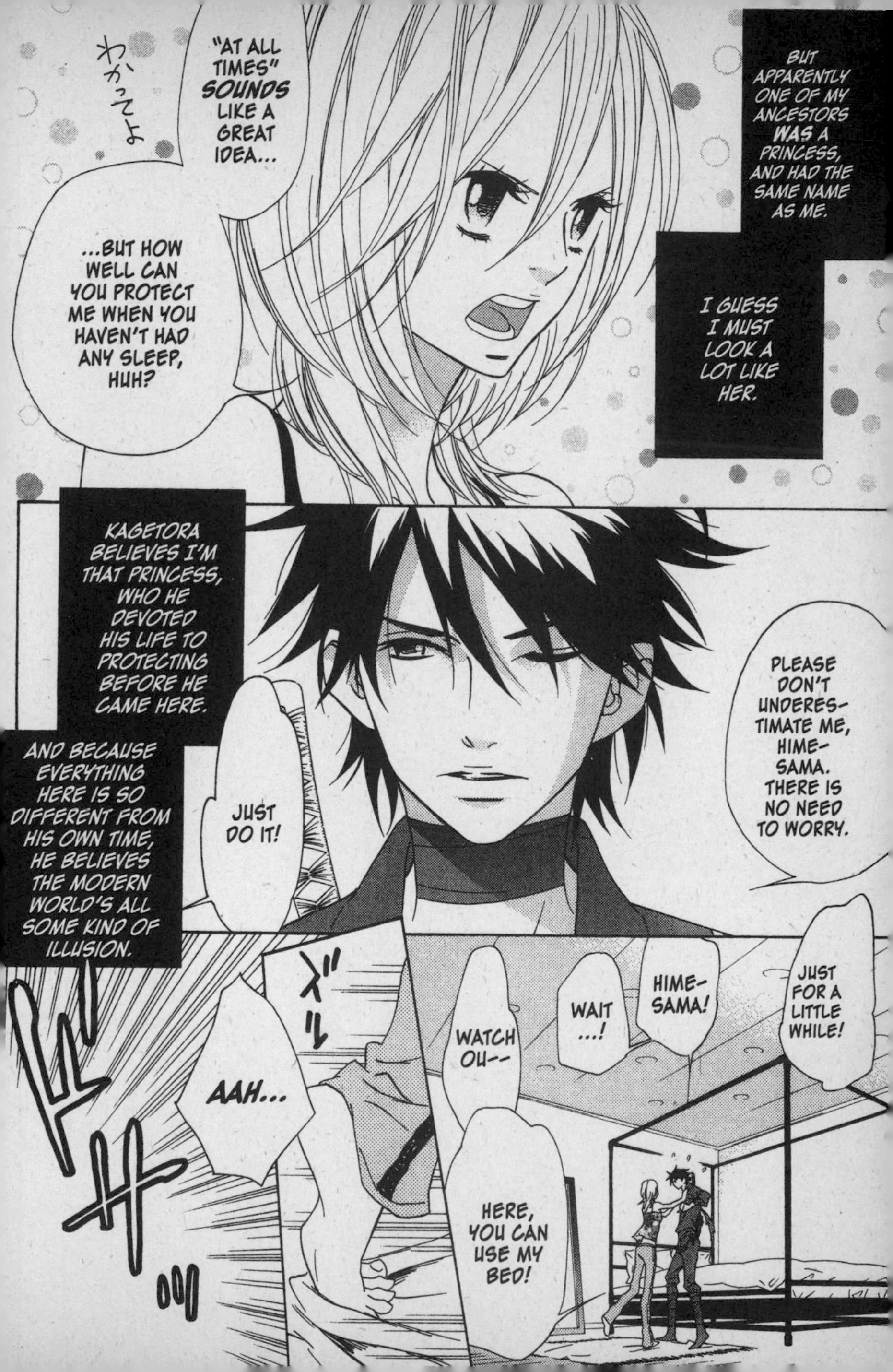
BUT APPARENTLY ONE OF MY ANCESTORS WAS A PRINCESS, AND HAD THE SAME NAME AS ME.
I GUESS I MUST LOOK A LOT LIKE HER.
"AT ALL TIMES" SOUNDS LIKE A GREAT IDEA...
わかってよ
...BUT HOW WELL CAN YOU PROTECT ME WHEN YOU HAVEN'T HAD ANY SLEEP, HUH?
KAGETORA BELIEVES I'M THAT PRINCESS, WHO HE DEVOTED HIS LIFE TO PROTECTING BEFORE HE CAME HERE.
PLEASE DON'T UNDERESTIMATE ME, HIME-SAMA. THERE IS NO NEED TO WORRY.
JUST DO IT!
AND BECAUSE EVERYTHING HERE IS SO DIFFERENT FROM HIS OWN TIME, HE BELIEVES THE MODERN WORLD'S ALL SOME KIND OF ILLUSION.
JUST FOR A LITTLE WHILE!
HIME-SAMA!
WAIT ...!
WATCH OU--
HERE, YOU CAN USE MY BED!
ズル
AAH...

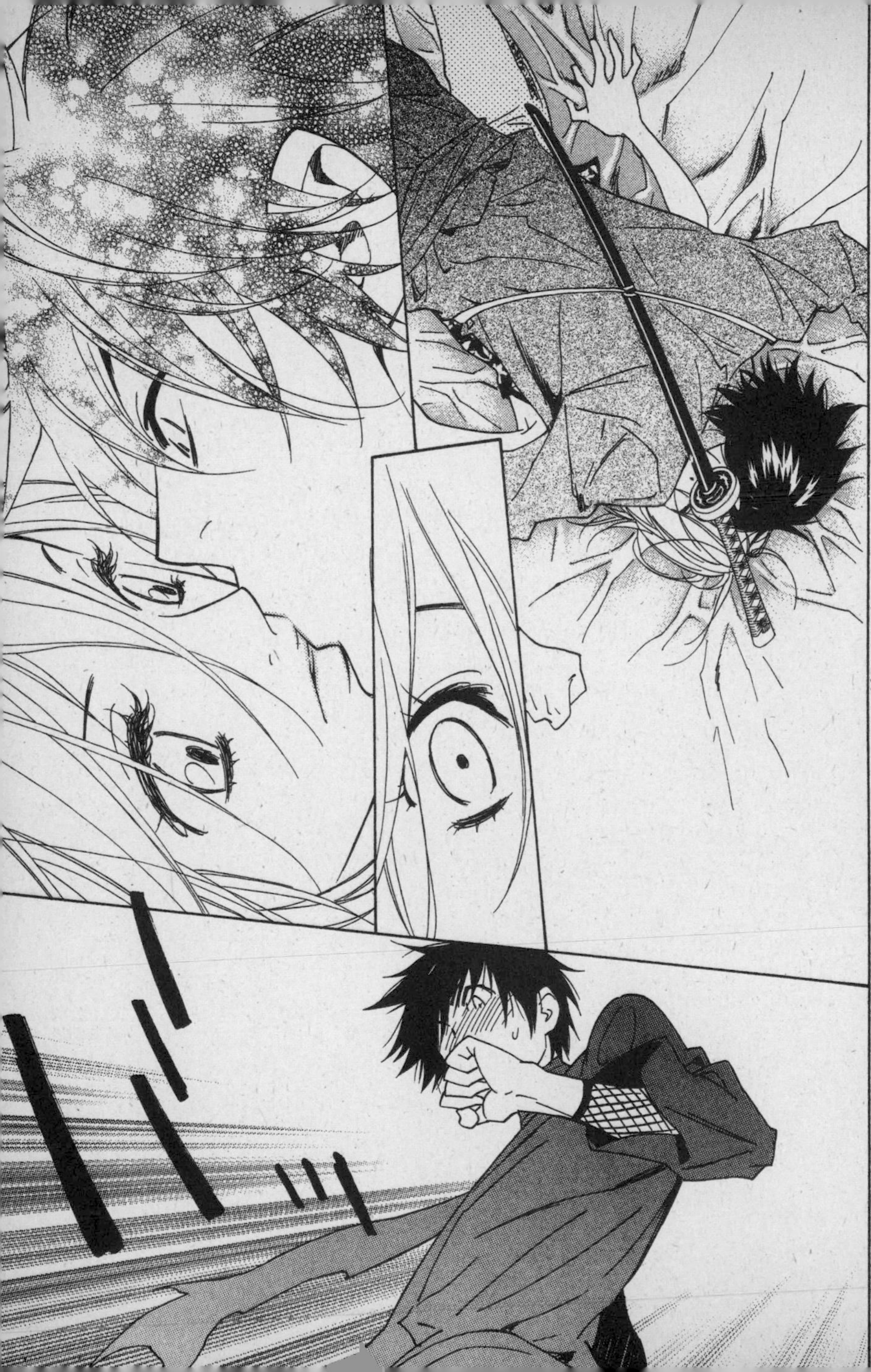

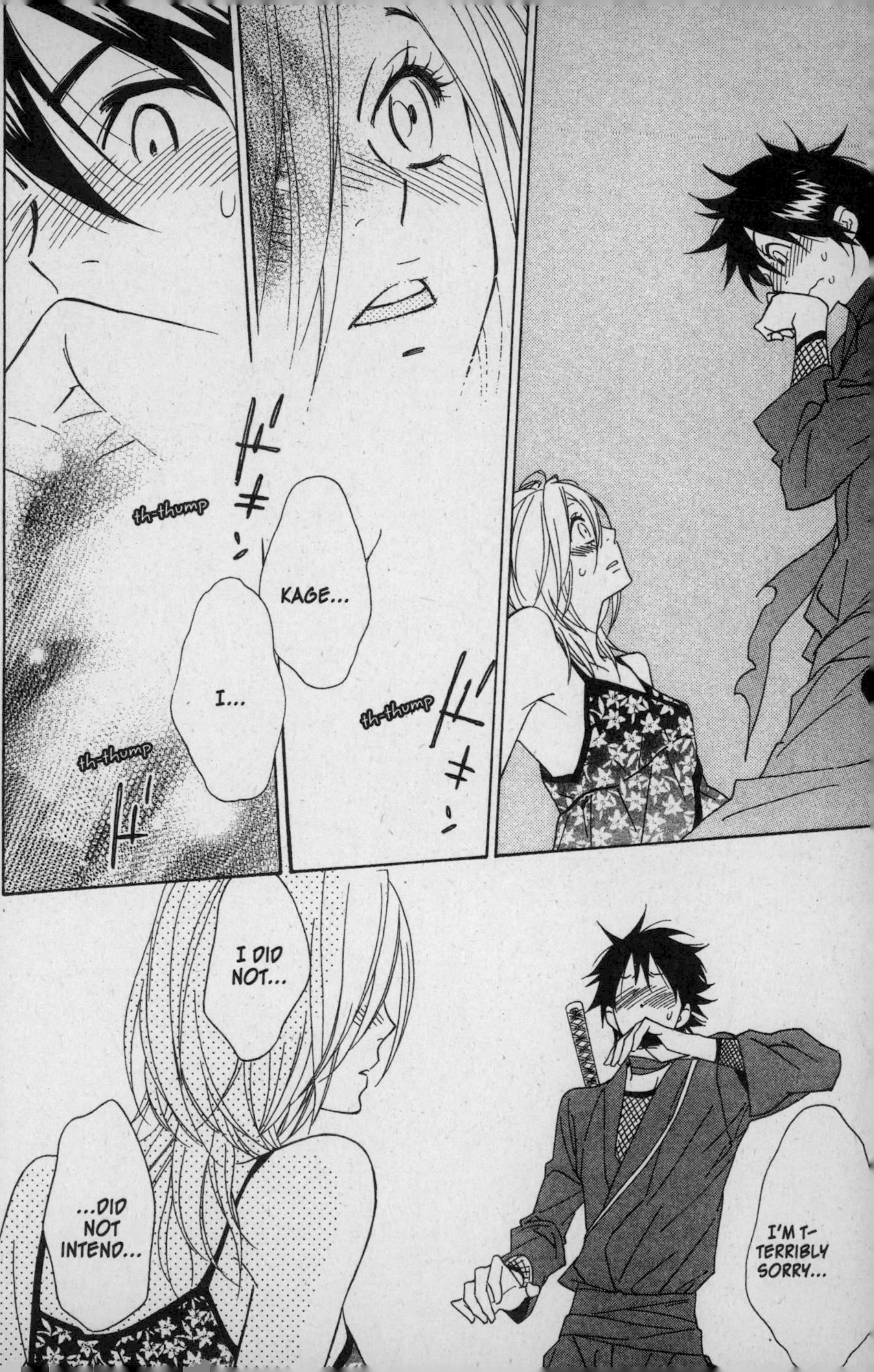
th-thump
KAGE...
I...
th-thump
th-thump
I'M T-TERRIBLY SORRY...
I DID NOT...
...DID NOT INTEND...

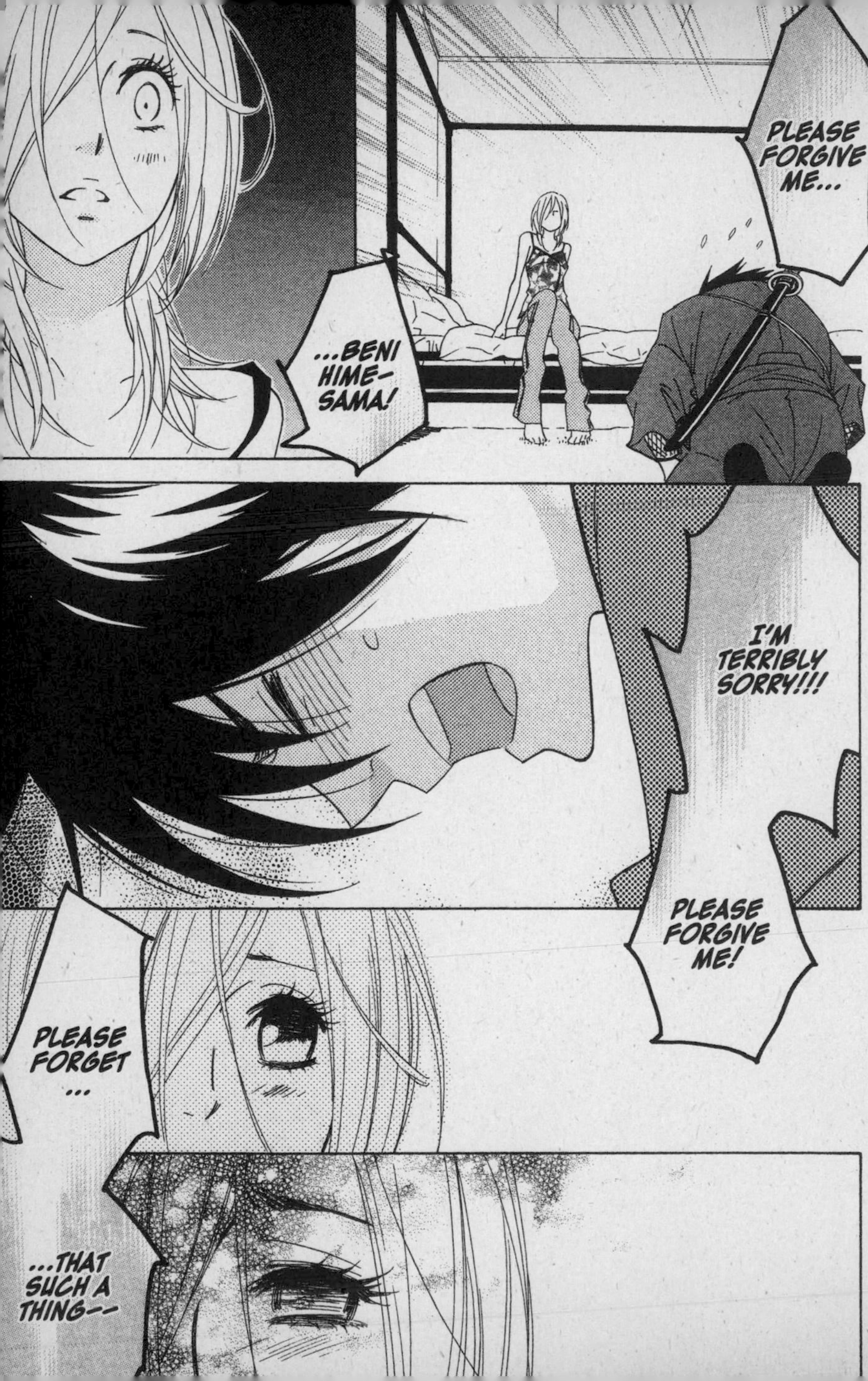
PLEASE FORGIVE ME...
...BENI HIME-SAMA!
I'M TERRIBLY SORRY!!!
PLEASE FORGIVE ME!
PLEASE FORGET ...
...THAT SUCH A THING--

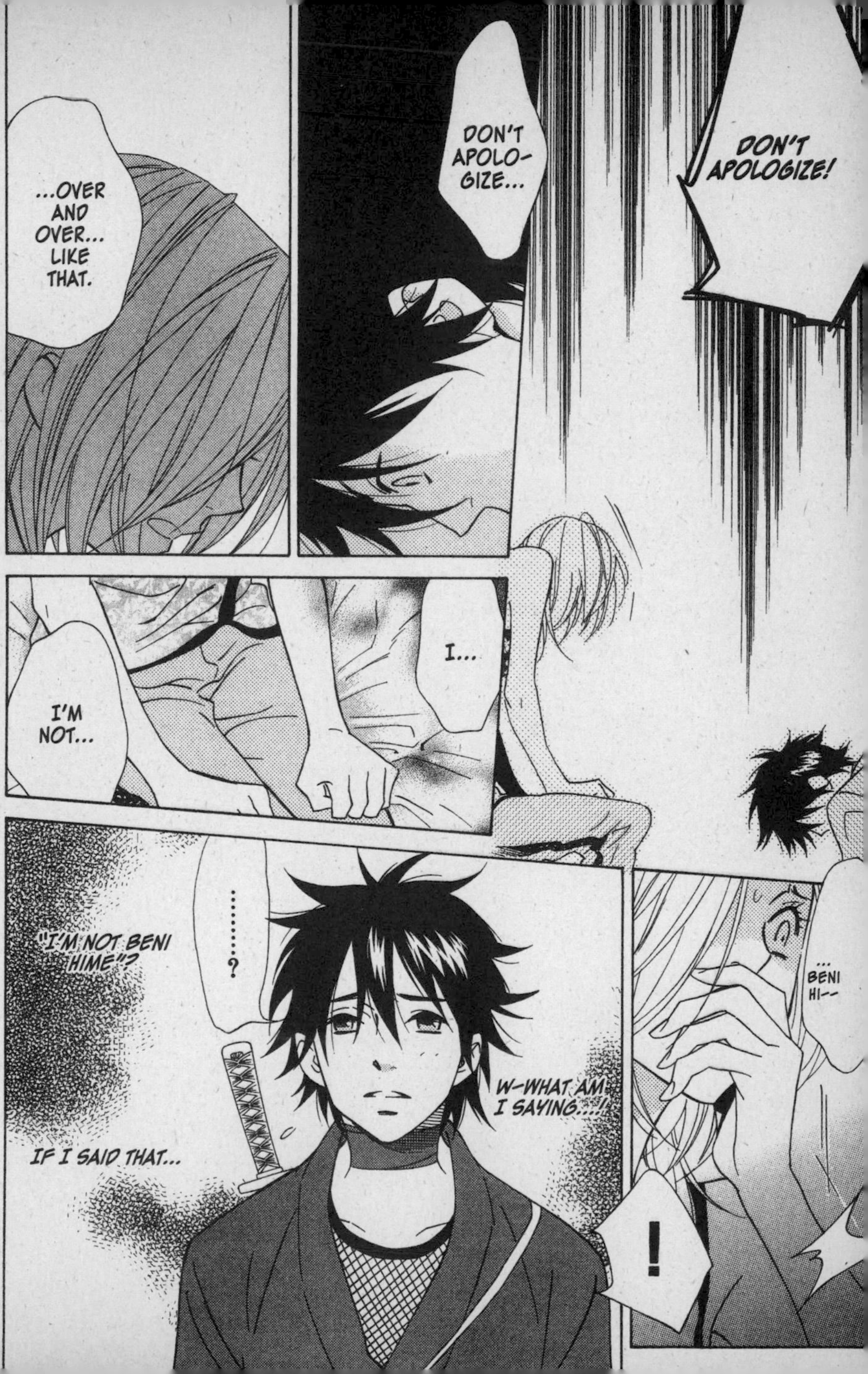
DON'T APOLOGIZE!
DON'T APOLO-GIZE...
...OVER AND OVER... LIKE THAT.
I...
I'M NOT...
...BENI HI--
!
......?
"I'M NOT BENI HIME"?
W-WHAT AM I SAYING...!
IF I SAID THAT...

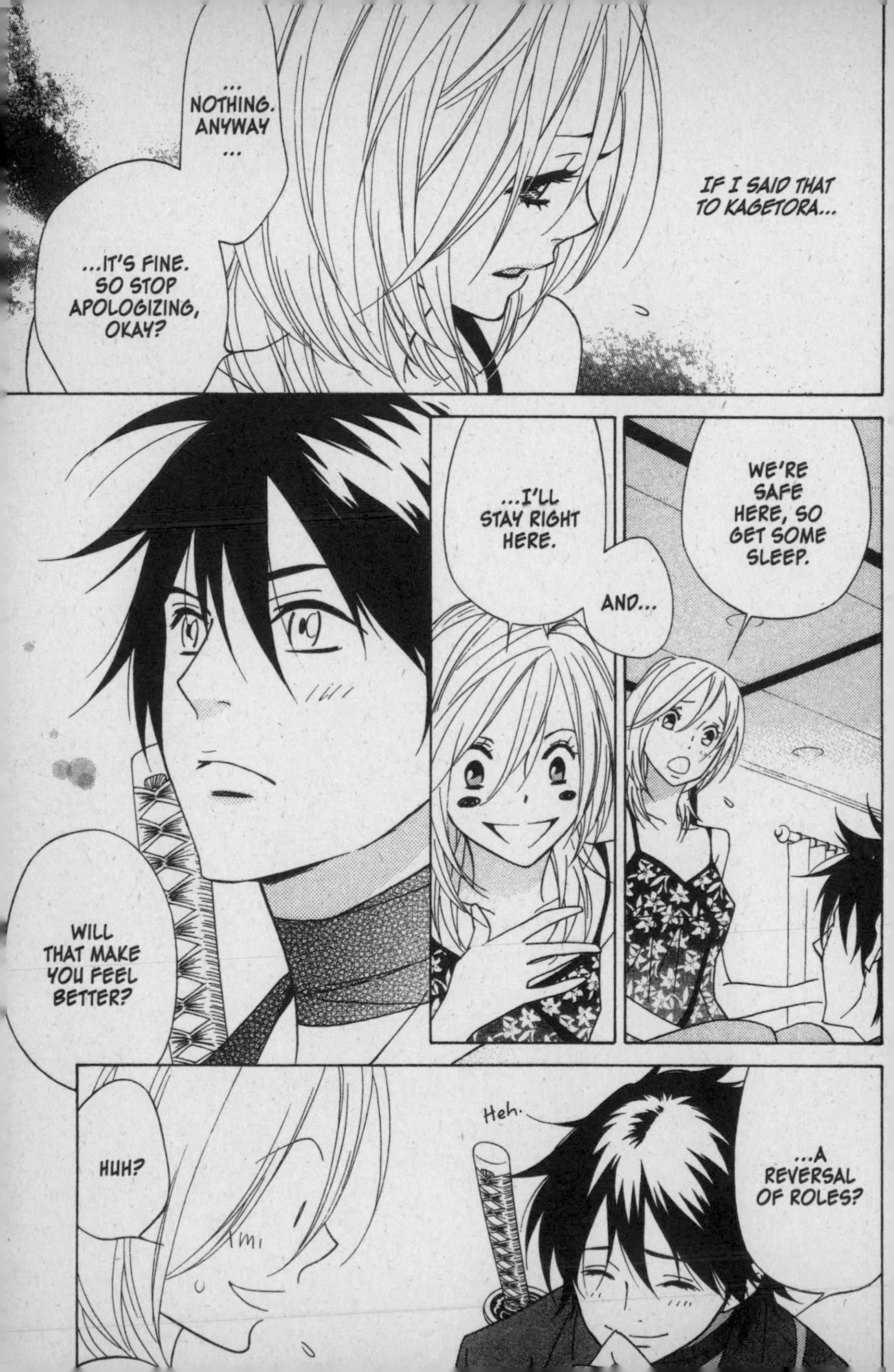
IF I SAID THAT TO KAGETORA...
... NOTHING. ANYWAY ...
...IT'S FINE. SO STOP APOLOGIZING, OKAY?
WE'RE SAFE HERE, SO GET SOME SLEEP.
AND...
...I'LL STAY RIGHT HERE.
WILL THAT MAKE YOU FEEL BETTER?
Heh.
...A REVERSAL OF ROLES?
HUH?

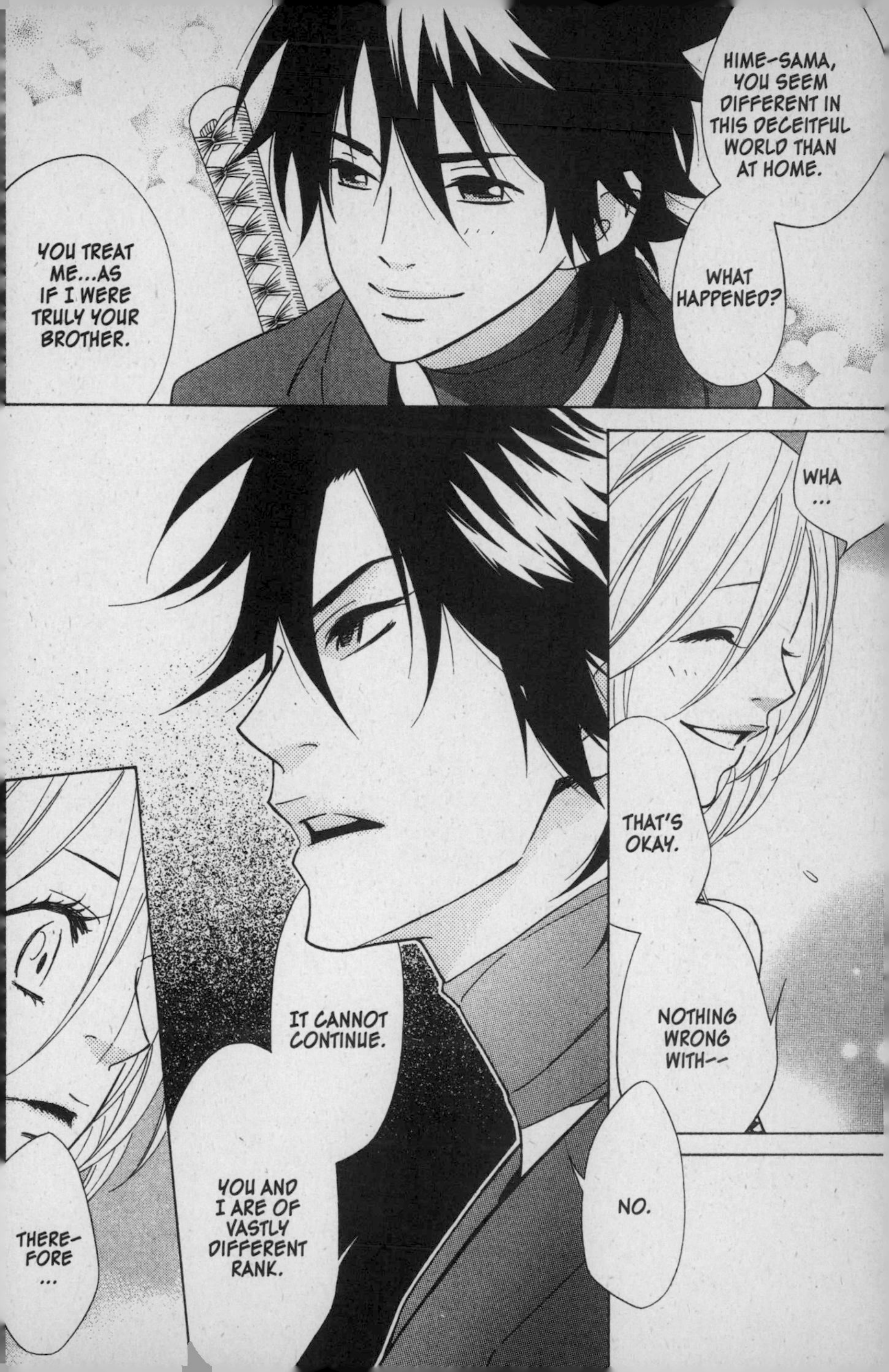
HIME-SAMA, YOU SEEM DIFFERENT IN THIS DECEITFUL WORLD THAN AT HOME.
WHAT HAPPENED?
YOU TREAT ME...AS IF I WERE TRULY YOUR BROTHER.
WHA...
THAT'S OKAY.
NOTHING WRONG WITH--
NO.
IT CANNOT CONTINUE.
YOU AND I ARE OF VASTLY DIFFERENT RANK.
THERE-FORE...

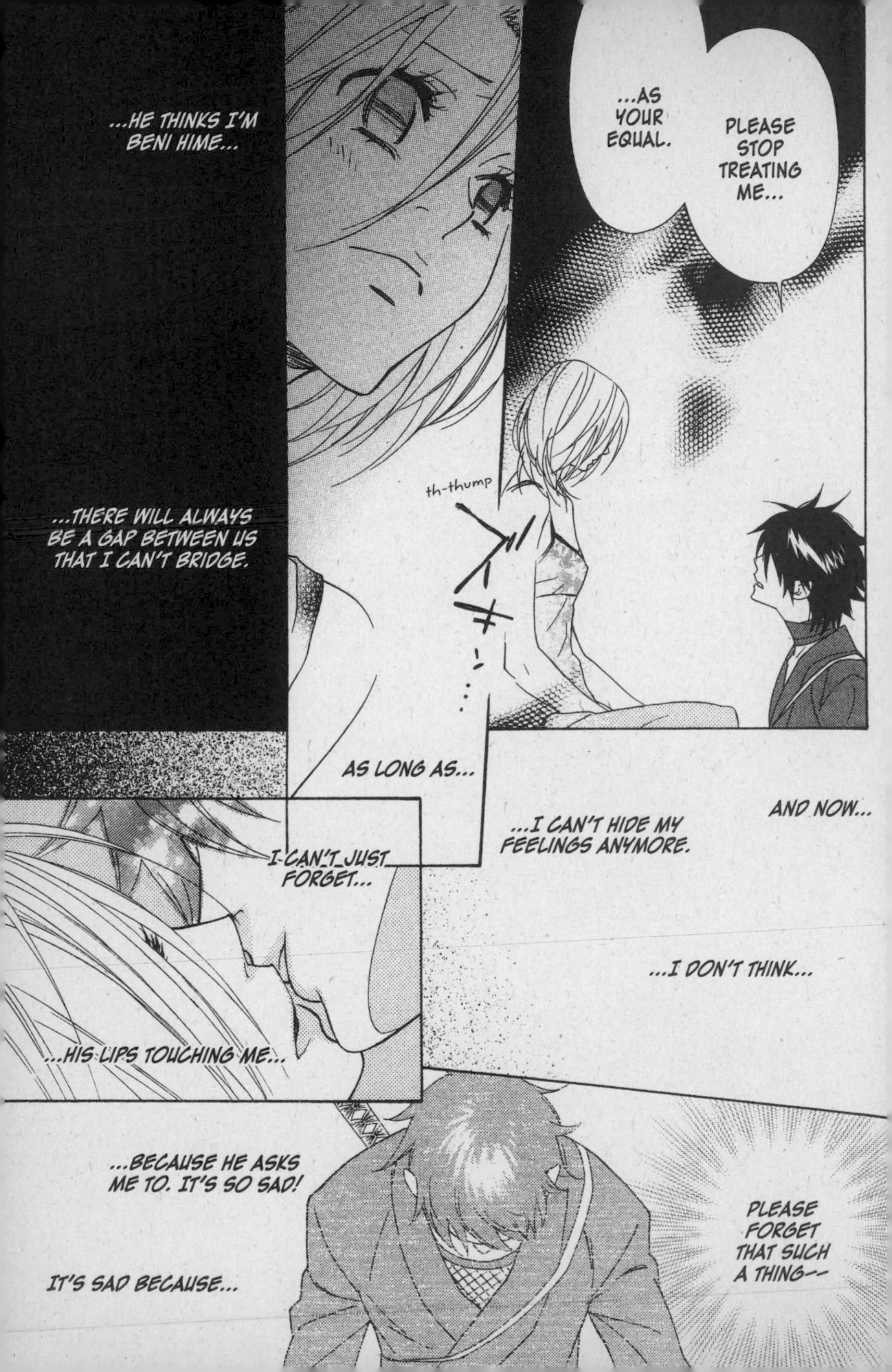
PLEASE STOP TREATING ME...
...AS YOUR EQUAL.
th-thump
...HE THINKS I'M BENI HIME...
...THERE WILL ALWAYS BE A GAP BETWEEN US THAT I CAN'T BRIDGE.
AND NOW...
...I CAN'T HIDE MY FEELINGS ANYMORE.
AS LONG AS...
I CAN'T JUST FORGET...
...HIS LIPS TOUCHING ME...
...I DON'T THINK...
PLEASE FORGET THAT SUCH A THING--
...BECAUSE HE ASKS ME TO. IT'S SO SAD!
IT'S SAD BECAUSE...

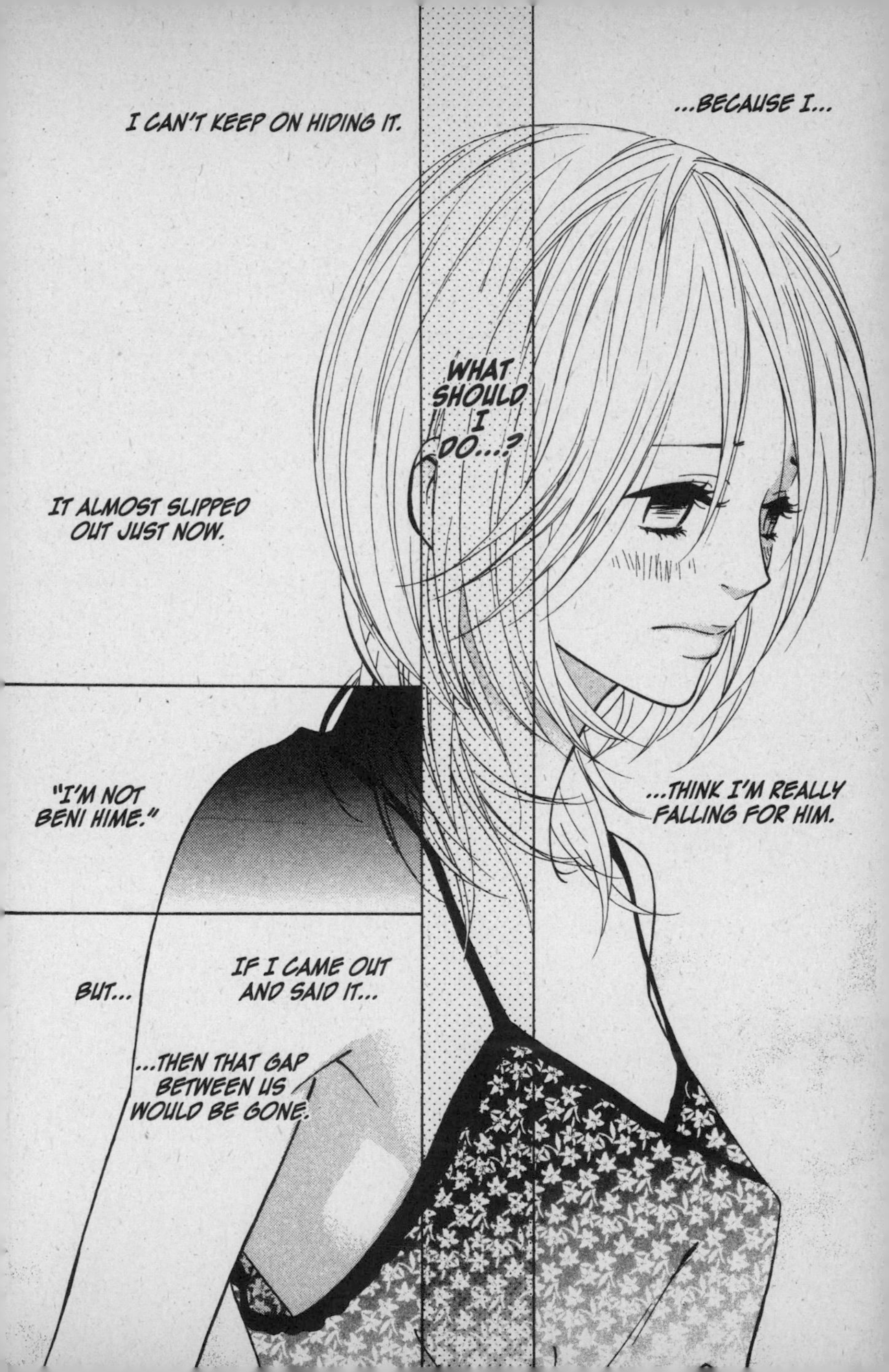
...BECAUSE I...
WHAT SHOULD I DO...?
...THINK I'M REALLY FALLING FOR HIM.
I CAN'T KEEP ON HIDING IT.
IT ALMOST SLIPPED OUT JUST NOW.
"I'M NOT BENI HIME."
BUT...
IF I CAME OUT AND SAID IT...
...THEN THAT GAP BETWEEN US WOULD BE GONE.

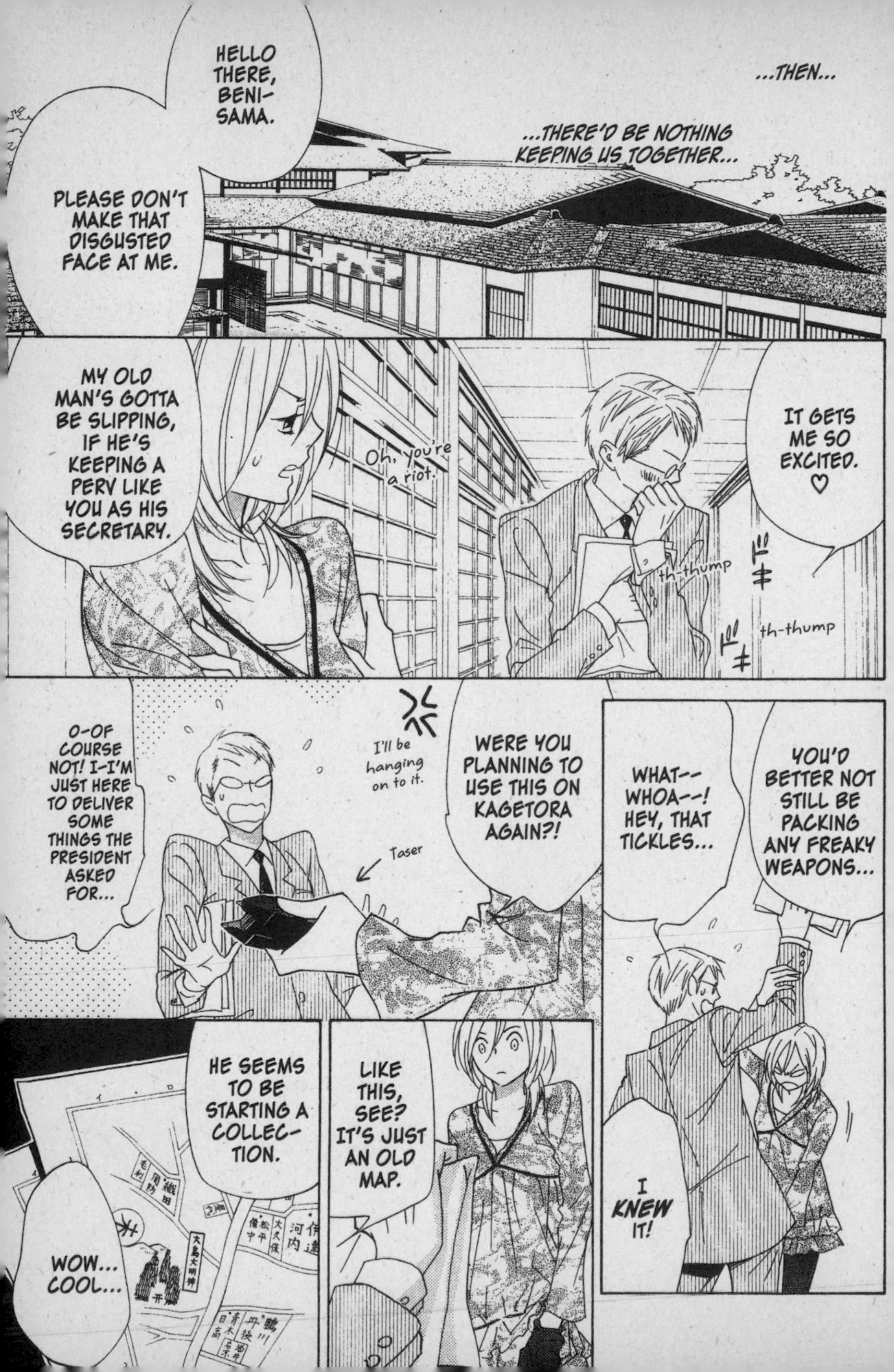
...THEN...
...THERE'D BE NOTHING KEEPING US TOGETHER...
HELLO THERE, BENI-SAMA.
PLEASE DON'T MAKE THAT DISGUSTED FACE AT ME.
IT GETS ME SO EXCITED. ♡
ドキ th-thump
ドキ th-thump
Oh, you're a riot.
MY OLD MAN'S GOTTA BE SLIPPING, IF HE'S KEEPING A PERV LIKE YOU AS HIS SECRETARY.
YOU'D BETTER NOT STILL BE PACKING ANY FREAKY WEAPONS...
WHAT--WHOA--! HEY, THAT TICKLES...
I KNEW IT!
WERE YOU PLANNING TO USE THIS ON KAGETORA AGAIN?!
I'll be hanging on to it.
Taser
O-OF COURSE NOT! I-I'M JUST HERE TO DELIVER SOME THINGS THE PRESIDENT ASKED FOR...
LIKE THIS, SEE? IT'S JUST AN OLD MAP.
HE SEEMS TO BE STARTING A COLLECTION.
WOW... COOL...

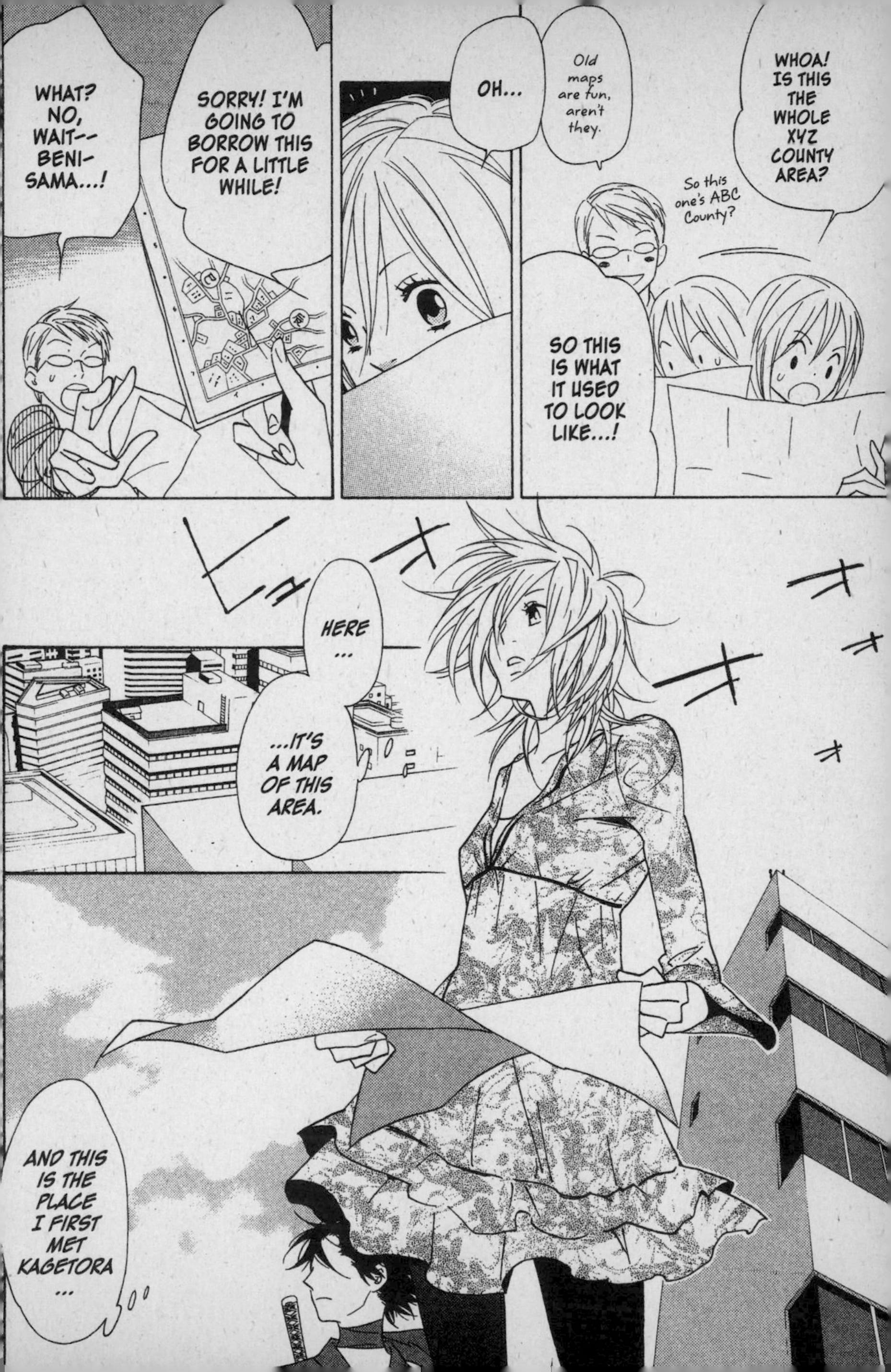
WHOA! IS THIS THE WHOLE XYZ COUNTY AREA?
Old maps are fun, aren't they.
So this one's ABC County?
SO THIS IS WHAT IT USED TO LOOK LIKE...!
OH...
SORRY! I'M GOING TO BORROW THIS FOR A LITTLE WHILE!
WHAT? NO, WAIT-- BENI-SAMA...!
HERE...
...IT'S A MAP OF THIS AREA.
AND THIS IS THE PLACE I FIRST MET KAGETORA...

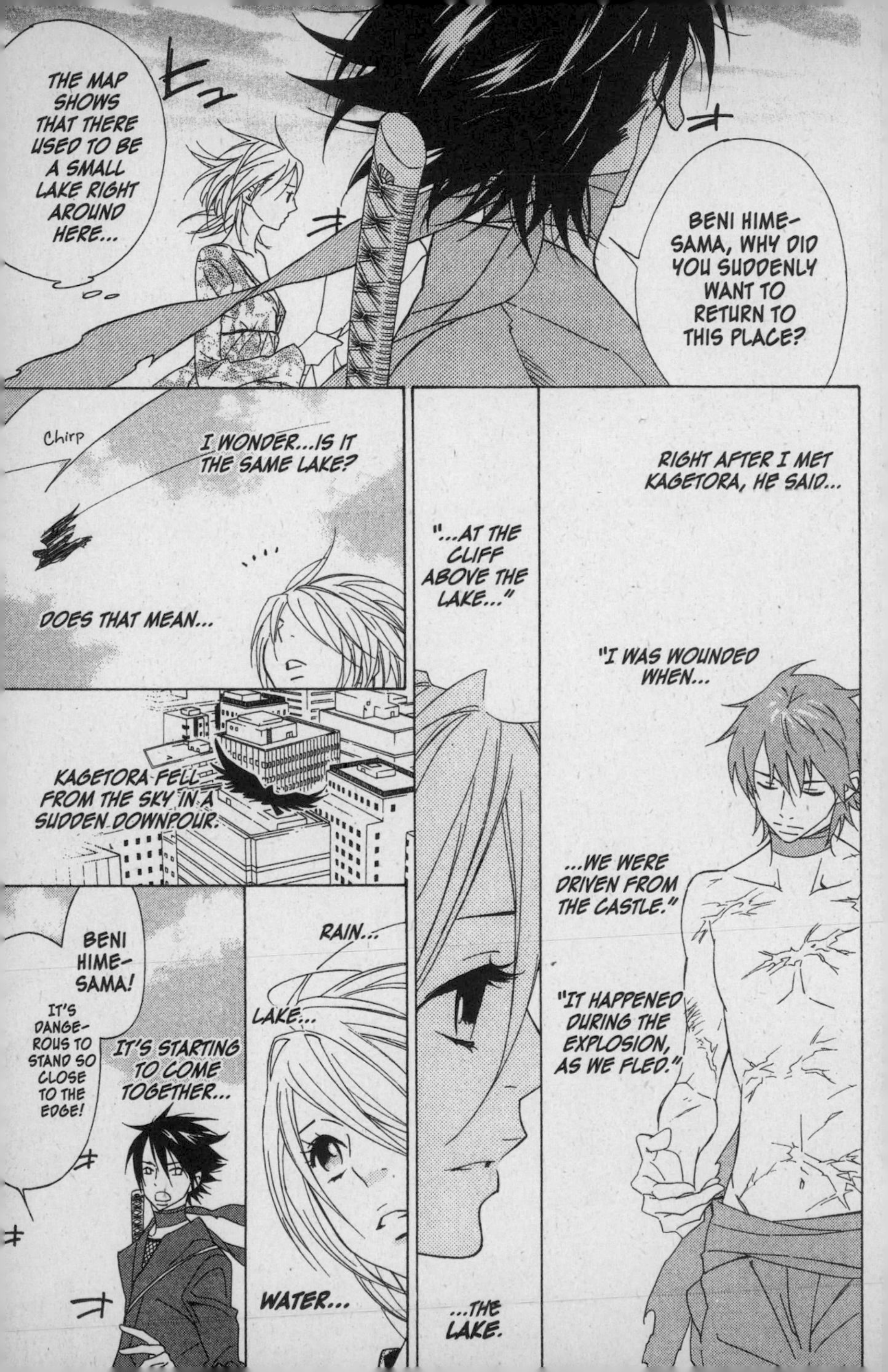
BENI HIME-SAMA, WHY DID YOU SUDDENLY WANT TO RETURN TO THIS PLACE?
THE MAP SHOWS THAT THERE USED TO BE A SMALL LAKE RIGHT AROUND HERE...
RIGHT AFTER I MET KAGETORA, HE SAID...
"I WAS WOUNDED WHEN...
...WE WERE DRIVEN FROM THE CASTLE."
"IT HAPPENED DURING THE EXPLOSION, AS WE FLED."
"...AT THE CLIFF ABOVE THE LAKE..."
...THE LAKE.
Chirp
I WONDER...IS IT THE SAME LAKE?
...
DOES THAT MEAN...
KAGETORA FELL FROM THE SKY IN A SUDDEN DOWNPOUR.
RAIN...
LAKE...
WATER...
BENI HIME-SAMA!
IT'S DANGEROUS TO STAND SO CLOSE TO THE EDGE!
IT'S STARTING TO COME TOGETHER...

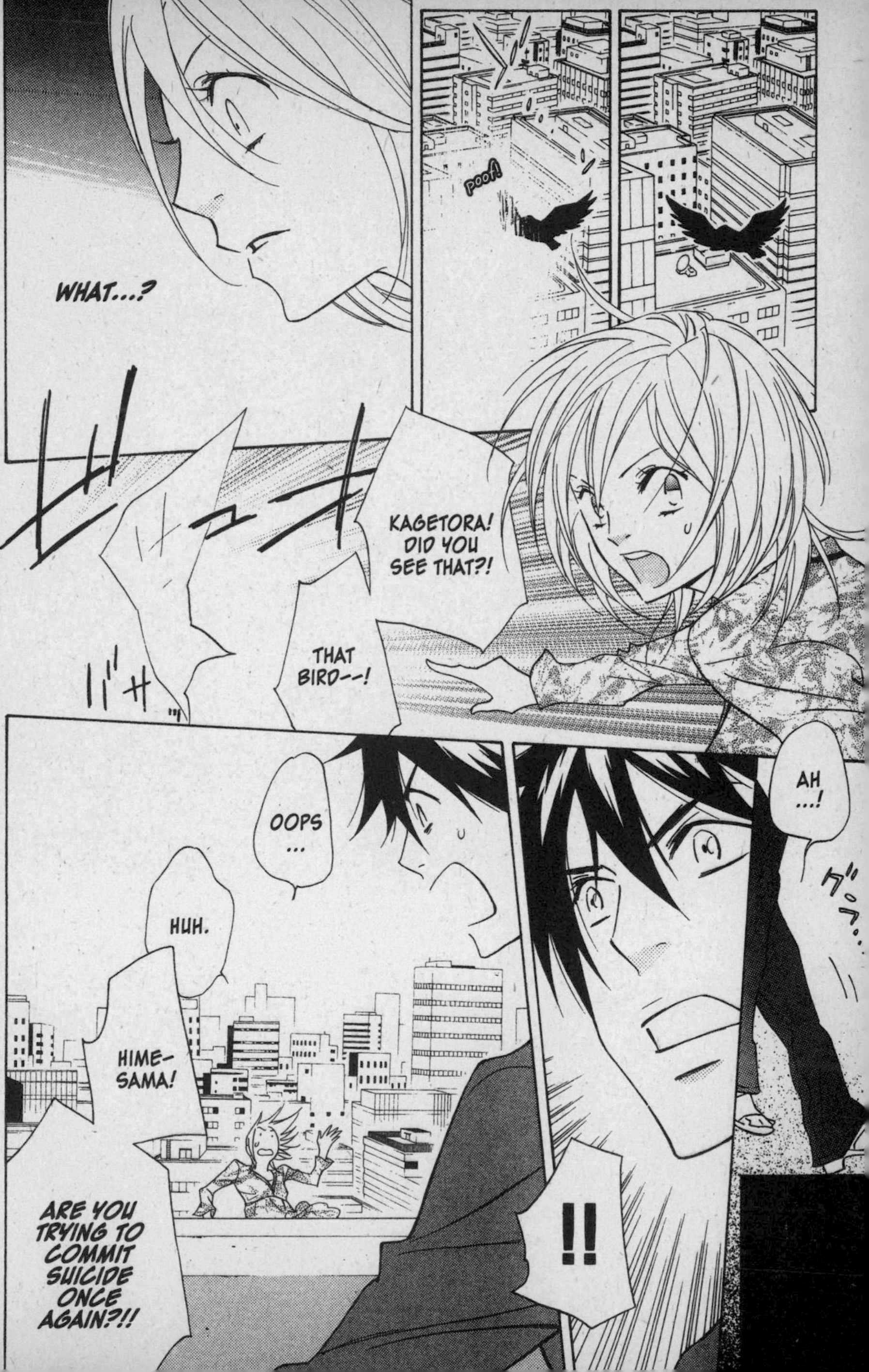
poof!
WHAT...?
KAGETORA! DID YOU SEE THAT?!
THAT BIRD--!
AH ...!
!!
OOPS ...
HUH.
HIME-SAMA!
ARE YOU TRYING TO COMMIT SUICIDE ONCE AGAIN?!!

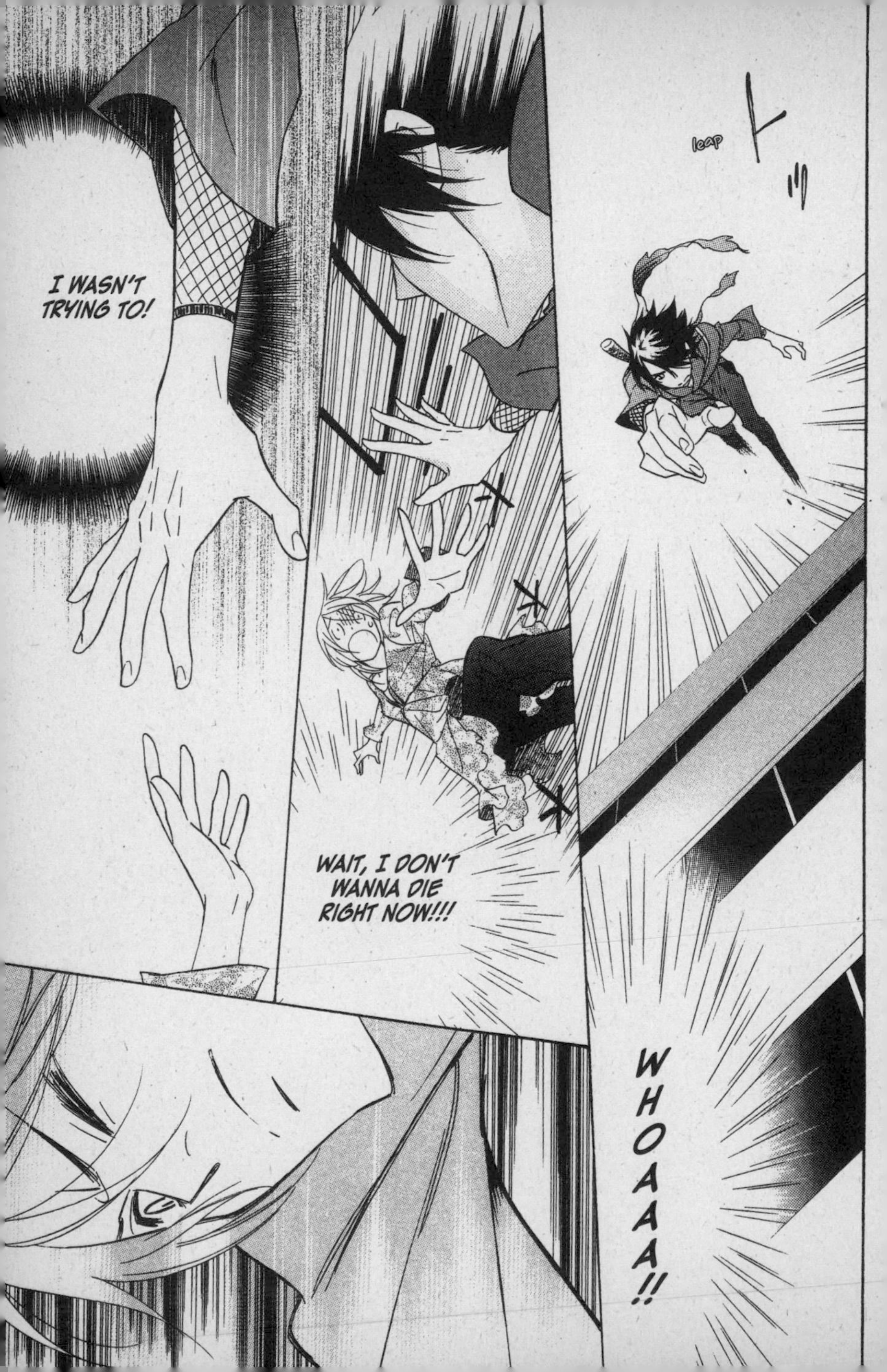
leap
WHOAAA!!
WAIT, I DON'T WANNA DIE RIGHT NOW!!!
I WASN'T TRYING TO!

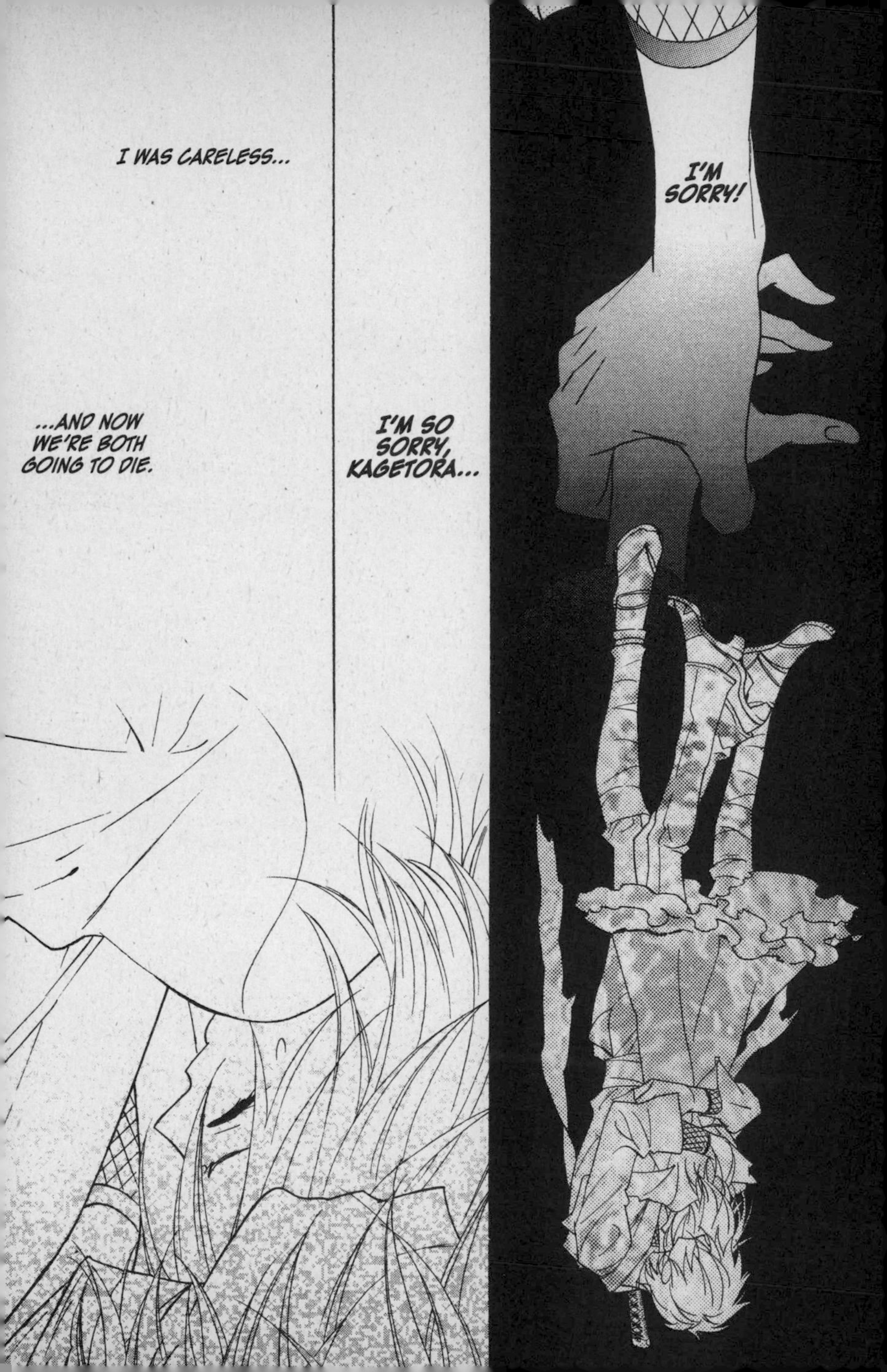
I'M SORRY!
I'M SO SORRY, KAGETORA...
I WAS CARELESS...
...AND NOW WE'RE BOTH GOING TO DIE.

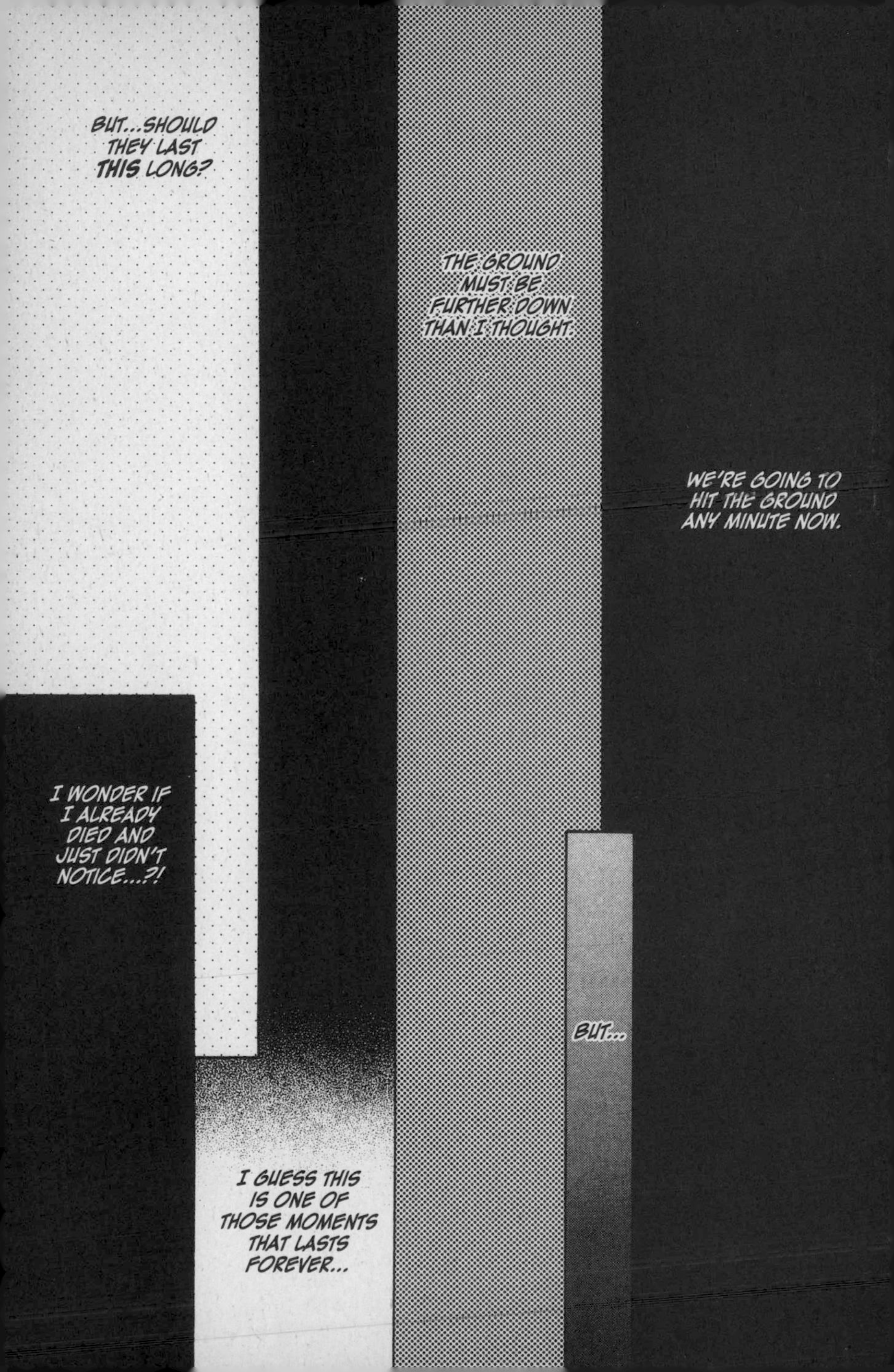
WE'RE GOING TO HIT THE GROUND ANY MINUTE NOW.
BUT...
THE GROUND MUST BE FURTHER DOWN THAN I THOUGHT.
BUT...SHOULD THEY LAST THIS LONG?
I GUESS THIS IS ONE OF THOSE MOMENTS THAT LASTS FOREVER...
I WONDER IF I ALREADY DIED AND JUST DIDN'T NOTICE...?!

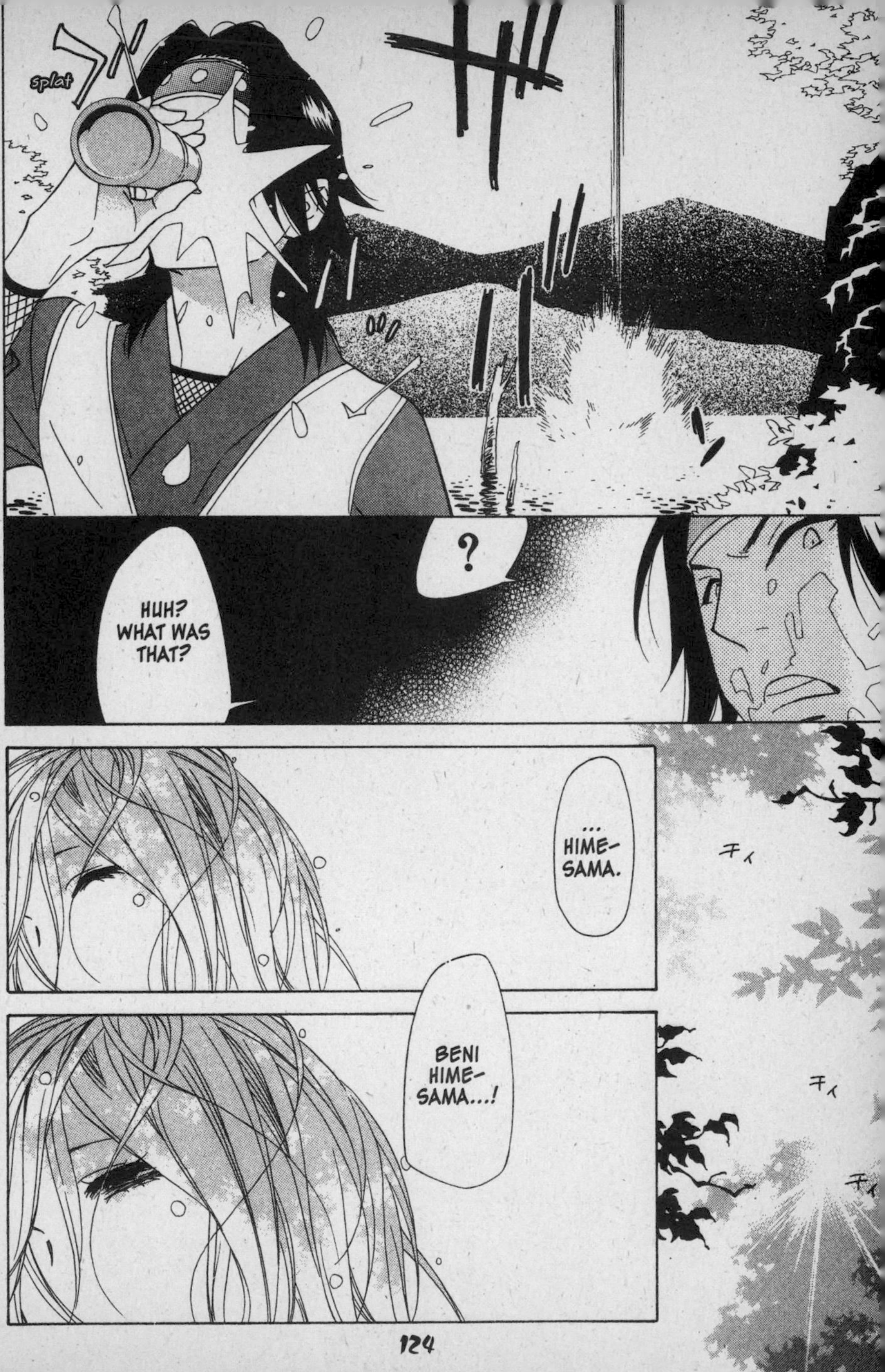
splat
?
HUH? WHAT WAS THAT?
チィ
... HIME-SAMA.
チィ
チィ
BENI HIME-SAMA...!

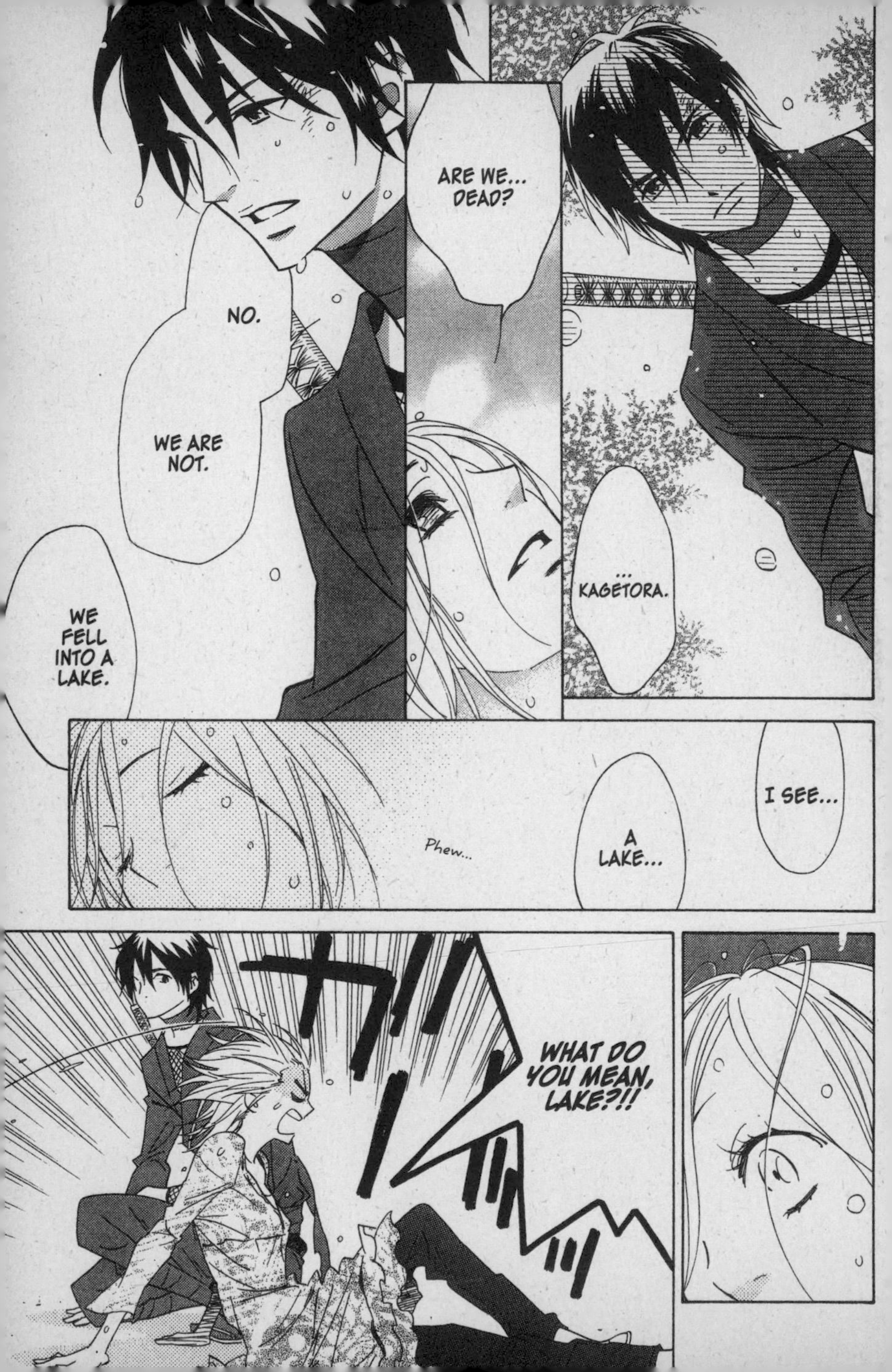
...KAGETORA.
ARE WE... DEAD?
NO.
WE ARE NOT.
WE FELL INTO A LAKE.
I SEE...
A LAKE...
Phew...
WHAT DO YOU MEAN, LAKE?!!

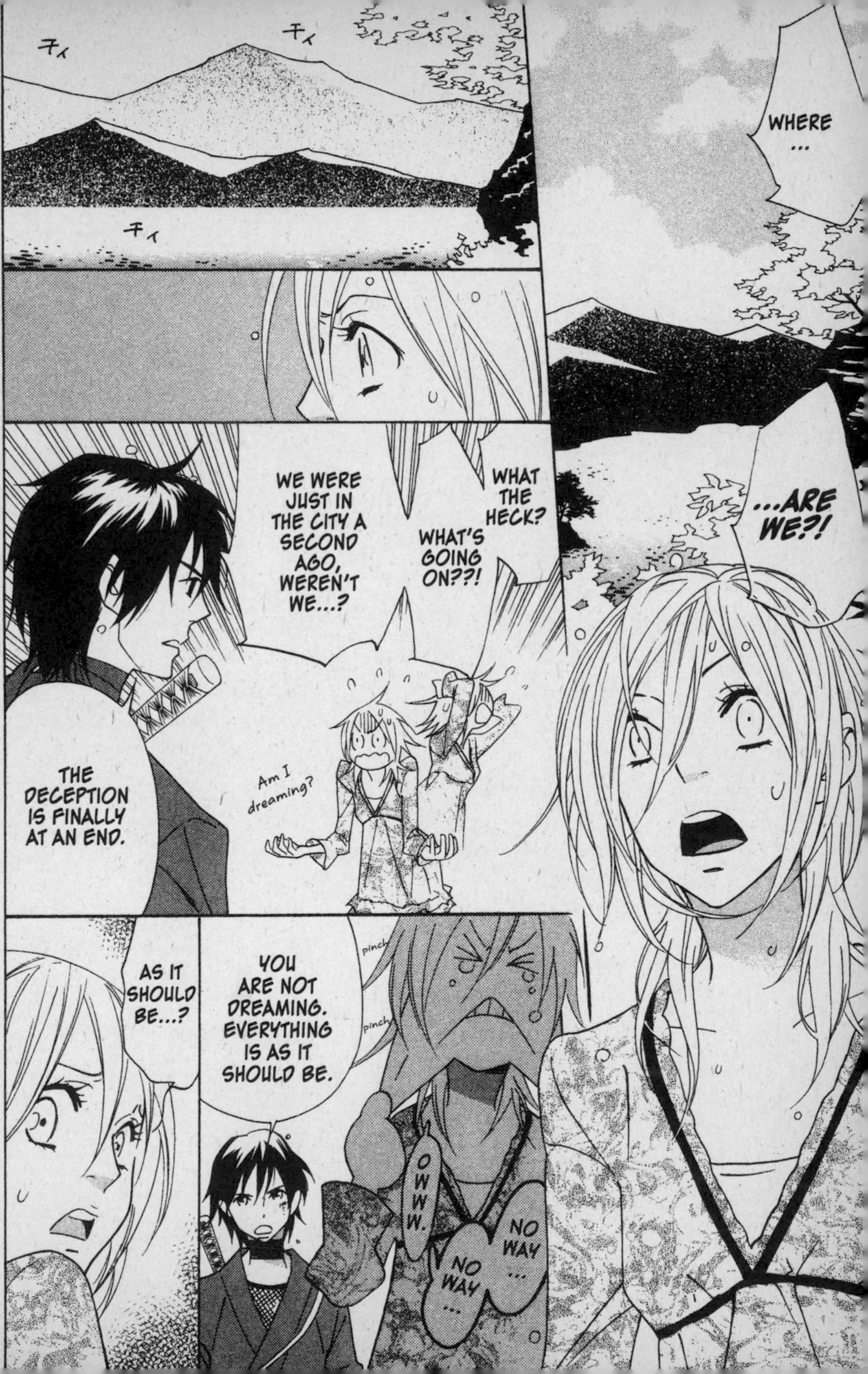
WHERE ...
...ARE WE?!
チィ
チィ
チィ
WHAT THE HECK?
WHAT'S GOING ON??!
WE WERE JUST IN THE CITY A SECOND AGO, WEREN'T WE...?
Am I dreaming?
THE DECEPTION IS FINALLY AT AN END.
pinch
pinch
OWWW.
NO WAY ...
NO WAY ...
YOU ARE NOT DREAMING. EVERYTHING IS AS IT SHOULD BE.
AS IT SHOULD BE...?

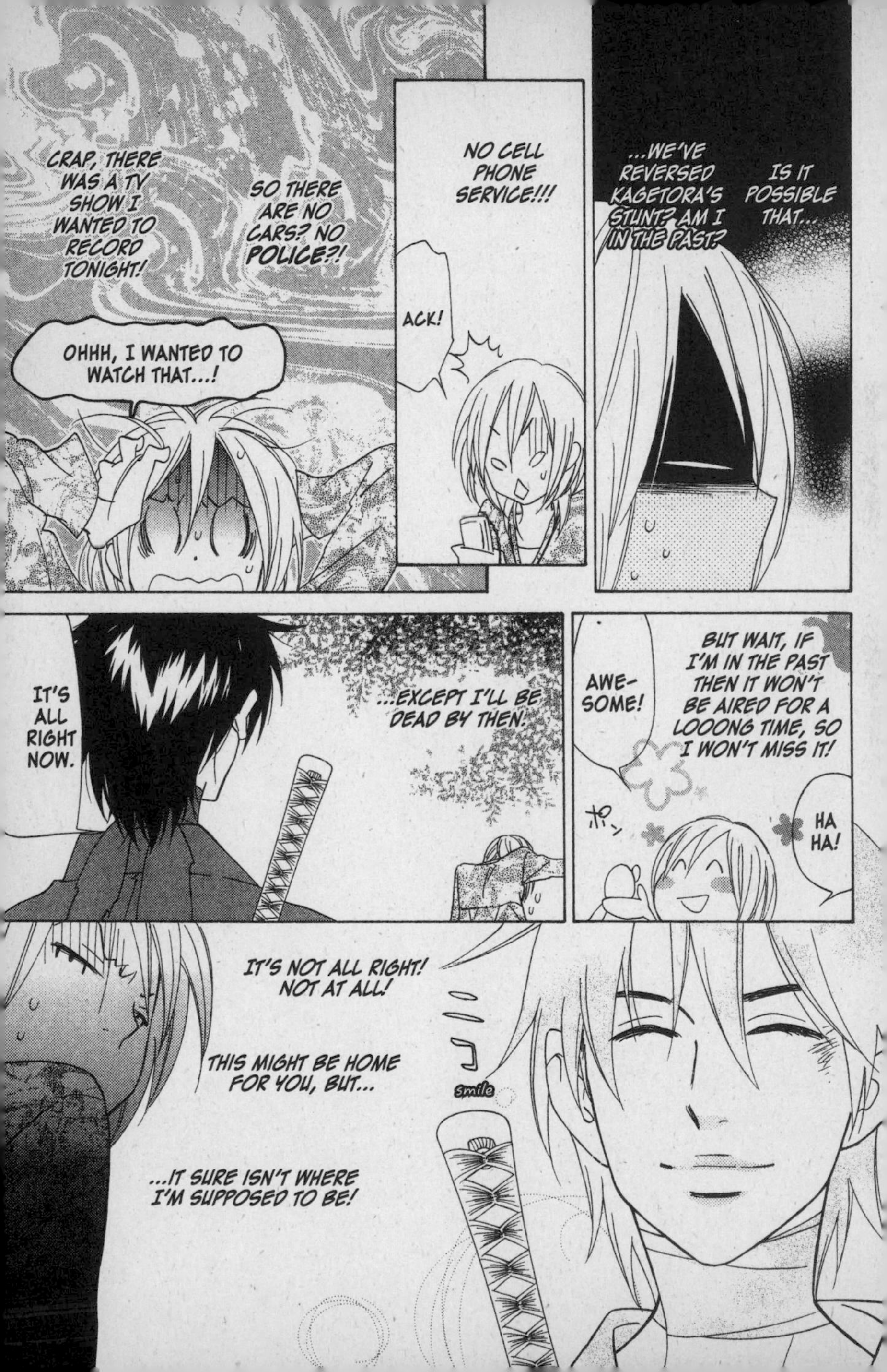
IS IT POSSIBLE THAT...
...WE'VE REVERSED KAGETORA'S STUNT? AM I IN THE PAST?
NO CELL PHONE SERVICE!!!
ACK!
SO THERE ARE NO CARS? NO POLICE?!
CRAP, THERE WAS A TV SHOW I WANTED TO RECORD TONIGHT!
OHHH, I WANTED TO WATCH THAT...!
BUT WAIT, IF I'M IN THE PAST THEN IT WON'T BE AIRED FOR A LOOONG TIME, SO I WON'T MISS IT!
AWE-SOME!
HA HA!
...EXCEPT I'LL BE DEAD BY THEN.
IT'S ALL RIGHT NOW.
smile
IT'S NOT ALL RIGHT! NOT AT ALL!
THIS MIGHT BE HOME FOR YOU, BUT...
...IT SURE ISN'T WHERE I'M SUPPOSED TO BE!

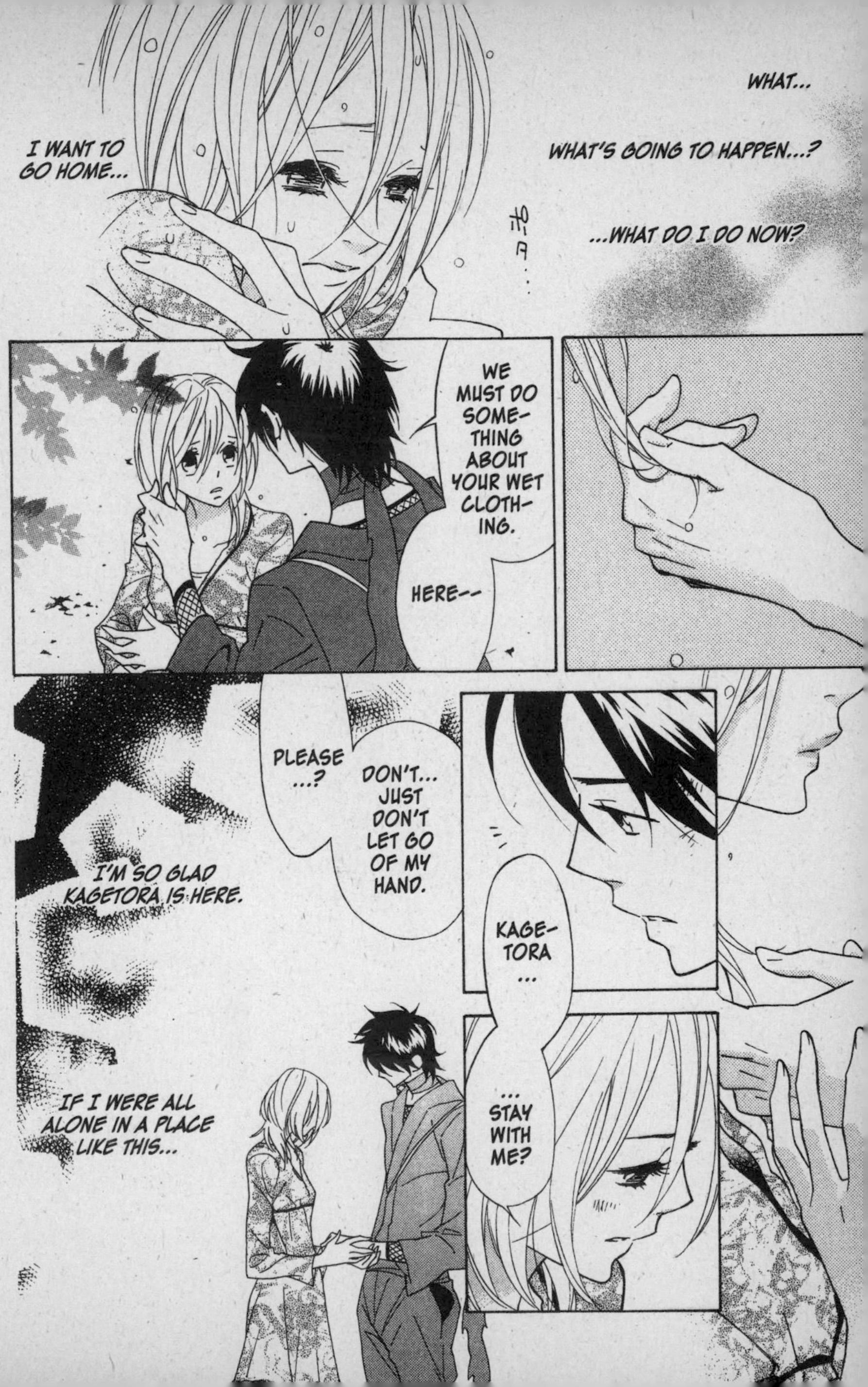
WHAT...
WHAT'S GOING TO HAPPEN...?
...WHAT DO I DO NOW?
ポタ…
I WANT TO GO HOME...
WE MUST DO SOME-THING ABOUT YOUR WET CLOTH-ING.
HERE--
KAGE-TORA...
DON'T... JUST DON'T LET GO OF MY HAND.
PLEASE...?
I'M SO GLAD KAGETORA IS HERE.
...STAY WITH ME?
IF I WERE ALL ALONE IN A PLACE LIKE THIS...

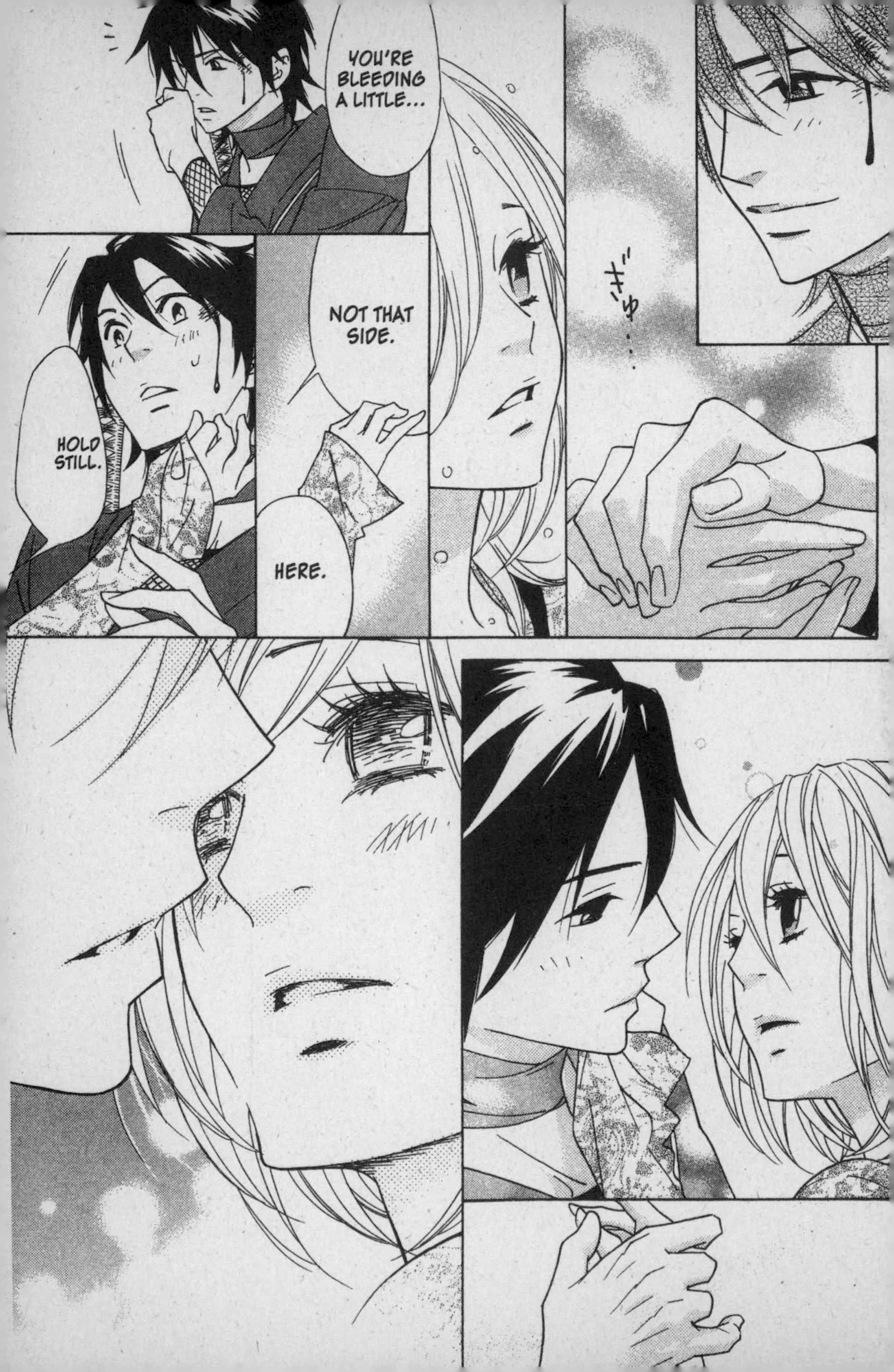

ぎゅ・・・
YOU'RE BLEEDING A LITTLE...
NOT THAT SIDE.
HERE.
HOLD STILL.

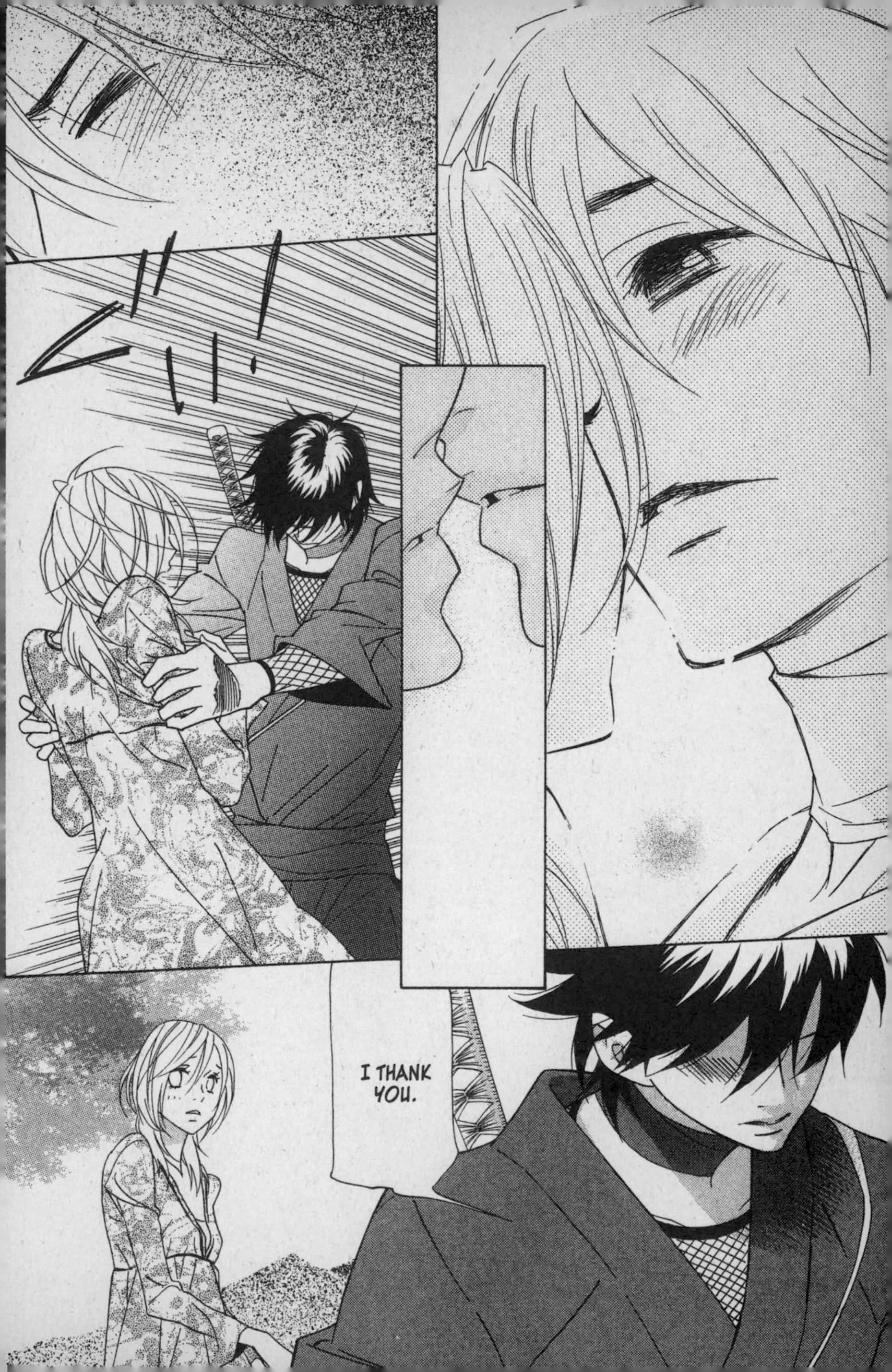
I THANK YOU.

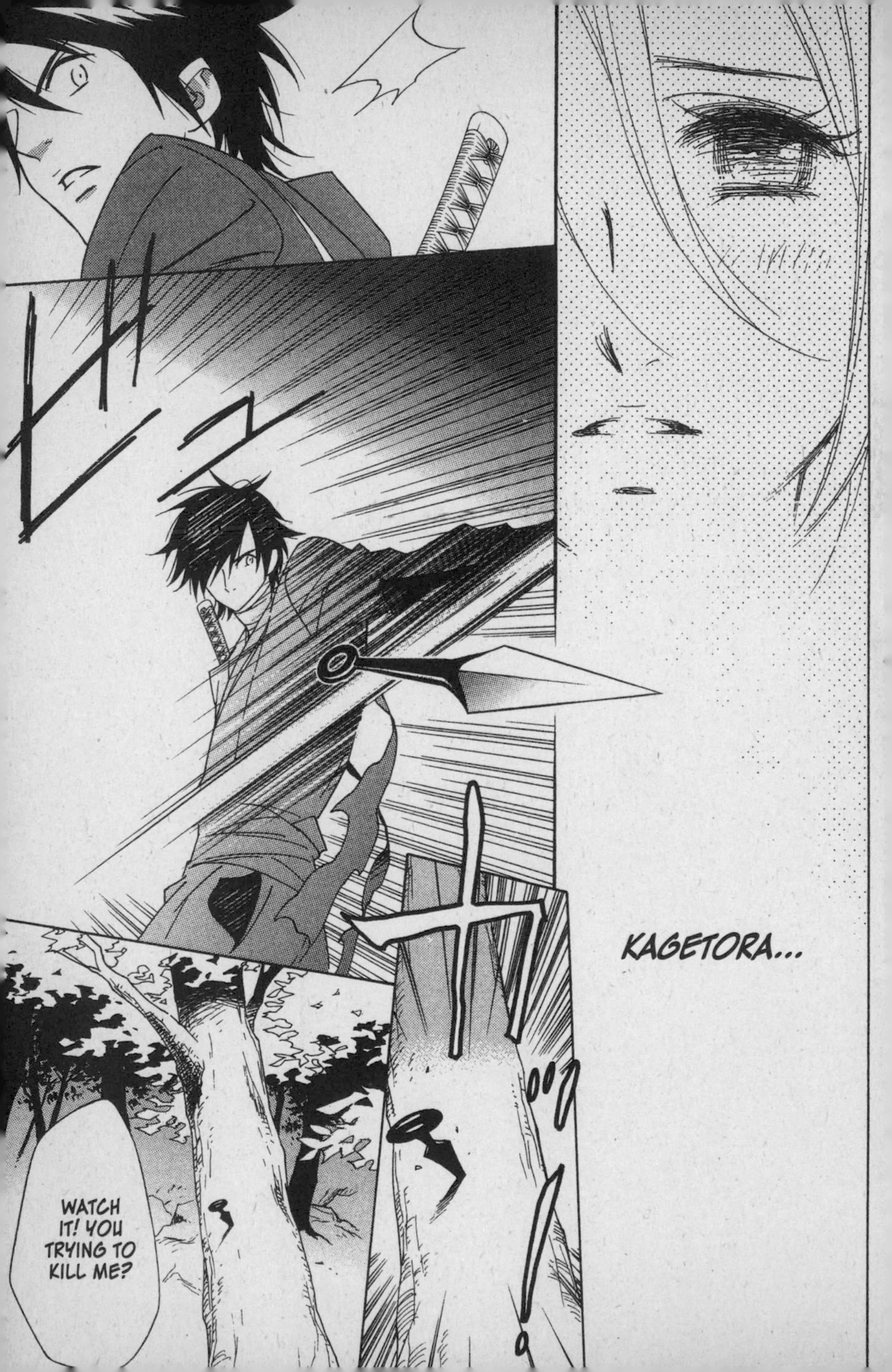
KAGETORA...
WATCH IT! YOU TRYING TO KILL ME?

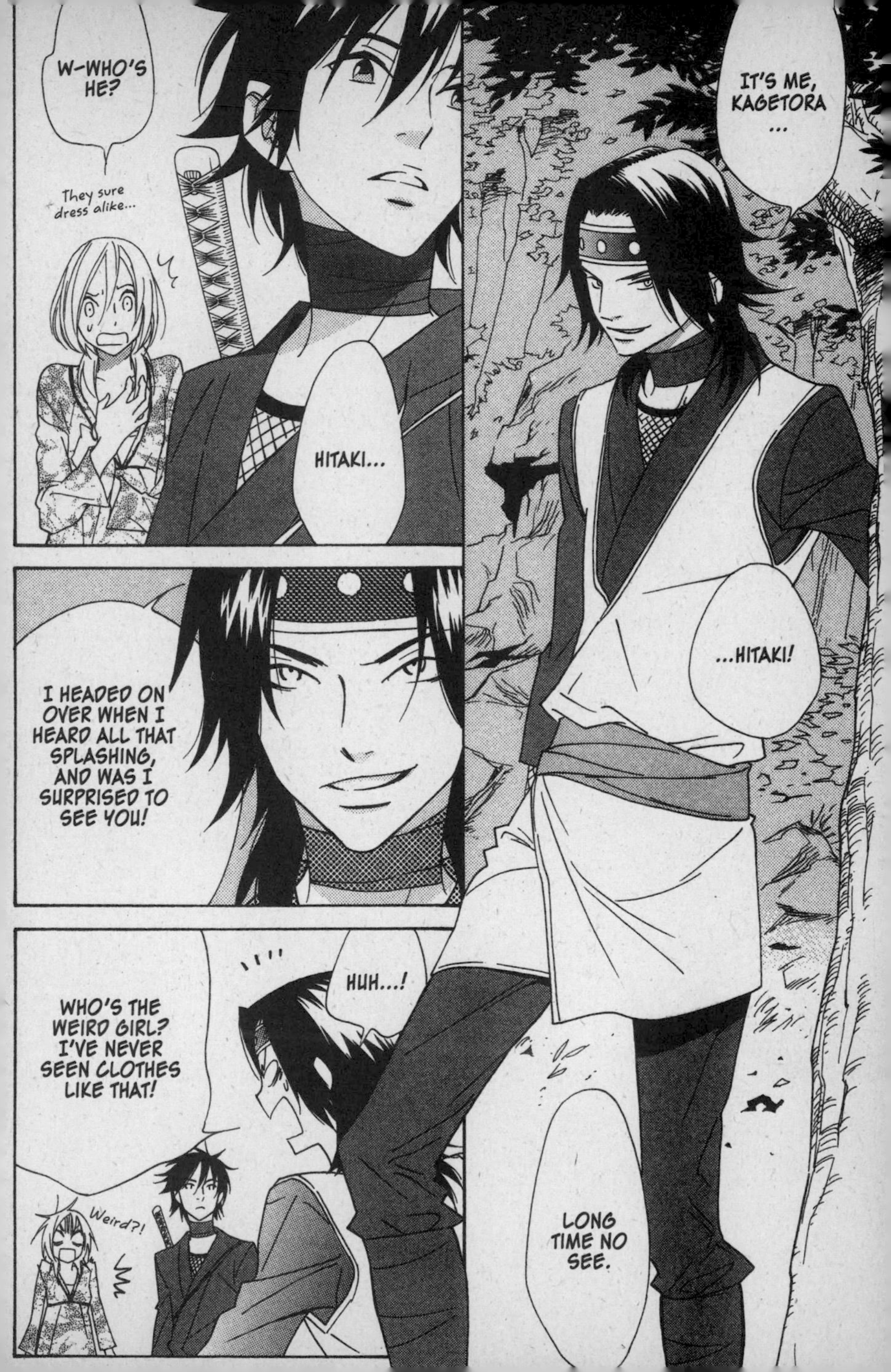
IT'S ME, KAGETORA ...
...HITAKI!
LONG TIME NO SEE.
W-WHO'S HE?
They sure dress alike...
HITAKI...
I HEADED ON OVER WHEN I HEARD ALL THAT SPLASHING, AND WAS I SURPRISED TO SEE YOU!
HUH...!
WHO'S THE WEIRD GIRL? I'VE NEVER SEEN CLOTHES LIKE THAT!
Weird?!

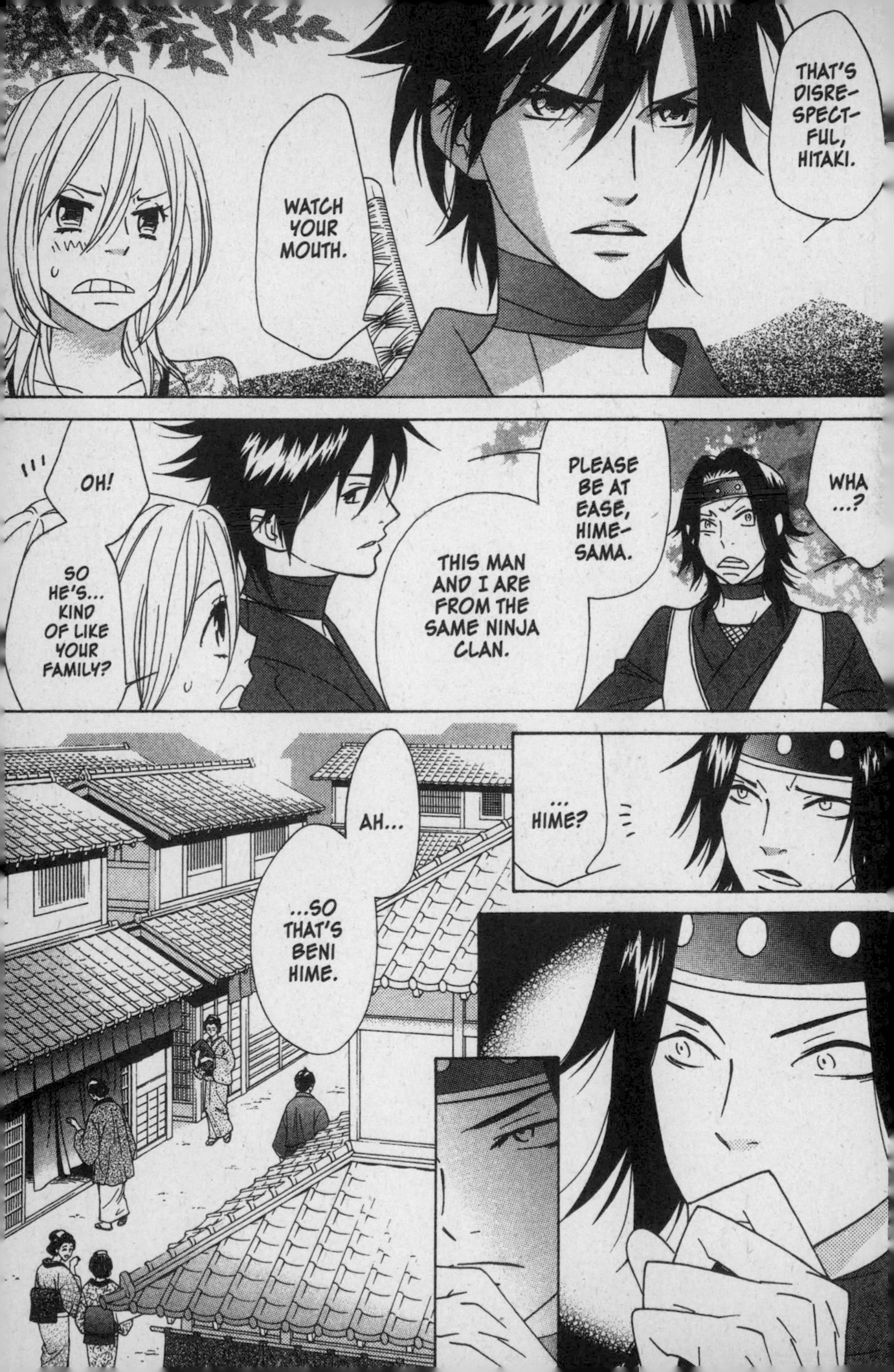
THAT'S DISRE-SPECT-FUL, HITAKI.
WATCH YOUR MOUTH.
WHA ...?
PLEASE BE AT EASE, HIME-SAMA.
THIS MAN AND I ARE FROM THE SAME NINJA CLAN.
OH!
SO HE'S... KIND OF LIKE YOUR FAMILY?
... HIME?
AH...
...SO THAT'S BENI HIME.

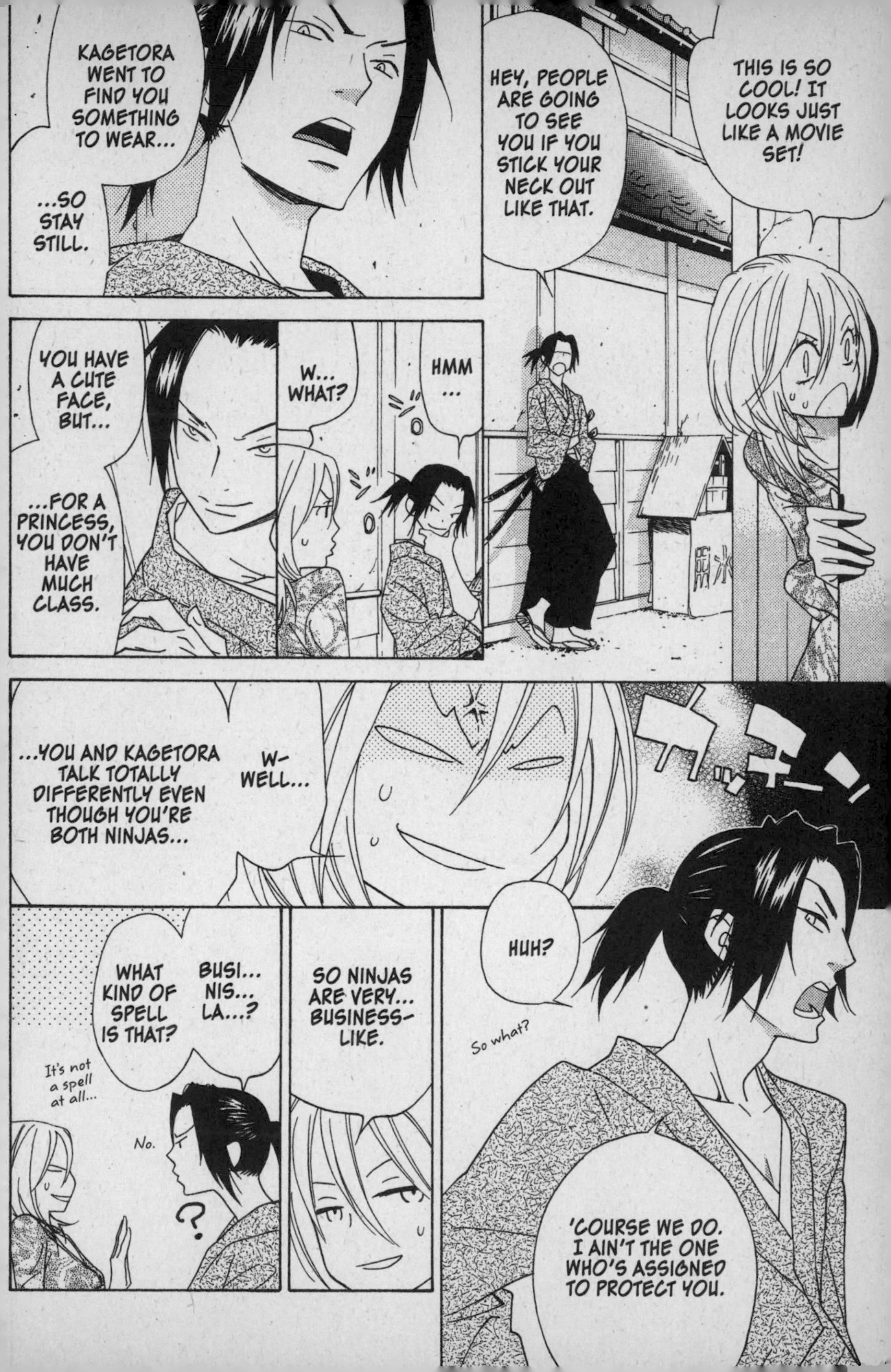
THIS IS SO COOL! IT LOOKS JUST LIKE A MOVIE SET!
HEY, PEOPLE ARE GOING TO SEE YOU IF YOU STICK YOUR NECK OUT LIKE THAT.
KAGETORA WENT TO FIND YOU SOMETHING TO WEAR...
...SO STAY STILL.
HMM...
W... WHAT?
YOU HAVE A CUTE FACE, BUT...
...FOR A PRINCESS, YOU DON'T HAVE MUCH CLASS.
W-WELL...
...YOU AND KAGETORA TALK TOTALLY DIFFERENTLY EVEN THOUGH YOU'RE BOTH NINJAS...
HUH?
So what?
'COURSE WE DO. I AIN'T THE ONE WHO'S ASSIGNED TO PROTECT YOU.
SO NINJAS ARE VERY... BUSINESS-LIKE.
BUSI... NIS... LA...?
WHAT KIND OF SPELL IS THAT?
It's not a spell at all...
No.
?

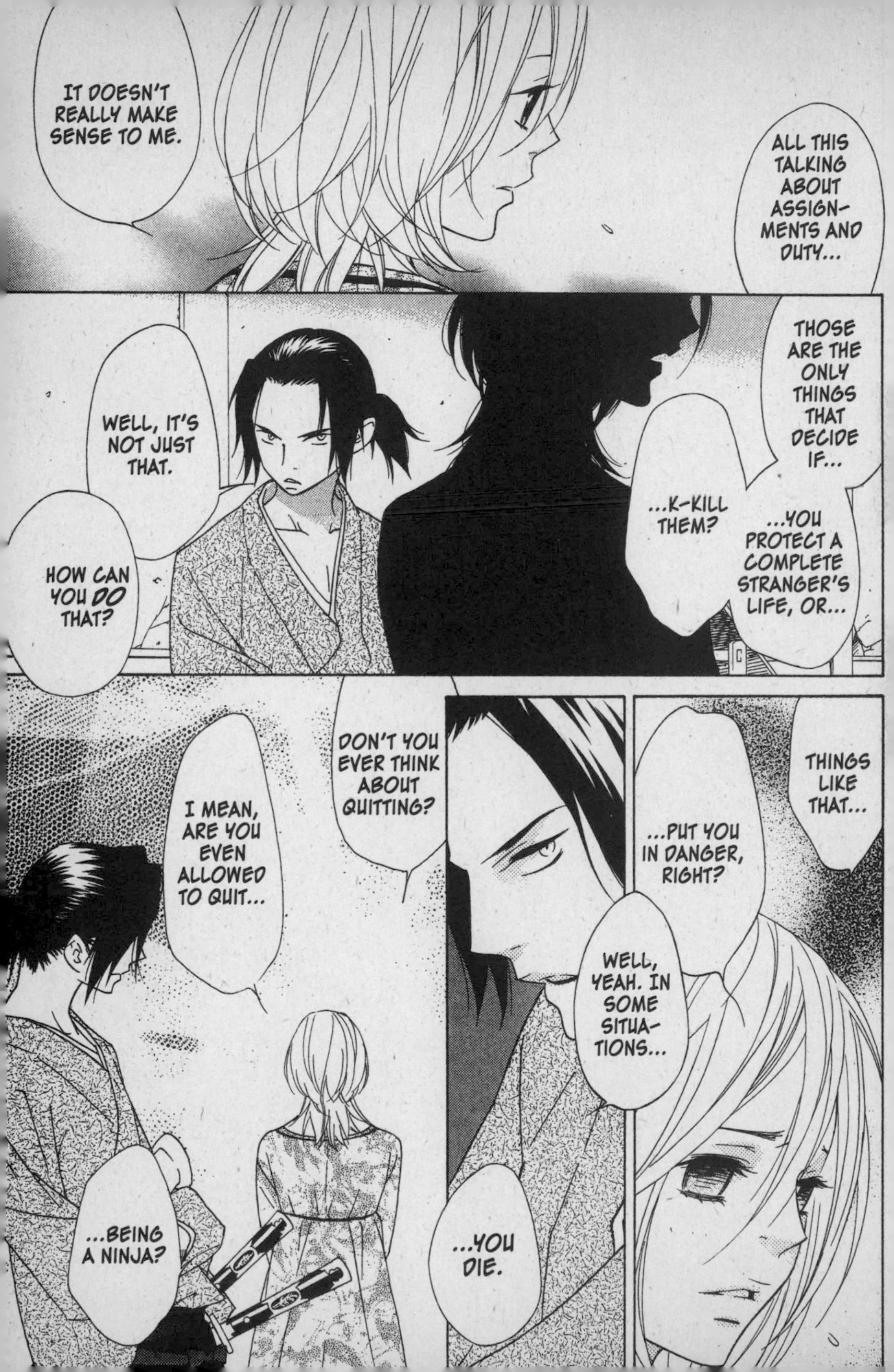
ALL THIS TALKING ABOUT ASSIGNMENTS AND DUTY...
IT DOESN'T REALLY MAKE SENSE TO ME.
THOSE ARE THE ONLY THINGS THAT DECIDE IF...
...YOU PROTECT A COMPLETE STRANGER'S LIFE, OR...
...K-KILL THEM?
WELL, IT'S NOT JUST THAT.
HOW CAN YOU *DO* THAT?
THINGS LIKE THAT...
...PUT YOU IN DANGER, RIGHT?
WELL, YEAH. IN SOME SITUATIONS...
...YOU DIE.
DON'T YOU EVER THINK ABOUT QUITTING?
I MEAN, ARE YOU EVEN ALLOWED TO QUIT...
...BEING A NINJA?

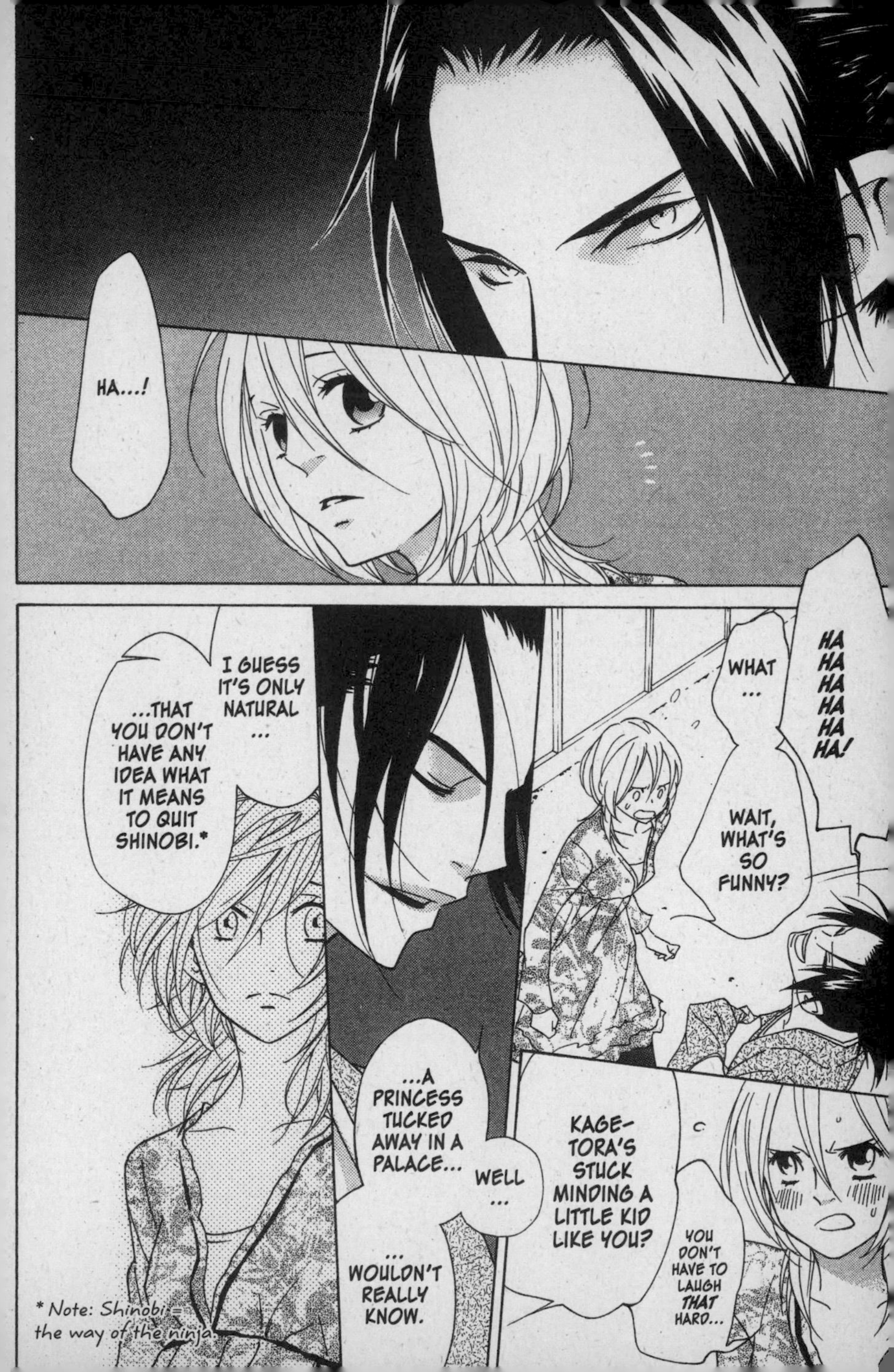
HA...!
HA HA HA HA HA HA HA!
WHAT...
WAIT, WHAT'S SO FUNNY?
KAGE-TORA'S STUCK MINDING A LITTLE KID LIKE YOU?
YOU DON'T HAVE TO LAUGH *THAT* HARD...
I GUESS IT'S ONLY NATURAL...
...THAT YOU DON'T HAVE ANY IDEA WHAT IT MEANS TO QUIT SHINOBI.*
...A PRINCESS TUCKED AWAY IN A PALACE...
WELL...
...WOULDN'T REALLY KNOW.

* Note: Shinobi = the way of the ninja.

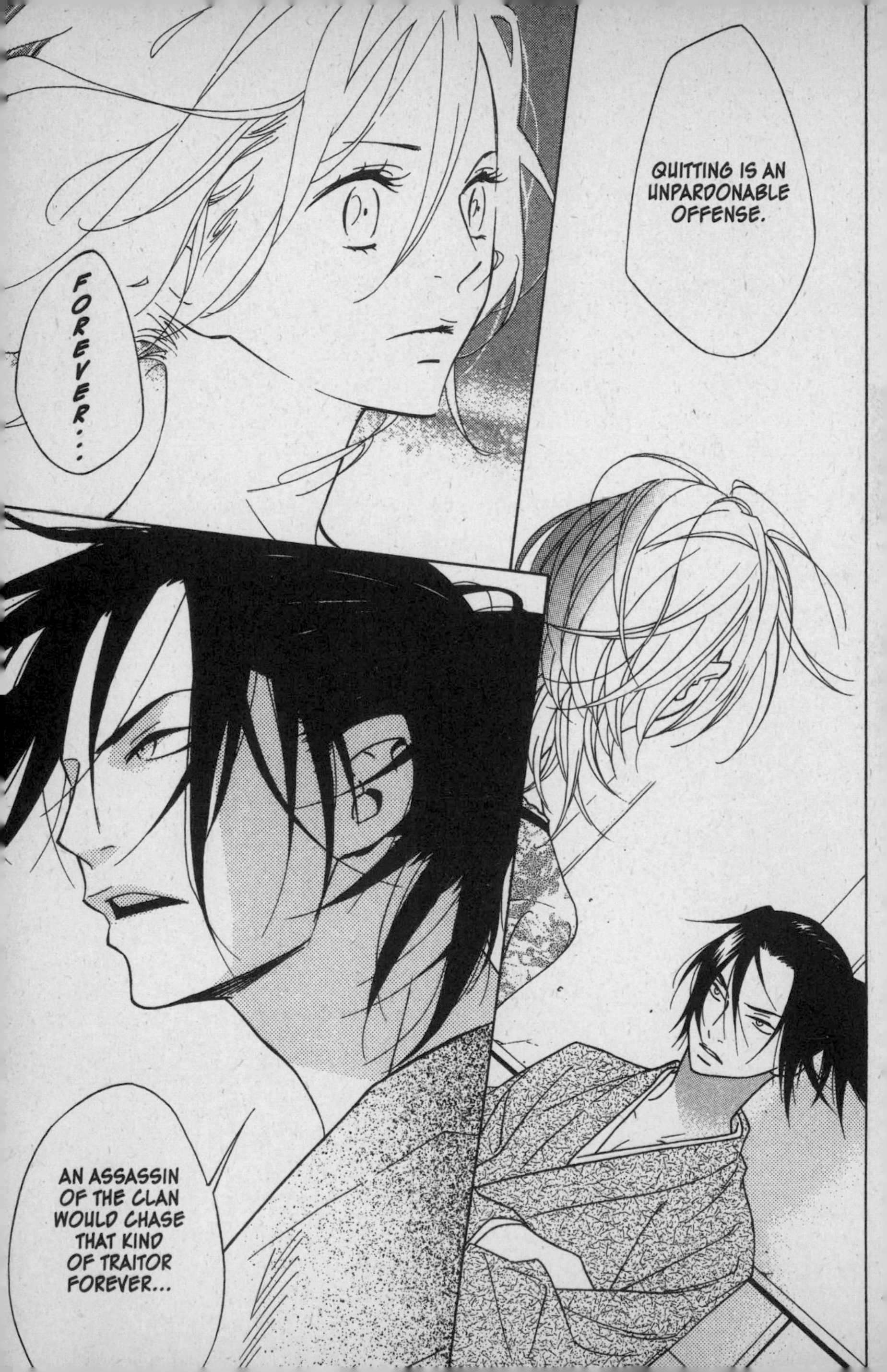
QUITTING IS AN UNPARDONABLE OFFENSE.
FOREVER...
AN ASSASSIN OF THE CLAN WOULD CHASE THAT KIND OF TRAITOR FOREVER...

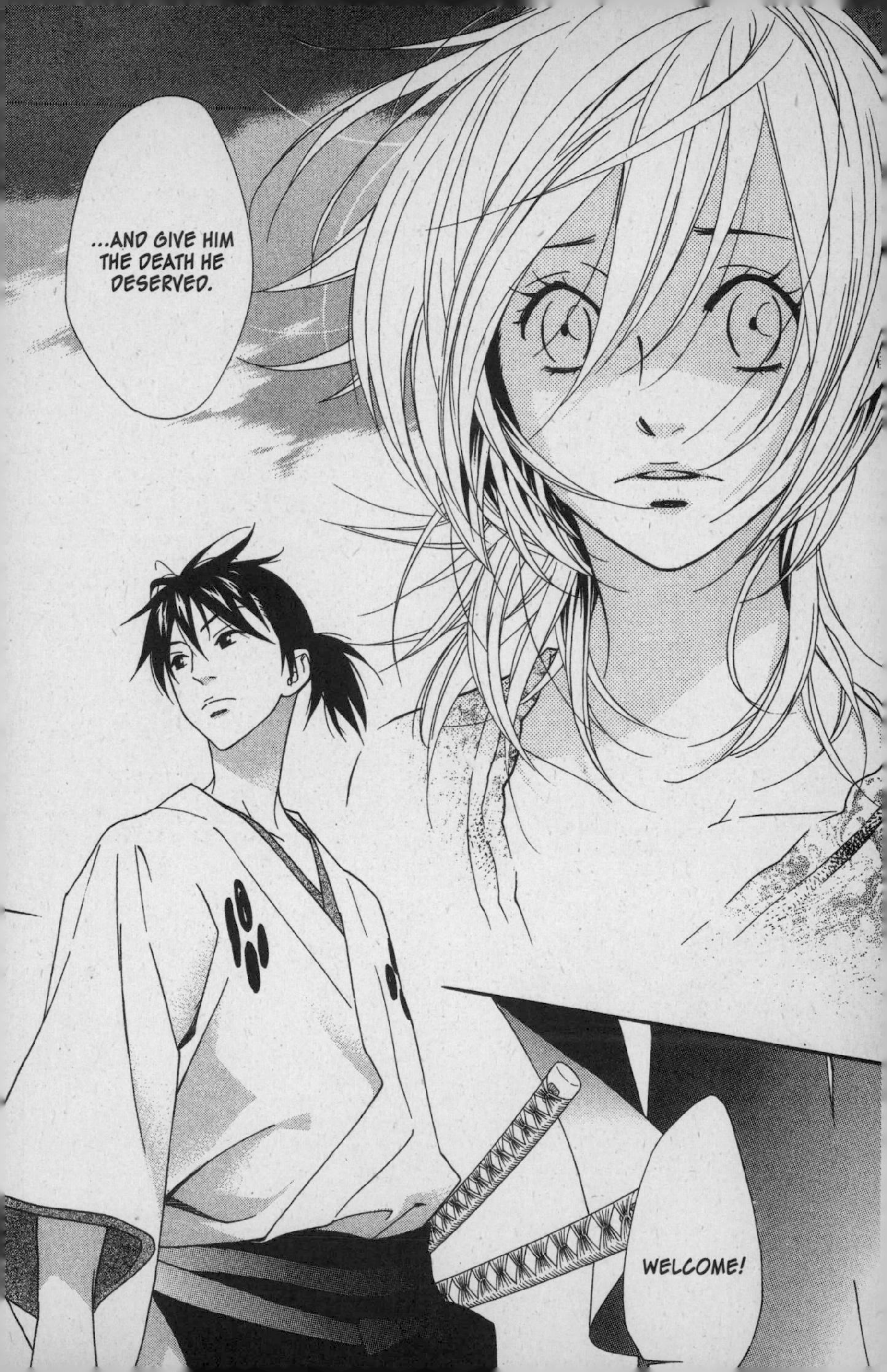
...AND GIVE HIM THE DEATH HE DESERVED.
WELCOME!

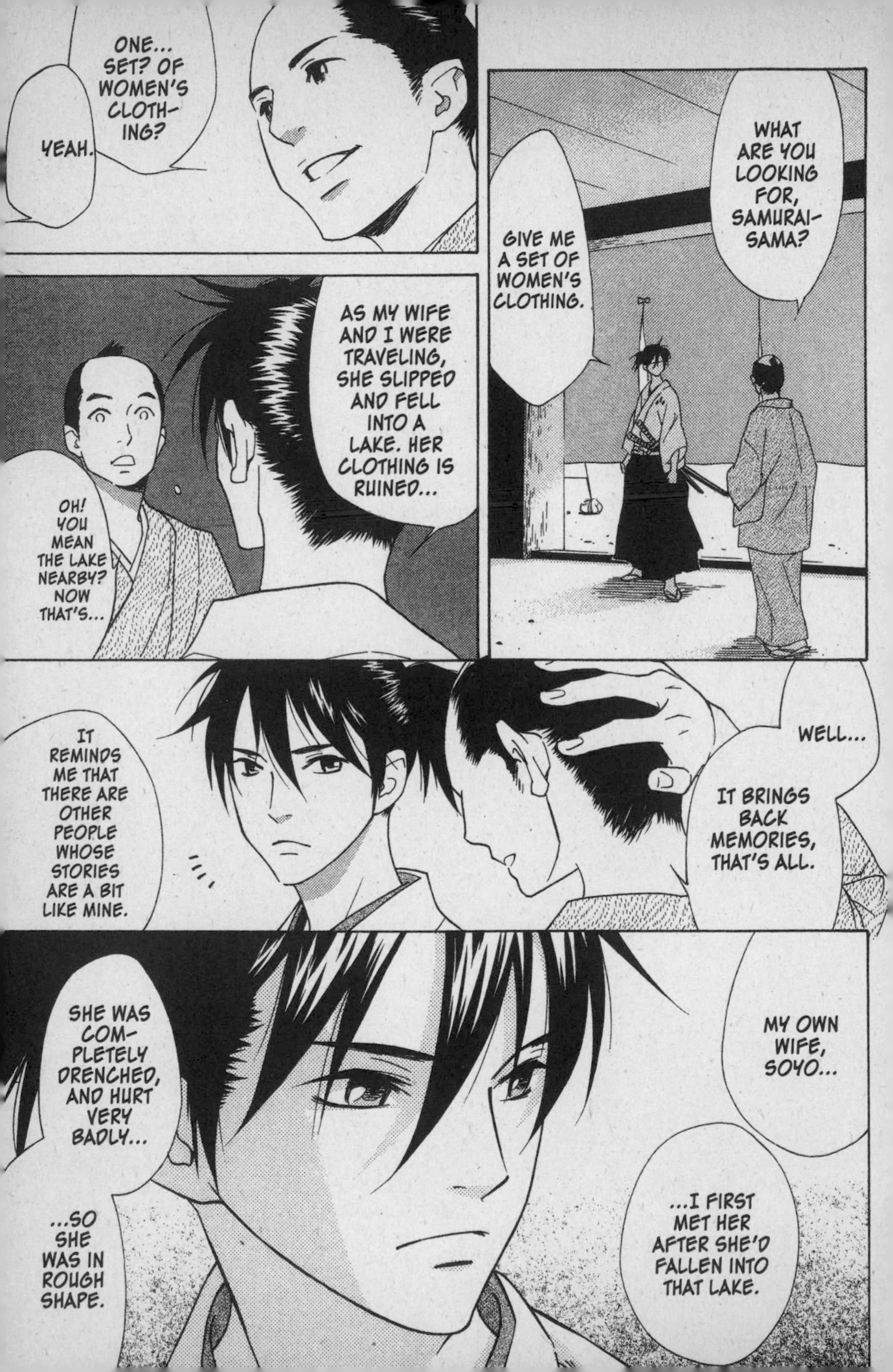
WHAT ARE YOU LOOKING FOR, SAMURAI-SAMA?
GIVE ME A SET OF WOMEN'S CLOTHING.
ONE... SET? OF WOMEN'S CLOTH-ING?
YEAH.
AS MY WIFE AND I WERE TRAVELING, SHE SLIPPED AND FELL INTO A LAKE. HER CLOTHING IS RUINED...
OH! YOU MEAN THE LAKE NEARBY? NOW THAT'S...
WELL...
IT BRINGS BACK MEMORIES, THAT'S ALL.
IT REMINDS ME THAT THERE ARE OTHER PEOPLE WHOSE STORIES ARE A BIT LIKE MINE.
MY OWN WIFE, SOYO...
...I FIRST MET HER AFTER SHE'D FALLEN INTO THAT LAKE.
SHE WAS COM-PLETELY DRENCHED, AND HURT VERY BADLY...
...SO SHE WAS IN ROUGH SHAPE.

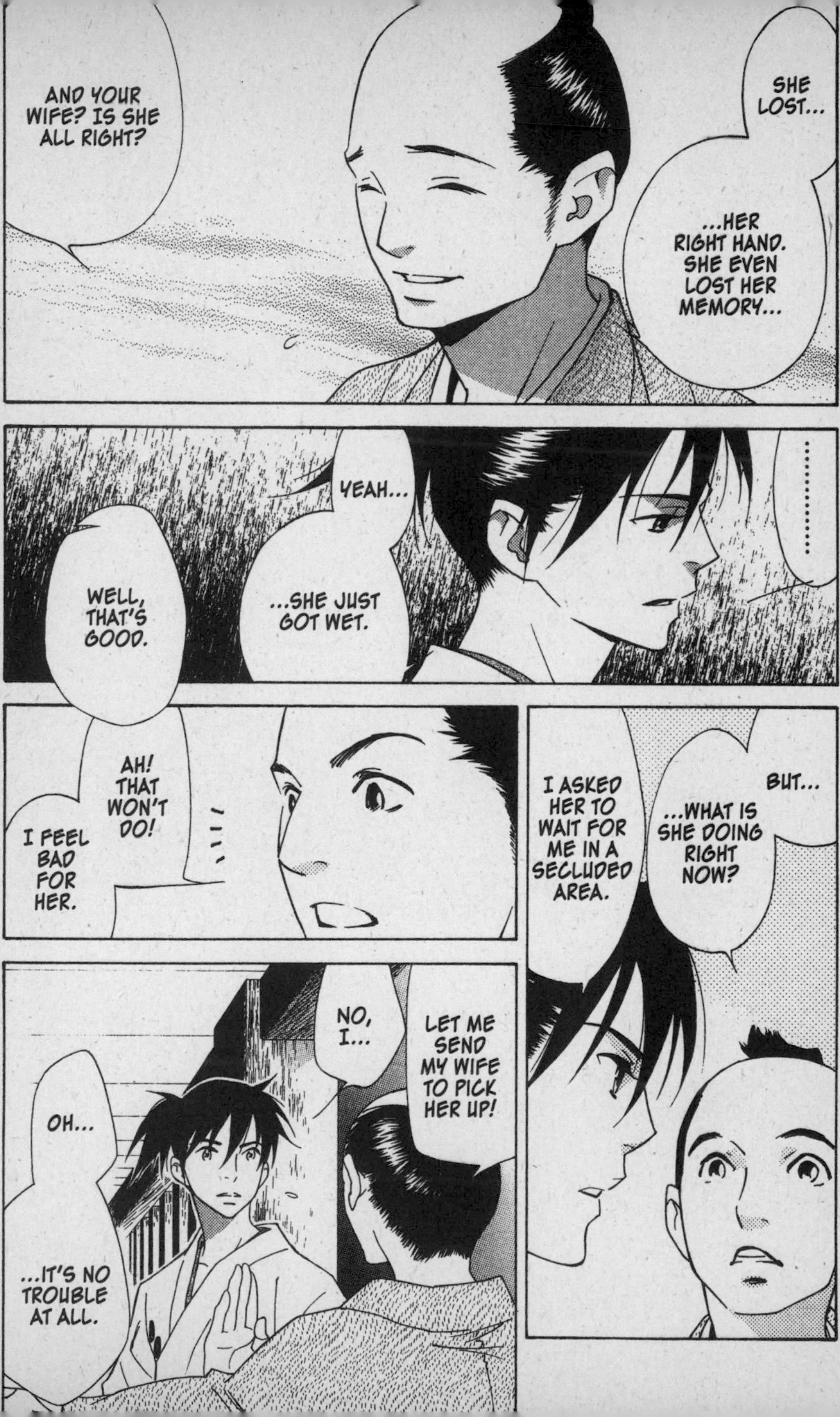
SHE LOST...
...HER RIGHT HAND. SHE EVEN LOST HER MEMORY...
AND YOUR WIFE? IS SHE ALL RIGHT?
......
YEAH...
...SHE JUST GOT WET.
WELL, THAT'S GOOD.
BUT...
...WHAT IS SHE DOING RIGHT NOW?
I ASKED HER TO WAIT FOR ME IN A SECLUDED AREA.
AH! THAT WON'T DO!
I FEEL BAD FOR HER.
LET ME SEND MY WIFE TO PICK HER UP!
NO, I...
OH...
...IT'S NO TROUBLE AT ALL.

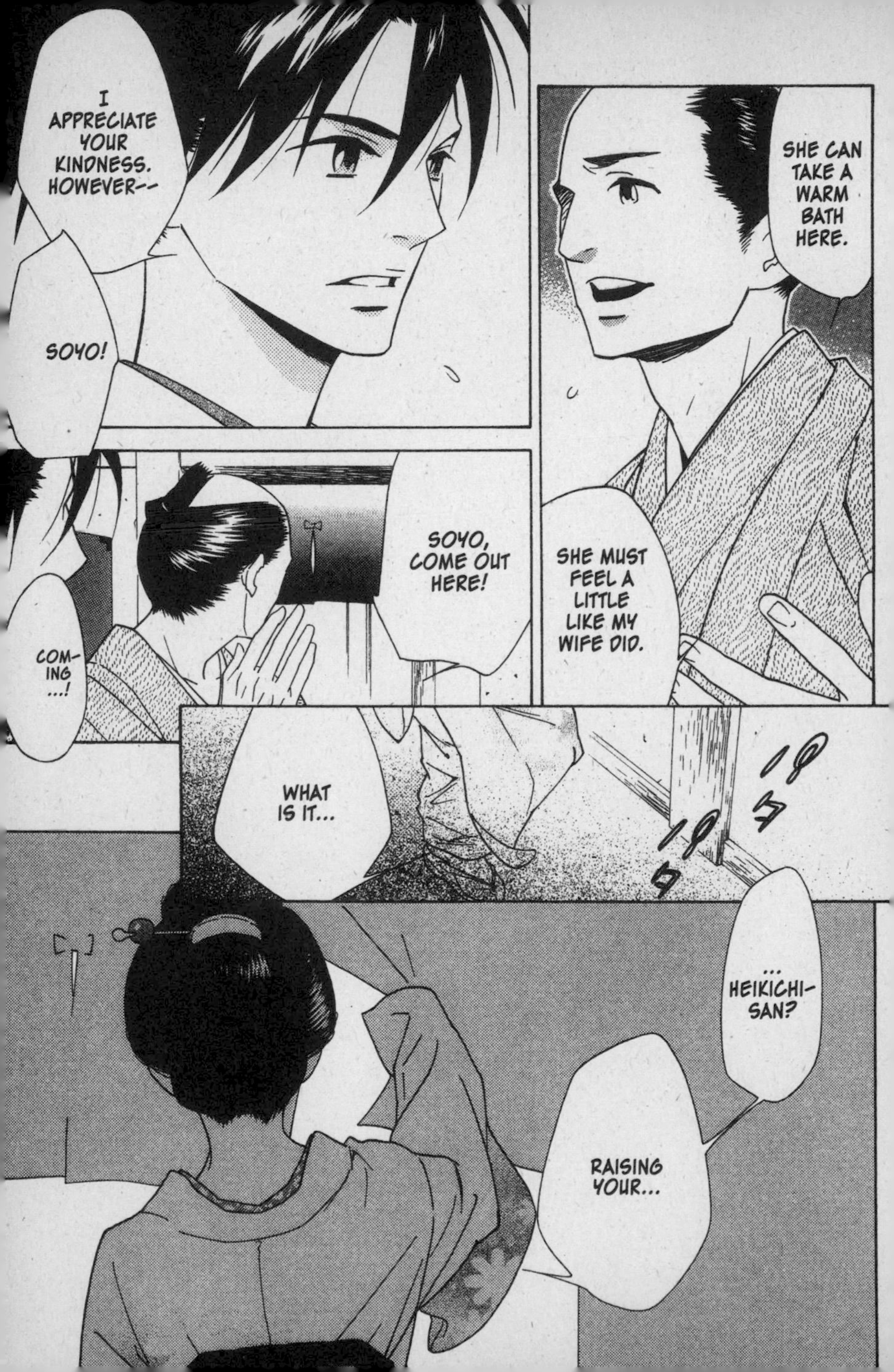

SHE CAN TAKE A WARM BATH HERE.
SHE MUST FEEL A LITTLE LIKE MY WIFE DID.
I APPRECIATE YOUR KINDNESS. HOWEVER--
SOYO!
SOYO, COME OUT HERE!
COMING...!
WHAT IS IT...
...HEIKICHI-SAN?
RAISING YOUR...

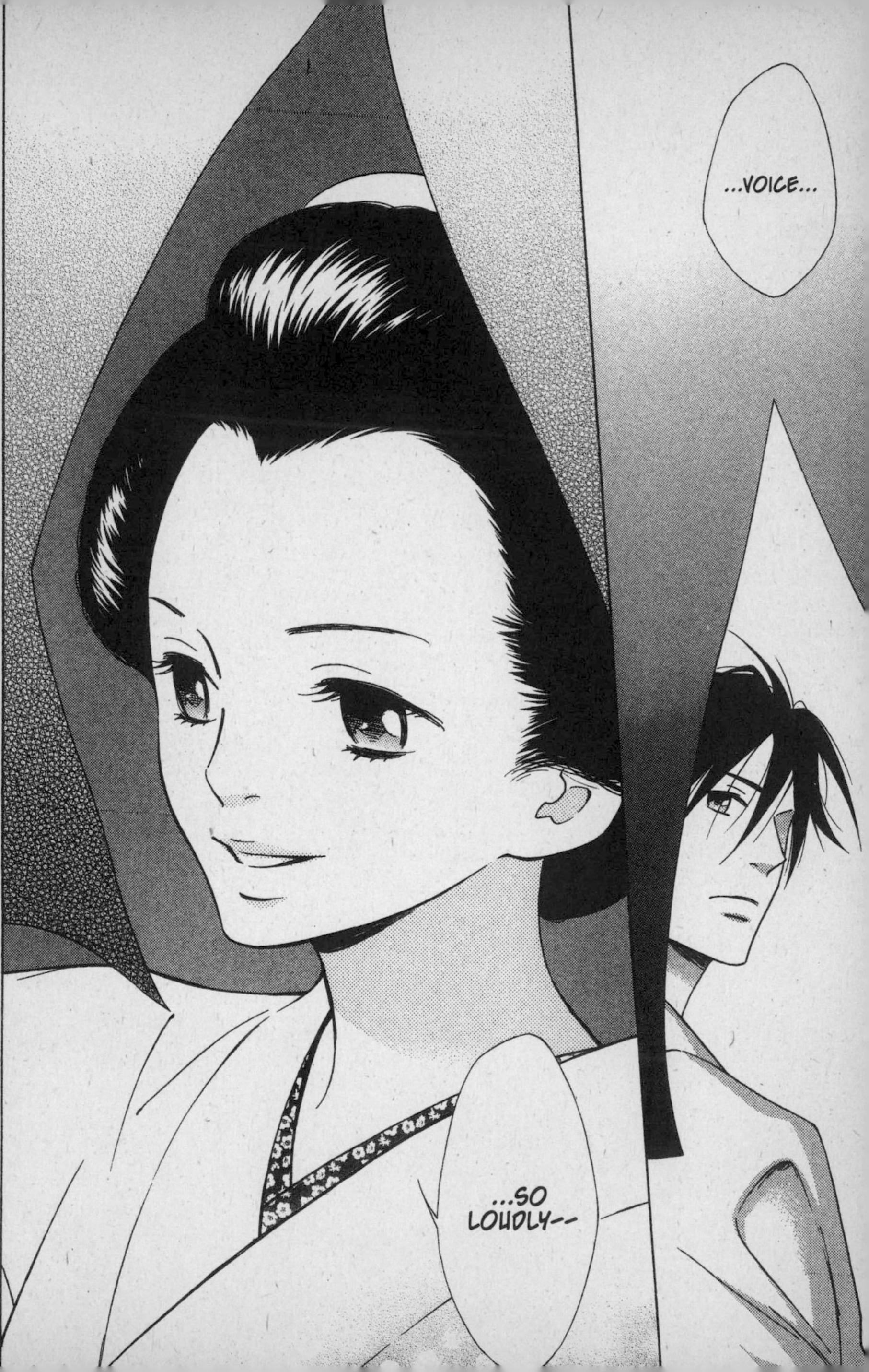
...VOICE...
...SO LOUDLY--

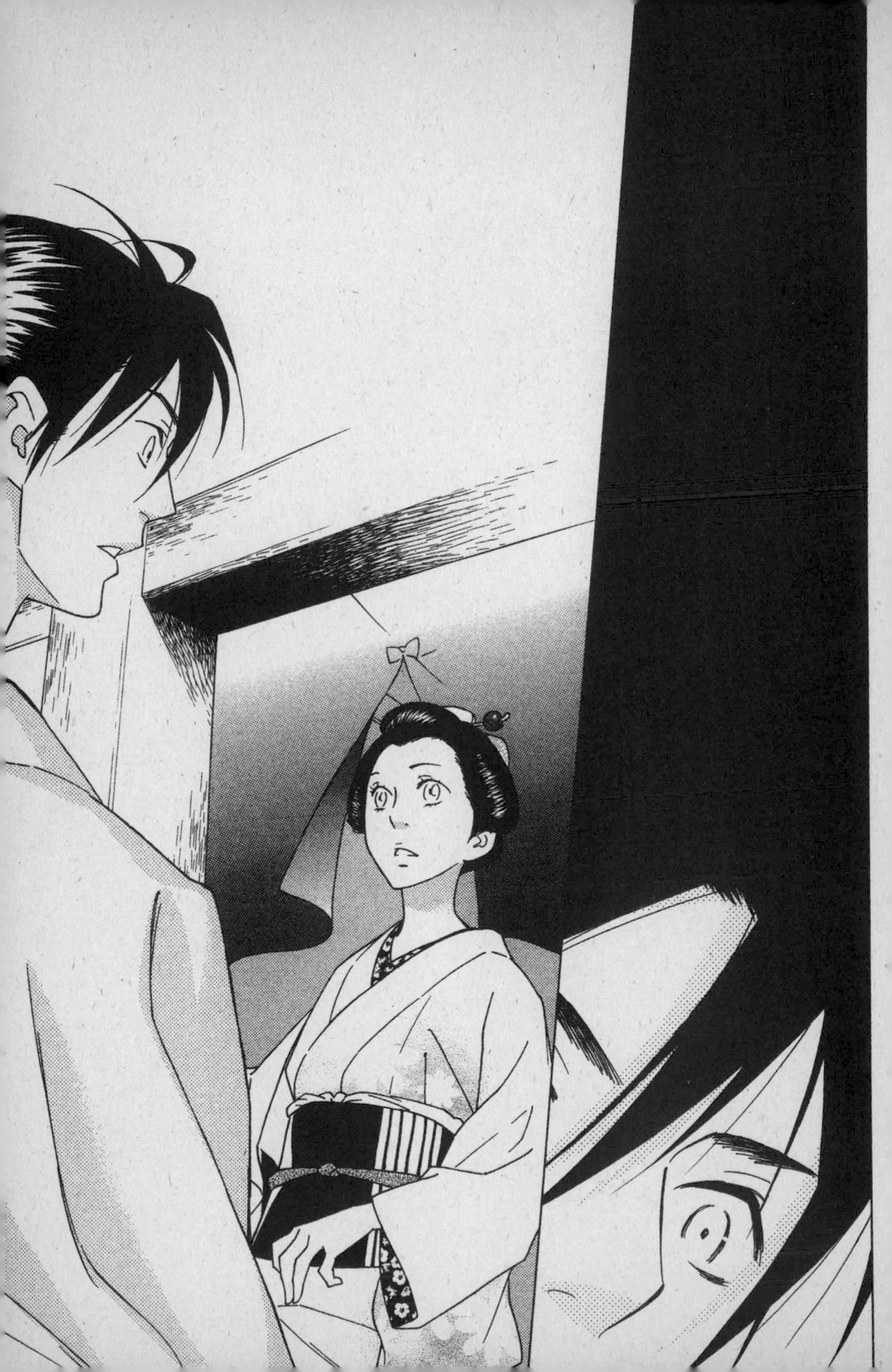

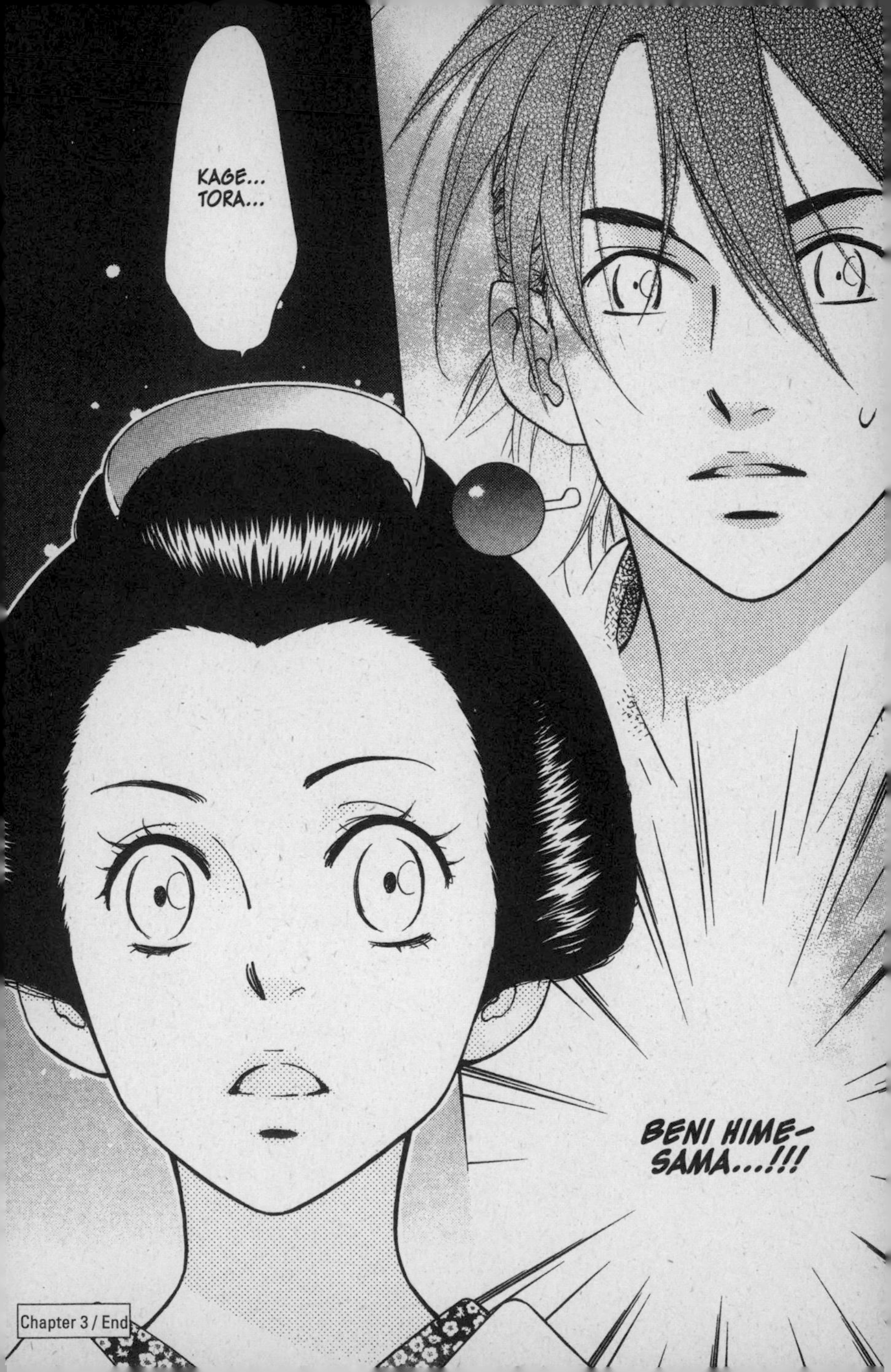
BENI HIME-
SAMA...!!!
KAGE...
TORA...
Chapter 3 / End

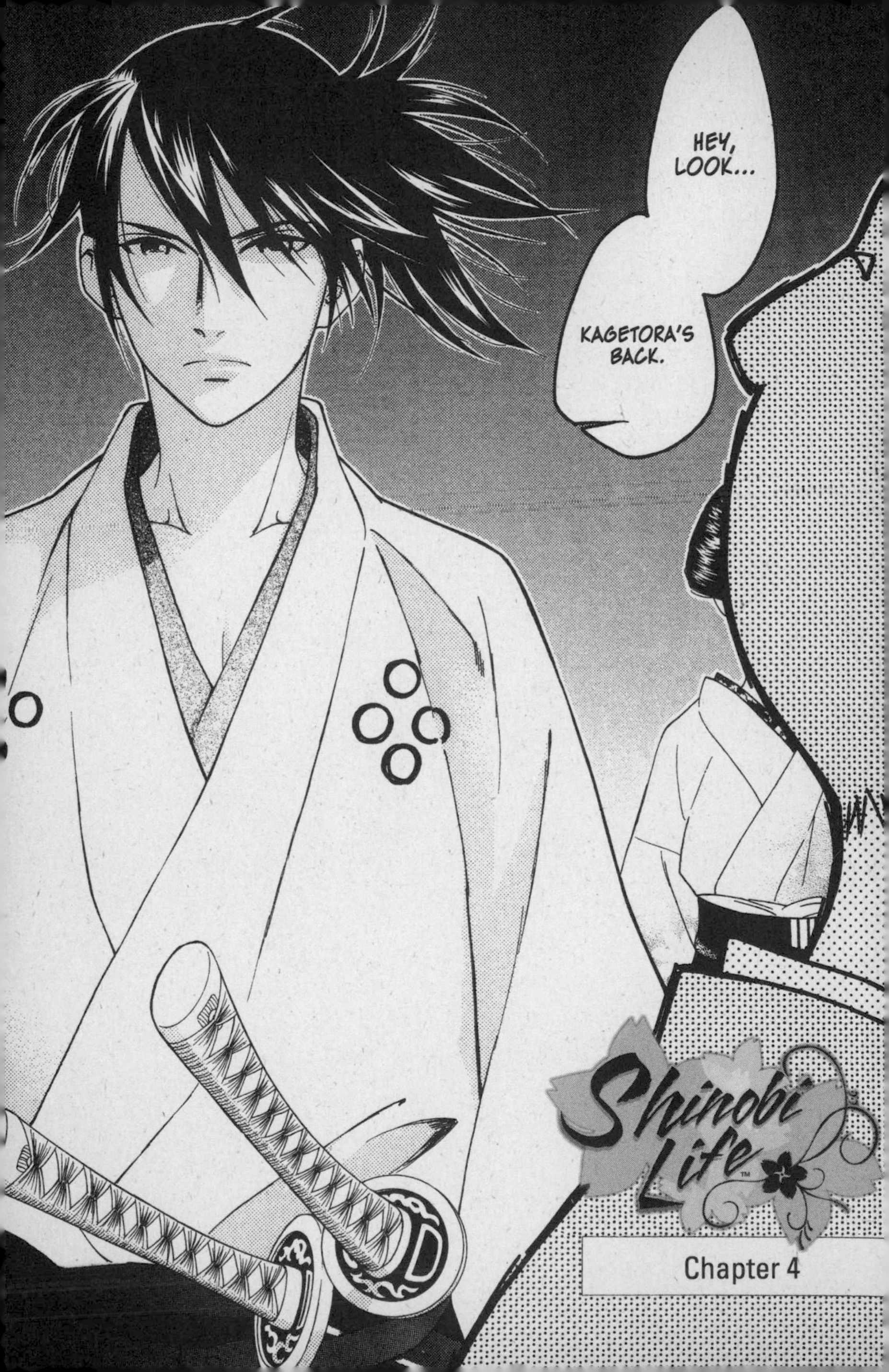
HEY, LOOK...
KAGETORA'S BACK.
Shinobi Life™
Chapter 4

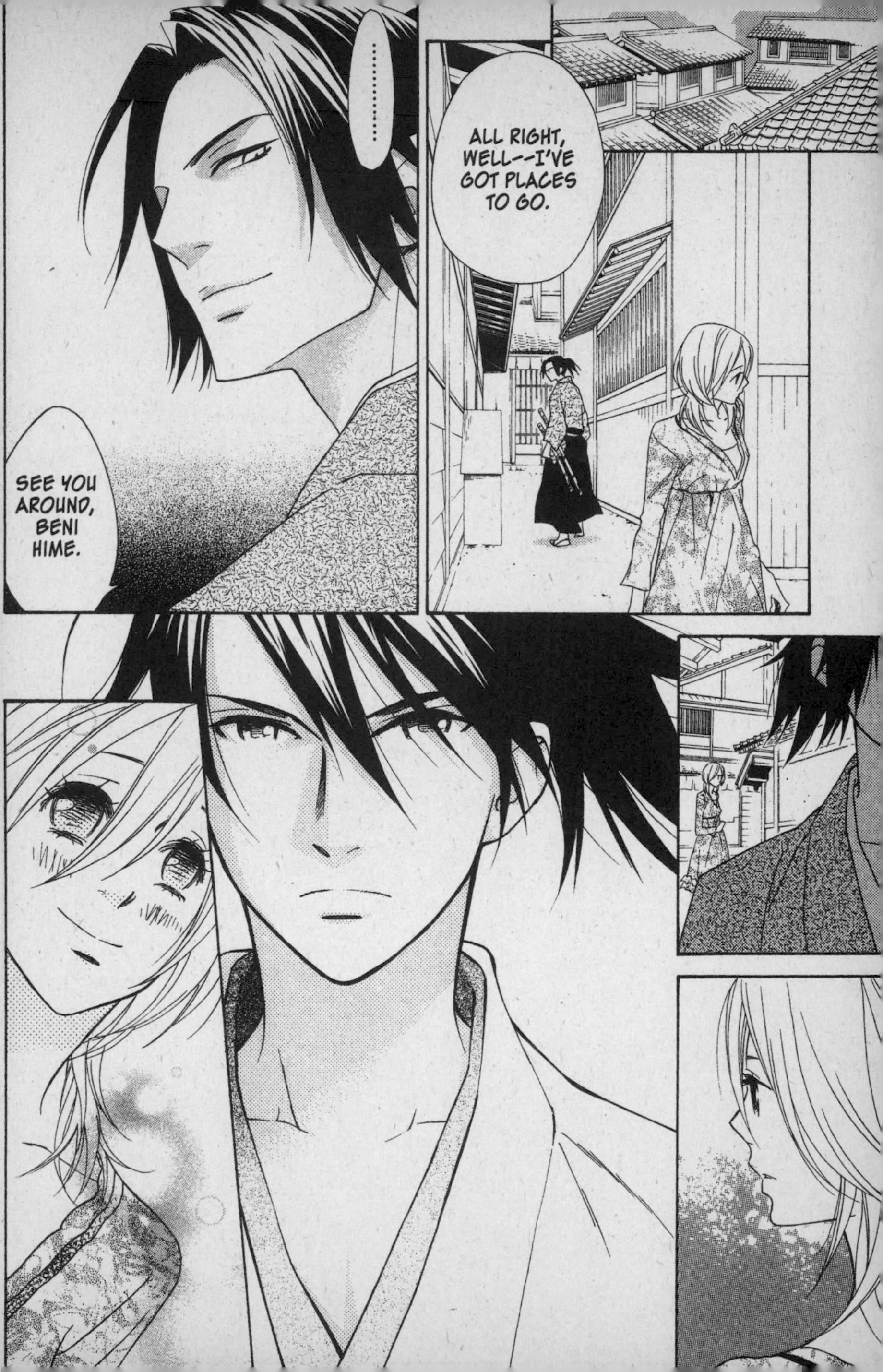
ALL RIGHT, WELL--I'VE GOT PLACES TO GO.
......
SEE YOU AROUND, BENI HIME.

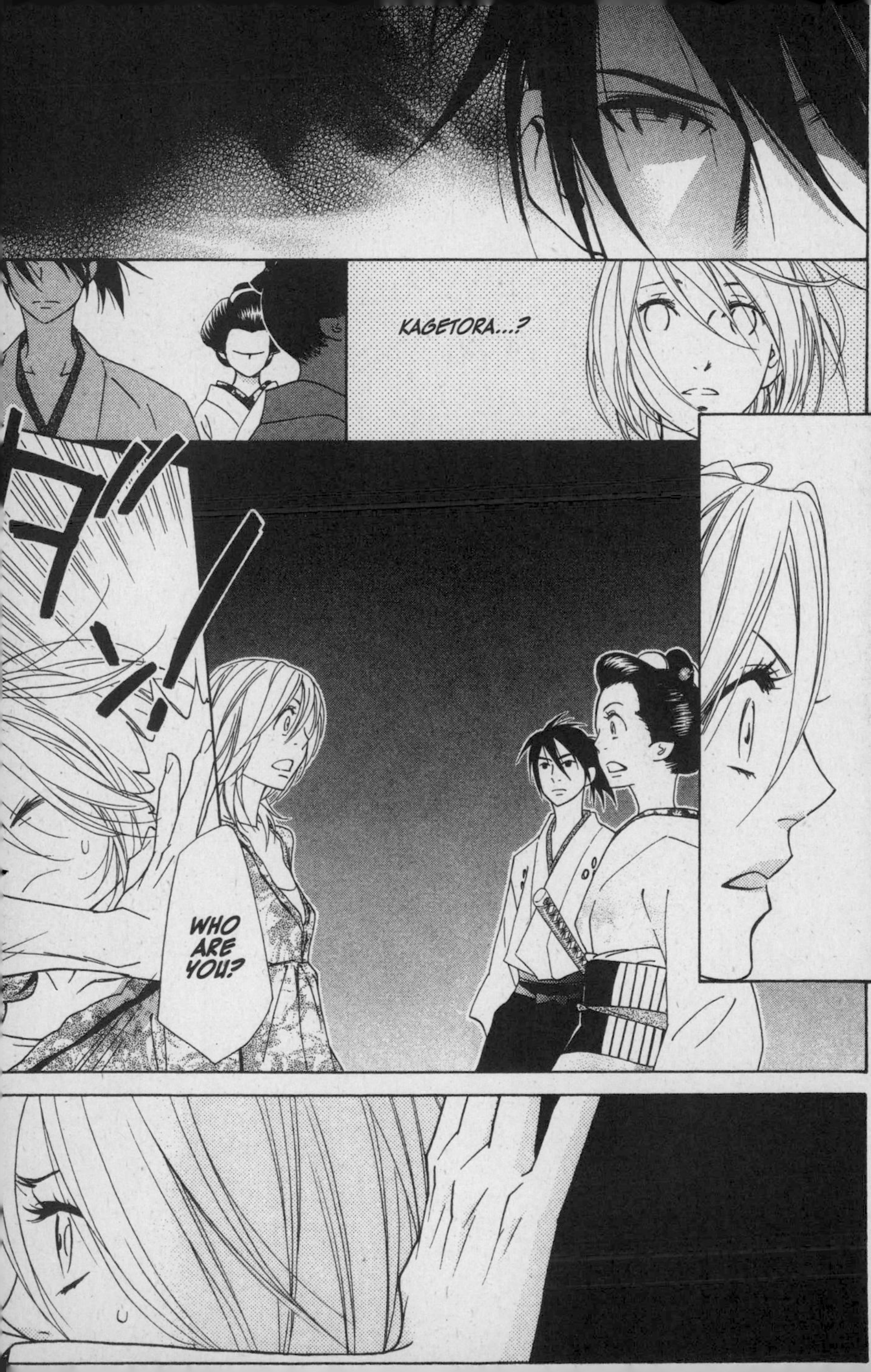
KAGETORA...?
WHO ARE YOU?

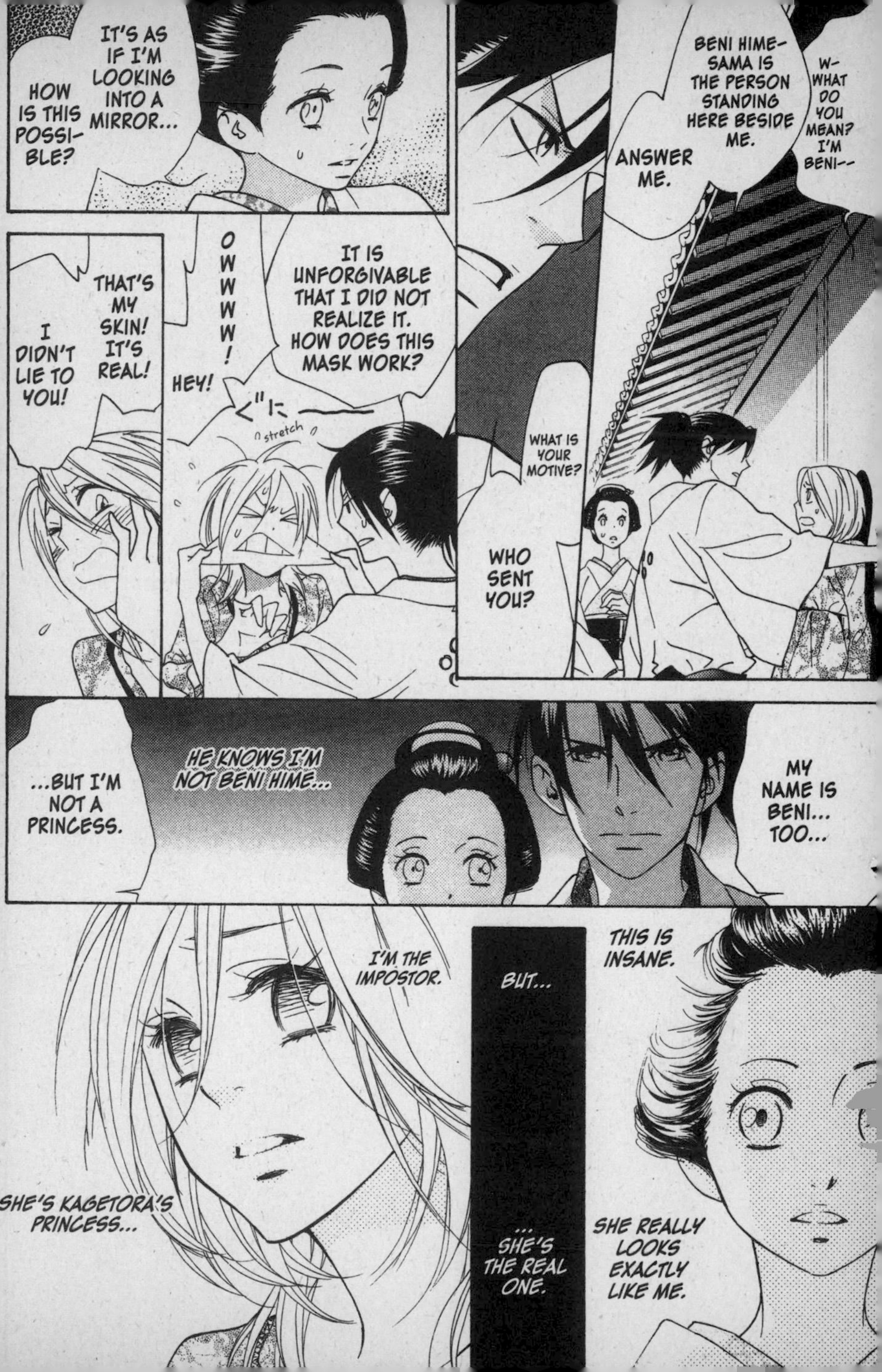
W-WHAT DO YOU MEAN? I'M BENI--
BENI HIME-SAMA IS THE PERSON STANDING HERE BESIDE ME.
ANSWER ME.
WHAT IS YOUR MOTIVE?
WHO SENT YOU?
IT'S AS IF I'M LOOKING INTO A MIRROR...
HOW IS THIS POSSIBLE?
IT IS UNFORGIVABLE THAT I DID NOT REALIZE IT. HOW DOES THIS MASK WORK?
OWWWWW!
HEY!
ぐに——
stretch
THAT'S MY SKIN! IT'S REAL!
I DIDN'T LIE TO YOU!
MY NAME IS BENI... TOO...
HE KNOWS I'M NOT BENI HIME...
...BUT I'M NOT A PRINCESS.
THIS IS INSANE.
SHE REALLY LOOKS EXACTLY LIKE ME.
BUT...
...SHE'S THE REAL ONE.
I'M THE IMPOSTOR.
SHE'S KAGETORA'S PRINCESS...

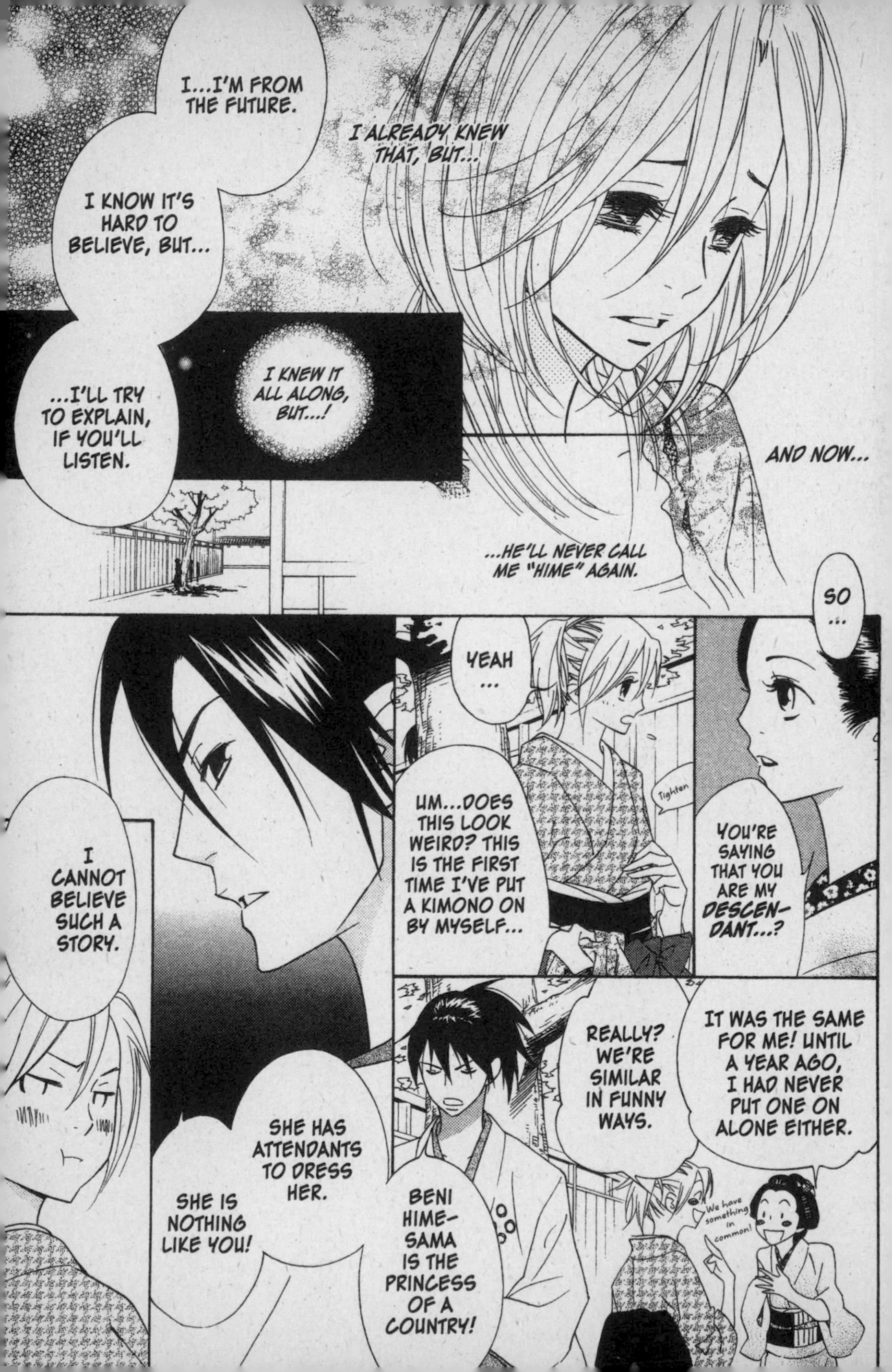

I...I'M FROM THE FUTURE.
I ALREADY KNEW THAT, BUT...
I KNOW IT'S HARD TO BELIEVE, BUT...
...I'LL TRY TO EXPLAIN, IF YOU'LL LISTEN.
I KNEW IT ALL ALONG, BUT...!
AND NOW...
...HE'LL NEVER CALL ME "HIME" AGAIN.
SO ...
YOU'RE SAYING THAT YOU ARE MY DESCENDANT...?
YEAH ...
Tighten
UM...DOES THIS LOOK WEIRD? THIS IS THE FIRST TIME I'VE PUT A KIMONO ON BY MYSELF...
IT WAS THE SAME FOR ME! UNTIL A YEAR AGO, I HAD NEVER PUT ONE ON ALONE EITHER.
REALLY? WE'RE SIMILAR IN FUNNY WAYS.
We have something in common!
BENI HIME-SAMA IS THE PRINCESS OF A COUNTRY!
SHE HAS ATTENDANTS TO DRESS HER.
SHE IS NOTHING LIKE YOU!
I CANNOT BELIEVE SUCH A STORY.

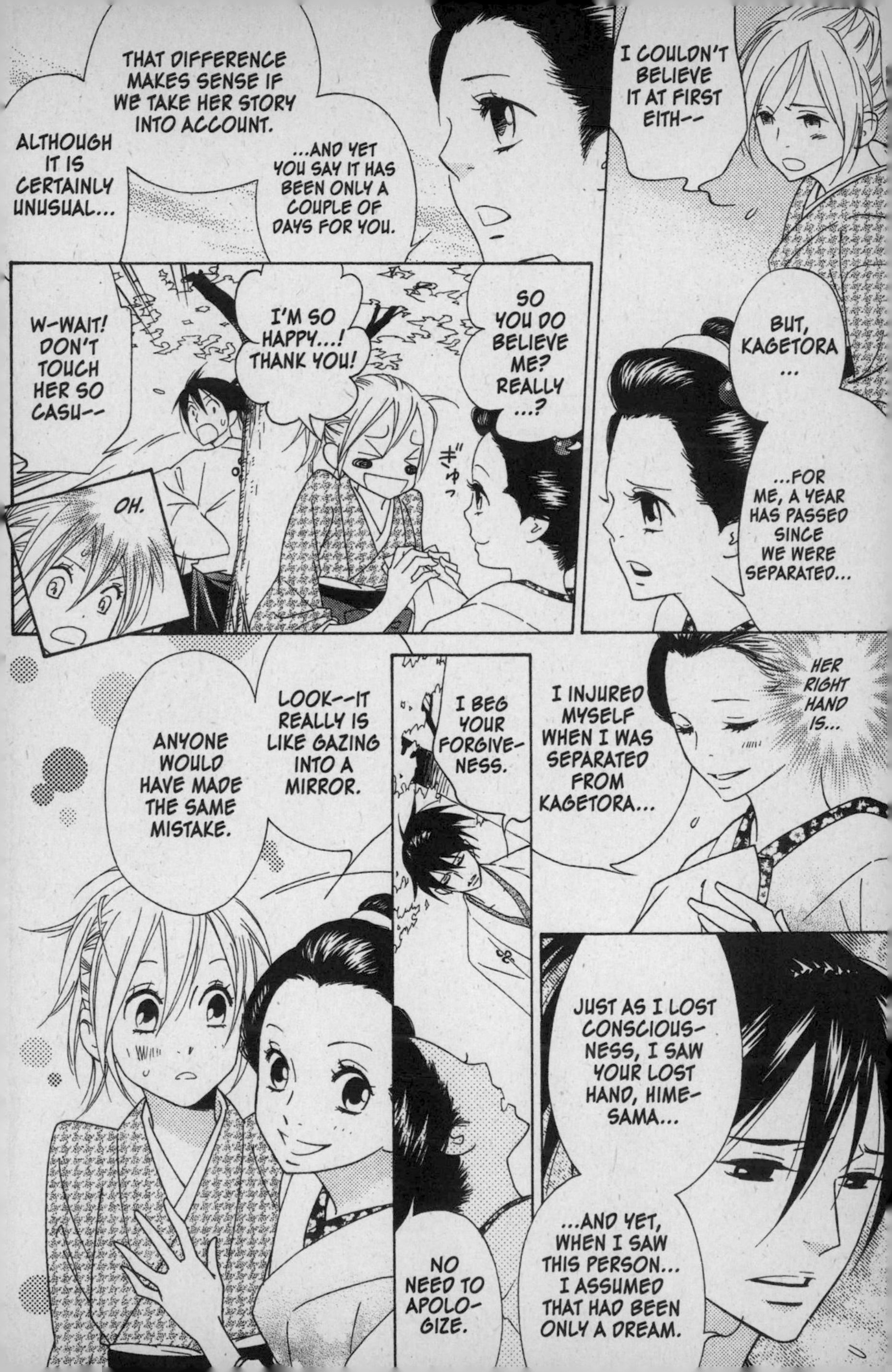
BUT, KAGETORA...
...FOR ME, A YEAR HAS PASSED SINCE WE WERE SEPARATED...
...AND YET YOU SAY IT HAS BEEN ONLY A COUPLE OF DAYS FOR YOU.
ALTHOUGH IT IS CERTAINLY UNUSUAL...
THAT DIFFERENCE MAKES SENSE IF WE TAKE HER STORY INTO ACCOUNT.
I COULDN'T BELIEVE IT AT FIRST EITH--
SO YOU DO BELIEVE ME? REALLY...?
ぎゅっ
I'M SO HAPPY...! THANK YOU!
W-WAIT! DON'T TOUCH HER SO CASU--
OH.
HER RIGHT HAND IS...
I INJURED MYSELF WHEN I WAS SEPARATED FROM KAGETORA...
JUST AS I LOST CONSCIOUS-NESS, I SAW YOUR LOST HAND, HIME-SAMA...
...AND YET, WHEN I SAW THIS PERSON... I ASSUMED THAT HAD BEEN ONLY A DREAM.
I BEG YOUR FORGIVE-NESS.
NO NEED TO APOLO-GIZE.
LOOK--IT REALLY IS LIKE GAZING INTO A MIRROR.
ANYONE WOULD HAVE MADE THE SAME MISTAKE.

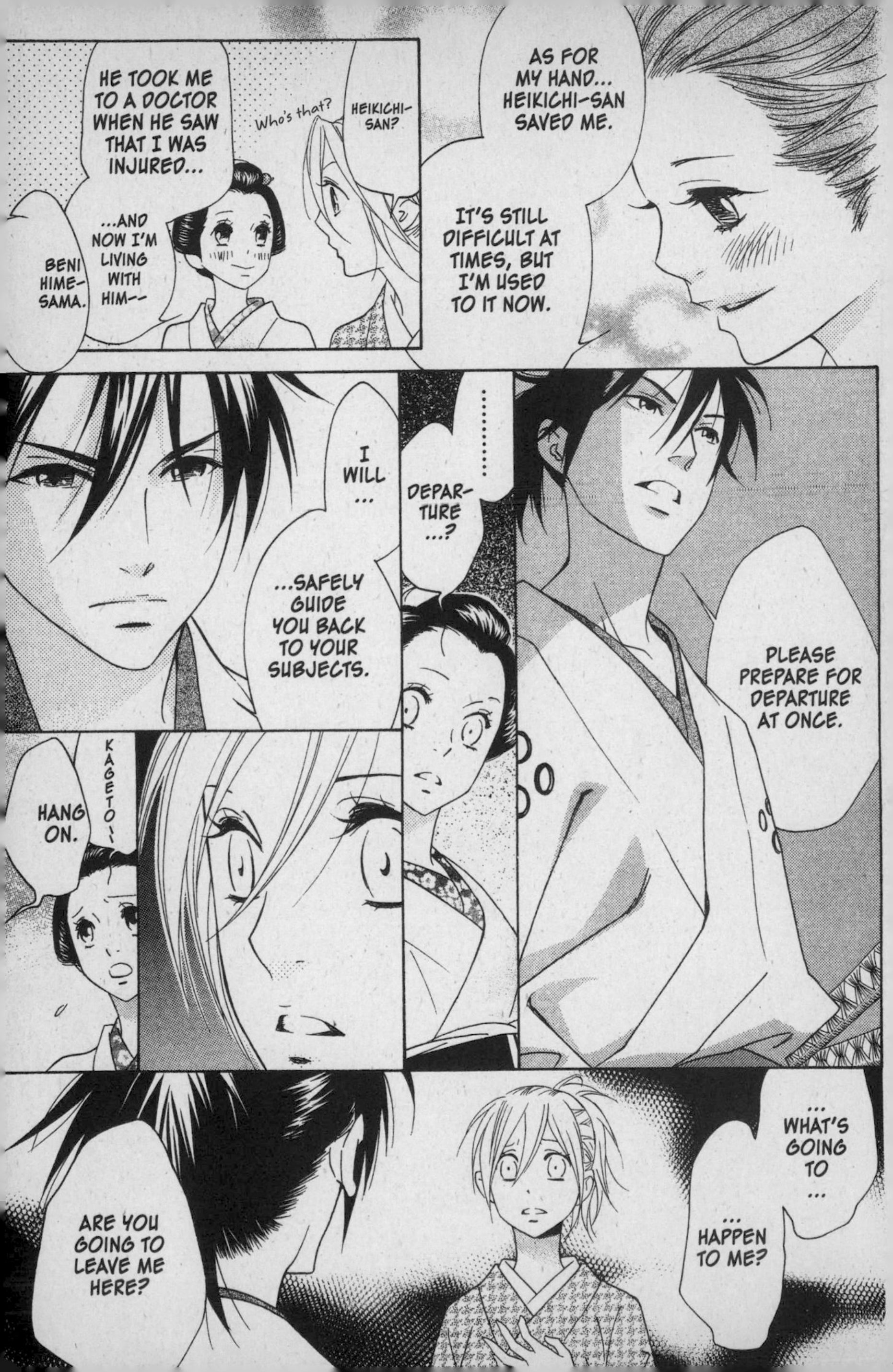
AS FOR MY HAND... HEIKICHI-SAN SAVED ME.
IT'S STILL DIFFICULT AT TIMES, BUT I'M USED TO IT NOW.
HEIKICHI-SAN?
Who's that?
HE TOOK ME TO A DOCTOR WHEN HE SAW THAT I WAS INJURED...
...AND NOW I'M LIVING WITH HIM--
BENI HIME-SAMA.
PLEASE PREPARE FOR DEPARTURE AT ONCE.
......
DEPARTURE...?
I WILL...
...SAFELY GUIDE YOU BACK TO YOUR SUBJECTS.
KAGETO!!
HANG ON.
...WHAT'S GOING TO...
...HAPPEN TO ME?
ARE YOU GOING TO LEAVE ME HERE?

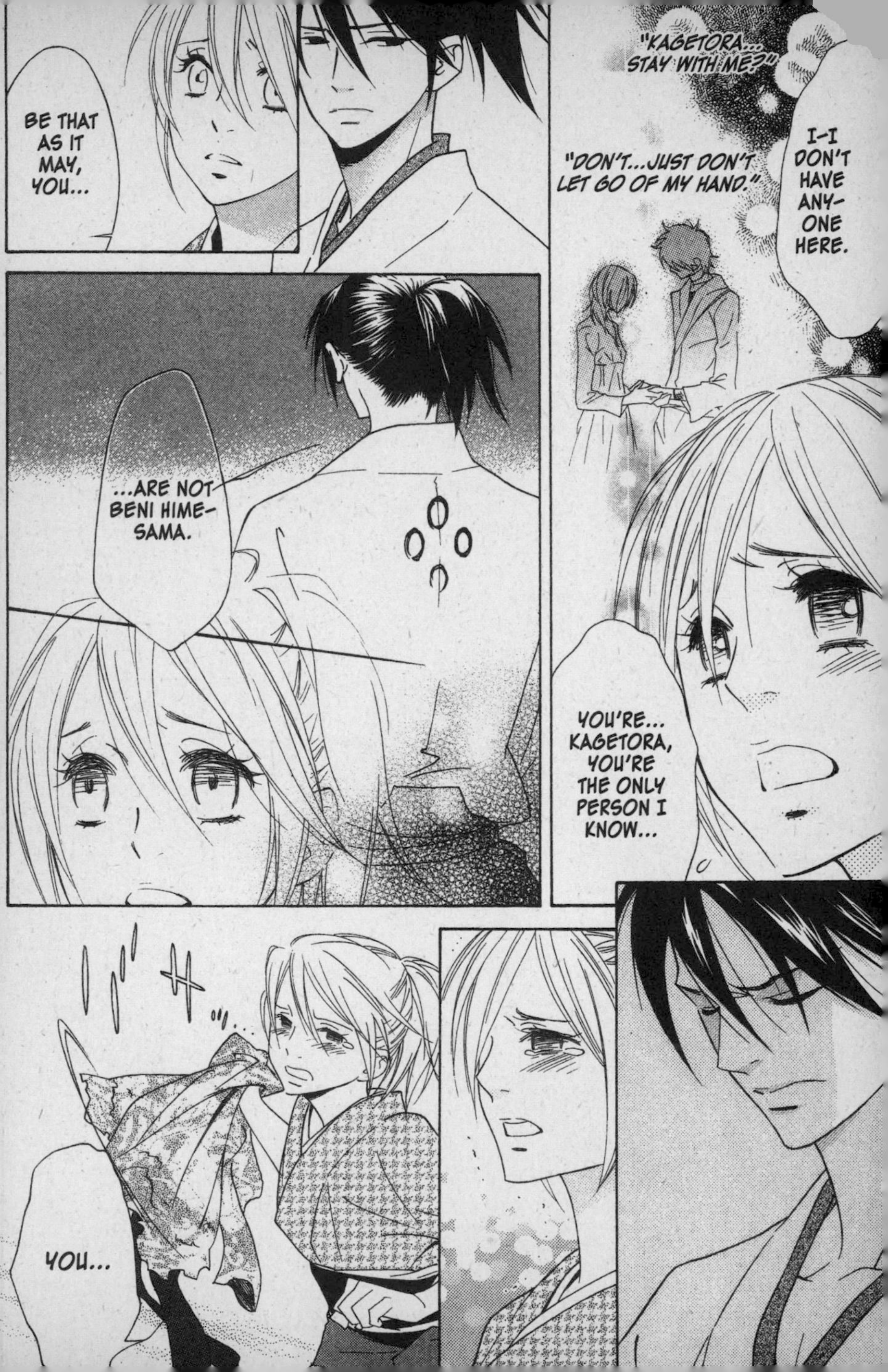
"KAGETORA... STAY WITH ME?"
"DON'T...JUST DON'T LET GO OF MY HAND."
I-I DON'T HAVE ANY-ONE HERE.
YOU'RE... KAGETORA, YOU'RE THE ONLY PERSON I KNOW...
BE THAT AS IT MAY, YOU...
...ARE NOT BENI HIME-SAMA.
YOU...

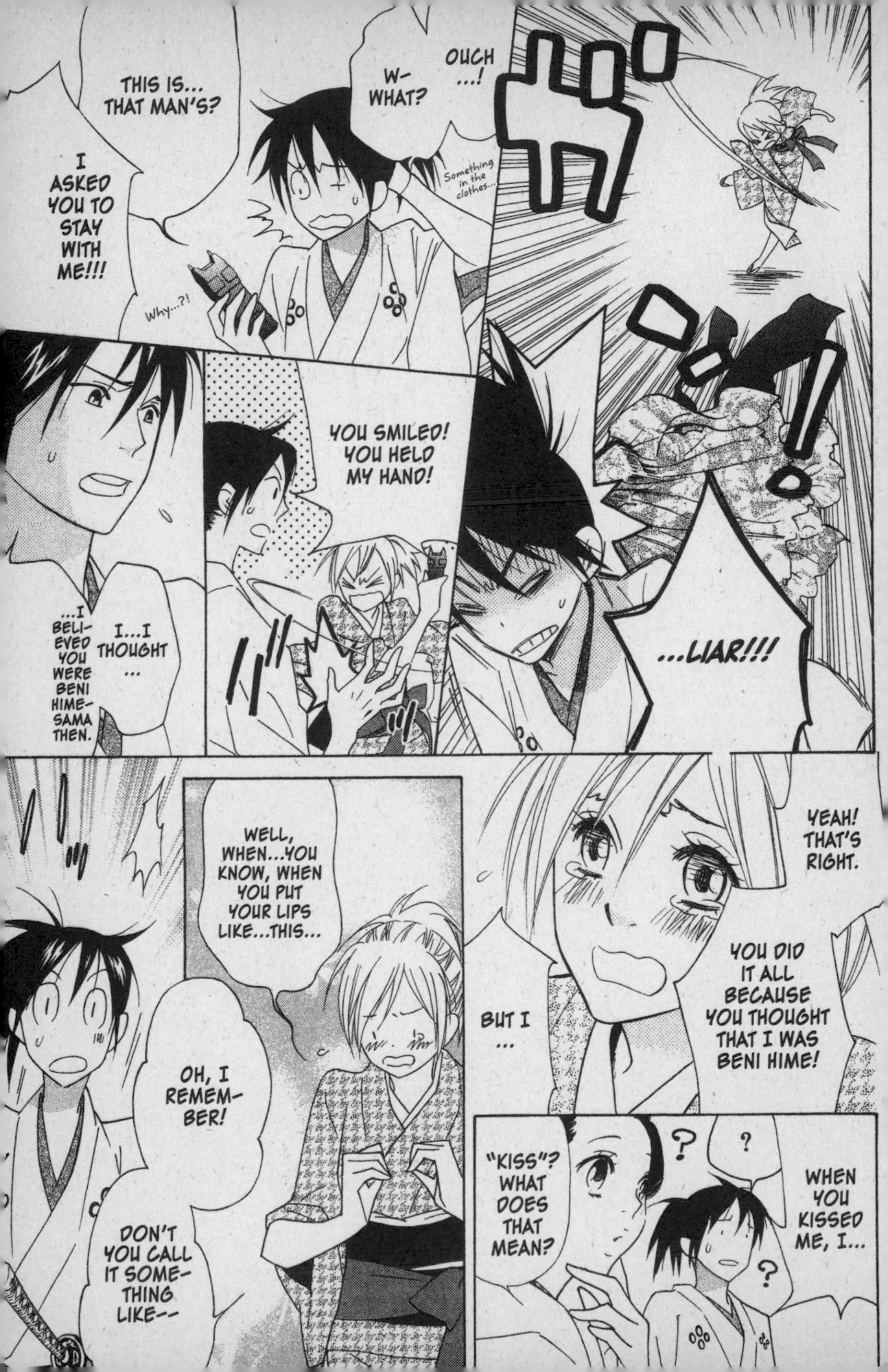
OUCH ...!
W- WHAT?
Something in the clothes...
THIS IS... THAT MAN'S?
I ASKED YOU TO STAY WITH ME!!!
Why...?!
...LIAR!!!
YOU SMILED! YOU HELD MY HAND!
I...I THOUGHT ...
...I BELIEVED YOU WERE BENI HIME-SAMA THEN.
YEAH! THAT'S RIGHT.
YOU DID IT ALL BECAUSE YOU THOUGHT THAT I WAS BENI HIME!
BUT I ...
WHEN YOU KISSED ME, I...
"KISS"? WHAT DOES THAT MEAN?
WELL, WHEN...YOU KNOW, WHEN YOU PUT YOUR LIPS LIKE...THIS...
OH, I REMEMBER!
DON'T YOU CALL IT SOMETHING LIKE--

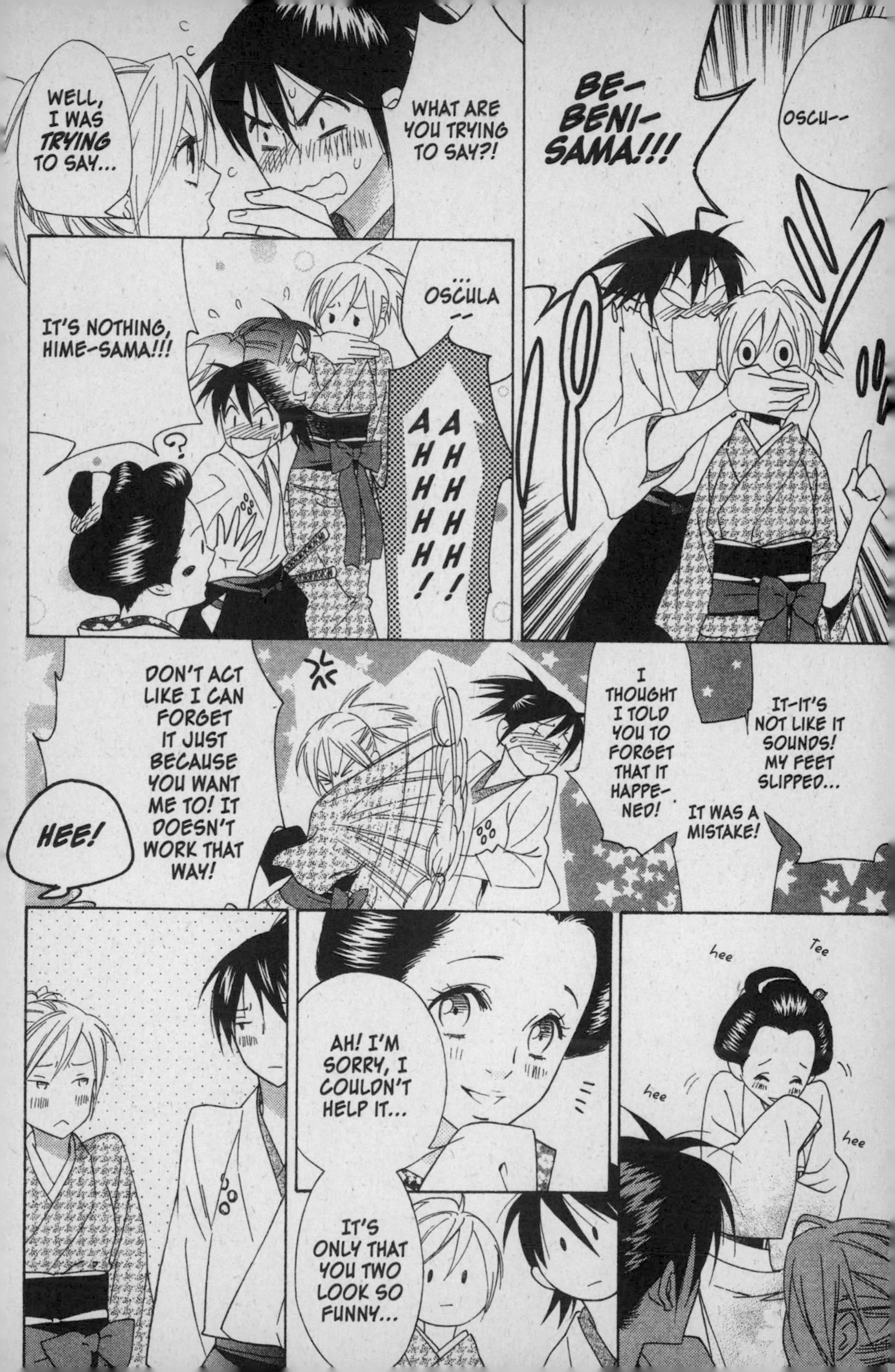
OSCU--
BE-BENI-SAMA!!!
WHAT ARE YOU TRYING TO SAY?!
WELL, I WAS TRYING TO SAY...
...OSCULA--
AHHHHH!
AHHHHH!
IT'S NOTHING, HIME-SAMA!!!
?
IT-IT'S NOT LIKE IT SOUNDS! MY FEET SLIPPED...
IT WAS A MISTAKE!
I THOUGHT I TOLD YOU TO FORGET THAT IT HAPPENED!
DON'T ACT LIKE I CAN FORGET IT JUST BECAUSE YOU WANT ME TO! IT DOESN'T WORK THAT WAY!
HEE!
Tee
hee
hee
hee
AH! I'M SORRY, I COULDN'T HELP IT...
IT'S ONLY THAT YOU TWO LOOK SO FUNNY...

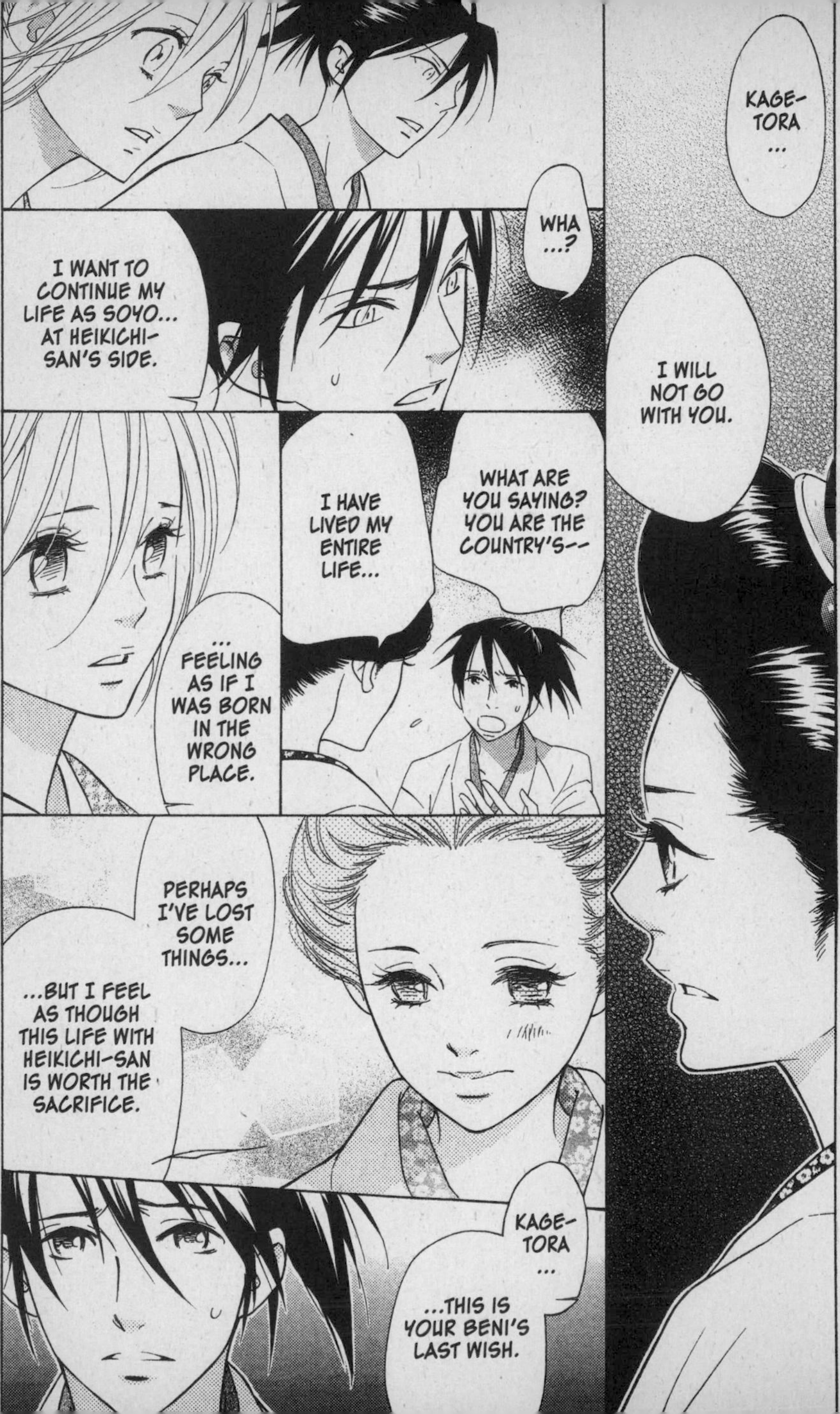
KAGE-TORA ...
I WILL NOT GO WITH YOU.
WHA ...?
I WANT TO CONTINUE MY LIFE AS SOYO... AT HEIKICHI-SAN'S SIDE.
WHAT ARE YOU SAYING? YOU ARE THE COUNTRY'S--
I HAVE LIVED MY ENTIRE LIFE...
... FEELING AS IF I WAS BORN IN THE WRONG PLACE.
PERHAPS I'VE LOST SOME THINGS...
...BUT I FEEL AS THOUGH THIS LIFE WITH HEIKICHI-SAN IS WORTH THE SACRIFICE.
KAGE-TORA ...
...THIS IS YOUR BENI'S LAST WISH.

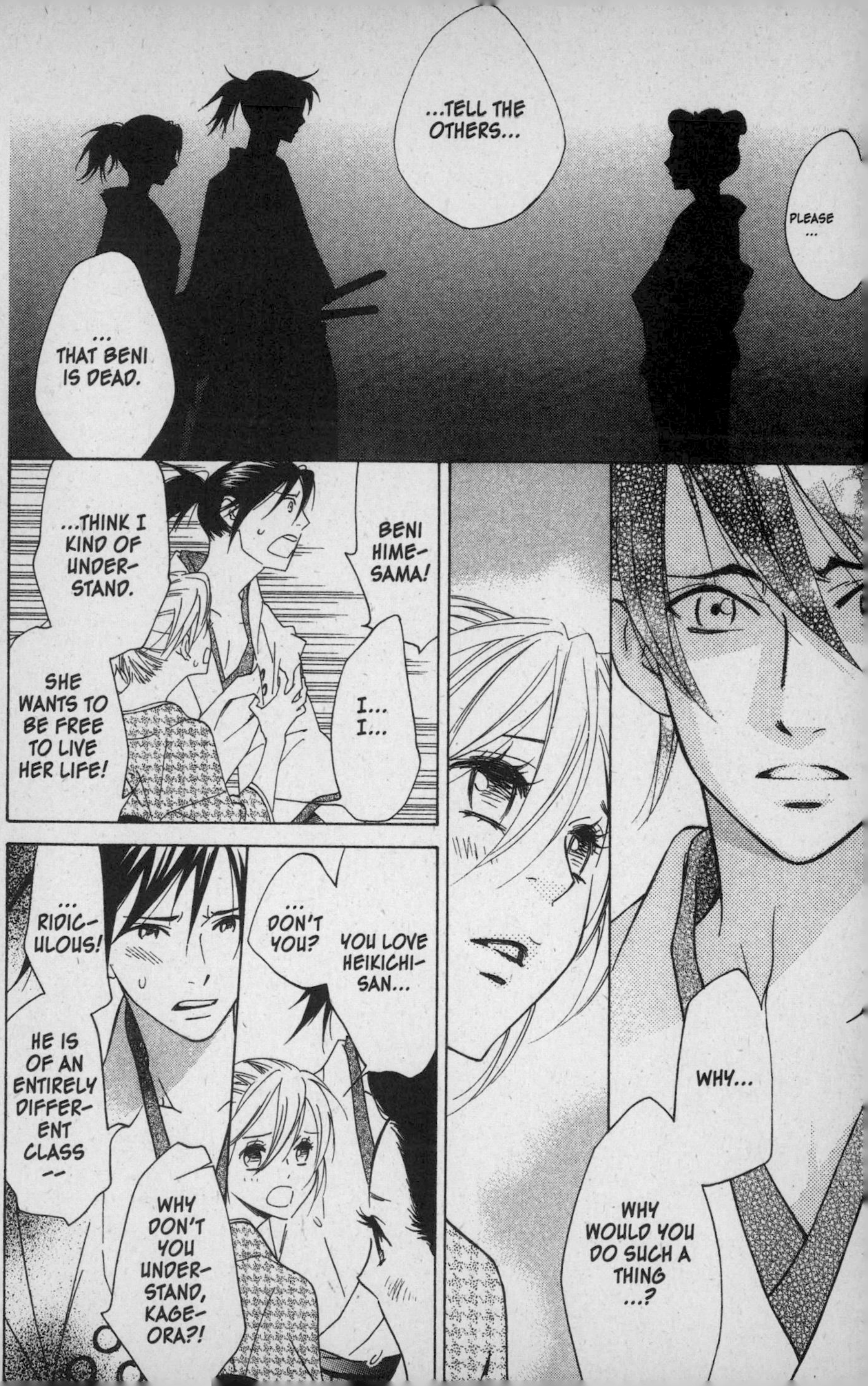
PLEASE ...
...TELL THE OTHERS...
... THAT BENI IS DEAD.
WHY...
WHY WOULD YOU DO SUCH A THING ...?
BENI HIME-SAMA!
I... I...
...THINK I KIND OF UNDER-STAND.
SHE WANTS TO BE FREE TO LIVE HER LIFE!
YOU LOVE HEIKICHI-SAN...
... DON'T YOU?
... RIDIC-ULOUS!
HE IS OF AN ENTIRELY DIFFER-ENT CLASS --
WHY DON'T YOU UNDER-STAND, KAGE-ORA?!

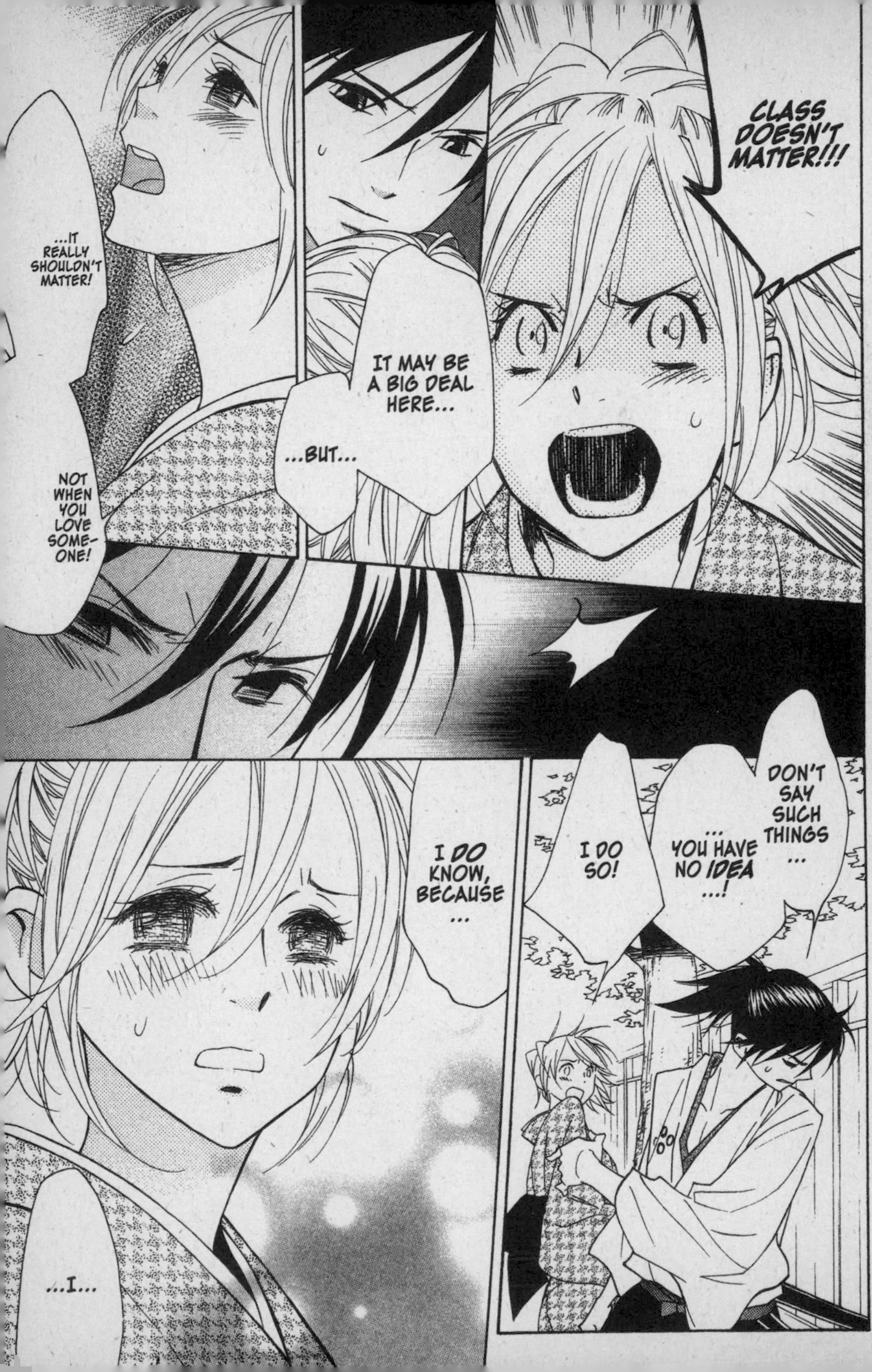
CLASS DOESN'T MATTER!!!
IT MAY BE A BIG DEAL HERE...
...BUT...
...IT REALLY SHOULDN'T MATTER!
NOT WHEN YOU LOVE SOME-ONE!
DON'T SAY SUCH THINGS ...
... YOU HAVE NO IDEA ...!
I DO SO!
I DO KNOW, BECAUSE ...
...I...

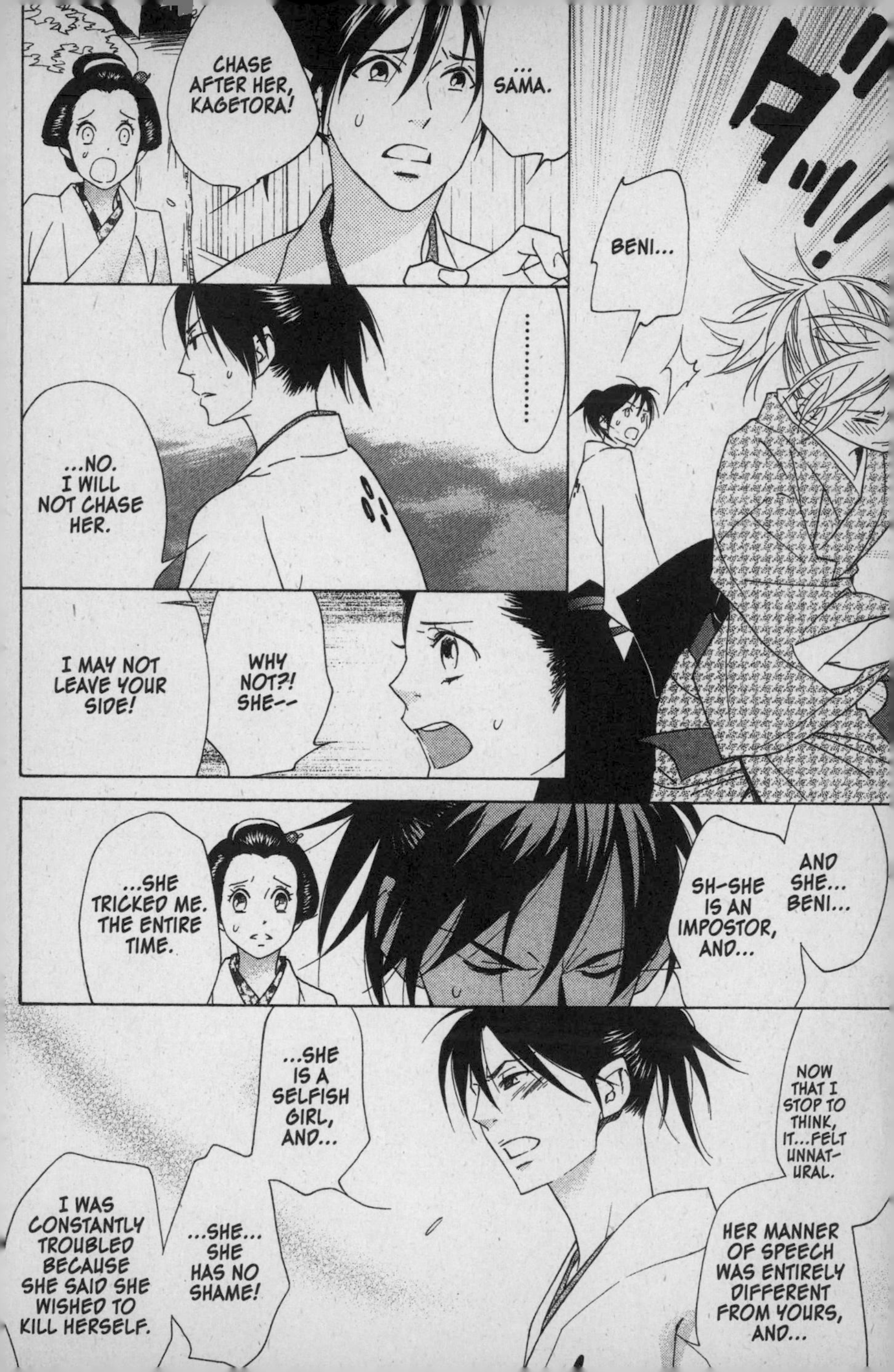
ダッ!!
BENI...
...SAMA.
CHASE AFTER HER, KAGETORA!
......
...NO. I WILL NOT CHASE HER.
WHY NOT?! SHE--
I MAY NOT LEAVE YOUR SIDE!
AND SHE... BENI...
SH-SHE IS AN IMPOSTOR, AND...
...SHE TRICKED ME. THE ENTIRE TIME.
NOW THAT I STOP TO THINK, IT...FELT UNNAT-URAL.
HER MANNER OF SPEECH WAS ENTIRELY DIFFERENT FROM YOURS, AND...
...SHE IS A SELFISH GIRL, AND...
...SHE... SHE HAS NO SHAME!
I WAS CONSTANTLY TROUBLED BECAUSE SHE SAID SHE WISHED TO KILL HERSELF.

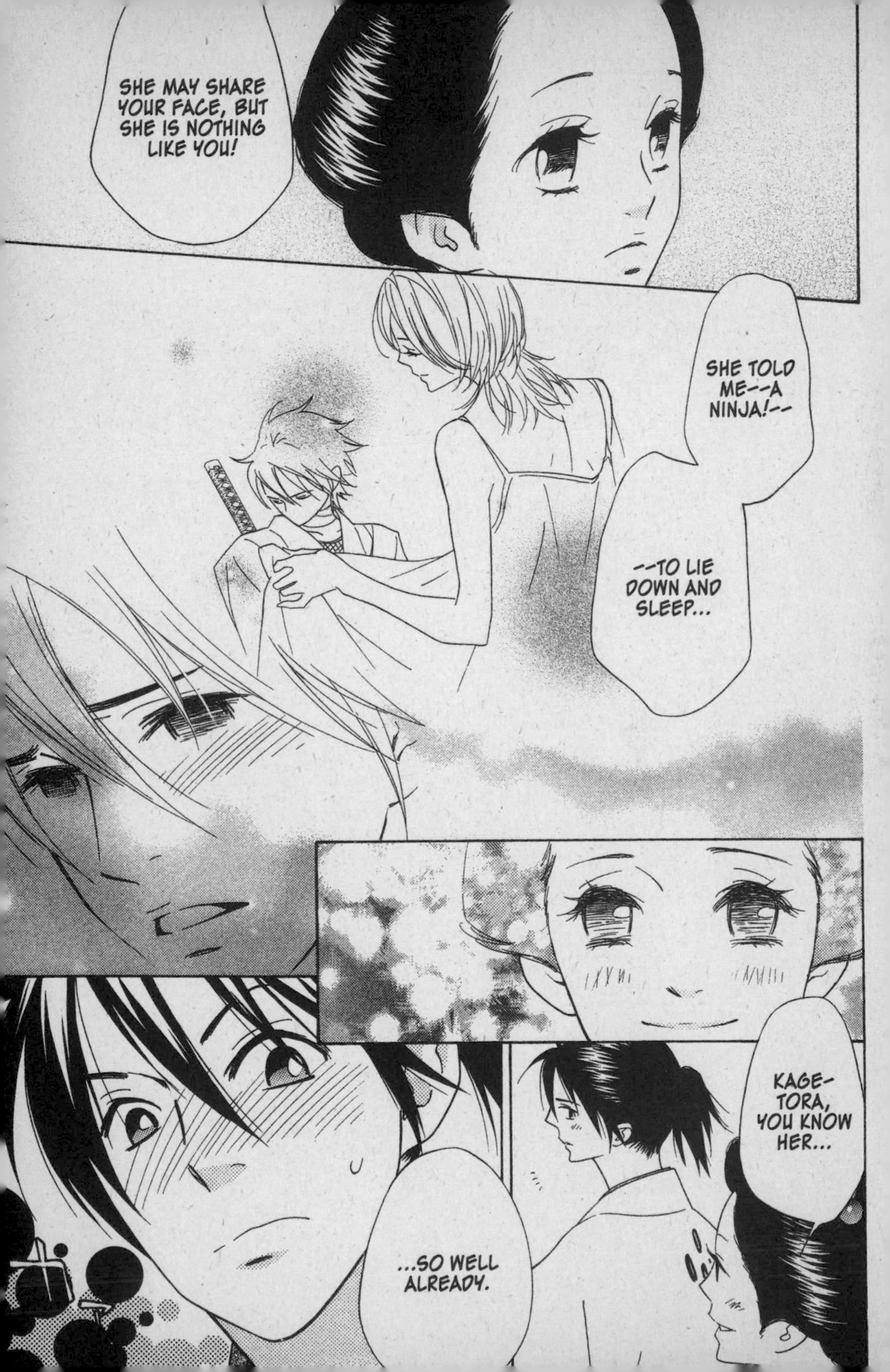
SHE MAY SHARE YOUR FACE, BUT SHE IS NOTHING LIKE YOU!
SHE TOLD ME--A NINJA!--
--TO LIE DOWN AND SLEEP...
KAGE-TORA, YOU KNOW HER...
...SO WELL ALREADY.

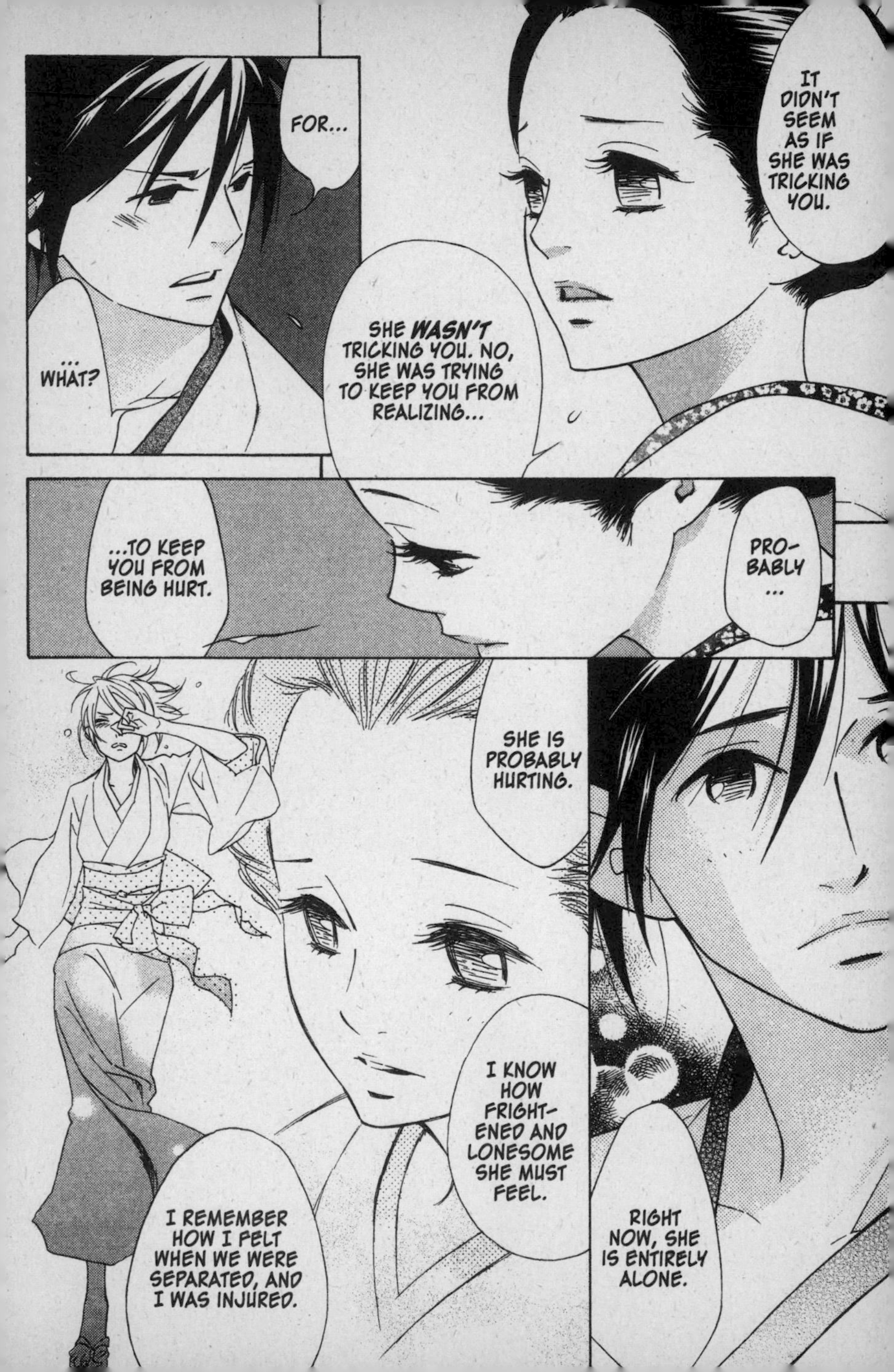
IT DIDN'T SEEM AS IF SHE WAS TRICKING YOU.
SHE *WASN'T* TRICKING YOU. NO, SHE WAS TRYING TO KEEP YOU FROM REALIZING...
FOR...
... WHAT?
PRO-BABLY ...
...TO KEEP YOU FROM BEING HURT.
RIGHT NOW, SHE IS ENTIRELY ALONE.
SHE IS PROBABLY HURTING.
I KNOW HOW FRIGHT-ENED AND LONESOME SHE MUST FEEL.
I REMEMBER HOW I FELT WHEN WE WERE SEPARATED, AND I WAS INJURED.

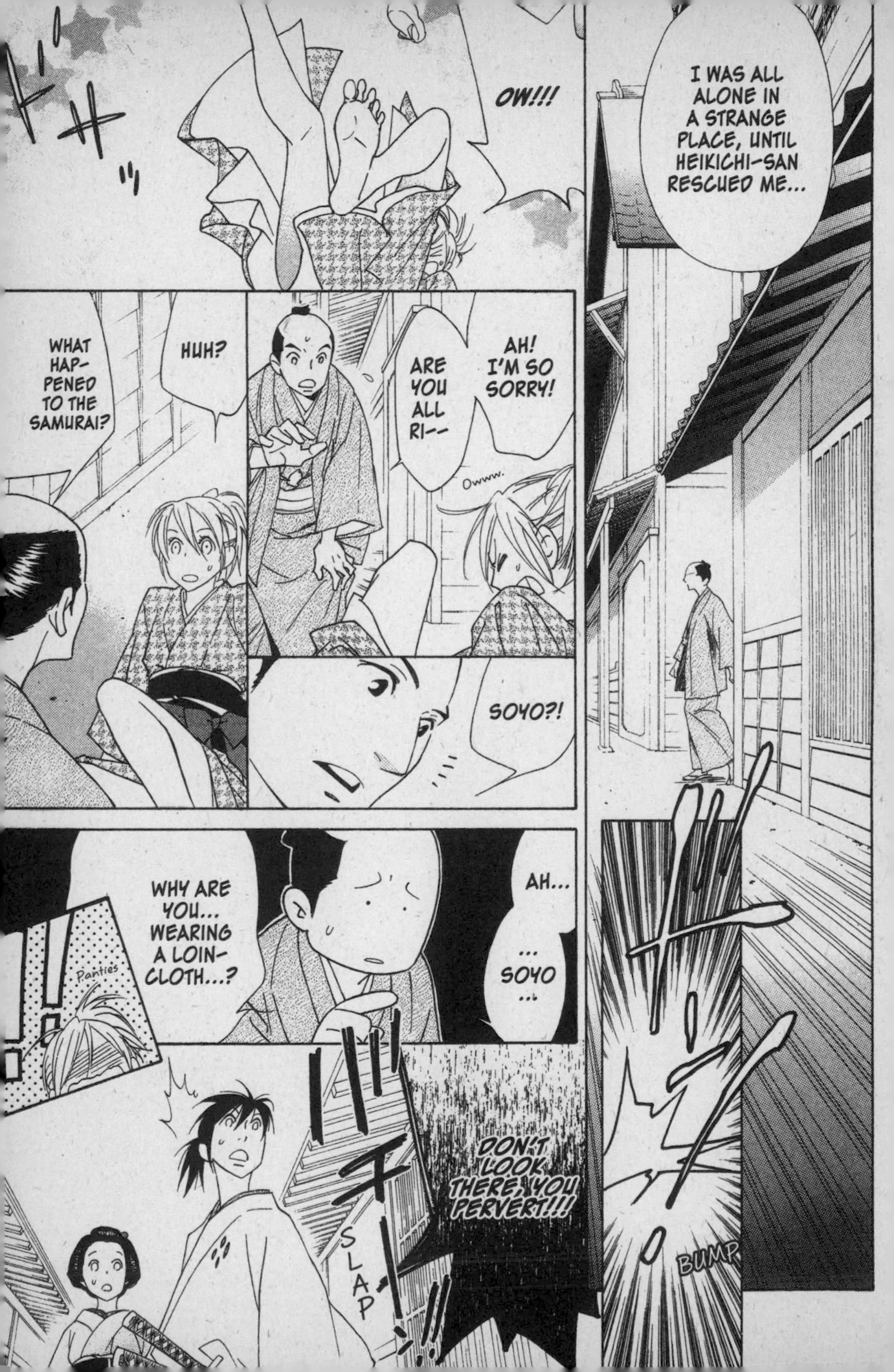
I WAS ALL ALONE IN A STRANGE PLACE, UNTIL HEIKICHI-SAN RESCUED ME...
BUMP
OW!!!
AH! I'M SO SORRY!
ARE YOU ALL RI--
Owww.
SOYO?!
HUH?
WHAT HAPPENED TO THE SAMURAI?
AH...
... SOYO ...
WHY ARE YOU... WEARING A LOIN-CLOTH...?
Panties
DON'T LOOK THERE, YOU PERVERT!!!
SLAP

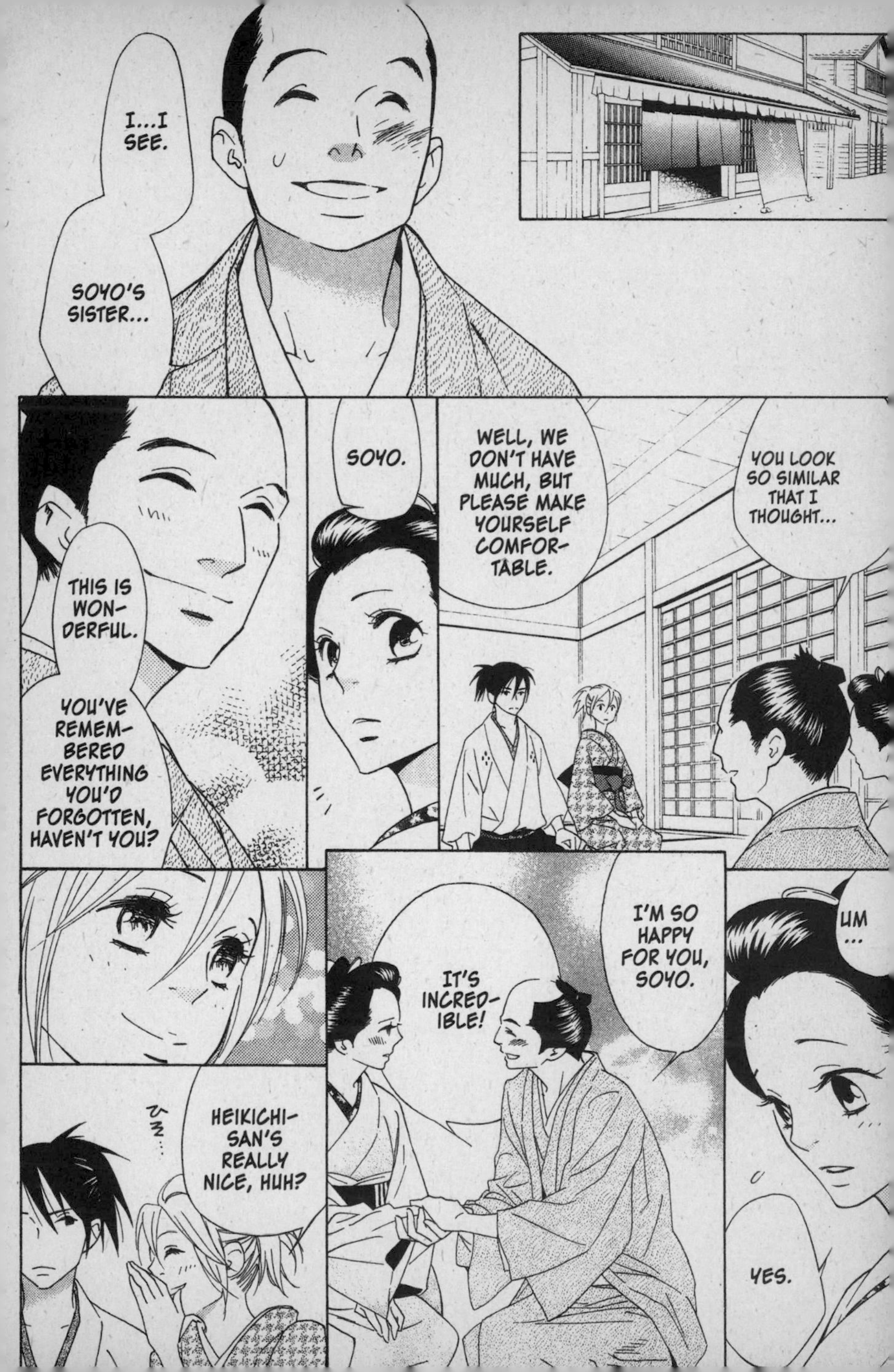
I...I SEE.
SOYO'S SISTER...
YOU LOOK SO SIMILAR THAT I THOUGHT...
WELL, WE DON'T HAVE MUCH, BUT PLEASE MAKE YOURSELF COMFORTABLE.
SOYO.
THIS IS WONDERFUL.
YOU'VE REMEMBERED EVERYTHING YOU'D FORGOTTEN, HAVEN'T YOU?
UM...
YES.
I'M SO HAPPY FOR YOU, SOYO.
IT'S INCREDIBLE!
HEIKICHI-SAN'S REALLY NICE, HUH?

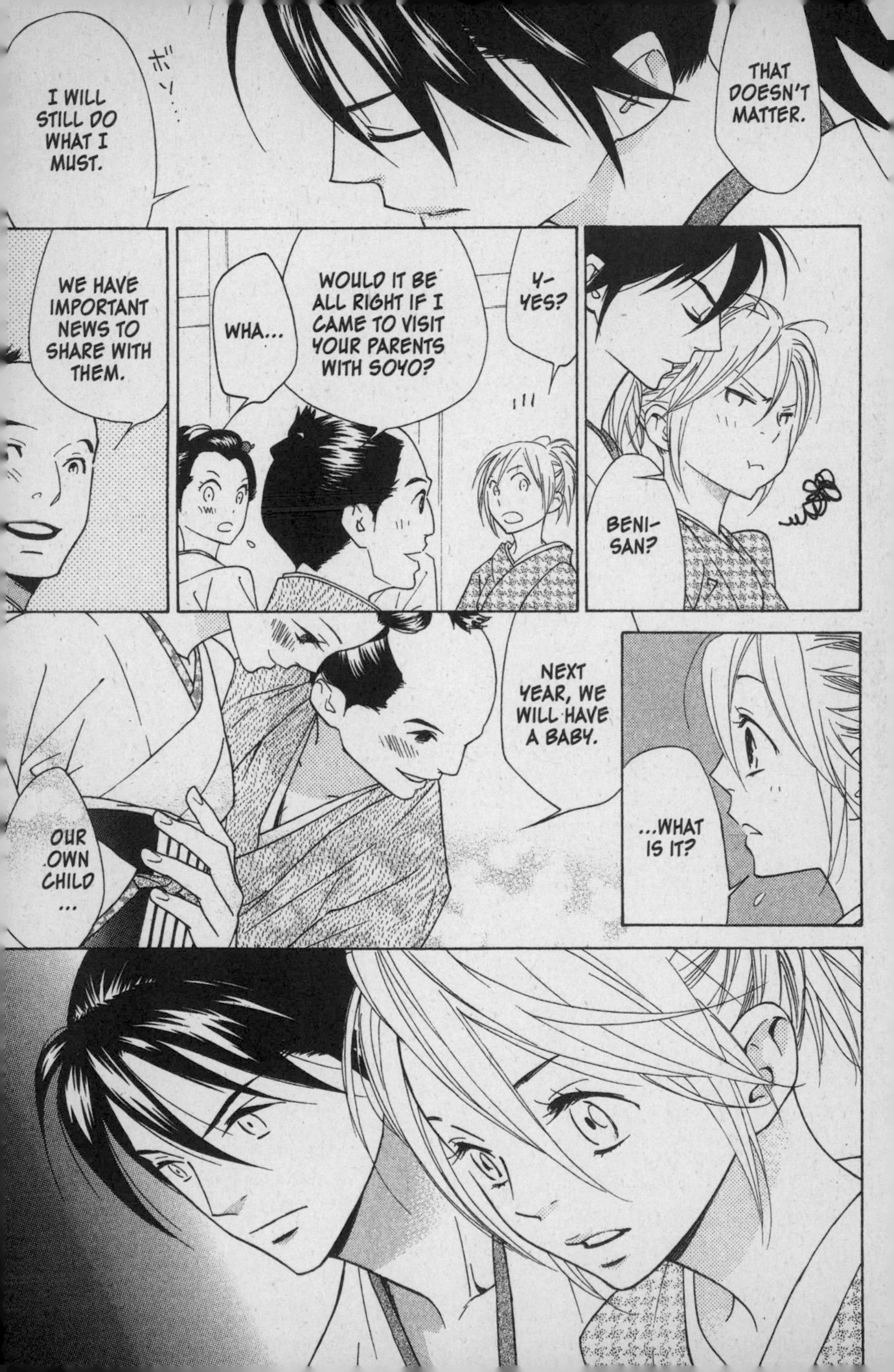
THAT DOESN'T MATTER.
ボソ…
I WILL STILL DO WHAT I MUST.
BENI-SAN?
Y-YES?
WOULD IT BE ALL RIGHT IF I CAME TO VISIT YOUR PARENTS WITH SOYO?
WHA...
WE HAVE IMPORTANT NEWS TO SHARE WITH THEM.
...WHAT IS IT?
NEXT YEAR, WE WILL HAVE A BABY.
OUR OWN CHILD ...

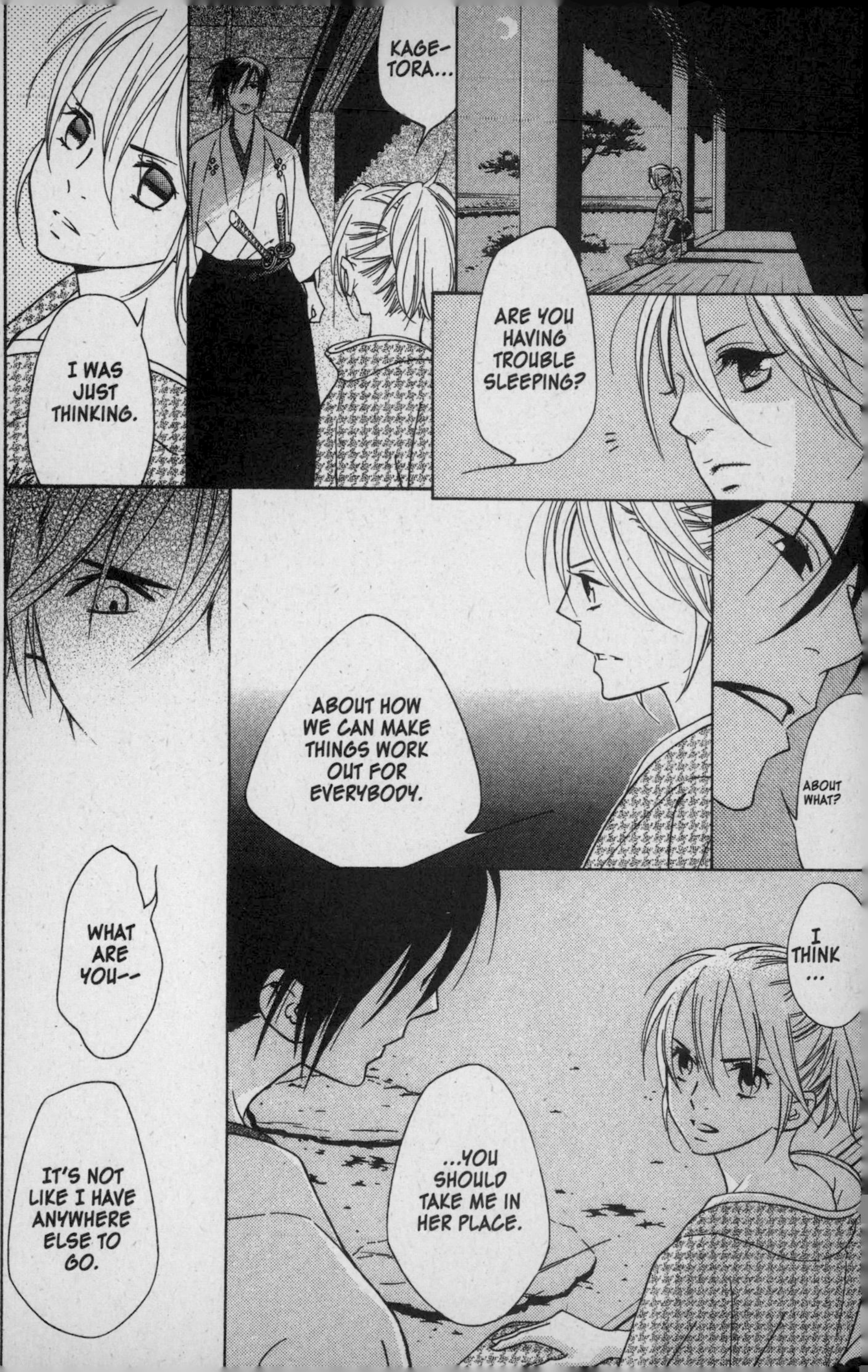
ARE YOU HAVING TROUBLE SLEEPING?
KAGE-TORA...
I WAS JUST THINKING.
ABOUT WHAT?
ABOUT HOW WE CAN MAKE THINGS WORK OUT FOR EVERYBODY.
I THINK...
...YOU SHOULD TAKE ME IN HER PLACE.
WHAT ARE YOU--
IT'S NOT LIKE I HAVE ANYWHERE ELSE TO GO.

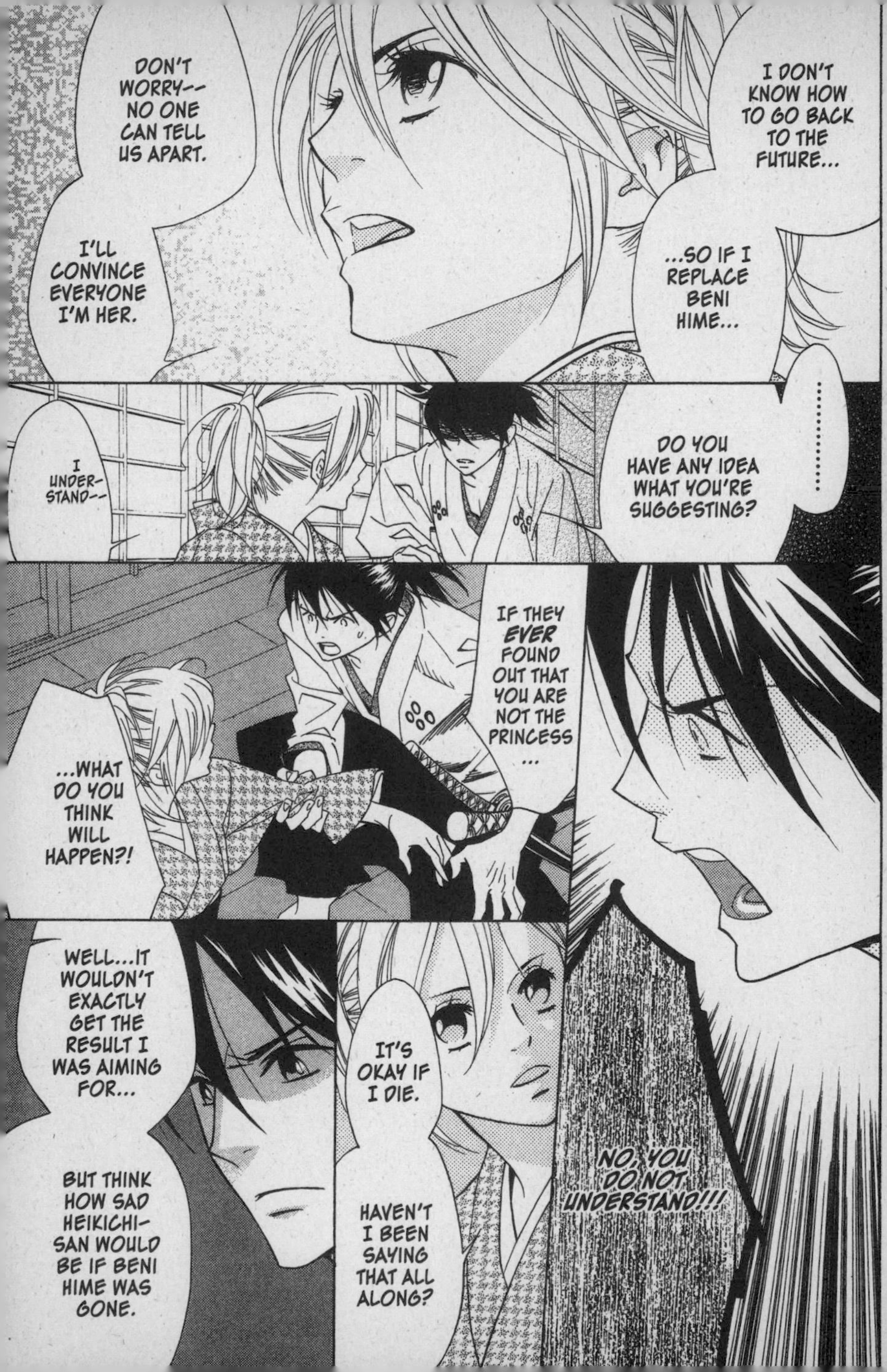
I DON'T KNOW HOW TO GO BACK TO THE FUTURE...
...SO IF I REPLACE BENI HIME...
DON'T WORRY-- NO ONE CAN TELL US APART.
I'LL CONVINCE EVERYONE I'M HER.
......
DO YOU HAVE ANY IDEA WHAT YOU'RE SUGGESTING?
I UNDERSTAND--
IF THEY EVER FOUND OUT THAT YOU ARE NOT THE PRINCESS...
...WHAT DO YOU THINK WILL HAPPEN?!
NO, YOU DO NOT UNDERSTAND!!!
IT'S OKAY IF I DIE.
HAVEN'T I BEEN SAYING THAT ALL ALONG?
WELL...IT WOULDN'T EXACTLY GET THE RESULT I WAS AIMING FOR...
BUT THINK HOW SAD HEIKICHI-SAN WOULD BE IF BENI HIME WAS GONE.

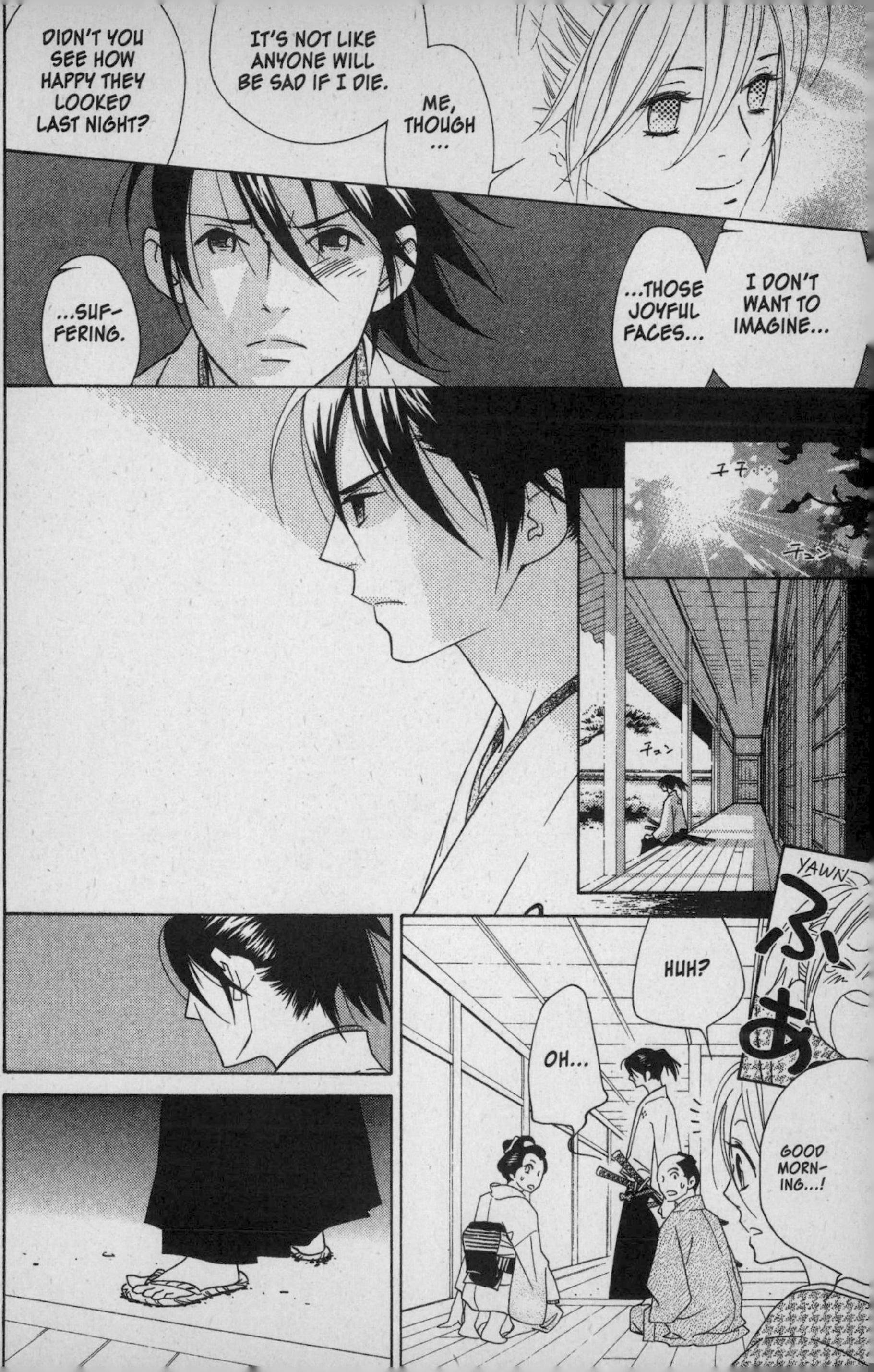
IT'S NOT LIKE ANYONE WILL BE SAD IF I DIE.
DIDN'T YOU SEE HOW HAPPY THEY LOOKED LAST NIGHT?
ME, THOUGH ...
I DON'T WANT TO IMAGINE...
...THOSE JOYFUL FACES...
...SUF-FERING.
チチ
チュン
チュン
YAWN
ふあ
HUH?
OH...
GOOD MORN-ING...!

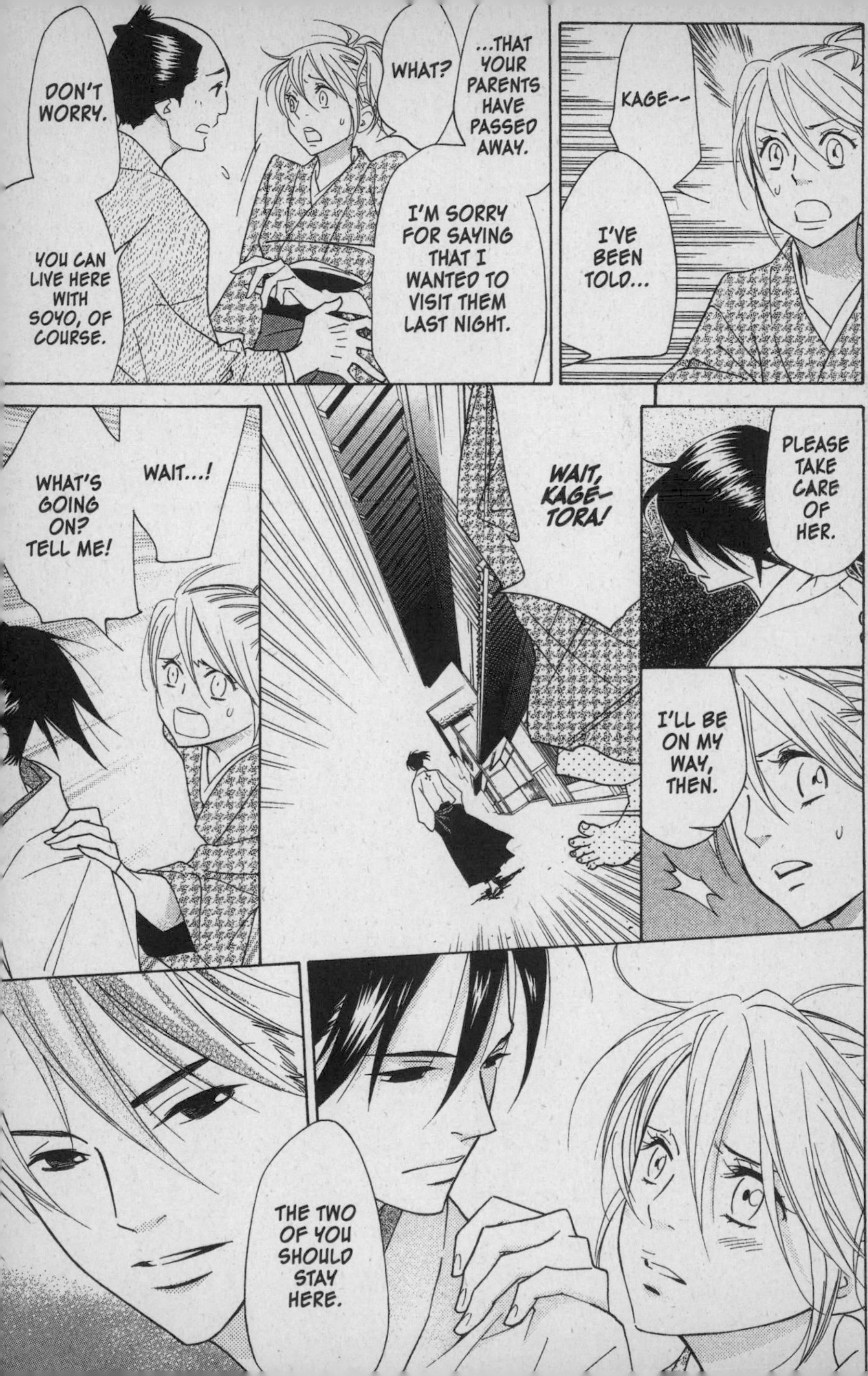
KAGE--
I'VE BEEN TOLD...
...THAT YOUR PARENTS HAVE PASSED AWAY.
WHAT?
I'M SORRY FOR SAYING THAT I WANTED TO VISIT THEM LAST NIGHT.
DON'T WORRY.
YOU CAN LIVE HERE WITH SOYO, OF COURSE.
PLEASE TAKE CARE OF HER.
I'LL BE ON MY WAY, THEN.
WAIT, KAGE-TORA!
WAIT...!
WHAT'S GOING ON? TELL ME!
THE TWO OF YOU SHOULD STAY HERE.

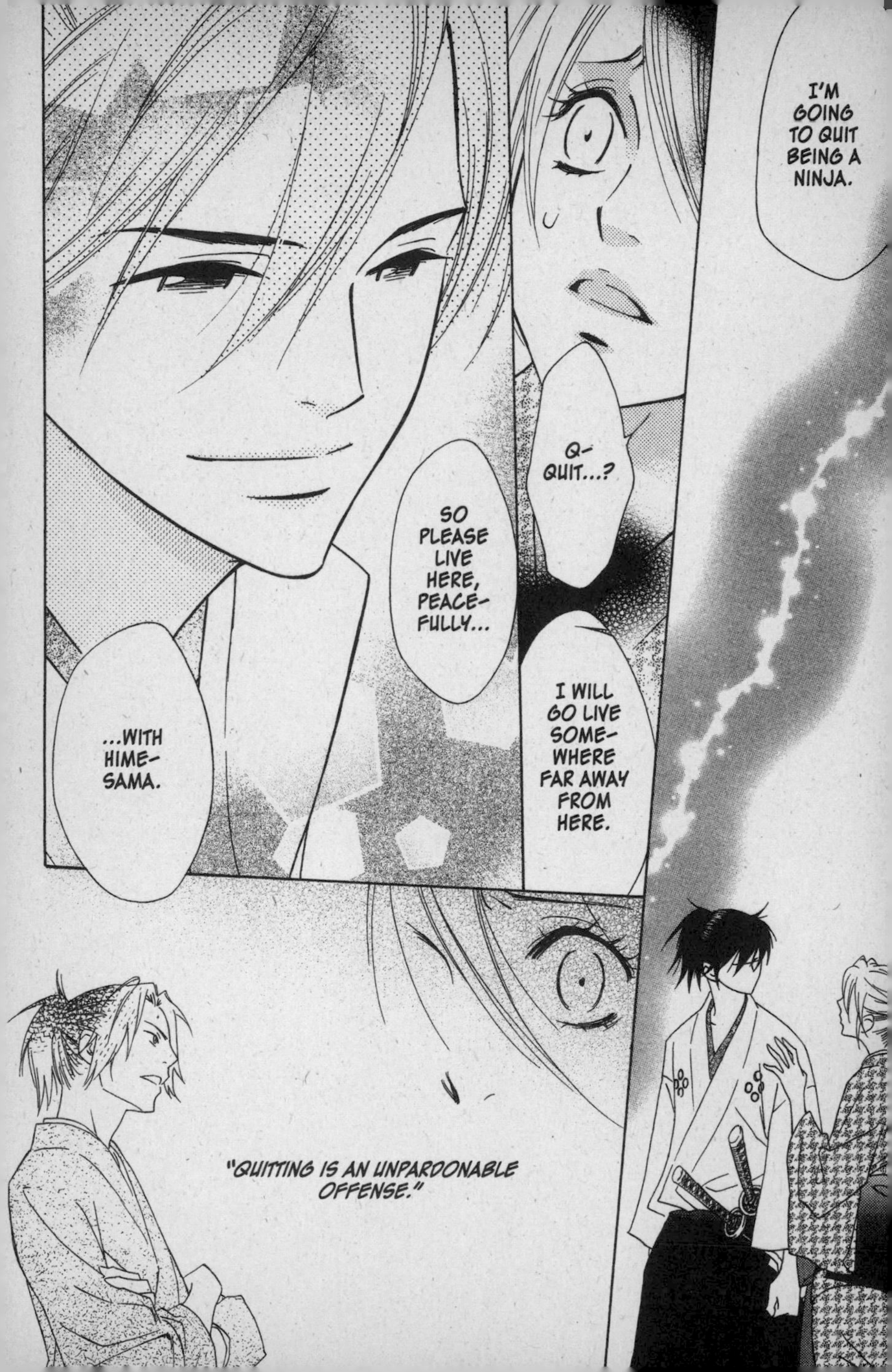
I'M GOING TO QUIT BEING A NINJA.
Q-QUIT...?
I WILL GO LIVE SOMEWHERE FAR AWAY FROM HERE.
SO PLEASE LIVE HERE, PEACEFULLY...
...WITH HIME-SAMA.
"QUITTING IS AN UNPARDONABLE OFFENSE."

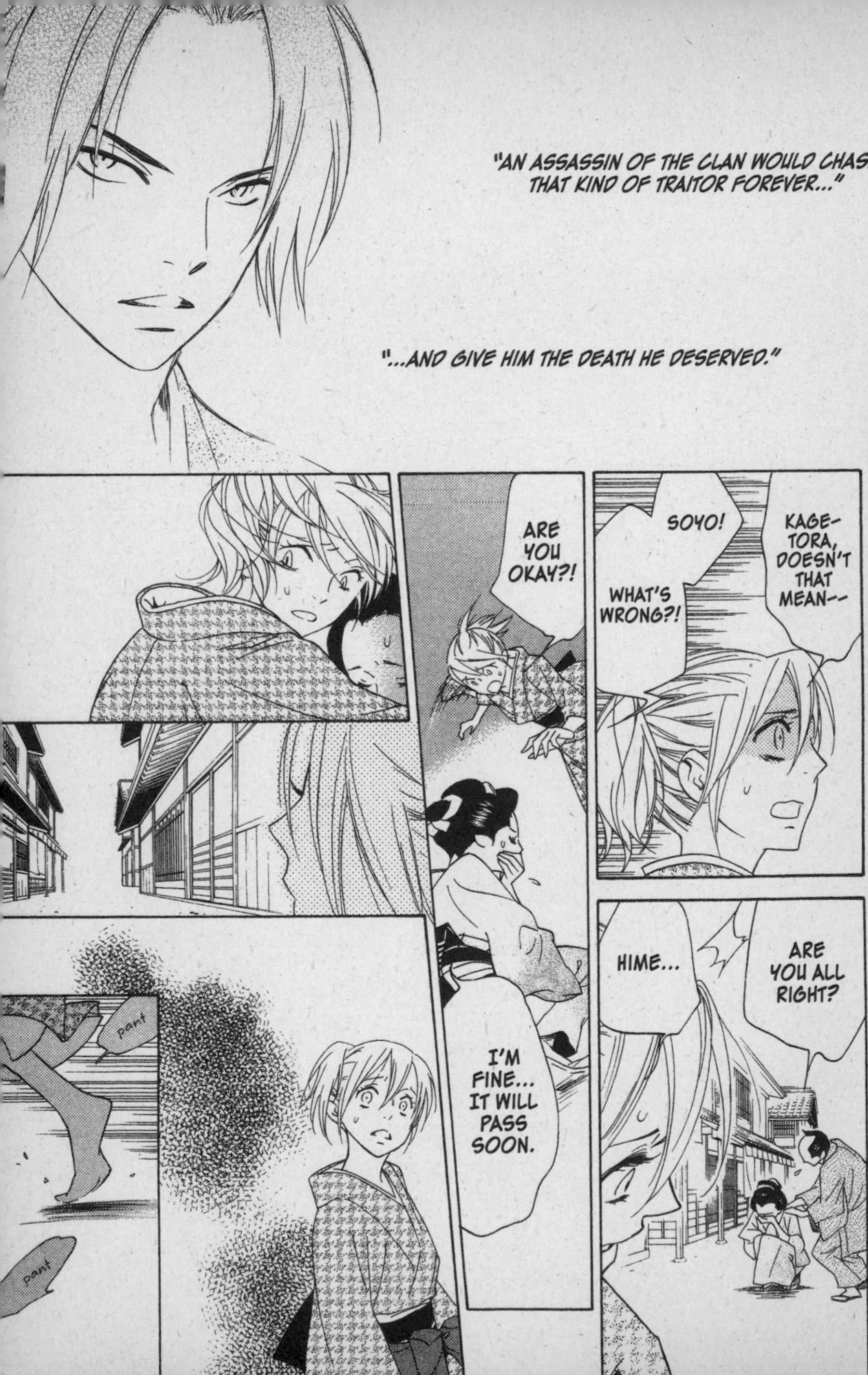
"AN ASSASSIN OF THE CLAN WOULD CHASE THAT KIND OF TRAITOR FOREVER..."
"...AND GIVE HIM THE DEATH HE DESERVED."
KAGE-TORA, DOESN'T THAT MEAN--
SOYO!
WHAT'S WRONG?!
ARE YOU OKAY?!
ARE YOU ALL RIGHT?
HIME...
I'M FINE... IT WILL PASS SOON.
pant
pant

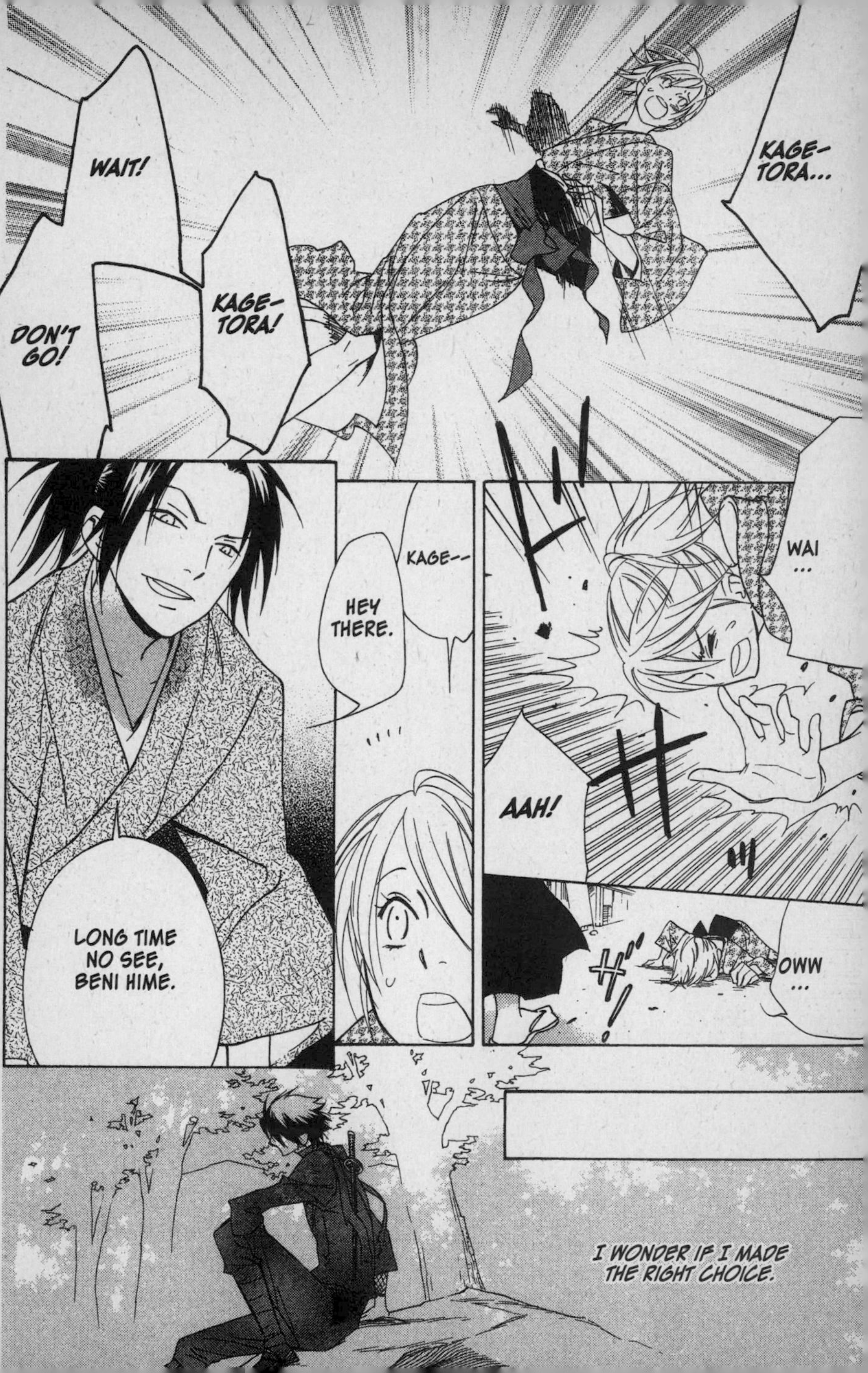
KAGE-TORA...
KAGE-TORA!
WAIT!
DON'T GO!
WAI ...
AAH!
OWW ...
KAGE--
HEY THERE.
LONG TIME NO SEE, BENI HIME.
I WONDER IF I MADE THE RIGHT CHOICE.

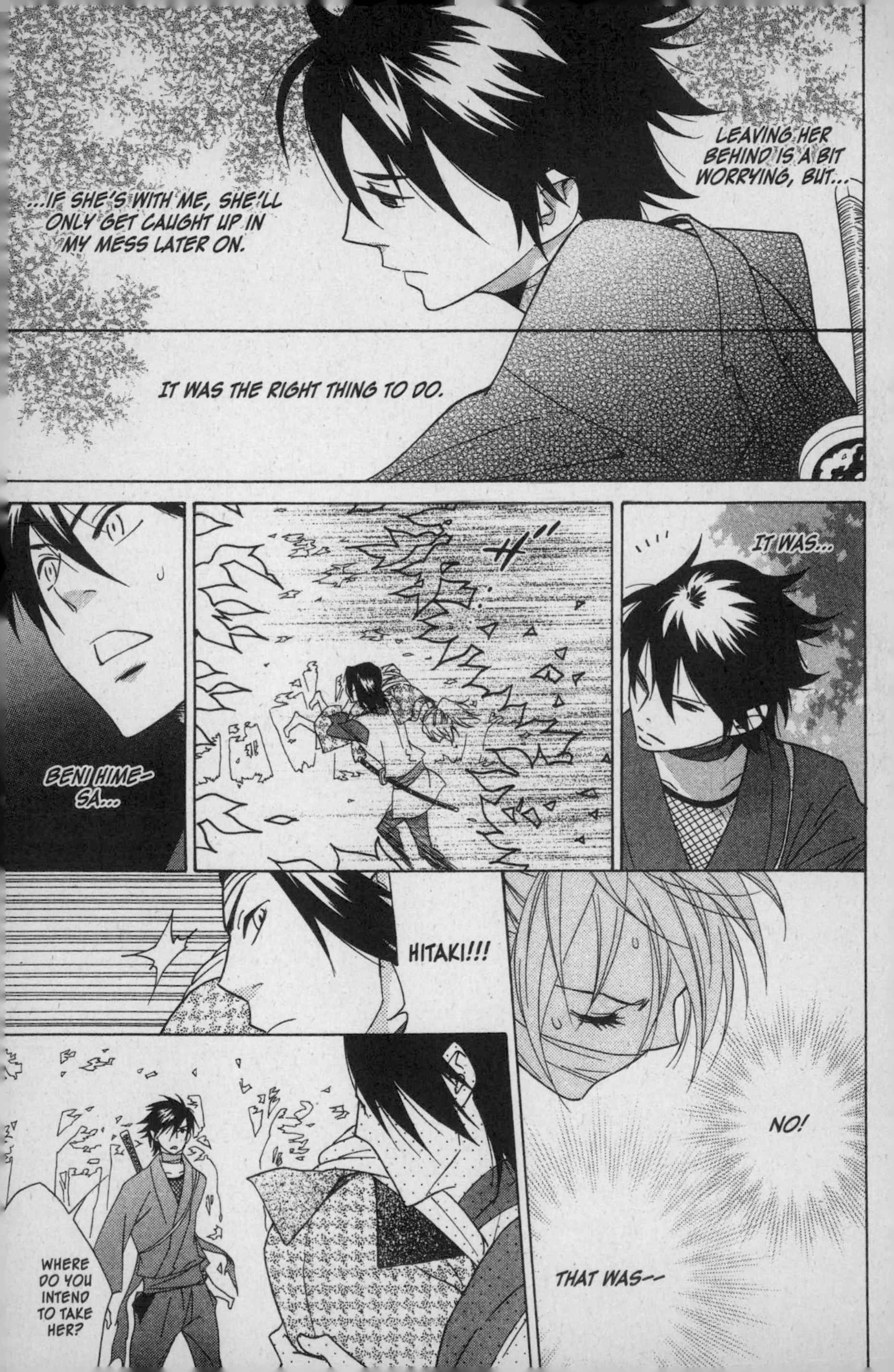
LEAVING HER BEHIND IS A BIT WORRYING, BUT...
...IF SHE'S WITH ME, SHE'LL ONLY GET CAUGHT UP IN MY MESS LATER ON.
IT WAS THE RIGHT THING TO DO.
IT WAS...
BENI HIME-SA...
NO!
THAT WAS--
HITAKI!!!
WHERE DO YOU INTEND TO TAKE HER?

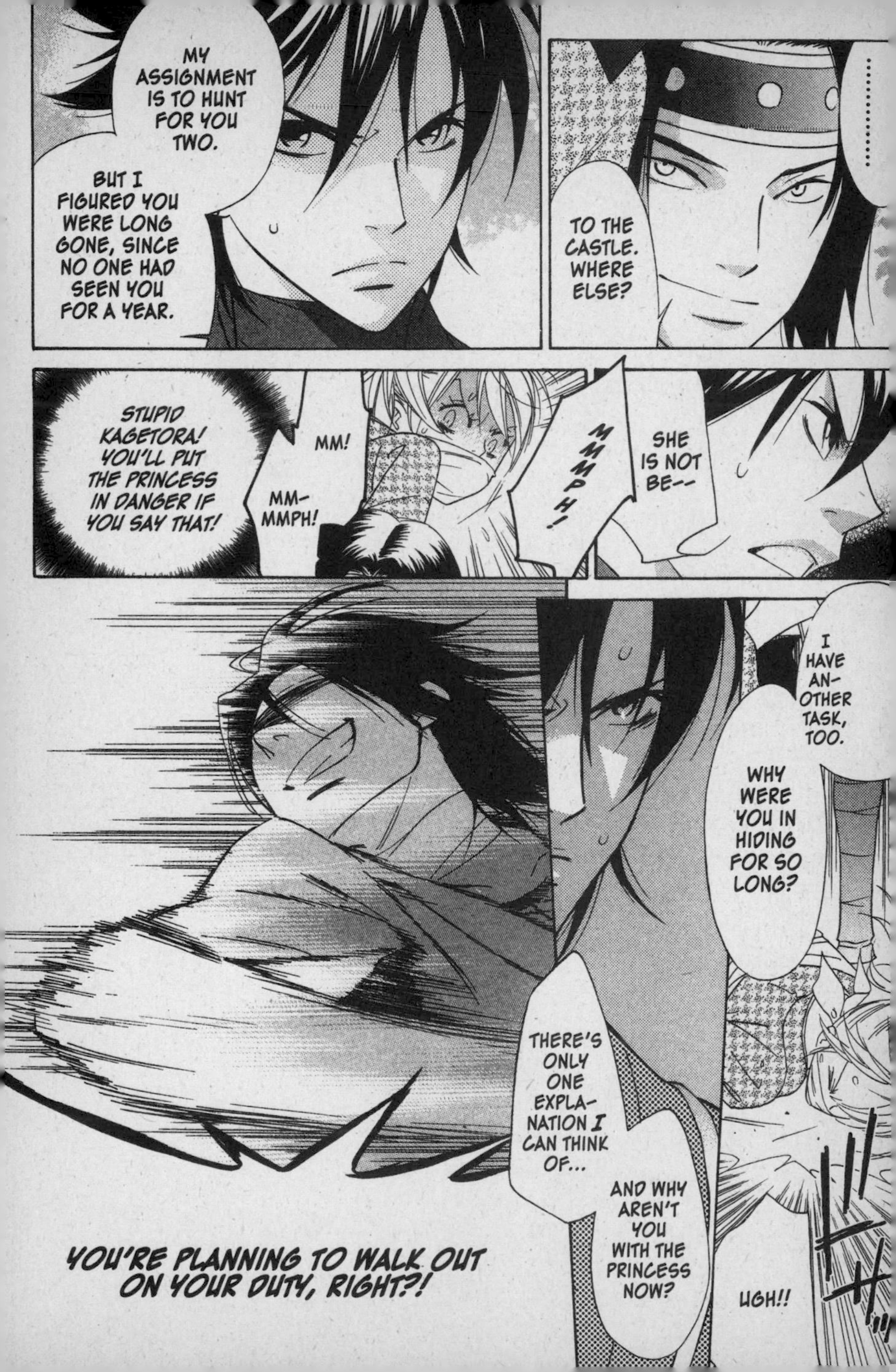
......
TO THE CASTLE. WHERE ELSE?
MY ASSIGNMENT IS TO HUNT FOR YOU TWO.
BUT I FIGURED YOU WERE LONG GONE, SINCE NO ONE HAD SEEN YOU FOR A YEAR.
SHE IS NOT BE--
MMMPH!
MM!
MM-MMPH!
STUPID KAGETORA! YOU'LL PUT THE PRINCESS IN DANGER IF YOU SAY THAT!
I HAVE AN-OTHER TASK, TOO.
WHY WERE YOU IN HIDING FOR SO LONG?
AND WHY AREN'T YOU WITH THE PRINCESS NOW?
THERE'S ONLY ONE EXPLA-NATION I CAN THINK OF...
UGH!!
YOU'RE PLANNING TO WALK OUT ON YOUR DUTY, RIGHT?!

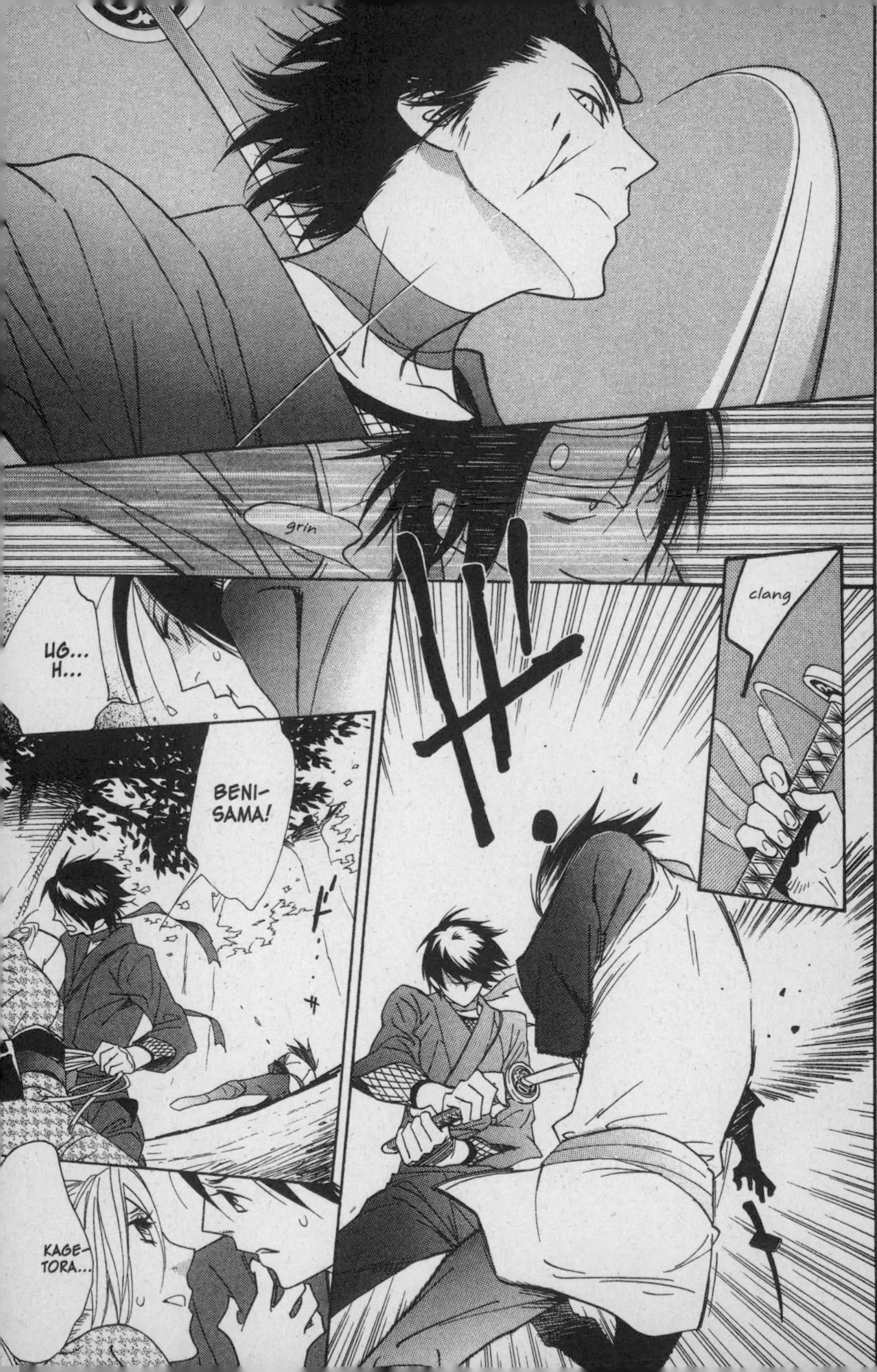
grin
clang
UG...
H...
BENI-
SAMA!
KAGE-
TORA...

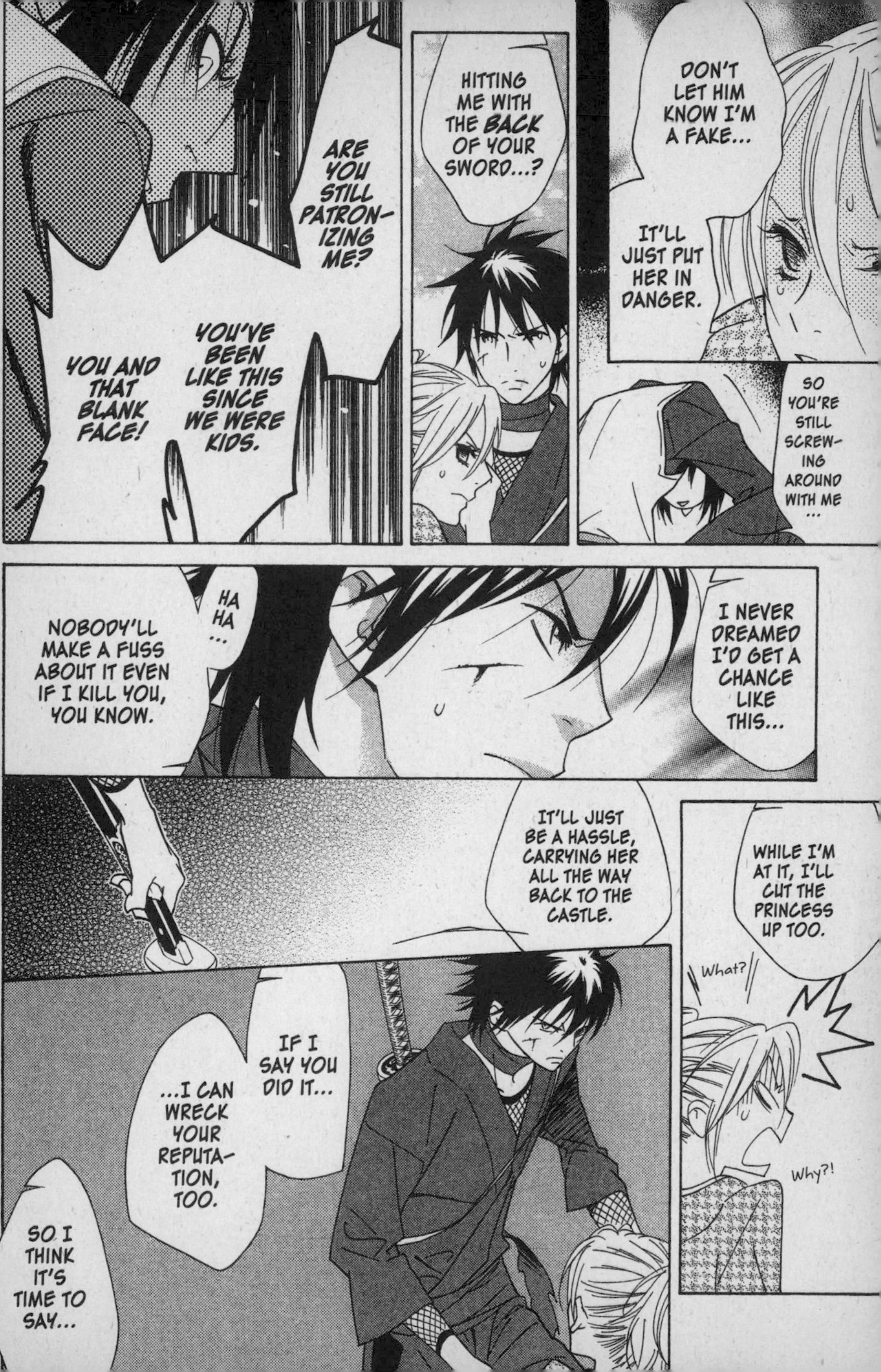
DON'T LET HIM KNOW I'M A FAKE...
IT'LL JUST PUT HER IN DANGER.
SO YOU'RE STILL SCREWING AROUND WITH ME...
HITTING ME WITH THE BACK OF YOUR SWORD...?
ARE YOU STILL PATRONIZING ME?
YOU'VE BEEN LIKE THIS SINCE WE WERE KIDS.
YOU AND THAT BLANK FACE!
I NEVER DREAMED I'D GET A CHANCE LIKE THIS...
HA HA...
NOBODY'LL MAKE A FUSS ABOUT IT EVEN IF I KILL YOU, YOU KNOW.
WHILE I'M AT IT, I'LL CUT THE PRINCESS UP TOO.
What?
Why?!
IT'LL JUST BE A HASSLE, CARRYING HER ALL THE WAY BACK TO THE CASTLE.
IF I SAY YOU DID IT...
...I CAN WRECK YOUR REPUTATION, TOO.
SO I THINK IT'S TIME TO SAY...

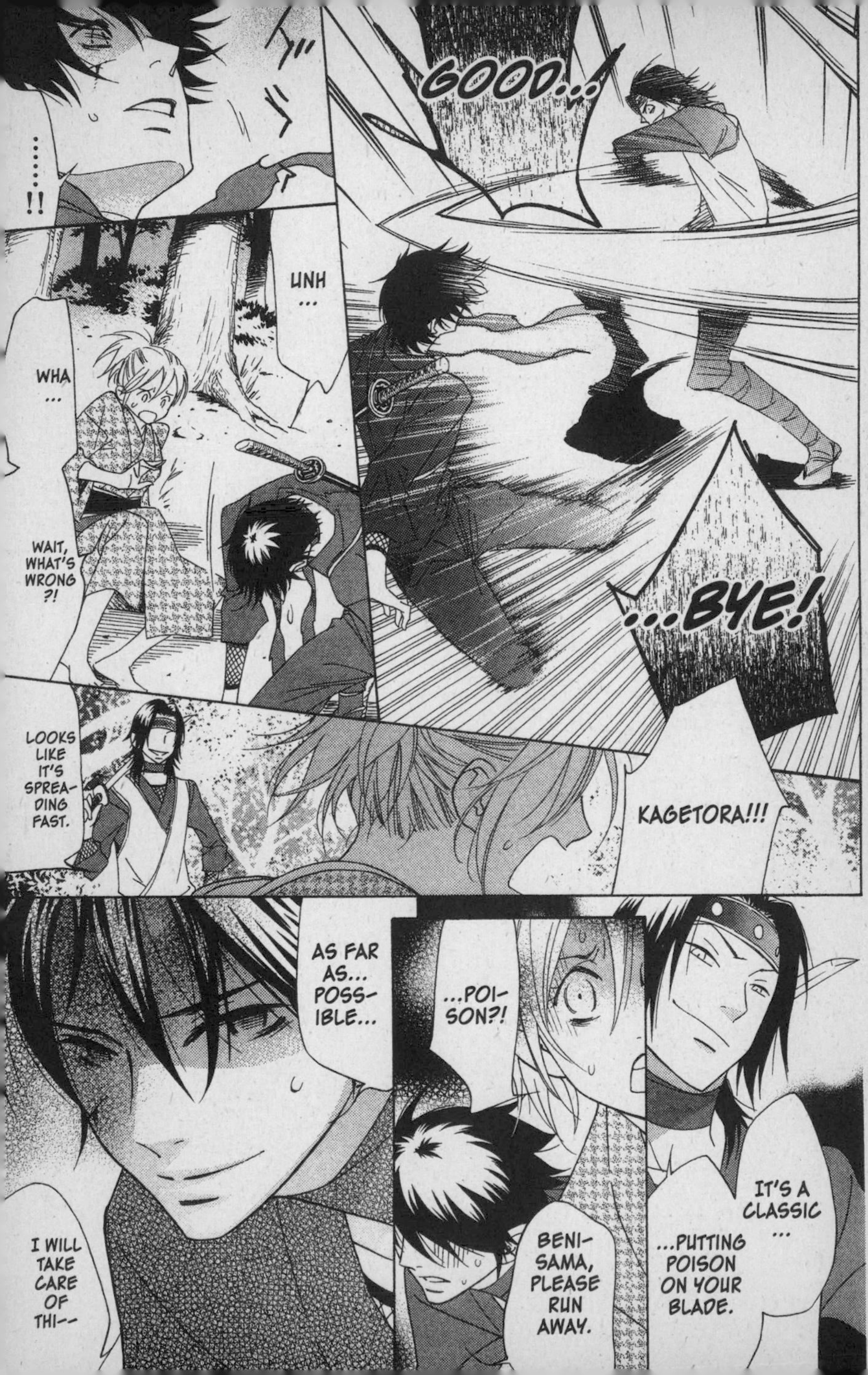

GOOD...!
...BYE!
......!!
UNH...
WHA...
WAIT, WHAT'S WRONG?!
KAGETORA!!!
LOOKS LIKE IT'S SPREADING FAST.
...POI-SON?!
IT'S A CLASSIC...
...PUTTING POISON ON YOUR BLADE.
BENI-SAMA, PLEASE RUN AWAY.
AS FAR AS... POSS-IBLE...
I WILL TAKE CARE OF THI--

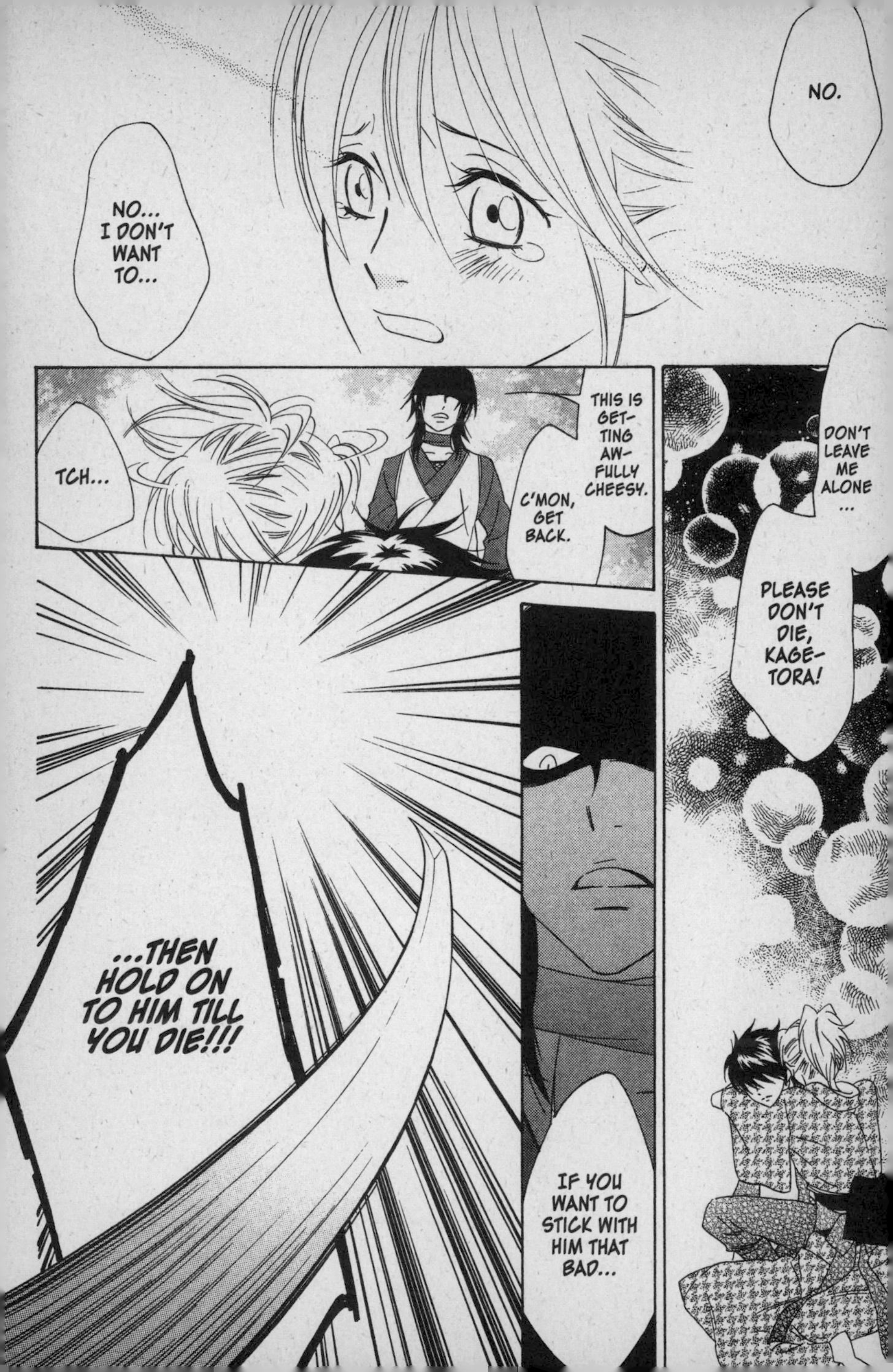
NO.
NO... I DON'T WANT TO...
DON'T LEAVE ME ALONE ...
PLEASE DON'T DIE, KAGE-TORA!
THIS IS GET-TING AW-FULLY CHEESY.
C'MON, GET BACK.
TCH...
IF YOU WANT TO STICK WITH HIM THAT BAD...
...THEN HOLD ON TO HIM TILL YOU DIE!!!

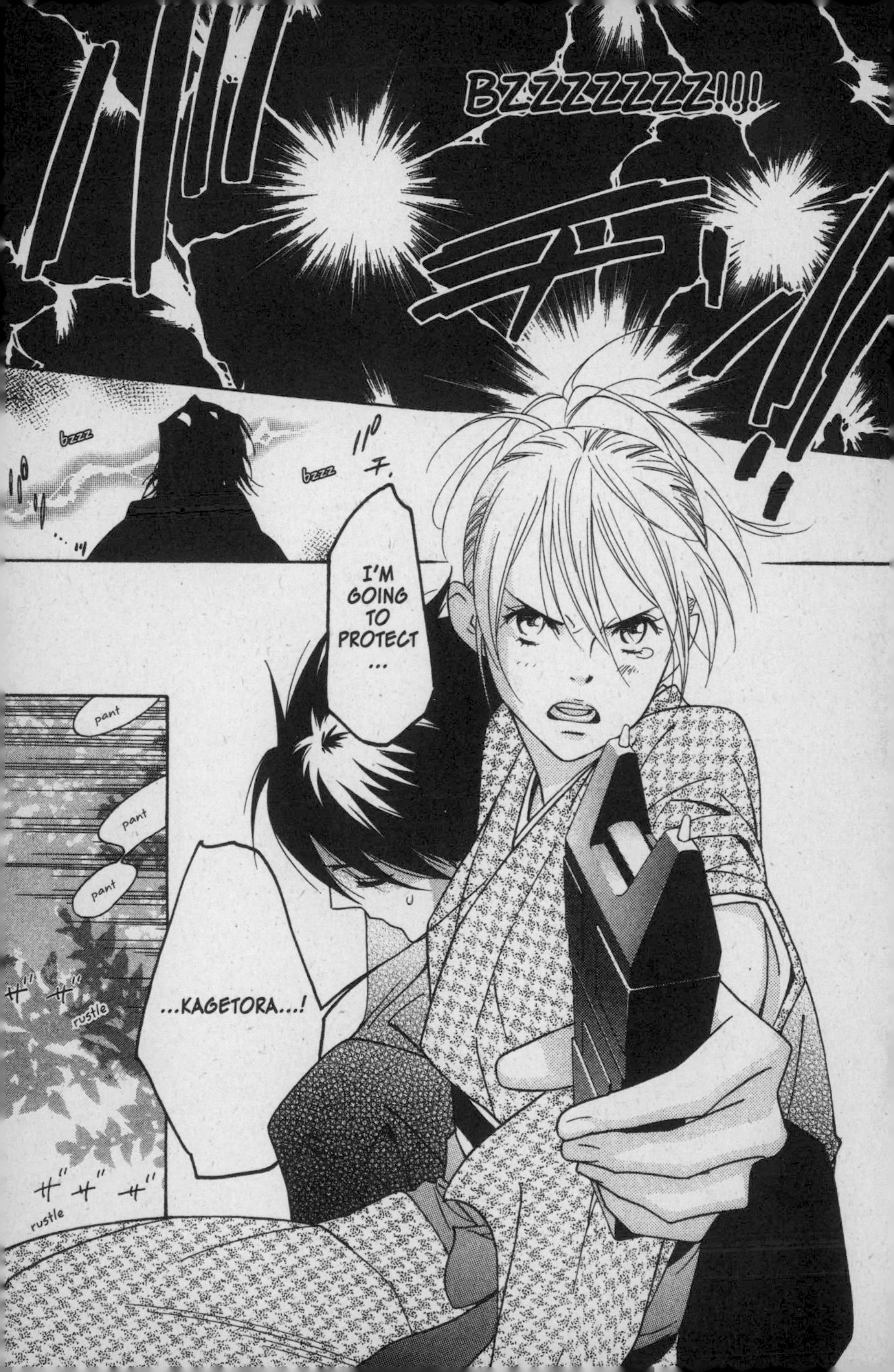
BZZZZZZZZ!!!
bzzz
bzzz
I'M GOING TO PROTECT ...
pant
pant
pant
...KAGETORA...!
rustle
rustle

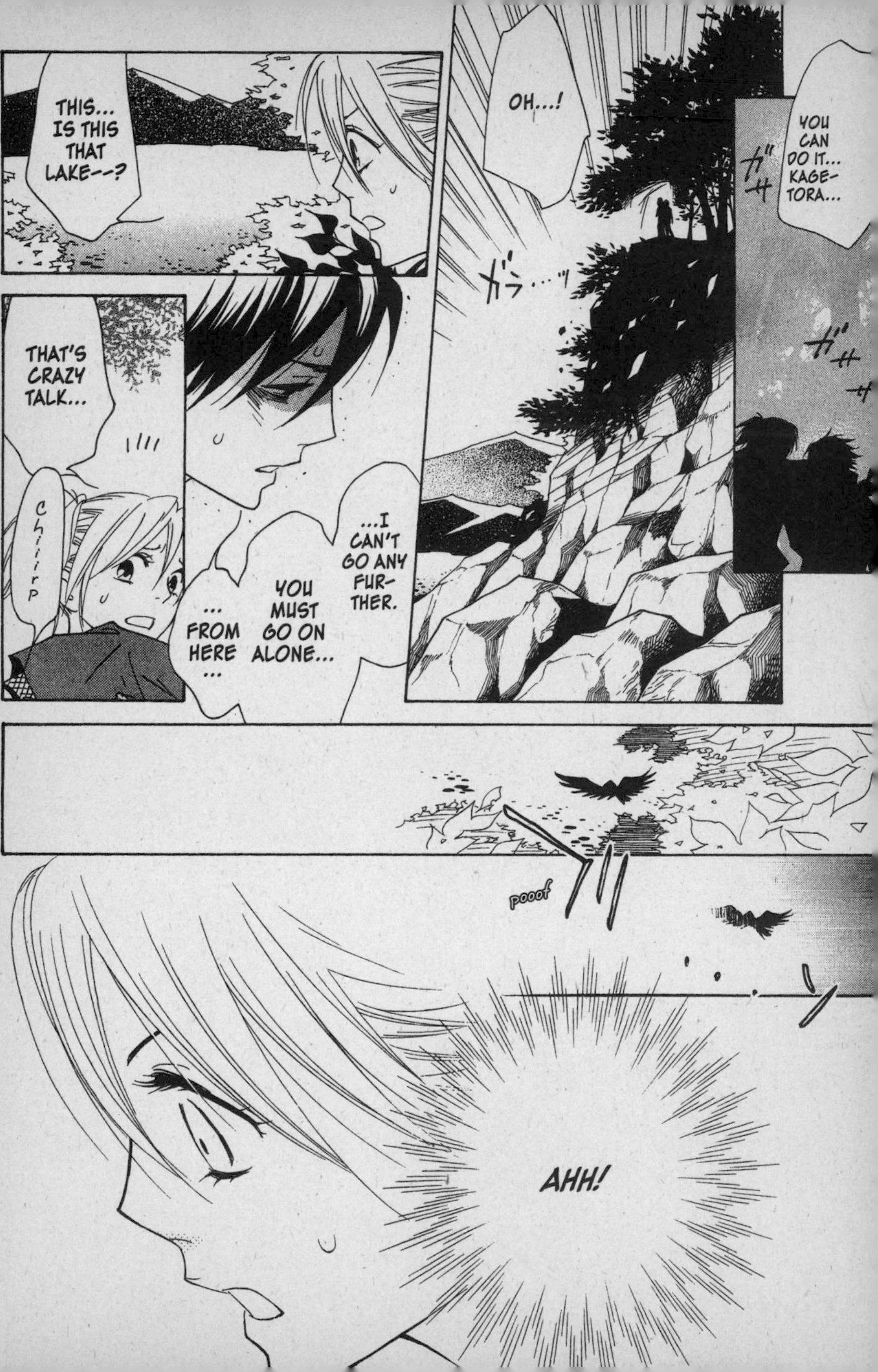
YOU CAN DO IT... KAGE-TORA...
OH...!
THIS... IS THIS THAT LAKE--?
...I CAN'T GO ANY FUR-THER.
YOU MUST GO ON ALONE...
...FROM HERE...
THAT'S CRAZY TALK...
Chiiirp
pooof
AHH!

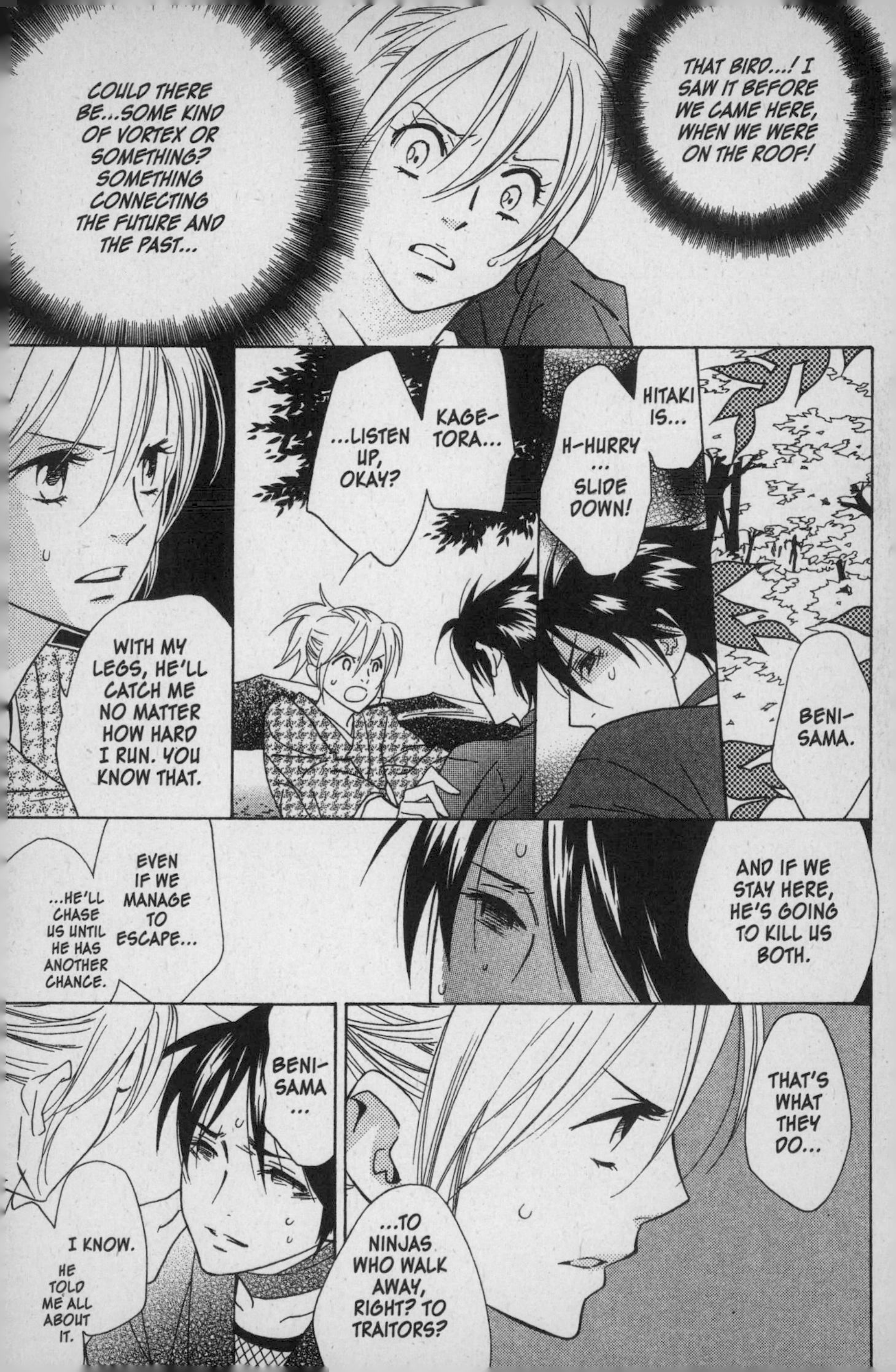
THAT BIRD...! I SAW IT BEFORE WE CAME HERE, WHEN WE WERE ON THE ROOF!
COULD THERE BE...SOME KIND OF VORTEX OR SOMETHING? SOMETHING CONNECTING THE FUTURE AND THE PAST...
BENI-SAMA.
HITAKI IS...
H-HURRY ... SLIDE DOWN!
KAGE-TORA...
...LISTEN UP, OKAY?
WITH MY LEGS, HE'LL CATCH ME NO MATTER HOW HARD I RUN. YOU KNOW THAT.
AND IF WE STAY HERE, HE'S GOING TO KILL US BOTH.
EVEN IF WE MANAGE TO ESCAPE...
...HE'LL CHASE US UNTIL HE HAS ANOTHER CHANCE.
THAT'S WHAT THEY DO...
...TO NINJAS WHO WALK AWAY, RIGHT? TO TRAITORS?
BENI-SAMA ...
I KNOW.
HE TOLD ME ALL ABOUT IT.

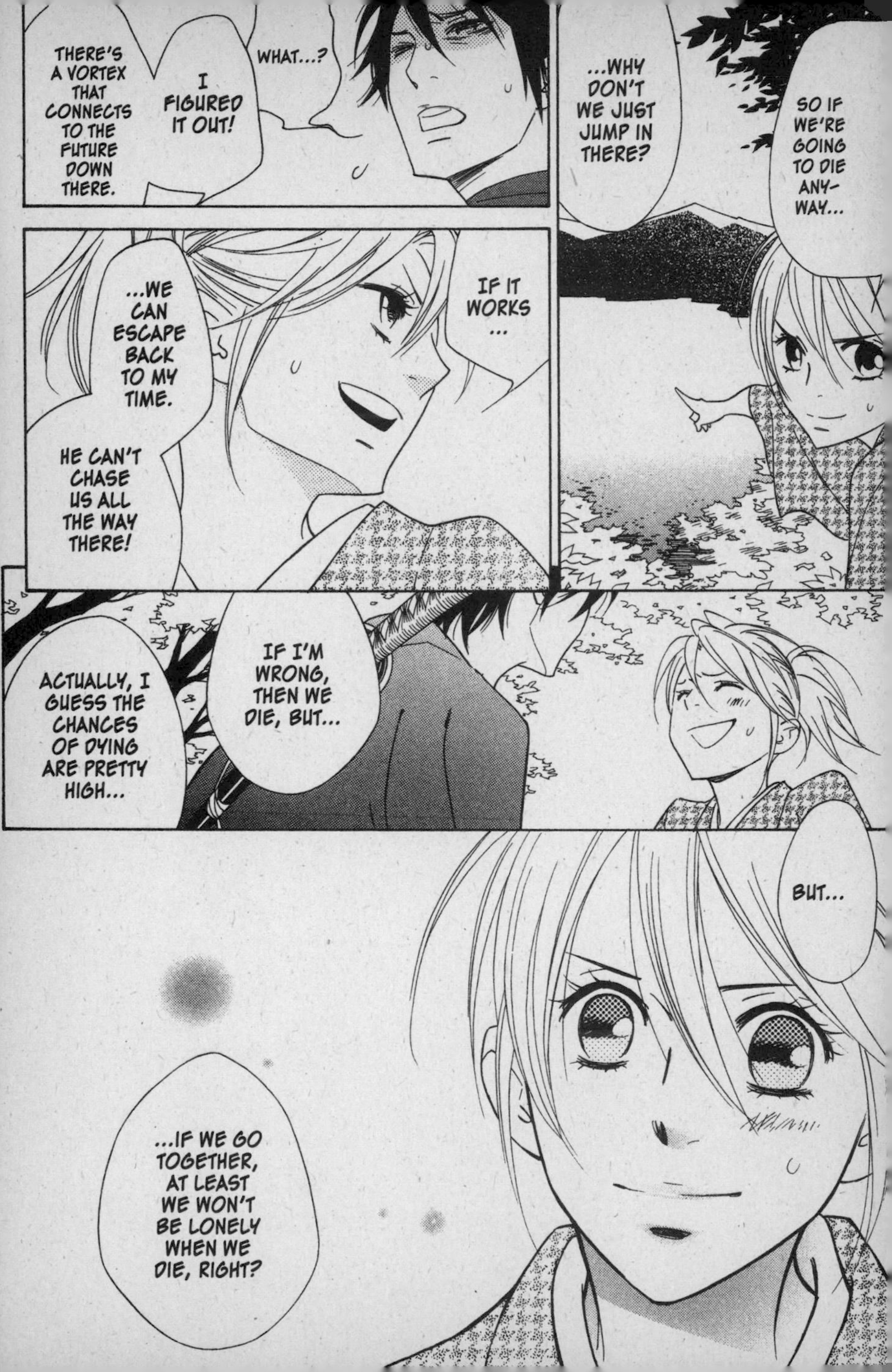
SO IF WE'RE GOING TO DIE ANY-WAY...
...WHY DON'T WE JUST JUMP IN THERE?
WHAT...?
I FIGURED IT OUT!
THERE'S A VORTEX THAT CONNECTS TO THE FUTURE DOWN THERE.
IF IT WORKS...
...WE CAN ESCAPE BACK TO MY TIME.
HE CAN'T CHASE US ALL THE WAY THERE!
IF I'M WRONG, THEN WE DIE, BUT...
ACTUALLY, I GUESS THE CHANCES OF DYING ARE PRETTY HIGH...
BUT...
...IF WE GO TOGETHER, AT LEAST WE WON'T BE LONELY WHEN WE DIE, RIGHT?

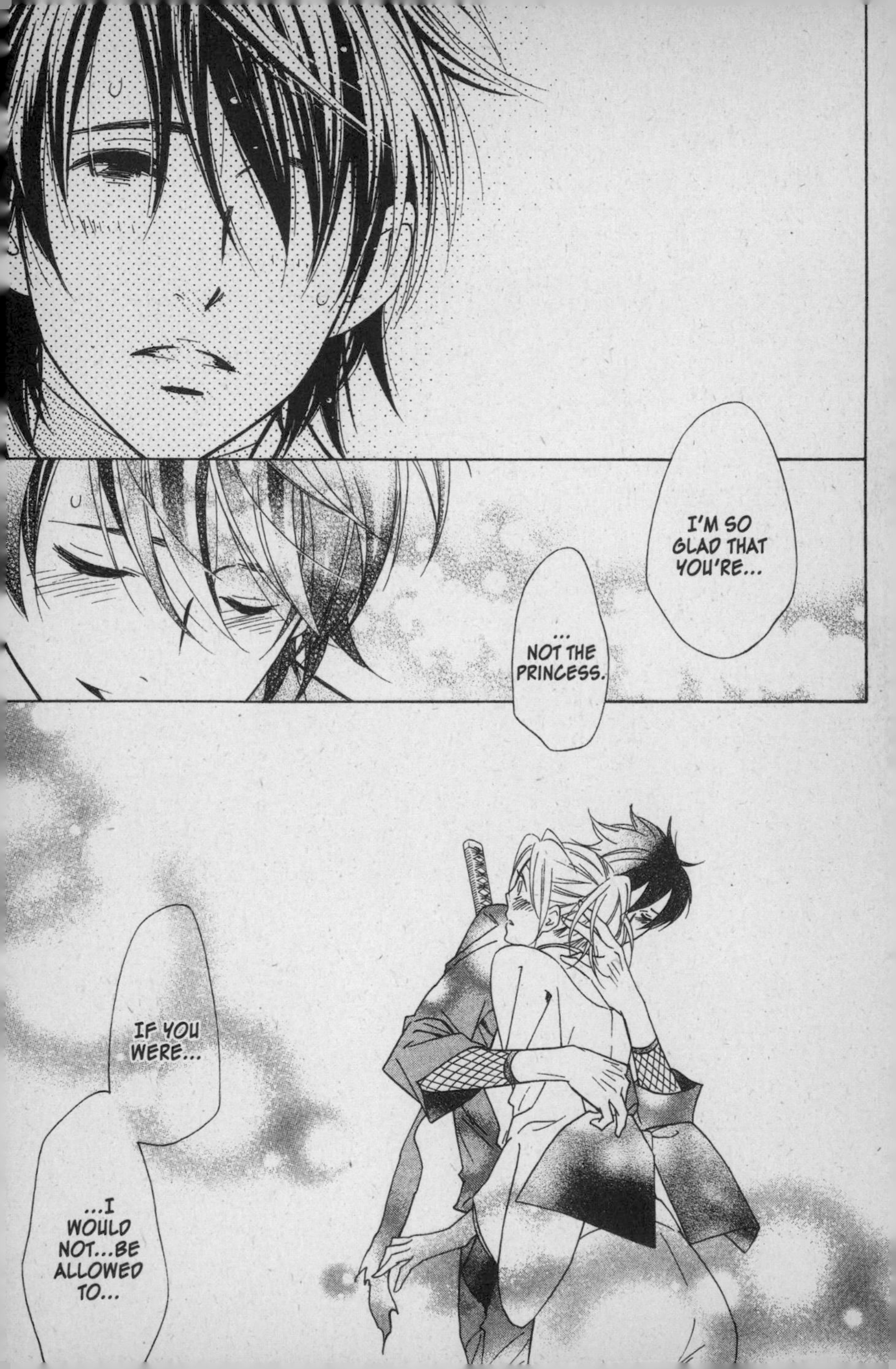
I'M SO GLAD THAT YOU'RE...
... NOT THE PRINCESS.
IF YOU WERE...
...I WOULD NOT...BE ALLOWED TO...

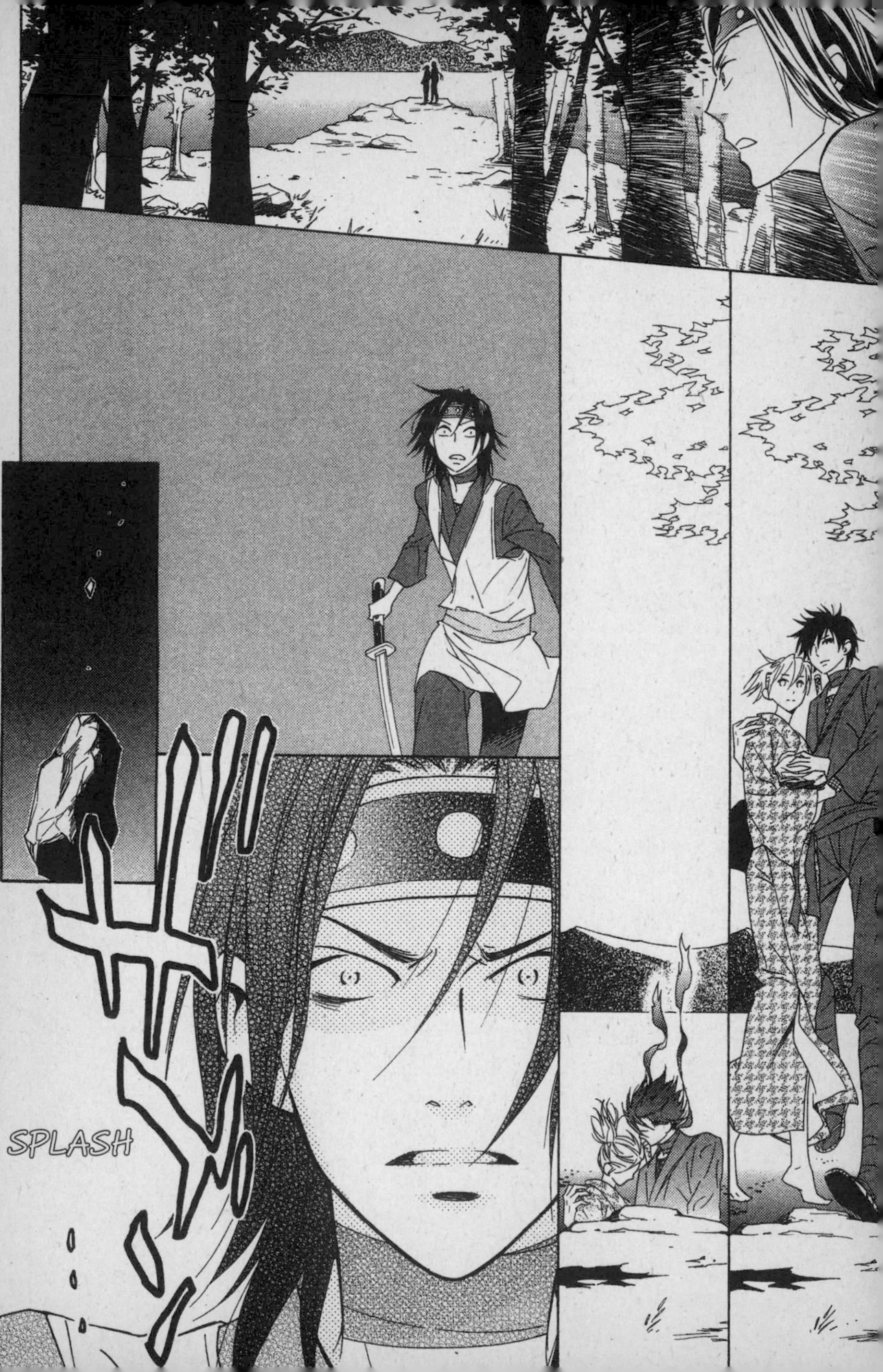
SPLASH

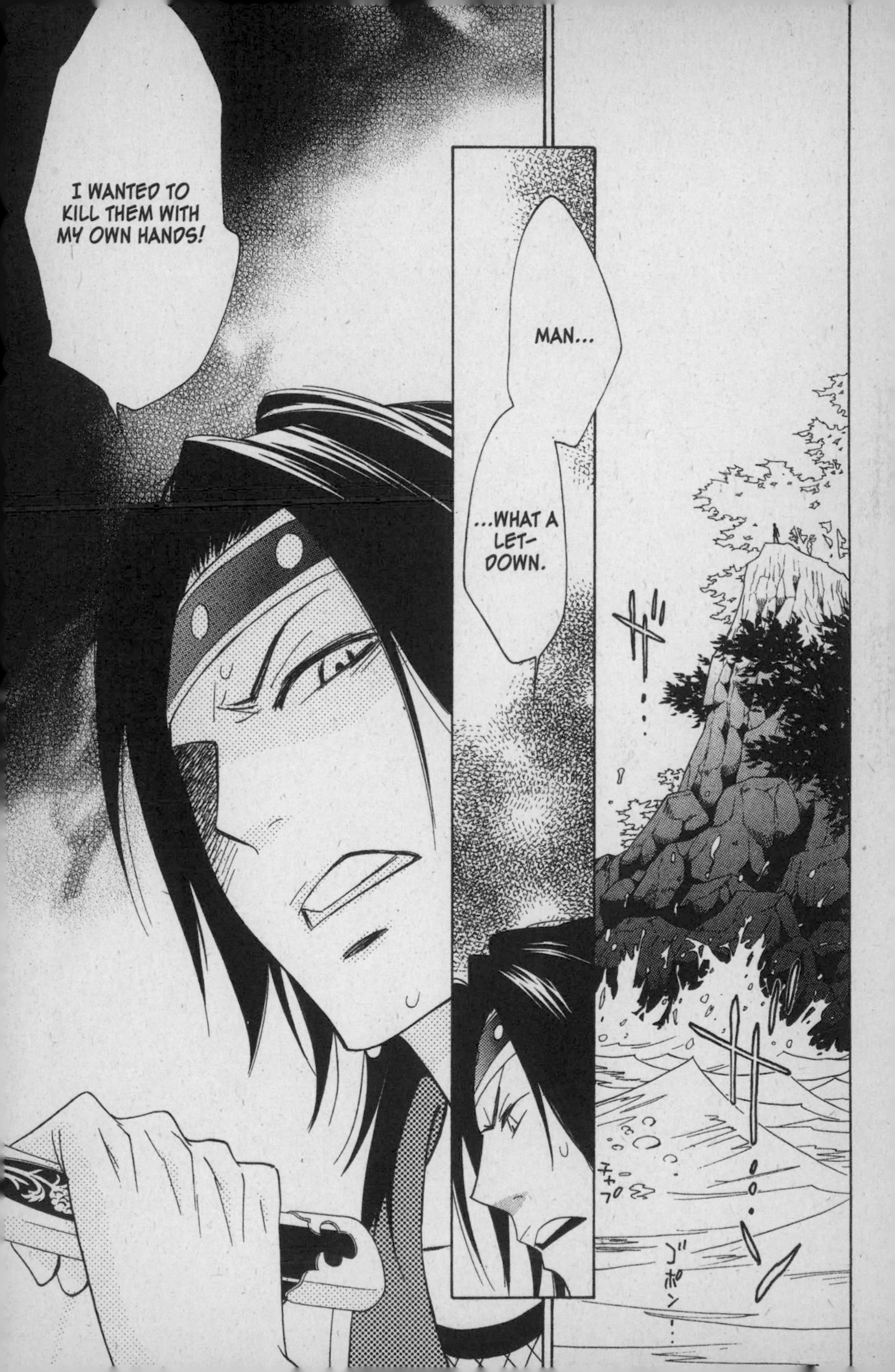
チャプ
MAN...
...WHAT A LET-DOWN.
I WANTED TO KILL THEM WITH MY OWN HANDS!

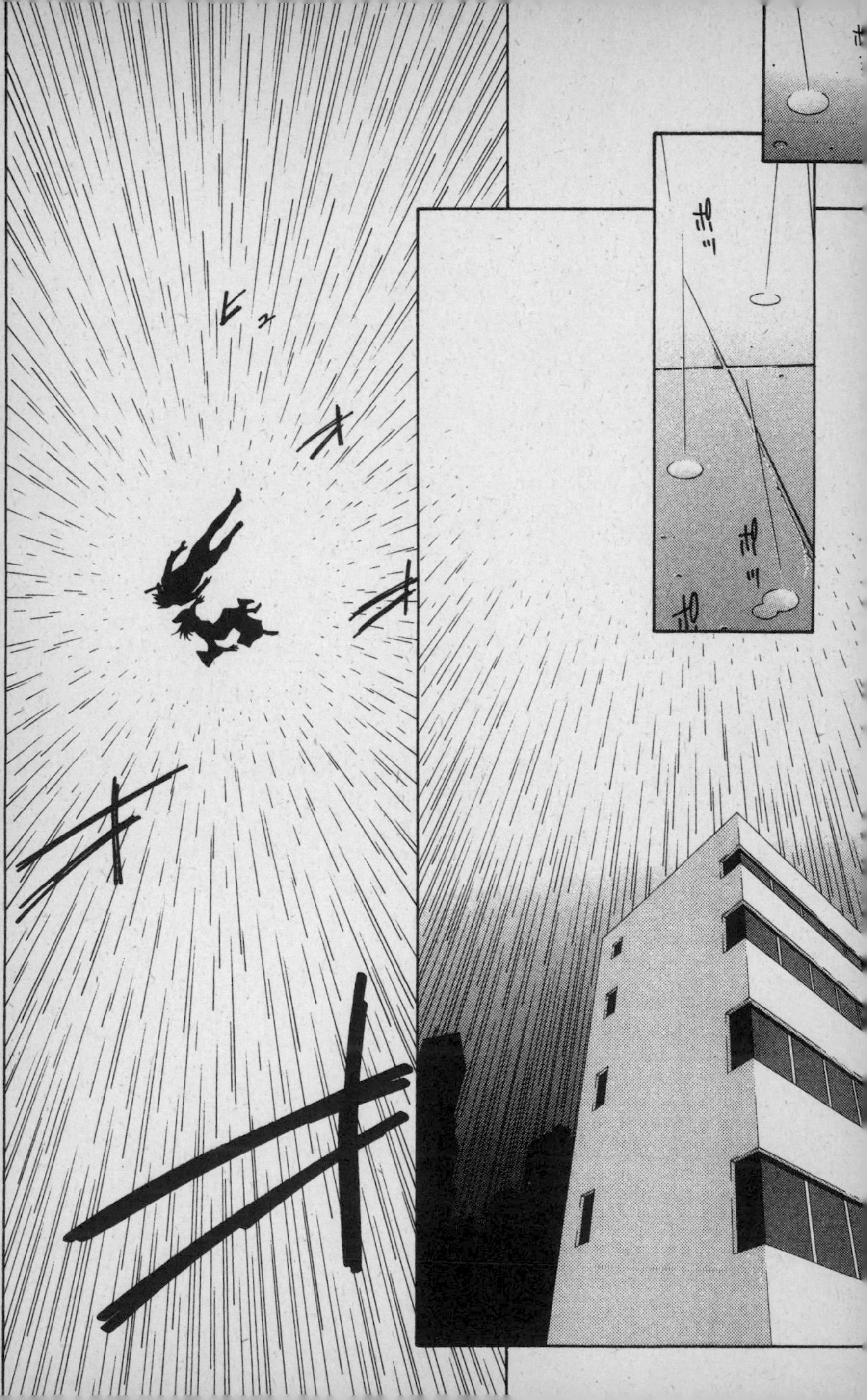
ポツ
ポツ
ポ
ヒュ

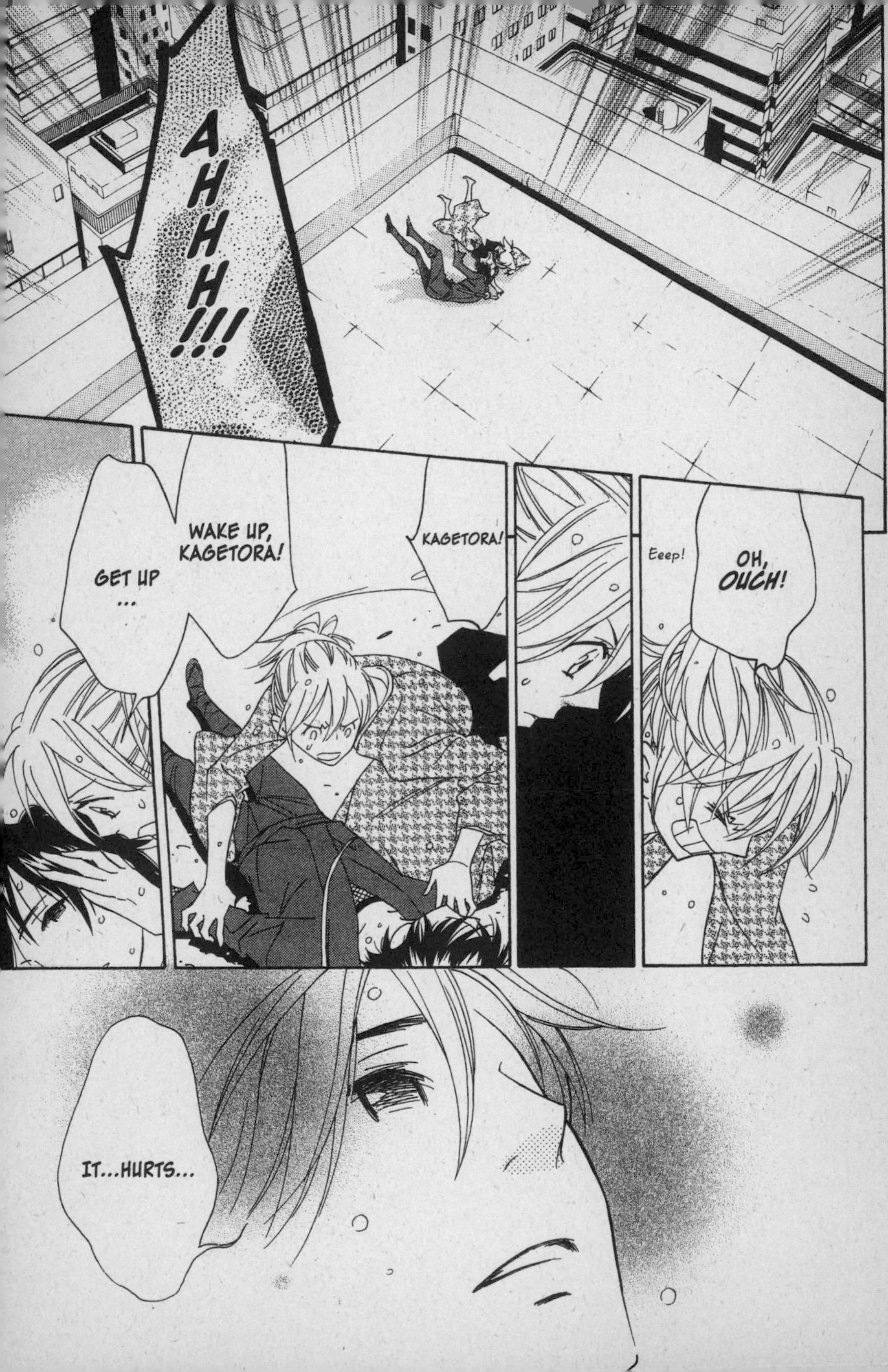
AHHH!!!
OH, OUCH!
Eeep!
KAGETORA!
WAKE UP, KAGETORA!
GET UP ...
IT...HURTS...

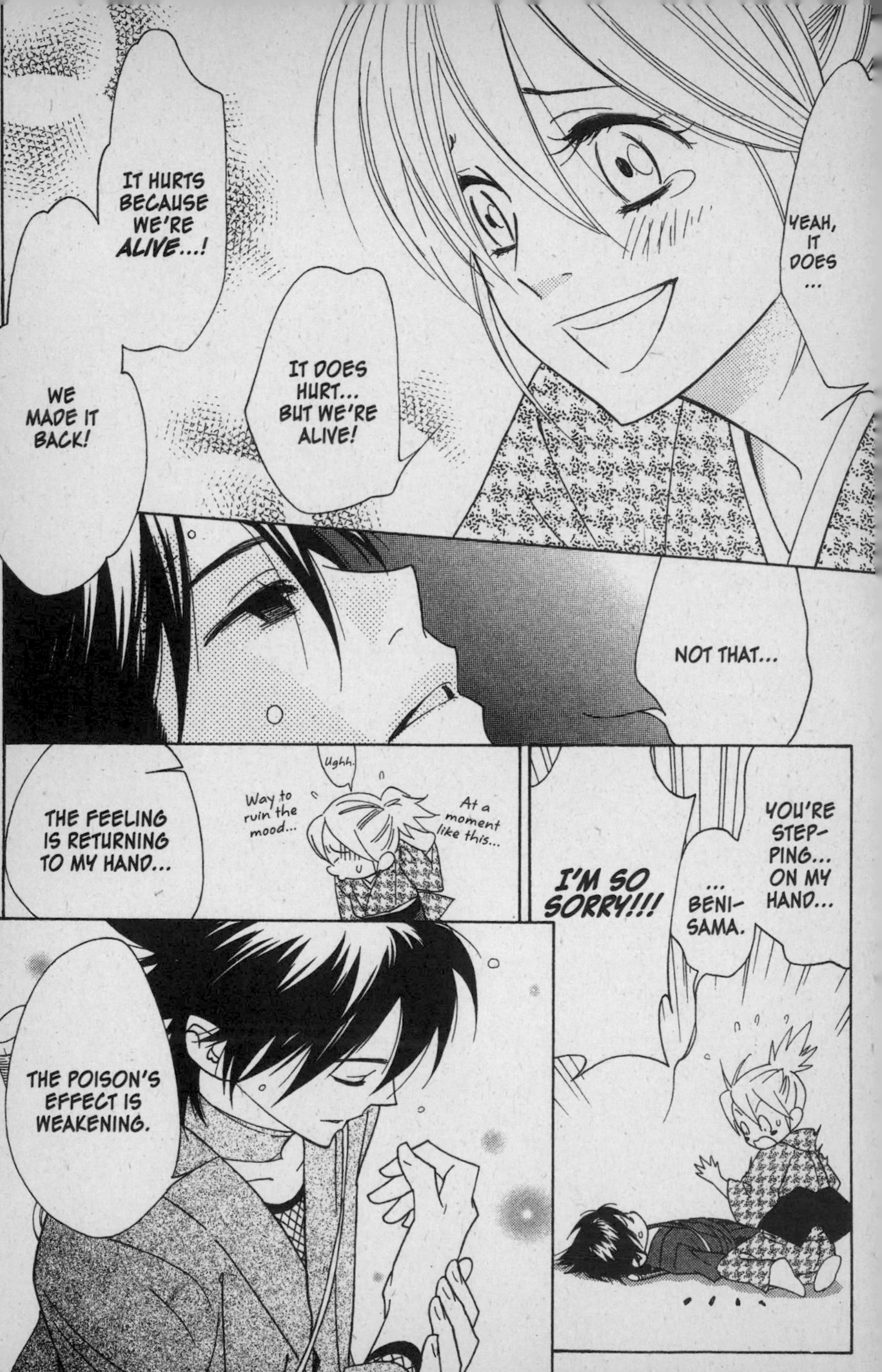
YEAH, IT DOES...
IT DOES HURT... BUT WE'RE ALIVE!
IT HURTS BECAUSE WE'RE ALIVE...!
WE MADE IT BACK!
NOT THAT...
YOU'RE STEPPING... ON MY HAND...
...BENI-SAMA.
I'M SO SORRY!!!
THE FEELING IS RETURNING TO MY HAND...
Ughh.
At a moment like this...
Way to ruin the mood...
THE POISON'S EFFECT IS WEAKENING.

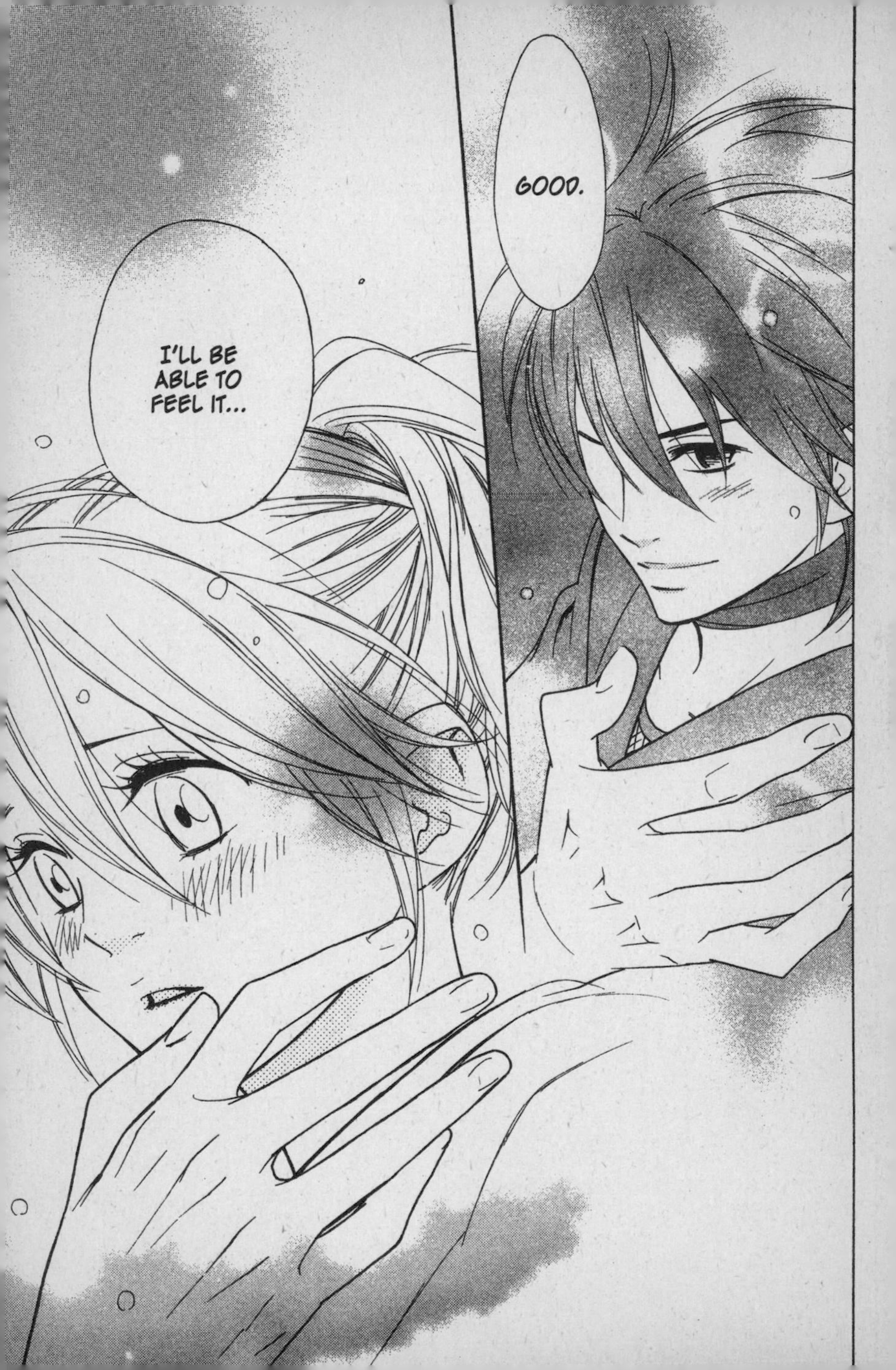
GOOD.
I'LL BE ABLE TO FEEL IT...

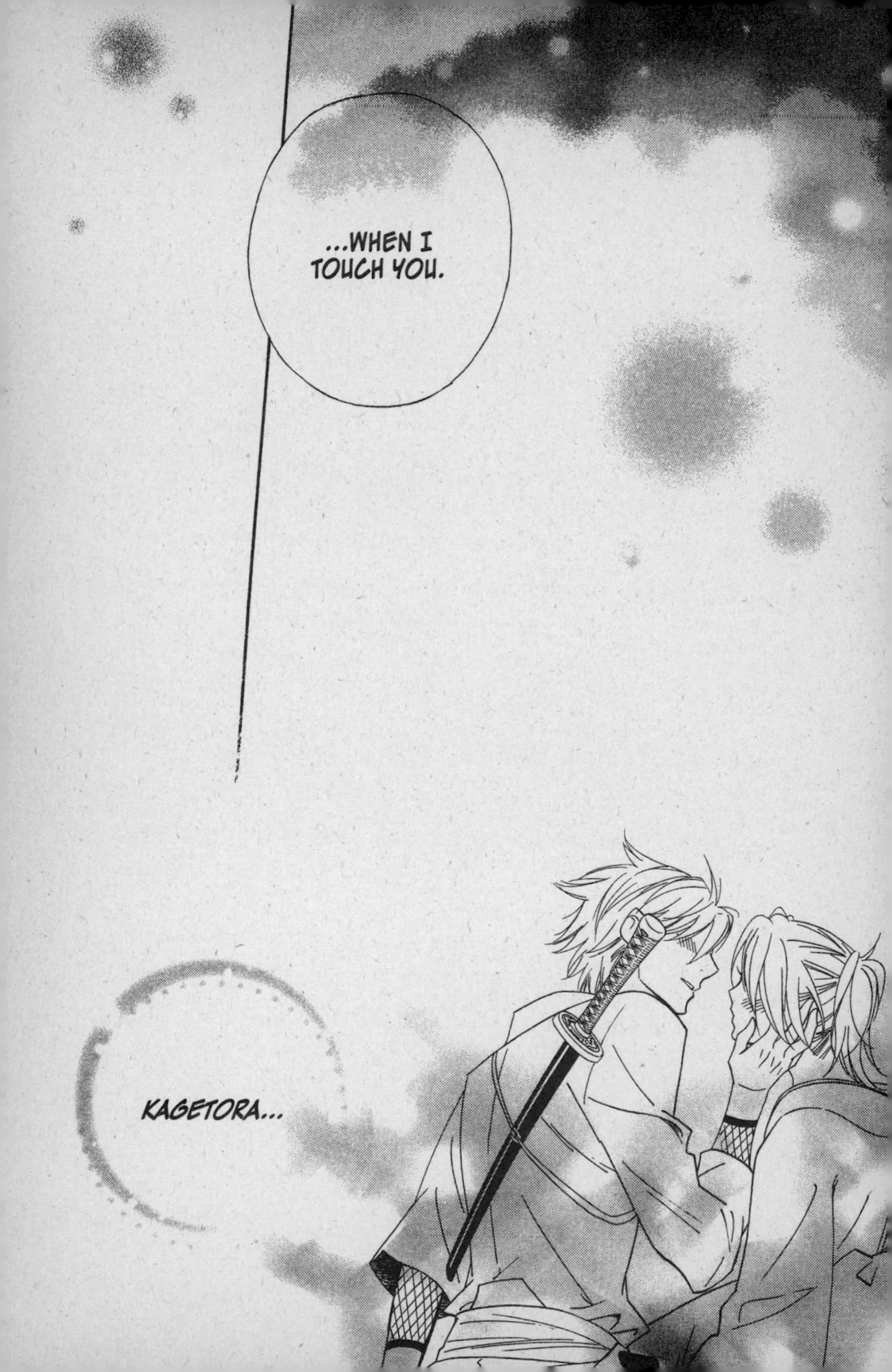
...WHEN I TOUCH YOU.
KAGETORA...

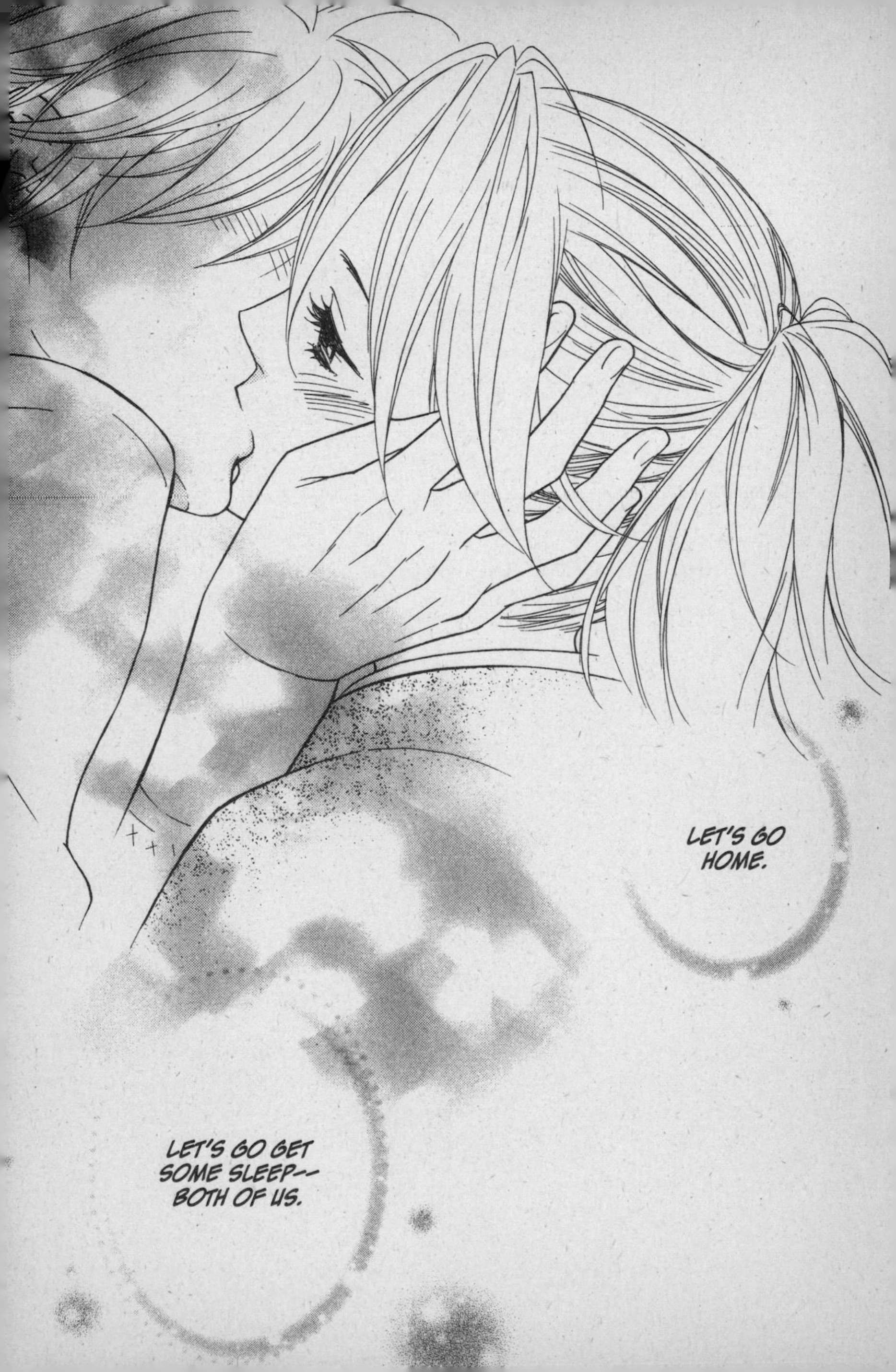
LET'S GO HOME.
LET'S GO GET SOME SLEEP-- BOTH OF US.

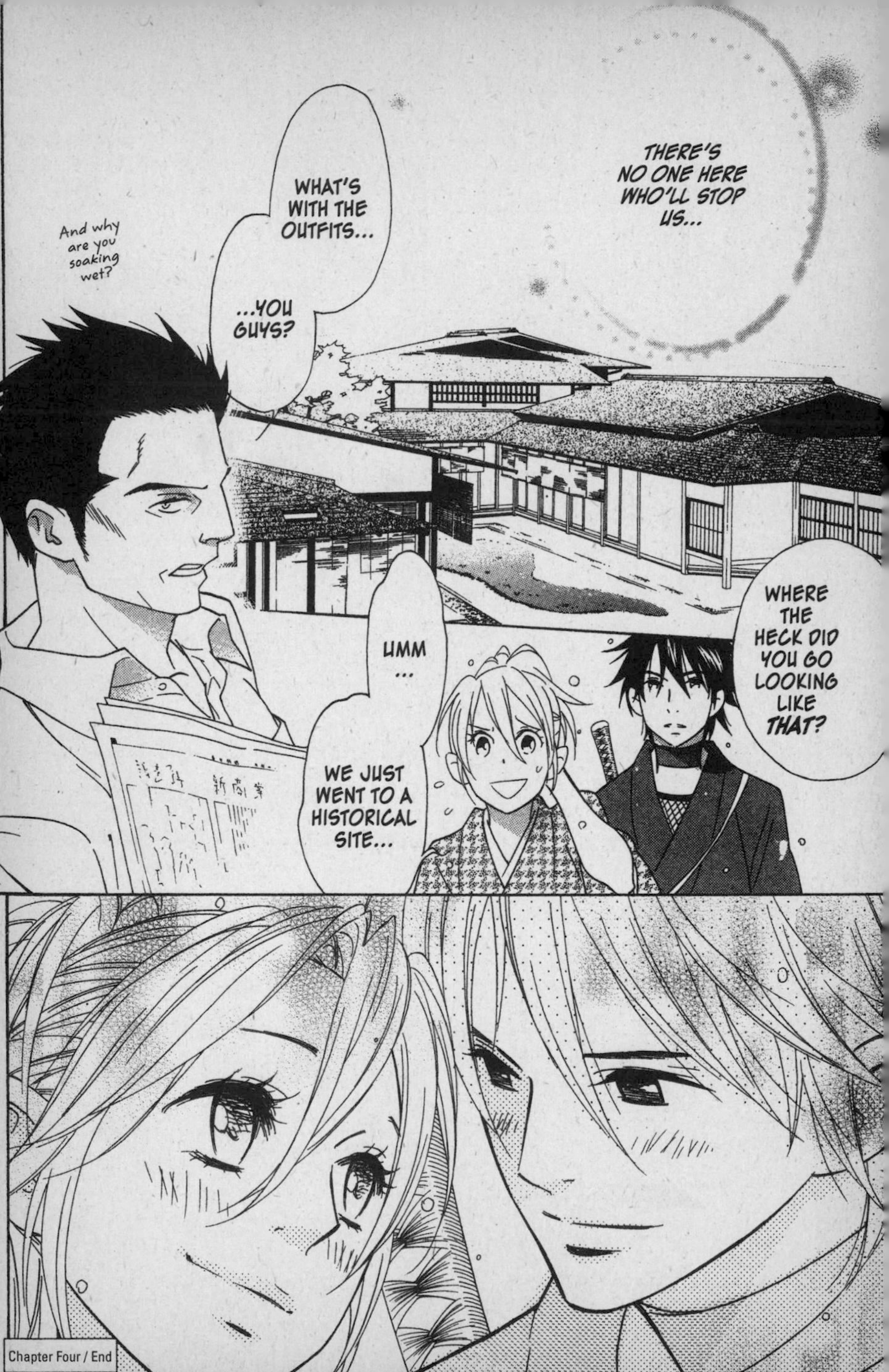
THERE'S NO ONE HERE WHO'LL STOP US...
WHAT'S WITH THE OUTFITS...
...YOU GUYS?
And why are you soaking wet?
WHERE THE HECK DID YOU GO LOOKING LIKE THAT?
UMM ...
WE JUST WENT TO A HISTORICAL SITE...
Chapter Four / End

Bonus Manga! ● Kagetora-kun the Ninja! ●

## Drying your eyes out

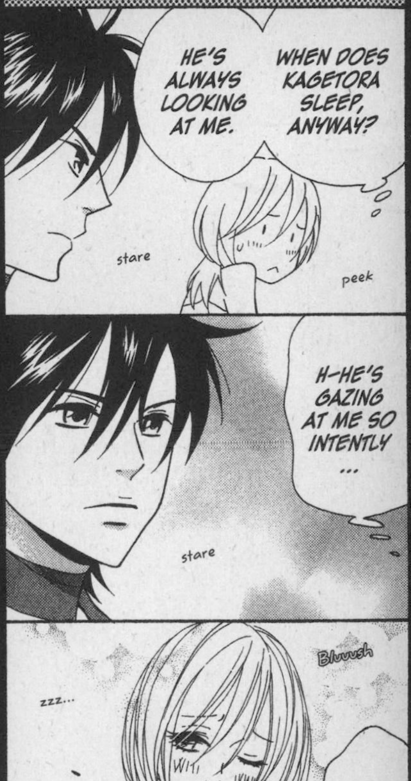
WHEN DOES KAGETORA SLEEP, ANYWAY?
HE'S ALWAYS LOOKING AT ME.
stare
peek
H-HE'S GAZING AT ME SO INTENTLY ...
stare
Bluuush
...IT MAKES ME A LITTLE UNCOMFORTABLE...
zzz...
zzz...
zzz...
HE'S SLEEPING?!!
With his eyes open...!

## What do you mean, "coaster"?

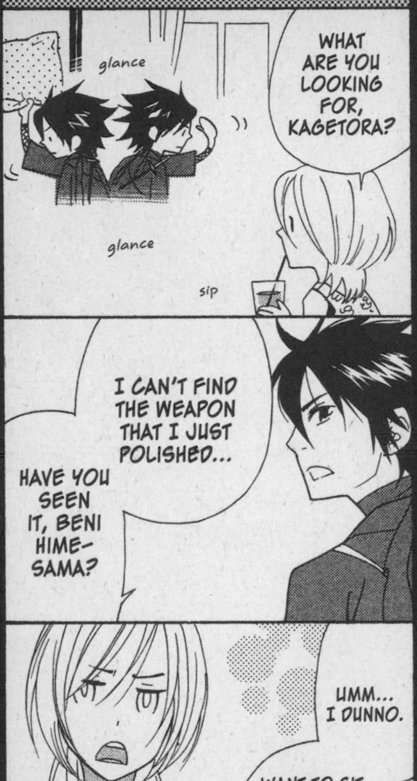
WHAT ARE YOU LOOKING FOR, KAGETORA?
glance
glance
sip
I CAN'T FIND THE WEAPON THAT I JUST POLISHED...
HAVE YOU SEEN IT, BENI HIME-SAMA?
UMM... I DUNNO.
WANT TO SIT DOWN AND HAVE SOME TEA BEFORE YOU TURN THE PLACE UPSIDE DOWN?
THANK YOU, I WILL...
Ninja star

Shinobi Life 1/End

● Shoko Conami's homepage: ● http://conami.cc/

(You can access it with your cell phone too!)

SEE YOU IN VOLUME 2!

# STOP!

## This is the back of the book.
## You wouldn't want to spoil a great ending!

This book is printed "manga-style," in the authentic Japanese right-to-left format. Since none of the artwork has been flipped or altered, readers get to experience the story just as the creator intended. You've been asking for it, so TOKYOPOP® delivered: authentic, hot-off-the-press, and far more fun!

# DIRECTIONS

If this is your first time reading manga-style, here's a quick guide to help you understand how it works.

It's easy... just start in the top right panel and follow the numbers. Have fun, and look for more 100% authentic manga from TOKYOPOP®!